P9-AQF-659

THE UNIVERSITY OF MICHIGAN

CENTER FOR SOUTH AND SOUTHEAST ASIAN STUDIES

MICHIGAN PAPERS ON SOUTH AND SOUTHEAST ASIA

Editorial Board

A. L. Becker
Peter E. Hook
Karl L. Hutterer
John K. Musgrave
Nicholas B. Dirks, Chair

Ann Arbor, Michigan
USA

KARAWITAN

SOURCE READINGS IN JAVANESE GAMELAN
AND VOCAL MUSIC

Judith Becker
editor

Alan H. Feinstein
assistant editor

Hardja Susilo
Sumarsam
A. L. Becker

consultants

Volume 3

MICHIGAN PAPERS ON SOUTH AND SOUTHEAST ASIA
Center for South and Southeast Asian Studies
The University of Michigan

Number 31

Library of Congress Catalog Card Number: 82-72445

ISBN 0-89148-034-X

Copyright

© 1988

by

Center for South and Southeast Asian Studies
The University of Michigan

All rights reserved

Publication of this book was assisted in part by a grant from the Publications Program of the National Endowment for the Humanities. Additional funding or assistance was provided by the National Endowment for the Humanities (Translations); the Southeast Asia Regional Council, Association for Asian Studies; The Rackham School of Graduate Studies, The University of Michigan; and the School of Music, The University of Michigan.

Printed in the United States of America

CONTENTS

This work is complete in three volumes.

Volume 1

Articles and monographs by Martopangrawit, Sumarsam, Sastrapustaka, Gitosaprodjo, Sindoesawarno, Poerbapangrawit, and Probohardjono.

Volume 2

Articles and monographs by Warsadiningrat, Sumarsam, Gitosaprodjo, Purbodiningrat, Poerbatjaraka, Sindoesawarno, and Paku Buwana X.

Volume 3

Appendix 1: Glossary of technical terms mentioned in the texts. Appendix 2: Javanese cipher notation *(titilaras kepatihan)* of musical pieces mentioned in the texts. Appendix 3: Biographies of authors. Appendix 4: Bibliography of sources mentioned by authors, translators, editors, and consultants. General Index. Index to Musical Pieces (Gendhing).

For information on obtaining the original versions of the translated texts, write to the Center for South and Southeast Asian Studies, Publications, 130 Lane Hall, The University of Michigan, Ann Arbor, Michigan 48109–1290, USA.

ACKNOWLEDGMENTS

Judith Becker

Four years have passed since the publication of volume 1 of *Karawitan: Source Readings in Javanese Gamelan and Vocal Music.* In that volume I thanked a number of people who since that time have continued to contribute to the editing of subsequent volumes such as R. Anderson Sutton and Susan Pratt Walton. In addition to the many scholars whose assistance is acknowledged individually in the introductions to the appendices that follow here, special appreciation is due to René T. A. Lysloff for the time he spent compiling an index that we both wanted to be of maximum use to our readers. No simple computer search could have resulted in the kind of educational index we hope we have achieved.

I wish to express my thanks for the editorial, secretarial, and production assistance of several people who labored on volume 3 employed by the publications division of the Center for South and Southeast Asian Studies, namely, Randal E. Baier, Margaret Becker, Alice Frye, Marta Stowell, Cara Murphy, and Nancy Manion.

Finally, I am especially grateful to the one person who has been intimately involved with every detail of the editing and production of these three volumes, the Center's general editor, Janet Opdyke. Her skill and experience have improved every aspect of these volumes.

APPENDIX 1

GLOSSARY OF TECHNICAL TERMS
MENTIONED IN THE TEXTS

INTRODUCTION

Judith Becker

Dictionaries, or glossaries, should not be thought of as arbiters of usage; they are only compilations of usage from the point of view of the compiler. The terms given here share with all natural language vocabularies the phenomenon of multiple usages and diverse meanings. Our intention is not to prescribe or standardize usage, but only to reflect some of the meanings of these terms according to (1) the understanding of the authors represented, and (2) the textual sources at our disposal. Except for a few entries provided to expand upon or help clarify the meanings of the rest, only terms mentioned in the texts in volumes 1 and 2 of *Karawitan* are included. No meaning should be attached to the numbered order of the definitions for terms with multiple referents; definition 1 is no more frequent or acceptable than definitions 2 or 3. A few outside references were consulted to provide definitions supplementing those given in the texts. These are Bandem 1975; Horne 1974; Kunst 1973; McPhee 1966; Soedarsono et al. 1976; Soeharto 1978; Soetrisno 1976; and *Udan Mas* 1960.

For critical readings of, and helpful suggestions concerning, this glossary, I wish to thank Alan H. Feinstein, Martin Hatch, René T. A. Lysloff, Sumarsam, R. Anderson Sutton, Susan Pratt Walton, and Richard Wallis.

GLOSSARY

aba: gestural signals performed in rehearsal or in performance to indicate to other musicians the correct pitch, a drum stroke, or the moment for a stroke on the *kethuk, kempul, kenong,* or *gong.*

aba-aba: see *aba.*

abon-abon: short phrases sung by the *pesindhèn* at unstressed positions within a *gendhing.* Contrasts with *sindhènan srambahan.*

ada-ada: a kind of song of the category *sulukan,* sung by a *dhalang* in a *wayang* performance in order to portray a tense atmosphere (*suasana tegang*) or a critical situation (*keadaan gawat*), accompanied by *gendèr* and *keprak* (*kepyak*), sometimes punctuated by *kendhang* and *gong.*

adangiah: see *odangiyah.*

adangiyah: see *odangiyah.*

adu manis: see *kempyung.*

aja ngono: a term that refers to a particular vocal melodic pattern, and the way in which it is realized on *rebab, gendèr, gambang, celempung, gendèr panerus,* and *suling.*

aksara: 1. a written syllable. 2. a letter of an alphabet. 3. a character of the Old Javanese script.

alok: lit., 'to shout/yell'. Short vocal phrases of indefinite or indeterminate pitch inserted within a *gendhing* to enhance the mood.

andhegan: stopping but not ending. With verbal prefix *m* it becomes *mandheg*: to come to a stop but not to end. Used in reference to *gendhing* in which the gamelan players stop, the *pesindhèn* sings alone briefly, then the musicians resume playing.

andhegan gawan: an *andhegan* melody in which the text and its melody are used exclusively with one piece.

andhegan gendhing: *andhegan* in which most of the instruments stop and the *pesindhèn* continues to sing.

andhegan selingan: a fixed song, usually from one of the *sekar* poetic forms, inserted into a piece. The remaining gamelan players wait silently until the song is ended, then continue playing the piece.

angkatan: 1. beginning. 2. transition.

angkat-angkatan: 1. section of a *gendhing.* 2. a *gendhing* of two movements.

angkatan ciblon: 1. the section of a *gendhing* in which the *ciblon* begins to
play; or the transition section between *irama II* and *irama III*. 2. the
part played by the *ciblon* to indicate the transition from *irama II* to *irama
III* (Surakarta).

angkatan dhawah: see *angkat dhawah*.

angkatan inggah: see *angkat dhawah*.

angkatan minggah: see *angkat dhawah*.

angkatan munggah: see *angkat dhawah*.

angkatan seseg: the transition to, or beginning of, the section of a *gendhing*
that is played fast (*seseg*).

angkatan sindhèn: the point in a *kenongan* at which the *pesindhèn* begins the
vocal melody for a particular musical phrase.

angkatan ungguh: see *angkat dhawah*.

angkat dhawah: the beginning of the *dhawah* (*inggah*) section or the transition
to the *dhawah* (*inggah*) section from the *mérong* section of a *gendhing*.

angkat inggah: see *angkat dhawah*.

angkat minggah: see *angkat dhawah*.

angkat munggah: see *angkat dhawah*.

angkat unggah: see *angkat dhawah*.

angkep: see *gembyangan*.

angklung: a bamboo idiophone.

antal: slow tempo.

antawacana: the specific speaking-style of each puppet in a *wayang kulit*
performance.

arang: lit., 'infrequent, sparse'. Refers to the *kethuk* marking "*kethuk* 2 (or 4)
arang (*awis*)."

awis: see *arang*.

ayak-ayakan: one of the formal structures of gamelan *gendhing*.

ayu kuning: one of a series of terms that refer to a particular vocal melodic
pattern and the text from which the term originates, and the way in
which it is realized on the *gendèr*, *gambang*, *rebab*, *gendèr panerus*, and
celempung.

babarangan: see *barangan*.

badhaya: see *bedhaya*.

bahiri: see *bèri*.

baku: basic, essential.

baku swara: tonic.

balungan: lit., 'skeleton, frame'. 1. an underlying melody, which may be realized on the *bonang panembung* (Yogyakarta) or implied by the *gendèr/
rebab* (Surakarta). 2. the part played by *slenthem*, *saron demung*, and/or
saron barung.

balungan dhawah: see *balungan nibani*.

balungan gendhing: see *balungan*.

balungan lampah: see *balungan mlaku*.

balungan mlaku: 1. stepwise *balungan* (no. 2) in which there are no rests. 2. stepwise *balungan* in which there may be rests, but not at regular intervals as in *balungan nibani*.

balungan mlampah: see *balungan mlaku*.

balungan narancag: a fast-moving *balungan*.

balungan ndhawahi: 1. see *balungan nibani*. 2. *balungan* as in the following example.

$$\begin{array}{cccc} \text{N} & \text{N} & \text{N} & \text{G} \\ ...6 & .356 & .532 & .356 \end{array}$$

balungan ngadhal: *balungan* in which each *sabetan* contains two or more notes, for example,

$$\overline{25} \ \overline{35} \ \overline{23} \ 1$$

balungan nggantung: *balungan* with no melodic motion, in which a single tone is sustained, for example, 3 3 . . .

balungan nibani: *balungan* characterized by alternating ciphers and rests (*pin*), for example, . 5 . 6 .

balungan pin mundur: *balungan* in which there are rests (*pin*) at the accented points, for example, 2 . 1 . 2 . 2 6 .

balungan plèsèdan: *balungan* in which the melodic line of the *sindhèn*, *kenong*, or *rebab* part ends on a pitch that is: first, not the *sèlèh* tone; and, second, usually stressed in the succeeding *gatra*.

banyu mili: style of *gambang* playing almost entirely in octaves, evenly subdivided in fast, regular pulses involving continuous motion in both hands.

barang: one of the tones of the gamelan. In the *kepatihan* system of notation, *sléndro*, tone *barang* = 1; *pélog*, tone *barang* = 7.

barangan: 1. supporting instrumental parts in the gamelan. 2. the *gamelan bebarangan*. 3. itinerant street musicians.

barang miring: 1. a tuning that is neither *sléndro* nor *pélog*, sometimes employed by the *rebab* and *pesindhèn*. *Barang miring* is said to approach the scale of *pélog barang*, but is played in the context of *sléndro*. 2. a tuning that is basically *sléndro* but is mixed with *pélog* vocal pitch-levels. 3. the name of a *gendhing*, that is, *Barang Miring*.

barungan: the melodic phrases played by the upper-octave *bonang* of the *gamelan sekatèn* between the strokes of the *balungan* (*demung*) and/or the lower-octave *bonang* (*panembung*).

bawa: 1. a vocal composition used as an introduction to a *gendhing*. The poetic form may be *sekar ageng*, *sekar tengahan*, or *sekar macapat*.   2. voice/singing.

bawa suara: a short vocal melody for introducing a *gendhing*. Also see *celuk*.

bebarangan: see *barangan*.

bebendé: see *bendhé*.

bebuka: see *buka*.

bedhaya: a court dance of the palaces of Surakarta and Yogyakarta, usually performed only on such special occasions as a royal wedding or the anniversary of the coronation of a king.

bedhayan: 1. *bedhaya*-like.   2. the style of vocal music used to accompany *bedhaya*.

bedhug: a large pegged drum suspended from a rack and played with a padded mallet.

beksan: dance.

bem: 1. one of the tones of the *pélog* scale, *bem* = *panunggul* = 1 (*kepatihan* notation system).   2. a modal classification that groups together *pélog nem* and *pélog lima* (Yogyakarta).   3. a deep-sounding, right-hand stroke of the *kendhang ageng*.

bendhé: a thick-walled hanging gong used in archaic ensembles such as the *gamelan sekati/sekatèn* of Yogyakarta.

bère: see *bèri*.

bèri: 1. a bossless hanging gong.   2. a pair of cymbals beaten with a hard mallet. Also see *rojèh* (no. 2).

berpathut lima: see *patut lima*.

bléru: lit., 'dissonant, inharmonious, false'. Unintentional changes in gamelan or vocal tunings. Out of tune.

bonang: a rack of ten, twelve, or fourteen small, horizontally suspended gongs arranged in two rows. 2. *bonang barung*.

bonang barung: a mid-range set of *bonang* gongs.

bonang gedhé: see *bonang barung*.

bonang klenang: an archaic *bonang* found in *gamelan monggang* and *gamelan kodhok ngorèk*.

bonang panembung: 1. a low-range, large set of *bonang* gongs (Yogyakarta).   2. the lower octave of the *bonang* of the *gamelan sekatèn* (Surakarta).

bonang panerus: a high-range, small set of *bonang* gongs.

bonang penerus: see *bonang panerus*.

bonang telu: a three-gong *bonang*.

buka: the opening phrase, or introduction, of a *gendhing*.

buka celuk: a *buka* that is a solo song. Also see *celuk*.

buka gambang: a buka that is played on the gambang.

buka gendèr: a *buka* that is played on the *gendèr*.

buka kendhang: a *buka* that is played on the *kendhang*.

buka rebab: a *buka* that is played on the *rebab*.

byong: a Turkish crescent or bell tree found in the archaic gamelan *Kangjeng Kyai Kebo Ganggang*.

byur: see *rebab byur*.

calapita: see *kemanak*.

calong: 1. see *jublag*. 2. *gambang*.

caluri: *suling*.

caluring: 1. *suling*. 2. see *celuring*.

carita: narration of the *dhalang* without gamelan accompaniment.

cariyos: see *carita*.

cekak: brief, abridged.

celempung: a trapezoidal zither.

celuk: 1. the giving of a signal, to call. 2. a vocal introduction to a *gendhing* in which the text is taken from the same poem as that sung within the *gendhing*.

celuring: 1. small cymbals played by striking one hand-cymbal against a cymbal mounted on a frame. Same as Balinese *cèng-cèng*. 2. a small *saron* with keys that look like overturned cups.

cempala: the round, wooden knocker used by the *dhalang* to give signals to the gamelan, to punctuate sentences, and to create tension by fast, repeated knocking on the puppet box or against the *kepyak*.

cèng-cèng: two small pair of Balinese cymbals in which one cymbal of each pair is mounted on a wooden frame.

cèngkok: 1. melodic pattern, sometimes used interchangeably with *wilet*, played by the *gendèr*, *rebab*, *gambang*, *suling*, or *celempung*. 2. *gongan/* melodic pattern of one-*gongan* duration. 3. style, such as *cèngkok Surabaya*, or *cèngkok Cirebon*. 4. a melodic pattern consisting of two *wilet*, that is, a *padhang* and *ulihan*.

cèngkok gawan: 1. *cèngkok* that are exclusive to only one *gendhing*. 2. texts that are exclusive to only one *cèngkok* in only one *gendhing*.

cèngkok mati: fixed *cèngkok*.

cèngkok rangkep: lit., 'doubled' *cèngkok*. Refers to the doubling of the melodic patterns when moving from *irama III* (*irama wilet*) to *irama IV* (*irama rangkep*).

cenguk: a single exclamation such as "*sooooo*" or "*ooooo*" inserted in a piece, usually sung by the *gérong*.

Chevé: refers to the *Galin/Paris/Chevé* system of notation (Paris, 1894) that served as the basis for the *kepatihan* system of notation.

ciblon: see *kendhang ciblon*.
dados: 1. *irama dados* = *irama II*. 2. the section of a *gendhing* that occurs after the tempo has settled and the *saron* part is *mlaku* (Yogyakarta). 3. to continue with another piece of the same formal structure as the preceding piece.
daya swara: dominant and/or subdominant tone.
degung: see *gamelan degung*.
demung: 1. see *saron demung*. 2. see *slenthem gantung*.
demung ageng: see *saron demung ageng*.
demung lantakan: see *saron demung lantakan*.
demung pencon: see *saron demung ageng*.
denggung: part of the title of some *gendhing bonangan*.
dhadha: one of the tones of the gamelan scale. In the *kepatihan* system of notation, *dhadha* = 3.
dhalang: 1. the puppeteer in a *wayang kulit* performance. 2. the person who sings the *suluk* from the *wayang kulit* repertoire while narrating and commenting upon the action of a *wayang orang* performance.
dhawah: 1. the section of a *gendhing* that follows the *dados* section. Also see *inggah*. 2. the second section of a *gendhing*, in which the melody (*lagu*) is basically the same as in the *mérong* section. This definition contrasts *dhawah* with *inggah* (no. 2). 3. the second section of a *gendhing*, in which the first section has two or four *kethuk* per *kenong* and the second section is in *ladrang* form. See also *inggah ladrang*. 4. see *balungan nibani*.
dhawahan: the playing of the *saron* and *demung* on stressed notes in the *racikan*.
dhing: the least important pitch-level of a given *pathet*.
dhing-dhong: the stress system of gamelan *gendhing*; *dhing* = unstressed beat, *dhong* = stressed beat. *Dhong* usually falls on the second and fourth beat of a four-beat unit, that is,

```
    .        .        .        .
  dhing    dhong    dhing    dhong
   alit     alit    gedhe    gedhe
```

(*Dhong alit* = small *dhong*, *dhong gedhé* [*ageng*] = large *dhong*.)

dhodhogan: the sounds made by the striking of the *cempala* against the puppet box by the *dhalang* during a *wayang kulit* performance.

dhong: 1. the most important pitch-level of a given *pathet*. 2. see *dhing-dhong*.

dhong dhèng dhung dhang dhing: 1. mnemonics for the five tones of a *sléndro* or *pélog* scale. 2. see *pupuh*, no. 1.

dhong-dhing: 1. the name for the ordering of the vowel sounds in the last syllable of each line of a *sekar tengahan* or *sekar macapat*. See *guru-lagu*. 2. a kind of Balinese musical notation (*pupuh dhong-dhing*).

dolanan: 1. light songs often accompanied by gamelan. Since the song is primary, *dolanan* played by the gamelan often do not represent one of the regular formal structures of gamelan *gendhing*. 2. children's songs.

dongèng: story.

druta laya: fast tempo.

eluk: lit., 'arc, curve, or wave'. 1. a vocal ornament. 2. a division of a *gendhing* consisting of two *gatra*.

embat: 1. the raising or lowering of the pitch of the keys of the gamelan instruments. The nuances or 'correction' of a tuning system. 2. a comparison of the smallness or largeness of a particular gamelan tuning, the relative tuning of a gamelan or the intervallic structure of a gamelan.

embat alam: natural tuning.

embat buatan: an artificial tuning.

embat colongan: a tuning in which the interval between two neighboring tones is made smaller or larger according to the desires of the tuner.

embat kodrat: see *embat alam*.

embat laras ati: 1. a tuning in which the intervals between the tone *dhadha* (3) and its lower neighbor, and between the tone *dhadha* and its upper neighbor, are widened. 2. a tuning that is 'energetic' and 'lively'. 3. a tuning that is lower than a basic tuning.

embat lugu: 1. a tuning lacking a clear sequence of larger and smaller intervals. 2. a 'straightforward' tuning.

embat nglaras ati: see *embat laras ati*.

embat nyendari: 1. a tuning that is higher than a basic tuning. 2. a tuning in which the interval between the tone *dhadha* (3) and the tone *gulu* (2) is made smaller, or a tuning in which the interval between the tone *dhadha* and the tone *lima* (5) or *pélog* (4) is made smaller. 3. a tuning that gives rise to an unassuming, soft-spoken mood (*rasa*). 4. a tuning that is peaceful.

embat nyenggani: a tuning that has the characteristic of 'senggani', or 'sounding together'.

embat nyundari: see *embat nyendari*.

embat sundari: see *embat nyendari*.

enam: alternate spelling for *nem*, meaning pitch 6.

enem: see *enam*.

engkuk: a small gong paired with the *kemong*, another small gong.

engkuk-kemong: the two small gongs, *engkuk* and *kemong*, referred to as a single instrument. They alternate strokes as do the more common *kempyang* and *kethuk*. Example: e k e t e k e . e k e t e k e (Key: e = *engkuk*; k = *kemong*; t = *kethuk*).

gambang: a xylophone with wooden or bamboo keys suspended over a wooden trough. Sometimes used interchangeably with *gambang kayu*.

gambang gangsa: like a *gambang* but with bronze keys.

gambang kayu: a *gambang* with wooden keys.

gambang salukat: 1. *celempung*. 2. *gambang gangsa*.

gambelan: see *gamelan*.

gamelan: generic term for ensemble, usually indicating an ensemble with bossed gongs.

gamelan angklung: 1. a Balinese ceremonial gamelan consisting of various metallophones, small gongs, and occasionally *angklung*. It is distinguished from other Balinese gamelan by (usually) a four-toned scale system. 2. a Sundanese ensemble consisting of several *angklung* (bamboo idiophone).

gamelan arja: a Balinese, seven-toned, *pélog* (*saih pitu*) gamelan, which accompanies the dance-drama *arja*. The gamelan consists of two *suling*, two drums, cymbals, and two *guntang* (single-stringed bamboo zither).

gamelan barong landung: a form of Balinese *gamelan semar pegulingan* with a five-toned *pélog* (*patut lima*) tuning.

gamelan batèl: the Balinese *gendèr* quartet to which are added several small, horizontally suspended gongs, cymbals, and drums when accompanying either a *wayang kulit* or a dance performance of the *Rāmāyaṇa* epic.

gamelan bebarangan: a small itinerant gamelan, street musicians.

gamelan bonangan: a gamelan that includes *bonang* and *saron* but does not include *gendèr*, *rebab*, *gambang*, or *suling*. Contrasts with *gamelan klenèngan*.

gamelan carabalèn: see *gamelan cara balèn*.

gamelan cara balèn: a type of archaic gamelan found in the palaces of Surakarta and Yogyakarta with either four or six tones per octave.

gamelan cokèk: 1. a small gamelan from the Jakarta area, which accompanies the dramatic form *wayang cokèk*. The instrumentation may include a small *gong*, *kenong*, *kethuk*, *siter*, and *kendhang*, plus a *gambang*, *suling*, and *rebab*, or a *gendèr* and *slenthem*. 2. see *gamelan gadhon*.

gamelan cokèkan: see *gamelan cokèk*.

gamelan degung: a small Sundanese gamelan, which always includes the instrument *degung* (a row of six, small, horizontally suspended gongs) and is characterized by a five-tone-per-octave tuning, which is neither *sléndro* nor *pélog*.

gamelan demung: see *gamelan tembung*.

gamelan gadhon: a small gamelan without *saron* or *bonang*. Sometimes used interchangeably with *gamelan cokèkan*.

gamelan gala ganjur: the same as *gamelan kodok ngorèk*, called *gala ganjur* when the *gendhing Gala Ganjur* is played.

gamelan gambang: a small, ceremonial, Balinese gamelan of four bamboo xylophones and one or two *saron* with a seven-toned *pélog* (*saih pitu*) tuning.

gamelan gambuh: a Balinese ensemble with a *saih pitu* tuning (seven-toned *pélog*), which accompanies the dance-drama *gambuh*. The instrumentation includes several very large *suling*, *rebab*, *kendhang*, small horizontal gongs, and cymbals.

gamelan gendèr: a Balinese ensemble with a *sléndro* tuning, consisting of two or four *gendèr*, which accompanies *wayang kulit*.

gamelan génggong: a Balinese ensemble consisting of jew's harps (*génggong*).

gamelan gong: a large, ceremonial, Balinese gamelan consisting of about twenty-five or more instruments, including a *trompong* (large *bonang*). *Gamelan gong* is a five-toned *pélog* gamelan (*patut lima*) in *selisir* tuning.

gamelan gong gedhé: see *gamelan gong*.

gamelan grantang: a Balinese ensemble of xylophones with keys made from bamboo tubes.

gamelan janger: a Balinese gamelan consisting of *gendèr*, *suling*, *terbang*, and *kendhang*, which accompanies the dance-drama *janger*.

gamelan jemblung: a bamboo gamelan found in the border areas between Sunda and Central Java.

gamelan jogèd: see *gamelan rindhik gegandrungan*.

gamelan kala ganjur: see *gamelan gala ganjur*.

gamelan kebyar: a large, Balinese, five-toned *pélog* gamelan (*patut lima*) in *selisir* tuning known for its brilliant style of performance.

gamelan kecapi: a Sundanese ensemble consisting of two or three *kecapi* and a *rebab* or *suling*.

gamelan klenèngan: 1. a large gamelan ensemble that plays without *saron demung* and *saron peking* or *bonang*, in which the *gong suwukan* or *gong kemodhong* may substitute for the large gong. 2. see *klenèngan*.

gamelan kliningan: a Sundanese gamelan.

gamelan kodhok ngorèk: a type of archaic gamelan found in the palaces of Surakarta and Yogyakarta, which includes only three tones per octave.

gamelan krumpyung: a gamelan in which all the instruments are made of bamboo.

gamelan lokananta: 1. the same as *gamelan monggang*. 2. a mythical gamelan said to have been created in: (a) ca. 347 A.D., consisting of three gongs (Ranggawarsita, *Kitab Jitapsara, n.d.*); (b) ca. 235 A.D., consisting of *gong, kendhang, kethuk, kenong,* and *kemanak* (Koesoemadilaga, *Pakem Sastramiroeda*, 1930); (c) ca. 404 A.D., instrumentation as in (b) above (Ranggawarsita, *Pustaka Raja*, 1884–92); (d) ca. 167 A.D., instrumentation as in (b) above (Warsadiningrat, *Wédha Pradangga*, translated in this volume).

gamelan Lokananta: see *gamelan lokananta*.

gamelan lokanata: see *gamelan lokananta*.

gamelan luang: a small, ceremonial, seven-toned *pélog (saih pitu)*, Balinese gamelan.

gamelan mardangga: an ancient war gamelan.

gamelan monggang: a type of archaic gamelan found in the palaces of Yogyakarta and Surakarta, which includes only three tones per octave.

gamelan monggang patalon: a *gamelan monggang* played in the palace square. See *gamelan patalon*.

gamelan munggang: see *gamelan monggang*.

gamelan patalon: an archaic gamelan, either *gamelan monggang, gamelan kodhok ngorèk*, or *gamelan cara balèn*, which plays in the palace square to honor the sultan when he approaches the field to witness sporting events, or to announce the arrival of important personages.

gamelan patut lima: any Balinese gamelan with five tones per octave (*patut lima*).

gamelan pegambuhan: see *gamelan gambuh*.

gamelan pelégongan: a Balinese gamelan (*patut lima, selisir* tuning) similar to, but larger than, the *gamelan semar pegulingan*.

gamelan pèrèrèt: see *gamelan serunèn*.

gamelan pramuni: a gamelan invented in the twentieth century with instruments in the shape of bamboo cylinders.

gamelan rèntèng: a small Sundanese village ensemble consisting of a *bonang*, a multi-octave *saron*, and one or two hanging gongs.

gamelan rindhik gegandrungan: a Balinese gamelan (*patut lima*, low *tembung* tuning) modelled on the *gamelan pelégongan* but consisting of only about a dozen players. The keys of all the instruments are made of bamboo and are suspended over bamboo resonators.

gamelan salundhing: an old-fashioned Balinese gamelan, of the seven-toned *pélog (saih pitu)* type, with large, iron keys resting on trough resonators.

gamelan sebarung: see *gamelan seprangkat*.

gamelan sekatèn: see *gamelan sekati*.

gamelan sekati: a kind of *pélog* gamelan played each year at the festival Garebeg Mulud to celebrate the birthday of the prophet Muhammad.

Gamelan sekati are characterized by the large size of the instruments and by the strong, powerful style of performance.

gamelan selisir: 1. any Balinese gamelan of the five-toned *pélog* (*patut lima*) type in a high register (*selisir*). 2. one of the modes of the *saih pitu* (seven-toned *pélog*) tuning system.

gamelan semar pegulingan: a Balinese gamelan smaller than the *gamelan gong* and more delicate in sound. It may be either seven-toned *pélog* (*saih pitu*) or five-toned *pélog* (*patut lima*) in a high tuning (*selisir*).

gamelan sengganèn: 1. a type of gamelan with glass keys. 2. a type of gamelan with iron keys. 3. a small gamelan without bossed gongs, having only keyed instruments, with the *kenong, kempul, bonang,* and *gong* all in a row. The whole ensemble may be packed into a box.

gamelan seprangkat: a single set of gamelan instruments, in either the *sléndro* or the *pélog* system.

gamelan serancak: see *gamelan seprangkat.*

gamelan serunai: see *gamelan serunèn.*

gamelan serunèn: a small gamelan ensemble possibly with only a *kendhang, gong,* and *kethuk,* but which must include the double-reed instrument *somprèt* (*serompèt/terompèt/serunai*).

gamelan Setu: an archaic gamelan, either *gamelan monggang, gamelan kodhok ngorèk,* or *gamelan cara balèn,* which plays for special ceremonies on Saturday (*setu*).

gamelan siteran: a small ensemble that includes a *siter.*

gamelan smara pegulingan: see *gamelan semar pegulingan.*

gamelan somprèt: see *gamelan serunèn.*

gamelan srunèn: see *gamelan serunèn.*

gamelan sukati: Sundanese term for *gamelan sekati.*

gamelan sunarèn: any Balinese gamelan of the *patut lima* type tuned to middle frequencies (*sunaren*).

gamelan talu: see *gamelan patalon.*

gamelan tembung: any Balinese gamelan of the *patut lima* type tuned to lower frequencies (*tembung*).

gamelan tètèt: see *gamelan serunèn.*

gancaran: 1. fluent, moving quickly. 2. pace, flow. 3. to paraphrase poetry into prose or to read poetry without singing. 4. a *gendhing* such as *Gangsaran* from the *gamelan cara balèn* repertoire with pitch 2 added and played continuously by the *saron.*

gangsa: 1. bronze. 2. a Balinese gamelan instrument similar to a Javanese *gendèr.* 3. gamelan.

gantungan: see *gatra gantungan.*

gara-gara: lit., 'turbulence in the realm of nature'. The term for the second section of a *wayang* performance in which the hero retires to the forest to meditate.

garap: 1. way of working or fashioning. 2. the creation of melodies (*wilet*) on the *gambang*, *gendèr*, or *rebab*.

garo: see *kempyang*.

gatra: lit., 'embryo'. 1. a metrical unit of gamelan *gendhing*, consisting of four *sabetan* (or beats), usually manifested as strokes of the *saron*. 2. a single sentence of poetry in a *sekar macapat*.

gatra gantung: see *balungan nggantung*.

gatra gantungan: see *balungan nggantung*.

gatra mlaku: see *balungan mlaku*.

gatra nibani: see *balungan nibani*.

gawan: a term used in vocal music to indicate that a particular *cèngkok* or a particular text is restricted in its use.

gawan gendhing: texts that are exclusive to only one *gendhing*.

gayor: the wooden rack for hanging the *kempul*, *gong*, *suwukan*, and *gong ageng*.

gecul: see *gendhing gecul*.

gembyakan: see *kendhang gembyakan*.

gembyang: 1. an interval separated by four keys on the *gendèr*. 2. an octave.

gembyangan: 1. a *bonang* technique involving octave playing. 2. an octave.

gembyung: an interval separated by one key of the *gendèr*.

gendèr: 1. an instrument with thin bronze keys, each suspended over a tube resonator. 2. *gendèr barung*.

gendèr barang: a *pélog gendèr* tuned to pitch-levels 2, 3, 5, 6, and 7.

gendèr barung: the middle-sized *gendèr* usually referred to simply as *gendèr*.

gendèr bem: see *gendèr nem*.

gendèr gedhé: see *gendèr barung*.

gendèr giying: a ten-keyed Balinese *gendèr*, larger than the *gendèr pamadé*.

gendèr kantil: the smallest Balinese one-octave *gendèr*.

gendèr nem: a *pélog gendèr* tuned to the pitch-levels 1, 2, 3, 5, and 6.

gendèr pamadé: a ten-keyed, Balinese *gendèr*.

gendèr panembung: see *slenthem gantung*.

gendèr panerus: the smallest, highest-pitched *gendèr*.

gendèr penerus: see *gendèr panerus*.

gendèr rambat: fourteen- or fifteen-keyed *gendèr*, leader of the gamelan *semar pegulingan*.

gendhèng: 1. songs accompanied by gamelan. 2. vocal music.

gendhing: 1. a generic term for any gamelan composition. 2. the designation of a class of formal gamelan structures characterized by relatively greater length (minimun *kethuk 2 kerep*) and the absence of *kempul*.

3. the section of a large piece which follows the *mérong*. 4. tunes that have *irama*, for example, *gendhing terbang*. 5. gamelan smith. 6. instrumental music as opposed to vocal music (*gendhèng*). 7. *kemanak*. 8. *rebab*. 9. gamelan.

gendhing ageng: lit., 'great *gendhing*'. Gamelan pieces with long *gongan* such as those with the formal structures *kethuk 16 kerepan* (*minggah*), *kethuk 8 kerep*, *kethuk 8 awis*, and *kethuk 4 awis*. *Gendhing ageng* are part of a tripartite category, which also includes *gendhing tengahan* and *gendhing alit*.

gendhing alit: lit., 'small *gendhing*'. Gamelan pieces with relatively small *gongan* such as the formal structures *kethuk 2 kerepan* (*ladrang* and *ketawang*) and *kethuk 2 kerep*.

gendhing bonang: 1. any *gendhing* in which the introduction is played on the *bonang* and the *gendhing* is played in loud style (Surakarta). See also *gendhing soran*. 2. *Gendhing tengahan* and *gendhing ageng* in which the *bonang* plays the introduction, the *bonang* is the principal melodic instrument, and the *rebab*, *gendèr*, and *gambang* do not play.

gendhing bonangan: see *gendhing bonang*.

gendhing cilik: see *gendhing alit*.

gendhing gambang: *gendhing* in which the *buka* is played on the *gambang*.

gendhing gecul: *gendhing* that are light in character.

gendhing gedhé: see *gendhing ageng*.

gendhing gendèr: *gendhing* in which the *buka* is played on the *gendèr barung*.

gendhing gérong: *gendhing* based upon a vocal form and including a *gérong*.

gendhing kemanak: vocal pieces played with a few gamelan instruments (*kemanak*, *kethuk*, *kendhang*, *kenong*, and *gong*) to accompany *bedhaya* and *srimpi* dances.

gendhing kendhang: *gendhing* in which the *buka* is played by the *kendhang*, that is, pieces of the categories *playon*, *sampak*, *srepegan*, *ayak-ayakan*, *gendhing cara balèn*, *gendhing monggang*, and *gendhing kodhok ngorèk*.

gendhing kethuk-kenong: see *gendhing kemanak*.

gendhing lancaran: see *lancaran*.

gendhing lésan: vocal pieces accompanied by gamelan.

gendhing monggangan: *gendhing* with the same formal or melodic structure as *gendhing monggang*.

gendhing pamijèn: lit., 'singular, one of a kind', from the root *siji* 'one'. 1. *gendhing* that do not conform to the usual kinds of gamelan formal structures, for example, a *gongan* with only three *kenongan*. 2. *gendhing* in regular formal structure with a nonstandard *kendhang* part.

gendhing prenès: *gendhing* that include an *inggah* with *ciblon* drumming and are lighthearted in character.

gendhing rebab: *gendhing* in which the *buka* is played on the *rebab*.

gendhing sabetan: loud-style *gendhing*.

gendhing sedhengan: see *gendhing tengahan*.

gendhing sindhèn: 1. *gendhing* based upon a vocal form in which the *buka* is sung by the *pesindhèn*. 2. *gendhing* in which the *pesindhèn* has a major role, originally without *gérong*.

gendhing soran: a loud-style gamelan piece (Yogyakarta). See also *gendhing bonang*.

gendhing talu: *gendhing* that are played before a *wayang kulit* performance.

gendhing tengahan: lit., 'middle-sized *gendhing*'. Gamelan pieces with *gongan* of medium size such as the formal structures *kethuk 8 kerepan* (*minggah*), *kethuk 4 kerep*, and *kethuk 2 awis*. See *gendhing ageng* and *gendhing alit*.

gendhing thuthuk: lit., 'struck *gendhing*'. 1. gamelan *gendhing* based upon an instrumental idiom as opposed to *gendhing* based upon vocal melodies. 2. gamelan *gendhing* played exclusively by percussive instruments, thus without *rebab* or *suling*.

gendhing tlèdhèk: 1. a repertoire of *gendhing*, which formerly accompanied the dancing of the *tlèdhèk*, featuring the *sindhèn* melody and often composed of nonstandard *gongan* structures. 2. Any *gendhing* arranged in the style used for the accompaniment of a *tlèdhèk* dancer, often including *gendhing* with closely spaced and irregular *kempul*, *kethuk*, and *kenong* strokes and special *kendhang* patterns.

gendhuk kuning: the name of a *gendèr* melodic pattern.

gentha: a prayer bell.

gentorag: a rod with small bronze bells attached in concentric circles. Also called "bell-tree" or "Turkish crescent." Found in certain archaic Javanese gamelan (*kodhok ngorèk*) and in some Balinese gamelan (*pelégongan*).

gérong: a unison male chorus, which sings with a gamelan.

gérongan: the part for the male chorus sung with the gamelan.

gérong mbalung: see *gérong milah*.

gérong milah: *gérongan* that is nearly identical to the *balungan* melody.

gineman: see *pathetan*.

gong: 1. a generic term for any kind of vertically or horizontally suspended gong. 2. the largest gong in the gamelan (*gong ageng*). 3. a gamelan (Balinese) that uses a large hanging gong.

gong ageng: see *gong*.

gongan: a formal structure marked at the end by a stroke on a hanging gong, *gong ageng*, *gong siyem*, or *kempul* (as in *sampak* and *srepegan*).

gong angklung: 1. a Balinese *gamelan angklung*. 2. a Javanese *angklung* ensemble. 3. a single bamboo instrument that functions as a gong. Also called *gong bumbung*.

gong gedhé: the largest hanging gong.

gong kemadha: see *gong kemodha*.

gong kemodha: an instrument with two large keys, often with a raised boss in the center, suspended over a box. *Gong kemodha* sometimes functions as a *gong ageng*.

gong kemodhong: see *gong kemodha*.

gong salahan: a gong played where normally no gong is expected.

gong siyem: a large hanging gong, smaller than *gong ageng*, larger than *kempul*.

gong suwuk: see *gong siyem*.

gong suwukan: see *gong siyem*.

goyang: see *kenong goyang*.

grambyangan: 1. a melodic unit indicating the *pathet*, played by the *gendèr* or *bonang* to alert the players before the beginning of a piece. 2. a melodic unit indicating the *pathet* played by the *gendèr* to accompany the talking of a *dhalang*. 3. a melodic unit, indicating the *pathet*, played by the *bonang* preceding the *racikan* (opening section) in *gendhing* from the repertoire of *gamelan sekati*.

grambyangan jugag: short *grambyangan*.

grambyangan wantah: long *grambyangan*, the usual or normal form.

grantang: 1. bamboo *gambang*. 2. *rebab*.

gregel: a vocal ornament of short duration like a Western turn or mordant.

grimingan: a style of rapid, nonmetric, *gendèr* playing used in a *wayang kulit* performance to indicate pitch and *pathet* register to the *dhalang* and to create a tense atmosphere.

grit: frame drum (*terbang*) struck with a mallet.

grobogan: 1. the wooden frame of the *gendèr barung*, *gendèr panerus*, and *slenthem*. 2. a boxlike resonator, the wooden frame of the *gambang* and *gong kemodhong*.

gropak: see *irama gropak*.

gubar: 1. bossless gong. 2. medium-sized gong.

gulu: one of the tones of the gamelan scale, notated 2 in the *kepatihan* system.

gupek: the smaller of the two drums in a Balinese *gamelan gong*.

gurnang: an instrument like a *kenong* but suspended by a cord like a *bendhé*, a kind of *penonthong*.

guru: 1. the stressed position in gamelan *gendhing* and *kakawin* poetry. Alternates with *lagu*, unstressed position. 2. the equivalent of *dhong*, stressed position in *gendhing*, which alternates with *dhing*, unstressed position. See *dhing-dhong*.

guru-laghu: see *guru-lagu*.

Appendix 1

guru-lagu: 1. the pattern of final syllables of each line in the forms *sekar tengahan* and *sekar macapat.* See *dhong-dhing.* 2. the stress pattern of a poetic line.

guru wilangan: the total number of syllables of a poetic line.

imbal: a style of playing in which two identical or similar instruments play interlocking parts forming a single repetitive melodic pattern.

imbal demung: *imbal* playing that is shared between two *saron demung.*

imbal-imbalan: see *imbal.*

imbal klénangan: a style of *bonang imbal* playing that is used in *gamelan cara balèn.*

imbal Surabayan: a style of *bonang imbal* playing popular in East Java (Surabaya).

inggah: 1. the section of a *gendhing* that follows a *mérong* and always has the form *kethuk* 2, or 4, or 8, or 16 *kerep.* Also see *dhawah.* 2. the section of a *gendhing* that follows a *mérong* and has a basic melody (*lagu*) that differs from the *mérong.*

inggah gendhing: 1. an *inggah* section in which the basic melody (*lagu*) differs from the *lagu* of the *mérong.* 2. an *inggah* section that has twice as many *kethuk* per *kenong* as the preceding *mérong.*

inggah-inggahan: 1. an alternate for *inggah.* 2. an *inggah* section of a *gendhing* that is in *ladrang* or *ketawang* form and consists of an *umpak* and a *ngelik.*

inggah kendhang: an *inggah* section of a *gendhing* that has the same basic melody (*lagu*) as the preceding *mérong.* Or, an *inggah* section in which the *saron* melody is an abstraction of the *saron* melody of the *mérong.*

inggah ladrang: an *inggah* section of a *gendhing* that has the formal structure of a *ladrang.*

inggah ladrangan: see *inggah ladrang.*

irama: 1. tempo, also known as *laya.* 2. rhythm. 3. refers to the different tempo relationships within a *gongan* or *gendhing.* Irama is the expanding and contracting of structural units such as the *gatra* and the degree or level at which the *gatra* is subdivided (or filled in). A *gongan* in *irama I* takes approximately half the time to perform as a *gongan* in *irama II.* Each change in *irama* either expands by two the time of the preceding *irama* level (*irama I* to *irama II*) or contracts by one-half the time of the succeeding *irama* level (*irama II* to *irama I*). The degree of subdivision can be measured according to the number of strokes on the *saron panerus* to one *sabetan* (beat) of the *balungan.* The chart below illustrates this and provides the common terms for the different levels of *irama.*

Irama Level	Irama Name	No. of Saron Penerus Strokes per Sabetan
1/2	lancar	1
I	tanggung	2
II	dados	4
III	wilet	8
IV	rangkep	16

irama ciblon: see *irama wilet*.

irama dadi: see *irama dados*.

irama dados: *irama II*; see *irama* (no. 3).

irama ditugal: see *irama mlumpat*.

irama gropak: a type of *irama* even faster than *irama lancar*.

irama lamba: fast *irama*.

irama lancar: *irama 1/2*; see *irama* (no. 3).

irama lancaran: see *irama lancar*.

irama mlumpat: the skipping over of one of the levels of *irama*, that is, moving from *irama III* to *irama I*. Also known as *irama ditugal*.

irama rangkep: *irama IV*; see *irama* (no. 3).

irama tamban: slow *irama*.

irama tanggung: *irama I*; see *irama* (no. 3).

irama wilet: *irama III*; see *irama* (no. 3).

isèn-isèn: see *abon-abon*.

jangga: one of the tones of the gamelan scale notated '2' in the *kepatihan* system. See *gulu*.

jangkep: unabridged.

janturan: 1. narration by the *dhalang*, introducing a major scene in a *wayang kulit* performance, accompanied by a softly playing gamelan. 2. the singing of a *sekar macapat* inserted into a *srepegan* accompanied by *kethuk*, *kempul*, *kenong*, *gong*, *gendèr*, *gambang*, *celempung*, and *kendhang*. The song is sung by a solo voice, or with a man and a woman alternating stanzas. Also see *uran-uran*.

jegogan: a Balinese gamelan instrument similar to a *slenthem*.

jejeging irama: the keeper of the *irama*. Refers to the function of some of the instruments in the gamelan.

jejer: a major court audience scene in a *wayang kulit* performance.

jengglong: a Sundanese gamelan instrument, consisting of a set of horizontally suspended gongs in the shape of an *L* or *U*.

jineman: 1. a gamelan accompaniment for a song whose structure does not necessarily represent one of the regular formal structures of gamelan *gendhing*. 2. Songs of a light character, which are accompanied by *gamelan gadhon*, without *rebab*. 3. a soft style of playing, without *rebab*, in which the *pesindhèn* has the prominent role. See *sekar lampah jineman*. 4. a section half-way through a *suluk* or a *bawa* in which the meter is regularized and the *kendhang, gong, kenong, kempul, kethuk*, and soft instruments (except *rebab*) join the singer.

jublag: a Balinese gamelan instrument similar to a *slenthem*.

jugag: abbreviated.

juru demung: a poetic verse-form of the category *sekar tengahan*.

kajar: a Balinese gamelan instrument similar to a *kethuk*.

kakawin: sung poetry in Old Javanese (Kawi) meters based on Sanskrit prosody.

kala: 1. *kendhang*. 2. *kenong*.

kalajengaken: (from the root *lajeng* 'to follow'). 1. to change to a *gendhing* of a form differing from the preceding one. 2. to proceed from an *inggah* section of a *gendhing* to a composition in a smaller formal structure.

kalimat lagu: melodic sentence or phrase.

kangsi: 1. a single pot gong. 2. a pair of very small cymbals mounted on a frame.

karawitan: gamelan music and associated singing.

kaseling: see *selingan*.

kata wilet: the last word of the text of one phrase of the *sindhènan*. The pitch of *kata wilet* must correspond with the pitch of *dhong gedhé* of a given phrase.

kebo giro: the name for a *gendhing* played for special occasions such as weddings or to welcome an honored guest.

kecapi: a Sundanese plucked zither.

kecèr: 1. a pair of small, round, bronze plates hit with a mallet. See *rojèh* (no. 1). 2. see *cèng-cèng*. 3. six tiny cymbals suspended from an iron bar and hit with a *saron tabuh*. Also called *rojèh*.

kekelèng: a small bell used for signalling meditation.

kemanak: a small bronze instrument in the shape of a hollow banana, slit on one side, held in the left hand, and struck with a mallet held in the right hand.

kembangan: see *sekaran*.

kemodhong: one or two large bronze or iron knobbed keys suspended over a sounding box. See also *gong kemodhong*.

kemong: a small gong. See *engkuk kemong*.

kempli: a Balinese gamelan instrument similar to a small *kenong*.

kempul: a hanging gong.

kempul kempyungan: a technique of playing the *kempul* in which the tones of the *kempul* are a *kempyung* distance (separated by two intervening pitches) from the tones of the *balungan*.

kempul mbalung: a technique of playing the *kempul* in which the tones of the *kempul* coincide with the tones of the *balungan*.

kempul monggangan: the technique of playing the *kempul* as heard in *gendhing monggang*.

kempul plèsèdan: a technique of playing the *kempul* in which the tones of the *kempul* anticipate the succeeding tone of the *balungan*.

kempur: a Balinese hanging gong, sometimes called *kempul*.

kempyang: 1. the octave as conceived without intervening pitches. See *gembyang*. 2. an interval with four intervening keys as played on a *gendèr*. 3. an instrument of the gamelan, a rack of two, small, horizontally suspended gongs. 4. two adjacent tones as played on the instrument *kempyang*. Also called *garo*.

kempyung: an interval separated by two keys as played on a *gendèr*.

kempyungan: see *kempyung*.

kemuda: one of the formal structures of gamelan *gendhing*. Same as *srepegan*.

kendhang: a generic term meaning 'drum'.

kendhangan: the term used to designate the type of pattern to be played for a given *gendhing*, such as *kendhangan Candra*, the drum pattern *Candra*. The *an* suffix is sometimes attached to the generic term *kendhang*, and sometimes to the modifying term, that is, *kendhang ladrangan/kendhangan ladrang*, the *ladrang* drum pattern.

kendhang batangan: a medium-sized drum used for lively playing and for dance accompaniment.

kendhang ciblon: see *kendhang batangan*.

kendhang cilik: see *ketipung*.

kendhang gedhé: the largest of the gamelan drums.

kendhang gembyakan: see *kendhang batangan*.

kendhang gendhing: see *kendhang gedhé*.

kendhang kalih: lit., 'two drums'. The drum style played on *kendhang gendhing* and *ketipung*.

kendhang satunggal: lit., 'one drum'. The drum style played on the *kendhang gendhing* alone.

kendhang wayangan: 1. the drum used to accompany *wayang kulit*, slightly larger than the *batangan* drum. 2. the style of drumming used to accompany *wayang kulit*.

kenong: a large, horizontally suspended gong.

kenongan: 1. a section of a *gongan* marked at the end by a stroke on the *kenong*. 2. the first word of a two-word, compound term designating a style of playing the *kenong*. The suffix *an* is sometimes attached to the first word of the compound (*kenong*), sometimes to the second word, and sometimes is omitted altogether.

kenongan goyang: see *kenongan sungsun*.

kenongan goyang sungsun: see *kenongan sungsun*.

kenongan jumbuh: see *kenong mbalung*.

kenongan mbalung: see *kenong mbalung*.

kenongan nibani: see *kenong nibani*.

kenongan nitir: see *kenong nitir*.

kenongan nunggal rasa: see *kenong kempyungan*.

kenongan plèsèdan: a style of playing the *kenong* in which the *kenong* anticipates the succeeding *balungan* tone or the next *sèlèh* tone.

kenongan salah gumun: a style of playing the *kenong* in which the *kenong* plays a pitch at the distance of one *salah gumun* (*gembyung*) interval from the pitch of the *balungan*.

kenongan sungsun: a style of playing the *kenong* in which the *kenong* tone is reiterated after the first and second *kenong* stroke of a *ladrang* form, for example,

```
.   .   .   .   .   .   N
                        .
N   N   P           N
.   .   .   .   .   .   .
N   N   P           N
.   .   .   .   .   .   .
        P           G
.   .   .   .   .   .   .
```

kenong goyang: see *kenongan sungsun*.

kenong japan: an archaic *kenong* tuned to pitch *nem* or pitch *lima* (low register).

kenong kempyungan: a style of playing the *kenong* in which the *kenong* plays a tone one *kempyung* distant from the tone of the *balungan*.

kenong lanang: 1. an archaic *kenong* tuned to *nem* or *lima* an octave below *kenong japan*. 2. lit., 'male kenong'. May refer to any *kenong* in the normal *kenong* range.

kenong mbalung: a style of playing the *kenong* in which the tones of the *kenong* are the same as the tones of the *balungan*.

kenong monggangan: the style of playing the *kenong* as heard in *gendhing monggang*.

kenong nibani: the style of playing the *kenong* as in the formal structures *ayak-ayakan*, *srepegan*, and *kebo giro*, for example,

```
        P       P
    N   N   N   N
. . . . . . . . , etc.
```

kenong nitir: a style of playing the *kenong* as in the formal structure *sampak*, for example,

```
    P   P
N   N   N   N, etc.
```

kenong plèsèdan: see *kenongan plèsèdan*.

kenthongan: a slit gong made of either bamboo or wood and used as a signalling device.

kepatihan: a system of cipher notation, devised ca. 1900 at the Kepatihan in Surakarta, based upon the Galin-Paris-Chevé system of 1894.

keplok: stylized, rhythmic clapping employed to enliven a *gendhing*.

keprak: a small wooden slit gong, or box, struck with a wooden mallet.

kepyak: a set of two or four bronze plates mounted on a box and struck by a *dhalang* with a wooden mallet.

kepyakan: the sounds made by a *dhalang* while striking the *kepyak* during a *wayang kulit* performance.

kepyak calapita: pieces of ivory that are held between the fingers.

kerep: lit., 'frequent, at short intervals'. Refers to the spacing of the strokes of the *kethuk* in a *gendhing*.

kerepan: refers to the spacing of the strokes of the *kethuk* in a *gendhing* at even shorter intervals than *kerep*.

ketawang: one of the formal structures of gamelan *gendhing*.

ketawang gendhing: one of the formal structures of gamelan *gendhing*.

keteg: 1. heartbeat. 2. musical pulse.

kethoprak: a theatrical genre, popular in Central and East Java, accompanied by gamelan.

kethuk: a small horizontally suspended gong.

kethuk banggèn: a special style of playing the *kethuk* after the third *kenong* of the *inggah* section of *gendhing*, whose *inggah* are *kethuk* 4.

```
             t      t        t         t          t    G
Example:     .  .  .  .    .  .  .    .  .  .  .    .  .  .  .
             _____/
```

kethuk salahan: a special style of playing the *kethuk* to signal approaching *gong*, for example:

```
                     t  t  t  t   G
(ladrang)            .  .  .  .  .  .  .  .
```

ketipung: a small drum used in conjunction with the *kendhang gedhé*.

kidung: narratives usually sung in *sekar macapat* meters. *Kidung* sometimes are sung in *sekar ageng* meters, in which case they may called *kidung sekar kawi* or *kidung sekar ageng*.

kinanthi: a *sekar macapat* meter.

klanthé: the cords that support the *kethuk, kempyang, kenong, kempul, gong suwukan*, and *gong gedhé*.

klènang: 1. a Balinese instrument, a small, horizontally suspended gong. 2. an archaic type of *bonang* found in the *gamelan cara balèn*.

klénangan: an old-fashioned style of *bonang imbalan*, also known as *cara balèn*.

klenèngan: gamelan playing for pleasure as opposed to playing for dance or theatrical accompaniment (Surakarta). Also called *uyon-uyon* (Yogyakarta).

klenong: a small Balinese gong.

kliningan: see *klenèngan*.

kocapan: see *carita*.

kodhok ngorèk: 1. a type of archaic gamelan. 2. the piece played on the gamelan of the same name, often used as a wedding piece and played on a modern gamelan. 3. a class of pieces performed in honor of special occasions at the palaces of Yogyakarta and Surakarta, played on a *pélog* gamelan accompanied by *gendèr* or *gambang gangsa* in *sléndro* (Surakarta), or a *saron barung* and *demung* in *sléndro* (Yogyakarta).

kombangan: 1. refers to an extension of a melodic phrase. See *plèsèdan*. 2. the sustained syllables "*eeee*" or "*oooo*" of a *suluk* sung by a *dhalang*. 3. the humming of a *dhalang* on certain pitches, sometimes as a signal to the musicians to make a transition to a new section or piece.

kosèkan: a fast, complex style of drumming played on the *kendhang wayangan* (Surakarta).

kosèk alus: 1. a style of drumming, slightly less lively and fast than *kosèk wayangan*, used in *ladrang* form and *inggah, irama III*. 2. a style of *kendhang satunggal* drumming used in the *inggah* section, *irama III*, of a *gendhing*.

kosèk wayangan: 1. the style of playing *kendhang wayangan* for *wayang* performance, the same as *kosèkan*. 2. *kosèkan*-style drumming for pieces in the formal structures *ladrang*, *kethuk kerep*, *mérong*, and *inggah*.

kosok wangsul: a *rebab* bowing technique.

kothèkan: 1. rice-pounding rhythms. 2. a term indicating interlocking rhythms played by two instruments.

kromong: see *bonang*.

kroncong: a popular song-style usually accompanied by a violin, ukulele, guitar, cello, and flute.

ladrang: one of the formal structures of gamelan *gendhing*.

ladrang lancaran: *lancaran* that include a *ladrang* section played when the *irama* is slow.

lagon: 1. another term for *pathetan*. 2. singing.

lagon cekak: see *lagon jugag*.

lagon jugag: a shortened *lagon*.

lagon pathet: see *lagon* (no. 1).

lagon wantah: a long version of a *lagon*, the usual or normal form.

lagu: 1. unstressed position in gamelan *gendhing*. Alternates with *guru*, stressed position. 2. melody, song. 3. a series of notes. 4. an underlying or abstracted melody of a *gendhing*. 5. one *pupuh* or a set of *padeswara* in *sekar* prosody. 6. the category *sekar ageng* or *kakawin*. 7. a particular *sekar ageng* or *kakawin*.

lagu gecul: a playful song.

lagu gedhé: long melodies.

lagu gendhing: melodies that originated in the instrumental, gamelan idiom.

lagu leutik: short melodies.

lagu mati: fixed melodies.

lagu pathet: see *pathetan*.

lagu rerenggongan: see *lagu leutik*.

lagu sedheng: medium-sized melodies.

lagu sekar: melodies that originated in the vocal idiom.

lagu tengah: see *lagu sedheng*.

lajengan: a continuation. See *kalajengaken*.

laku: see *lampah*.

lalagon: see *lagon*.

lamba: lit., 'single'. A section of a *gendhing* that is played fast while approaching a slower, stable tempo, usually just after the *buka*. The presence of a *lamba* implies that the *saron* part will double at some point.

lampah: 1. the ratio of instrumental strokes (*bonang*, *gendèr*) per *saron* stroke. 2. lines of poetry. See *pada dirga*. 3. the number of syllables per line in *sloka*, *kakawin*, or *sekar ageng* poetry. 4. stepwise. See *balungan lampah*.

lancaran: one of the formal structures of gamelan *gendhing*.

langen driya: a dance-opera based upon the *Damar Wulan* story, performed exclusively by women.

langgam: a kind of popular song with the structure AABA, usually 8 bars per section.

langgam jawa: 1. popular songs (*langgam*) accompanied by gamelan in the manner of *jineman*. 2. see *kroncong langgam jawa*.

laras: 1. tuning system. See also *embat*. 2. scale. See also *pathet*. 3. pitch.

laras bremara: see *laras mleng*.

laras cilik: high-register tuning.

laras gedhé: low-register tuning.

laras madya: pieces with *sekar* verse forms usually sung by men to the accompaniment of *terbang* and *kendhang* and sometimes *kemanak*.

laras mleng: perfectly tuned.

laras nyliring: see *laras silir*.

laras pleng: see *laras mleng*.

laras sedhengan: medium-register tuning.

laras silir: slightly out of tune but not necessarily undesirable.

laras umyung: tuning appropriate for loud playing.

laya: tempo. See *irama*.

lelagon: see *lagon*.

lengut: Balinese melodic pattern, similar to *wilet*.

let: interval of time or space.

lima: one of the tones of the gamelan scale, notated as 5.

logondhang: one of a number of melodies used in association with the *sinom sekar macapat* meter.

luk: see *eluk*.

macapat: 1. poetic meters and associated melodies. See *sekar macapat*.

madenda: a Sundanese tuning.

madya laya: moderate tempo.

maguru: gong.

maguru gangsa: one or two large bronze or iron knobbed keys suspended by a cord. Like *kemodhong* but without a sounding box.

maketeg: see *teteg*.

mandheg: see *andhegan*.

mas kumambang: a *sekar macapat* meter.

matra: 1. meter. 2. pulse.

mbalung: lit., 'to play the *balungan*'. A style of playing *bonang*, *gendèr*, or *rebab*, note for note with the *saron* (*balungan*).

mbalung nikeli: a style of playing *bonang panerus*, *mbalung* style, twice as fast as the *bonang barung*.

médoki: the stroke that falls on the *dhong* beat in the playing of *imbal demung*. See also *nglanangi*.

mengembat: to *embat*.

menggembyang: to *gembyang*.

mérong: a formal structure of gamelan *gendhing*, which cannot be played alone (it must be followed by an *inggah*), and is in one of the following formal structures: *kethuk 2 kerep, kethuk 2 awis, kethuk 4 kerep, kethuk 4 awis*, or *kethuk 8 kerep*. Contrastive with *inggah, kethuk kerepan*.

milah: 1. to play the keys (*wilahan*) of an instrument. 2. to play the *balungan*. 3. a *rebab* bowing-technique.

minggah: see *inggah*.

minggah gendhing: see *inggah gendhing*.

minggah kendhang: see *inggah kendhang*.

minggah ladrang: see *inggah ladrang*.

minjal: see *pinjalan*.

mipil: 1. a style of playing *bonang*. 2. see *pipilan*.

mipil lamba: a style of playing the *bonang*, as in the following example:

```
bonang:   2 3 2 3 2 1 2 1
balungan:   2   3   2   1
```

mipil nikeli: see *mipil rangkep*.

mipil rangkep: 1. see *pipilan*. 2. a style of playing the *bonang*, as in the following example.

```
bonang:   2 3 2 . . 3 2 3 2 1 2 . . 1 2 1   (Surakarta)
          2 3 2 . 2 3 2 3 2 1 2 . 2 1 2 1   (Yogyakarta)
balungan:     2       3       2       1
```

miring: lit., 'slanted'. 1. a notational device to indicate tones played on the *rebab* or sung, which are higher or lower than the indicated gamelan pitch. 2. the playing or singing of tones, which are higher or lower than the indicated gamelan pitch.

mirong: see *mérong*.

mlaku: 1. see *balungan mlaku*. 2. see *mipil*.

mlampah: see *mipil*.

mlaya: see *laya*.

mlèsèd: see *plèsèd*.

munggah: see *inggah*.

munggah gendhing: see *inggah gendhing*.

nacah: lit., 'chopping'. A style of playing the *saron panerus*.

nacah lamba: a style of playing the *saron panerus* with two strokes per *balungan*.

nacah rangkep: a style of playing the *saron panerus* with four strokes per *balungan*.

nada: tone, note.

nada-nada kelompok: tone groupings.

nadantara: interval.

nada sèlèh: 1. the goal tone, or ending tone, of a melodic phrase. 2. the last pitch of any even-numbered *gatra*.

ndhawah: 1. to continue with. 2. see *dhawah*.

ndhawahi: see *balungan ndhawahi*.

nduduk: 1. a type of *rebab* bowing in syncopated rhythm. 2. a *gendèr* melodic pattern.

nduduk gembyang: a *bonang* technique of playing octaves in rhythmic groupings of three.

nduduk tunggal: a *bonang* technique of playing single tones in rhythmic groupings of three.

nem: lit., 'six'. One of the tones of the gamelan scale, notated as 6.

ngadal: see *balungan ngadal*.

ngecèk: a bowing technique of the *rebab*.

ngecrèk: see *ngecèk*.

ngelik: 1. the section of a *gendhing* that rises in pitch and is not optional. 2. an optional section of a *gendhing*, which is signalled by the rising pitch of the *rebab*, *gendèr*, *gambang*, *bonang*, and *pesindhèn*. 3. a high-pitched voice.

nggandhul: lit., 'to delay slightly'. 1. a *rebab* bowing technique. 2. a delayed stroke of the *kenong*, *kempul*, or *gong*.

nggembyang: a style of octave playing by *gendèr*, *gambang*, or *bonang*. See also *gembyang*.

nggembyang lamba: 'single' or fast *gembyang*.

nggembyang nyegat: octave playing that anticipates the *sèlèh* tone.

nggembyang rangkep: 'double' or slow *gembyang*.

ngikik: a *rebab* bowing-technique.

nglanangi: the stroke that falls on the *dhing* beat in the playing of *imbal demung*. See also *médoki*.

ngracik: the style of playing the *bonang* in the opening section of a *gendhing* from the repertoire of *gamelan sekati*. See *racikan*.

nguyu-uyu: 1 a performance of *gendhing sabetan* on the day before a festival. 2. see *klenèngan*.

niba: see *dhawah*.

nibani: see *balungan nibani*.

nikeli: lit., 'to double'. A style of playing *bonang panerus*, playing the same tones as the *bonang barung* but twice as fast. See also *mbalung nikeli*.

niyaga: a gamelan musician.

nungkak: a *rebab* bowing-technique.

nut andha: see *titilaras andha*.

nut ranté: see *titilaras ranté*.

nyamat: see *pathet, pélog nyamat*.

nyela: a *rebab* bowing-technique.

nyodhèk: see *sodhèkan*.

odangiah: see *odangiyah*.

odangiyah: an introductory phrase to a *gendhing*, preceding the *buka*, which identifies the *pathet* of the *gendhing* to follow.

ombak: 1. the beats of a sound vibration. 2. the singing of the lengthened syllables "*aaaaaaa*" or "*yaaaaaa*" by a *dhalang*, usually at the end of a *sulukan*. See *umpak* (no. 4).

ombakan: see *ombak*.

ompak: see *umpak*.

ompak-ompak: see *embat*.

ompak-ompakan: see *umpak-umpakan*.

ompak-ompak merata: equidistant tuning.

pada: lit., 'foot'. 1. the end of a stanza. 2. a stanza. 3. a punctuation mark.

pada dirga: two or more *pada pala*.

pada lingsa: 1. the hook-shaped character of Javanese script commonly used as a comma. 2. a line of poetry.

pada pala: a *gatra*, or one line of poetry, consisting of two or more *wanda* and two or more *pedhotan*.

pada swara: the final vowel of one line of poetry.

padeswara: a single verse consisting of two or more *pada dirga*.

padhang: 1 an antecedent phrase that is followed by *ulihan*, a consequent phrase. 2. a question, an unresolved musical phrase.

padhoman: guide, directive, standard.

pakeliran: from the root *kelir*, the cloth screen used for a *wayang kulit* performance. The aspect of a *wayang* performance that deals with the action on the *kelir* rather than the literature.

pakem: printed scenarios of some of the plays of the *wayang kulit* repertoire.

palaran: a style of singing *sekar macapat* accompanied by *gong, kenong, kempul, kethuk, gendèr, gambang, celempung,* and *kendhang*, which may or may not be *rangkep* (Surakarta). See also *uran-uran*.

pamangku: see *pemangku*.

pamangku irama: see *pemangku irama*.

pamangku lagu: see *pemangku lagu*.

pamatut: 1. *kethuk*. 2. *kendhang*.

pamijèn: see *gendhing pamijèn*.

pamurba: leader, one who has authority.

pamurba irama: the instrument in charge of *irama*, that is, *kendhang*.

pamurba lagu: the one who has authority over melody, the instruments that lead the melody (*lagu*), that is, 1. *rebab*, *gendèr*, *bonang*; 2. *rebab*.

pamurba yatmaka: the one who has authority in presenting the inner feeling of a *gendhing*.

panakawan: the clowns of a *wayang kulit* performance, usually Semar, Garéng, Pétruk, and Bagong. 2. a term indicating the rank of a court musician (Surakarta).

pancer: a note, usually of constant pitch, inserted between every note of a *gendhing*.

pandhita: 1. priest. 2. holy hermit. 3. mystic teacher.

panembrama: a *gendhing* and a *gérongan* especially composed to welcome a distinguished guest from abroad.

panembung: see *bonang panembung*.

panerusan: instrumental parts that fill the gaps between the strokes of the slower instrumental parts.

pangkat dhawah: see *angkat dhawah*.

pangkat inggah: see *angkat dhawah*.

pangkat minggah: see *angkat dhawah*.

pangkat munggah: see *angkat dhawah*.

pangkat ndhawah: see *angkat dhawah*.

pangkat unggah: see *angkat dhawah*.

pangkon: the wooden frame of the *saron demung*, *saron barung*, and *saron penerus*.

pangkur: 1. a kind of *sekar macapat*. 2. the name of a *gendhing*.

panjanturan: see *janturan*.

panunggul: one of the tones of the *pélog* scale. In *kepatihan* notation, *panunggul* = 1.

papat: four.

papathet: see *pathetan*.

pathet: 1. *pathetan*. 2. a modal classification system implying tonal range, melodic patterns, and principle notes:

CENTRAL JAVA

sléndro: *pathet nem*
           pathet sanga
           pathet manyura

pélog: *pathet lima (gangsal)* ⎫ *pathet bem* (Yogyakarta)
           pathet nem (panunggul) ⎭
           pathet barang
           pathet manyura (nyamat); equivalent of *pélog*
                    pathet nem but with a range of 3̣ to 3̇.
                    Notation is the same as *sléndro manyura*.

           pathet sanga; the equivalent of *pélog pathet*
                nem but with a range of 5̣ to 2̇.

MADURA

sléndro: *pathet nem*
           pathet wolu
           pathet sanga

pélog: *pathet wolu*
           pathet nem
           pathet sanga

pathetan: one of the categories of songs *(suluk)*, sung by a *dhalang* during a *wayang kulit* performance, accompanied by *rebab, gendèr, gambang*, and *suling. Pathetan* are often played by the instruments alone as preludes or postludes to *gendhing* outside the context of a *wayang* performance.

pathokan: see *padhoman.*

patut lima: a type of *pélog* gamelan tuning, in Bali, in which there are five pitch-levels per octave.

pedhoman: see *padhoman.*

pedhotan: 1. small sections of poetic lines. 2. the caesura in the central section of a poetic line used by the singer for taking a breath.

pelengkap: the upper neighbor of the most important pitch-level *(dhong)* of a given *pathet.*

pélog: 1. the tuning system in which the octave is divided into seven nonequidistant intervals. 2. one of the tones of the *pélog* tuning system. In *kepatihan* notation, *pélog* = 4.

pemangku: the one who holds something in his lap, that is, the protector and upholder of a country or city, metaphorically extended to mean the upholder of *lagu* or *irama* in gamelan music.

pemangku irama: the instruments that have the task of helping the *kendhang* present the form of the *gendhing* and of indicating the levels of *irama*, that is, *kethuk, kenong, kempul,* and *gong.*

pemangku lagu: 1. the instruments that have the task of playing the basic melody (*lagu pokok, balungan*), sometimes designated as *saron demung, saron barung, saron peking,* and *slenthem,* and at other times as *gendèr, bonang, gambang, celempung, gendèr penerus, bonang penerus, slenthem, saron demung,* and *saron penerus.*

pen: see *pin.*

penacah: 1. a small *saron.* 2. a type of *bonang.*

penangis: a Sundanese tuning.

penerusan: see *panerusan.*

penggérong: see *gérong.*

pengisep: the tuning of the higher-pitched instrument of a pair of Balinese *gendèr.* When played with its mate (*pengumbang*) simultaneously on the same tone, acoustic beats will result.

pengumbang: the tuning of the lower-pitched instrument of a pair of Balinese *gendèr.* When played simultaneously on the same pitch as its mate (*pengisep*), acoustic beats will result.

penonthong: a gong shaped like a *kenong* but suspended vertically by a cord.

penunggul: see *panunggul.*

penunthung: the smallest of the gamelan drums, smaller than the *ketipung* and interchangeable with it.

penyacah: a Balinese gamelan instrument similar to a *gendèr.*

pesindhèn: 1. the solo female singer in the gamelan. 2. any singer, male or female, for example, the *pesindhèn bedhaya.*

petegakan: see *klenèngan.*

pin: a rest in which the previous tone is not damped. Notated in *kepatihan* notation as a dot.

pinjalan: 1. a style of playing interlocking parts with *bonang* or *slenthem.* 2. a style of *gambang* playing in which the right hand plays twice as fast as the left hand.

pipilan: 1. a *gendèr* technique in which the tones are not struck simultaneously, but in succession, producing a single melodic line. 2. see *mipil* (no. 1).

plangkan: 1. the generic term for the wooden frames of the instruments of the gamelan. 2. specifically, the wooden frame for the *kendhang.*

plèsèd: to slip off target.

plèsèdan: 1. the anticipation of a strong tone in the *gatra* preceding the *gatra* that includes the strong tone. 2. the extension of a melodic phrase by the *pesindhèn* beyond the goal tone (*nada sèlèh*) in which the final pitch of the *pesindhèn* is the same as the last pitch of the next *gatra.*

plèsèdan cèngkok: *plèsèdan* sung by the *pesindhèn* when there is a succession of repeated tones immediately after the *sèlèh* tone, but the repeated tones are not in stepwise relation to the *sèlèh* tone, for example, *balungan*:

$$\overset{\text{N}}{21\underset{\bullet}{2}6} \quad 33..$$

plèsèdan jujugan: *plèsèdan* sung by the *pesindhèn* when there is a succession of repeated tones immediately after the *sèlèh* tone, and in which the repeated tones are an octave or more distant from the *sèlèh* tone, for example, *balungan*:

$$\overset{\text{G}}{.16\underset{\bullet}{5}} \quad 66..$$

plèsèdan mbesut: *plèsèdan* sung by the *pesindhèn* when there is a succession of repeated tones immediately after the *sèlèh* tone, and the repeated tones are in stepwise relation to the *sèlèh* tone, for example, *balungan*:

$$\overset{\text{N}}{21\underset{\bullet}{2}6} \quad 11..$$

plèsèdan tungkakan: *plèsèdan* sung by the *pesindhèn* when there is a succession of repeated tones immediately after the *sèlèh* tone, and in which the tones leading to the *sèlèh* tone are too low for the *pesindhèn* to sing, for example, *balungan*:

$$..\underset{\bullet\bullet}{23} \quad \overset{\text{N}}{56\underset{\bullet\bullet\bullet\bullet}{35}} \quad \overset{\bullet\bullet}{11}..$$

plèsèdan wilet: *plèsèdan* sung by the *pesindhèn* when the tones following the *sèlèh* tone are not repeated and the *pesindhèn* is guided by the *rebab*, for example, *balungan*:

. N
.165 .621

pluntur: the ties that support the bronze keys of the *gendèr* or the horizontal gongs of the *bonang*.

pocapan: see *carita*.

ponthang: see *rebab ponthang*.

pranasmara: a sung theatrical genre invented in the twentieth century, based upon the stories of *wayang gedhog*, in which all parts are played by women.

prunggu: bronze. Also called *gangsa*.

puksur: frame drum played with a wooden mallet.

punakawan: see *panakawan*.

pupuh: 1. Balinese notation system using Balinese characters and the vocables *dhong, dhèng, dhung, dhang*, and *dhing*. Also called *pupuh dhong-dhing*. 2. a set of verses (*padeswara*).

puthut gelut: a melodic pattern whose name is derived from a specific *gendèr* melodic pattern.

rabana: see *terbang*.

racikan: the opening section of a *gendhing* played by the *gamelan sekati*, consisting of several *gongan*, in which the *bonang* is the featured instrument and the *saron* play only on the *kenong* tones.

rambangan: see *uran-uran*.

rancak: one set of gamelan instruments, either *sléndro* or *pélog*.

rancakan: the wooden frame of the *bonang barung*, *bonang penerus*, *kempyung*, *kethuk*, and *kenong*.

rangka: framework.

rangkep: 1. see *irama rangkep*. 2. see *cèngkok rangkep*. 3. see *thuthukan rangkep*.

raras: see *laras*.

rasa: mood, feeling, taste, emotive quality.

rebab: two-stringed fiddle. In a complete gamelan there are two *rebab*.

rebab byur: a *rebab* with an ivory or white wooden neck, which is played with a *pélog* gamelan.

rebab gadhing byur: see *rebab byur*.

rebab ponthang: a *rebab* with a black neck, or with ivory at the top and bottom and buffalo horn in the middle, played with a *sléndro* gamelan.

rebena: see *terbang*.

rerenggan: lit., 'fillers of the spaces'. Refers to the function of certain instruments of the gamelan.

réyong: a Balinese gamelan instrument consisting of a single row of small horizontally suspended gongs.

ricikan: 1. essential instrumental parts in gamelan playing. 2. instruments of the gamelan.

rijal: 1. small *saron*. 2. high pitch in the *Kodhok Ngorèk* melody.

rojèh: 1. an instrument found in certain *gamelan monggang* and *gamelan kodhok ngorèk* consisting of one or more round disks suspended from a center hole and played with a hard mallet. See *kecèr* (no. 1). 2. a pair of cymbals beaten with a hard mallet. Same as *béri* (no. 2). 3. see *kecèr* (no. 3).

ronggèng: a professional female dancer, accompanied by a small gamelan, who receives tips from the men with whom she dances. Also known as *tlèdhèk*.

rujak-rujakan: a *sindhèn* and *gendèr* melodic pattern.

rumus: a melodic formula more stereotyped than *wilet*.

sabetan: 1. manipulation of the shadow puppets. 2. the opening movements for various sections of a dance performance. 3. the four individual *balungan* beats of a *gatra*. 4. see *gendhing sabetan*.

sahuran: 1. *kenong*. 2. *gong*.

saih pitu: a type of Balinese *pélog* gamelan tuning in which there are seven pitches per octave.

salah gumun: see *gembyung*.

salisir: 1. a poetic meter sometimes classified as one of the *sekar macapat* meters, sometimes classified as *sekar ageng*. 2. a *wangsalan* meter. 3. a five-toned mode of the Balinese *saih-pitu* tuning system.

salomprèt: a wooden oboe.

salugi: *saron*.

salukat: *saron penerus*.

salundhing: 1. a metallophone or xylophone with floating suspended keys, with or without resonating tubes. Also called *salundhi*. 2. *kempul*. 3. *saron*.

sampak: one of the formal structures of gamelan *gendhing*.

samswara: see *samyaswara*.

samyaswara: 1. group singing. 2. chords.

sangka: 1. *gong* 2. *kethuk*. 3. conch-shell trumpet.

santi swara: pieces consisting of Islamic prayers, usually sung by men, to the accompaniment of *terbang* or *kendhang* and sometimes *kemanak*.

sarayuda: the end of a *pathetan* accompanied by *kendhang* and *gong* or *kempul* and sometimes *kenong* and *kethuk*.

saron: a metallophone whose keys rest on a low trough resonator.

saron barung: the middle-sized, medium-register *saron*.

saron demung: the large-sized, low-register *saron*. Also known as *demung*.

saron demung ageng: a *saron* one octave lower than the *saron demung*, with
a raised boss on each key.

saron demung lantakan: a *saron demung* with five keys.

saron demung pencon: a *saron demung* with a raised boss on each key.

saron panerus: the small-sized, high-register *saron*.

saron peking: see *saron panerus*.

saron penerus: see *saron panerus*.

saron slenthem: see *saron demung ageng*.

saron wayangan: 1. a style of *imbal* played by two *saron barung* during the
playing of *playon* or *srepegan*. 2. a *saron barung* with keys added in the
upper register.

sasmita: a partially disguised signal or hint.

sedheng: medium, usually referring to tempo.

sekar: song, generic term for vocal music.

sekar ageng: a category of poetic forms based upon Sanskrit meters characterized by having two or four adjacent lines with the same number of
syllables. The term *sekar ageng* was first used in the nineteenth century
and may refer to either Old Javanese *kakawin* poetry or to nineteenth-
century poetry based upon *kakawin* forms. In these manuscripts, the
two are distinguished as follows: *sekar ageng kakawin* for Old Javanese
poetry and *sekar ageng kawi miring* for nineteenth-century recreations of
Old Javanese *kakawin*.

sekar cilik: lit., 'small' songs. Refers to *sekar macapat*.

sekar gedhé: see *sekar ageng*.

sekar gendhing: *gendhing* that are based upon melodies traditionally
associated with the poetic forms *sekar tengahan* and *sekar macapat*,
usually in the form of a *ladrang* or *ketawang*.

sekar kawi: a subcategory of *sekar ageng* in the Kawi (Old Javanese)
language, conforming precisely to the rules of Sanskrit prosody. Also
called *sekar ageng kakawin*.

sekar lampah gendhing: *sekar* that closely follow the *balungan* of the
gendhing, usually in fast tempo, and in which the singing is somewhat
intermittent.

sekar lampah jineman: *sekar* that follow the melody of the *gendhing*, but in
which the *saron* and *bonang* do not play, thus giving the impression that
the gamelan is following the vocal melody.

sekar lampah lagon: the style of singing *pathetan* (*lagon*) accompanied by
rebab, *gendèr*, *gambang*, and *suling*.

sekar lampah sekar: the style of singing found in *gendhing kemanak* that
accompanies *bedhaya* and *srimpi* dances in which the *saron*, *slenthem* and
bonang do not play.

sekar lampah sekar gendhing: *sekar* that are sung continuously, usually in *irama rangkep*, and in which the gamelan follows the melody of the song.

sekar macapat: a category of poetic forms, which, like *sekar tengahan*, is characterized by meters of varying numbers of syllables per line and different final vowels for each line.

sekar madya: see *sekar tengahan*.

sekar palaran: see *palaran*.

sekar pedhalangan: the songs (*sulukan*) of the *dhalang*.

sekar tengahan: a category of poetic forms, which, like *sekar macapat*, is characterized by meters of varying numbers of syllables per line and different final vowels for each line.

sekaran: 1. ornamenting patterns, either vocal or instrumental, at the end of a regular melodic pattern or at the end of an *imbal* sequence. 2. melodies of instruments that elaborate the *balungan* melody. 3. the usual type of pattern played on the *ciblon* drum.

sekaran nyegat: abridged *sekaran*.

sekaran wetah: complete *sekaran*.

sekawan: four.

sèlèh: see *nada sèlèh*.

sèlèhan: the cadence of a melody when singing poetic forms.

selingan: from the root *seling* 'to insert'. An insertion of a *gendhing* with one formal structure into a *gendhing* of another formal structure.

selisir: see *salisir*.

senandhung macapat: *sekar macapat* sung quietly or hummed.

sendarèn: see *sundarèn*.

sendhal pancing: a *rebab* bowing technique.

sendhon: 1. one of the categories of *suluk*, sung by the *dhalang* to invoke a sad or moving atmosphere, accompanied by *gendèr*, *gambang*, and *suling* (Surakarta) or *gendèr*, *gambang*, *suling*, and *rebab* (Yogyakarta). 2. like a *pathetan* but in the *pélog* tuning system, that is, *sendhon lima*, *sendhon nem*, and *sendhon barang*.

sendhon pathet: *pathetan* specifically of vocal origin.

senggakan: nonsense syllables inserted within the main vocal melody of a *gendhing* sung by members of the *gérong*. They may be one, two, or four *gatra* in length.

sènggol: 1. (Sundanese) melodic pattern, similar to *wilet*. 2. (Sundanese) vocal ornament, like a turn.

senggrèngan: the last *rebab* phrase of a *pathetan*. Often played as a brief prelude to the *buka* of a *gendhing* or before the opening *pathetan* of a *gendhing*.

serancak: one *rancak* ('set').

serimpi: see *srimpi*.

seseg: fast, usually refers to tempo.

sesegan: the fast section of a *gendhing*, often occurring at the end of the piece.

sindhèn: singing.

sindhènan: songs sung by the *pesindhèn*. 2. songs sung by the *pesindhèn* and/ or *gérong*.

sindhènan baku: 'basic' *sindhènan*.

sindhènan bedhaya: *sindhènan* used with *gendhing* that accompany *bedhaya* dances.

sindhènan isèn-isèn: see *abon-abon*.

sindhènan limrah: see *sindhènan srambahan*.

sindhènan sekar: *sindhènan* texts that have their origin in *sekar* poetic forms sung with *gendhing*.

sindhènan srambahan: a *sindhènan* that has the same importance as any other instrument of the gamelan.

sinenggakan: see *senggakan*.

sinenggrèng: see *senggrèngan*.

singgetan: 1. sectioning. 2. section markers, referring to the function of some of the instruments of the gamelan. 3. patterns that mark boundaries, which are played on the *ciblon* drum.

sinom: a *sekar macapat* poetic form.

sirep: to play gamelan quietly.

sirepan: quiet gamelan playing while the *dhalang* narrates in a *wayang kulit* or *wayang orang* performance.

siter: a zither.

siter panerus: a small zither, tuned one octave above the regular *siter*.

slawatan: the singing, usually by men, of the *Koran* text concerning the birth of Muhammad, to the accompaniment of *terbang* or *kendhang*, and sometimes *kemanak*, while dancing in a sitting position.

sléndro: the tuning category in which the octave is divided into five intervals, which are more uniform than those of the *pélog* category.

sléndro miring: see *barang miring*.

slenthem: 1. a large-keyed, single-octave metallophone, tuned one octave below the *saron demung*, whose thin keys are suspended over bamboo or zinc resonators (*gendèr* family). 2. a large-keyed, single-octave metallophone, of the *gendèr* family but with a raised boss (*pencon*) in the middle of each key. See also *slenthem pencon*.

slenthem ageng: 1. a *slenthem* that sounds an octave lower than the usual *slenthem*. 2. a knobbed, single-octave metallophone whose keys are suspended over a trough resonator (that is, *saron* family). See also *saron demung ageng*.

slenthem gantung: 1. a single-octave *slenthem* whose range is the same as the lowest octave of the *gendèr barung*. 2. same as (1) but with a raised boss in the middle of each key.

slenthem pencon: see *slenthem ageng* (no. 2). See also *saron demung ageng*.

slentho: see *slenthem ageng* (no. 2). See also *saron demung ageng*.

slenthong: see *slenthem ageng* (no. 2). See also *saron demung ageng*.

sliring: deviating, out of tune.

slisir: see *salisir* or *sekar macapat*.

sloka: see *kakawin*.

sodhèkan: a simple style of *gendèr* playing in which the movement of the hands "is like a person pushing the ball in billiards."

sorogan: 1. alternate keys used in connection with the different *pathet* of the five-toned *pélog* scales. On the *gambang*, pitch-1 keys for *pathet lima* and *pathet nem* must be exchanged (*disorog*) for pitch-7 keys when playing in *pathet barang*. 2. *pélog* tones that sometimes alternate with the usual tones of a given *pélog pathet*. These alternate, or *sorogan*, tones are as follows.

pathet lima and *pathet nem*: pitch 7 is *sorogan* for pitch 1.
pitch 4 is *sorogan* for pitch 3.

pathet barang: pitch 1 is *sorogan* for pitch 7.
pitch 4 is *sorogan* for pitch 5.

srambahan: a *suluk* melody that can be used for several kinds of scenes or moods in a *wayang* performance.

srepegan: one of the formal structures of gamelan *gendhing*.

srimpi: a ceremonial dance from the Central Javanese court tradition usually performed by four females.

sruti: 1. interval. 2. set of intervals.

suara: 1. sound, tone. 2. voice.

suara berombak: two pitches, sounding together, producing beats, slightly out of tune but not necessarily undesirable.

suara bléro: two pitches, sounding together, very much out of tune.

suara nyliring: two pitches, sounding together, slightly out of tune but not necessarily undesirable.

suara pleng: two pitches, sounding together, perfectly in tune.

suling: a vertical bamboo flute.

suluk: a traditonal song sung by a *dhalang* during a *wayang kulit* performance.

sulukan: traditional song or songs sung by a *dhalang* during a *wayang kulit* performance.

sundarèn: self-sounding flute made of bamboo and attached to a kite.

sundari: a type of gamelan tuning. See *embat sundari*.

surupan: Sundanese modal categories.

sutra swara: finely woven sound.

suwuk: lit., 'end'. 1. the *gongan* on which a piece ends. 2. a special section added to the final *gongan* (*sampak*, *srepegan*, *ayak-ayakan*). 3. a substitute section at the end of the final *gongan*.

suwukan: 1. a special section for ending a *gendhing*. See *suwuk* (nos. 2 and 3). 2. *gong suwukan*.

swara: see *suara*.

swarantara: intervals.

swarawati: the *pesindhèn* with a gamelan.

tabang-tabang: see *terbang*.

tabuh: 1. mallet for striking instruments of the gamelan. 2. a Balinese classification system of the formal structures of gamelan pieces. Balinese terminology refers to the length of the unit marked off by a stroke on the largest gong. The terminology is not used consistently between different genres of gamelan. For *gamelan gong* the *tabuh* classification is as follows.

> *tabuh pisan* (one) = 8 strokes per *gongan*
> *tabuh dua* (two) = 32 strokes per *gongan*
> *tabuh telu* (three) = 48 strokes per *gongan*
> *tabuh pat* (four) = 64 strokes per *gongan*
> *tabuh kutus* = twice the *gongan* length of *tabuh pat*

tabuhan: an instrument of the gamelan struck with a mallet.

tabuhan barangan: instruments that play supporting parts.

tabuhan penerusan: see *tabuhan terusan*.

tabuhan ricikan: instruments that play essential parts in the gamelan.

tabuhan terusan: instruments that fill in between the essential parts.

talu: a *gendhing* or a series of *gendhing* played as an introduction to, or an opening of, a *wayang kulit* performance. The *gendhing* themselves are called *gendhing talu* or *patalon*.

tamban: see *irama tamban*.

tanggung: see *irama tanggung*.

tarawangsa: Sundanese spiked fiddle.

tari: dance.

tatabuhan: see *tabuhan*.

tebokan bem: the larger head of the *ciblon* drum.

tebokan kempyang: the smaller head of the *ciblon* drum.

tembang: see *sekar*.

tembang gedhé see *sekar ageng*.

tembang macapat: see *sekar macapat.*

tembang tengahan: see *sekar tengahan.*

terbang: a frame drum.

terompong: a Balinese gamelan instrument consisting of a row of small horizontally suspended gongs, similar to the Javanese *bonang.*

teteg: a small *bedhug* or *kendhang ageng* shaped like a *bedhug.*

tetembangan: singing.

thinthingan: 1. the playing of the four principal tones of the *pathet* in a descending order on the *gendèr.* 2. the style of accompanying *bawa* and *andegan* on *gendèr.*

thong-thong: a bronze slit-gong struck with a wooden mallet.

thuthukan: instruments of the gamelan struck with mallets.

thuthukan rangkep: a style of playing (*saron, gendèr, gambang,* and *bonang*) in which the patterns of one *irama* are doubled when played in the next highest *irama.*

thuthukan sabetan: vigorous playing.

thuthukan sodhèkan: see *sodhèkan.*

tingkat irama: levels of *irama,* that is, *irama I, irama II, irama III,* and so on.

titilaras: notaton.

titilaras andha: step or ladder notation.

titilaras damina: a variant of *sariswara* notation compiled by Machjar Angga Kusumadinata.

titilaras kepatihan: notation developed by Radèn Mas Tumenggung Wreksadiningrat, ca. 1900.

titilaras nut angka: see *titilaras kepatihan.*

titilaras ranté: a system of notation using a staff of five or seven lines.

titilaras sariswara: notation developed by Dr. Ki Hadjar Dewantara, the founder of the Taman Siswa schools, in 1928.

titiraras: see *titilaras.*

tlèdhèk: a female dancer/singer (or transvestite) who collects fees for street performances accompanied by a small gamelan. Also called *ronggèng.*

trompong: see *terompong.*

tumbuk: the common tone or tones between a particular *sléndro* gamelan and a particular *pélog* gamelan.

ulihan: a consequent phrase, preceded by *padhang,* an antecedent phrase.

umpak: 1. an opening *gongan* of a *gendhing,* usually played twice, followed by a *ngelik.* 2. a transition section of a *gendhing,* which indicates the form of the following *inggah* (*dhawah*), consisting of one or two *kenongan* or a whole *gongan.* 3. the section of a *gendhing* at the end of the piece but preceding the *suwuk.* 4. the metered *gendèr* part at the end of certain *sulukan.*

umpak inggah: same as *umpak* (no. 2), except that the transition is led by the rhythmic leader of the gamelan.

umpak-umpak: see *embat*.

umpak-umpakan: 1. a transition to an *inggah* in which the transition already has the structure and melody of the following *inggah*. See *umpak* (no. 2). 2. a transition to a *sesegan*.

umpak-umpak merata: see *ompak-ompak merata*.

unggah: see *inggah*.

ura-ura: 1. to sing for one's own pleasure in a quiet place such as the edge of a rice field or on a lonely road. 2. to sing nonclassical songs. 3. see *uran-uran*.

uran-uran: the singing of *sekar macapat* accompanied by *gendèr*, *gambang*, *kenong*, *kempul*, *gong*, and *kendhang*. Also called *rambangan* (Yogyakarta) or *palaran*.

uyon-uyon: see *klenèngan*.

uyon-uyon gadhon: playing gamelan *gadhon* for pleasure.

wanda: 1. syllable. 2. a particular manifestation of a *wayang* puppet.

wangsalan: a two-line, poetic riddle, with twelve syllables in each line, in which a word or group of words suggests through assonance or synonymity another word found later in the poem. Often used as a *sindhèn* text in a *gendhing*.

wantah: ordinary, basic, unadorned, nothing added.

wayang: lit., 'shadow'. 1. *wayang kulit*. 2. a generic term referring to any traditional dramatic performance accompanied by gamelan.

wayang bèbèr: a *wayang* performance in which the scenes of the story are depicted upon painted cloth.

wayang gedhog: a shadow-puppet play accompanied by a *pélog* gamelan depicting stories from the East Javanese *Panji* epic.

wayang klithik: a performance with flat, wooden puppets depicting stories from the East Javanese *Damar Wulan* epic, traditionally accompanied by a *pélog* gamelan.

wayang kulit: 1. a shadow-puppet performance, traditionally accompanied by a *sléndro* gamelan, depicting stories from the *Mahābhārata* and *Rāmāyaṇa* epics. 2. any shadow-puppet theater, for example, *wayang gedhog* or *wayang madya*.

wayang kulit purwa: 1. repertoire of shadow-puppet plays in which the stories are based upon (1) the Indian epics *Mahābhārata*, *Rāmāyana*, and *Bhārata Yudha*; (2) the *Arjuna Sasra Bau* cycle; and (3) stories set in prehistoric Java, traditionally accompanied by a *sléndro* gamelan. Often used interchangeably with *wayang kulit*.

wayang madya: a *wayang kulit* tradition created in the nineteenth century, accompanied by a *pélog* gamelan. *Wayang madya* stories begin at the point at which the *Mahābhārata* stories end.

wayang orang: dance-drama with spoken dialogue and stories based upon the *Mahābhārata* and *Rāmāyana* epics, accompanied by both a *sléndro* and a *pélog* gamelan.

wayang purwa: see *wayang kulit purwa.*

wayang wong: see *wayang orang.*

wetah: complete, nothing left out.

wilah: a single slab, or key, of a gamelan instrument.

wilahan: 1. the keys of the slab instruments of the gamelan. 2. the names of the tones in the *sléndro* and *pélog* tuning system, for example, *wilahan panunggul*, *wilahan gulu*, and so on.

wilambita laya: slow tempo.

wiled: see *wilet.*

wiledan: see *wiletan.*

wilet: 1. see *cèngkok* (no. 2). 2. melodic patterns played on *gendèr, gambang,* and *rebab*, sometimes used interchangeably with *cèngkok*. 3. the two sections of a *cèngkok*; the first *wilet* is called *padhang*, the second is called *ulihan*. 4. the melodic ornaments of a melody such as *luk* and *gregel.*

wiletan: 1. the creation of melodic patterns on a *gendèr, gambang,* or *rebab*. 2. (Sundanese) *gatra.*

wirama: 1. see *irama.* 2. (Balinese) Old Javanese or Sanskrit prosody observing long/short vowel qualities.

wirèng: a combat dance performed by two dancers (Surakarta).

APPENDIX 2

JAVANESE CIPHER NOTATION
(TITILARAS KEPATIHAN)
OF MUSICAL PIECES MENTIONED
IN THE TEXTS

INTRODUCTION

Judith Becker

This appendix of approximately 750 musical pieces, or *gendhing*, has been compiled for the convenience of the reader who may not know, or may not have access to, the notation of gendhing mentioned in the texts. The printed sources for this appendix are from different time periods and of varying provenance, although the majority represent the Surakarta style. The notation of a gendhing may vary widely, not only between areas but sometimes within a single tradition as well. To include in this appendix all the variants of a single gendhing would be cumbersome at best, and nearly impossible in some instances, as no collector nor any collection of gendhing can encompass all the diverse manifestations of a given piece. Some variant versions have been included here, however, to give the reader inexperienced with this phenomenon an idea of the kinds of variation encountered. The word *variant* is not intended to imply the presence of an "ur" text. *All* instances of a given gendhing are its variants.

In some respects, the notation system used here has been standardized, in some respects not. I have settled on a compromise between complete standardization, which would falsify the sources, and a faithful rendering of the notation from the sources, which would make comparisons difficult and put a heavy burden on the reader who is unfamiliar with the many notational styles used in Central Java. All the sources but two (Kunst 1973, "checkered script"; and Hood 1954, Western notation) use some version of *kepatihan* (cipher) notation. The standardization adopted here includes the following adjustments.

1. All instances of the cipher 7, which is used to indicate upper octave 1 in sléndro, have been changed to 1.
2. No upper or lower octave indicators (for example, 6 or 1) have been included. Often they do not appear in the sources, are not consistently included, or do not agree with other sources. Admittedly, for some kinds of research, this is a critical omission.
3. The symbols for *gong, kenong, kempul, kethuk, kempyang,* and repeats have been standardized as follows.

49

G = gong
N = kenong
P = kempul
t = kethuk
py = kempyang
[ ] = repeated section

The range of notational variation before the general adoption of kepatihan notation was substantial. Given below are examples of the kind of notational variants that are commonly encountered, particularly in older collections of gendhing.

Djakoeb and Wignjaroemeksa. *Serat Enoet Gendhing Slendro*. Batavia: Landsdrukkerij, 1919.

G = gong
N = kenong
● = kethuk
W = buka (wiwitan)

Poerbapangrawit, R. M. Kodrat. *Gendhing Djawa*. Jakarta: Harapan Masa, 1955.

° = gong (for example, 2 1 2 5°)
" = kenong (for example, 2 1 2 5")
* = kempul (for example, 2 1 2 5*)

Probohardjono, R. Ng. S. *Gendhing-gendhing ingkang kanggé Nabuhi Wajangan Purwa*. Yogyakarta: Usaha Penerbitan P. T. Sinduniti, 1957.

G = gong
N = kenong
P = kempul
k = kethuk

Tiknopranoto, R. M. Ng. *Titi Laras Gendhing Djawa Muljaning Agesang*. Trijasa, Surakarta, 1963.

G = gong
N = kenong
P = kempul
K = kethuk

pj = kempyang
W = buka (wiwitan)

Gitosapradja, S. *Titilaras Gendhing Djawi.* Malang, 1971.

○ = gong
∩ = kenong
∪ = kempul
∧ = kethuk
′ = kempyang

For the most part, in this appendix, only kethuk, kenong, and gong are indicated. In many instances, the kethuk markings have been added by the editor. Kempul is marked only for the categories *sampak*, *srepegan*, and *ayak-ayakan* in which kempul is a substitute gong, and in special instances, such as *Srundèng Gosong*, in which the kempul cannot be predicted.

4. The amount of information found after the title of a gendhing and the style of presentation of that information have been standardized. If kethuk markings were not indicated in the original work after the title of a gendhing they have been added to the notation but not added to the title.

5. Another kind of standardization involves the convention of halving note values. According to the Galin-Paris-Chevé system (1894) on which kepatihan notation is based, the symbols $\overline{56}$ $\overline{76}$ are read as

in which the first cipher of the halved unit falls on the beat. However, in Javanese gamelan music, the note between two stressed notes conceptually "belongs" to the following, not the preceding, note. Thus a confusion of usage is found in Javanese notation: sometimes $\overline{56}$ means

and sometimes it means

I have decided that, in spite of the possible conceptual distortion, it is generally simpler to print $\overline{56}$ as meaning

as in the Galin-Paris-Chevé model. Thus, kethuk or kenong will
always fall on the first cipher of such a unit, that is,

$$\frac{\text{t}}{56}$$

6. For the ease of the reader, all notations have been divided into
   gatra, or four-note units (2353, 6532, etc.).

Aspects of the notation that have not been standardized—in other words,
those that retain some of the diversity of the sources—are as follows.

1. The use or non-use of dots to indicate *irama*. Irama changes are
   explicit in some notations, for example, Gendhing *Majemuk*, irama
   III, but more generally are not marked or are not consistently
   marked.
2. A number of different but equivalent terms are used in the sources
   and retained in this appendix. These terms refer to the sections of
   a gendhing (for example, *buka* or *bubuka*) and to certain terms for
   kethuk markings for a gendhing (for example, *awis* or *arang*). In
   addition, the variant terms for one kind of formal structure,
   bubaran and *bibaran*, have been retained. These terms are as
   follows.

> buka/ bubuka
>
> odangiah/ adangiah
>
> umpak/ ompak/ umpak minggah/ ompak inggah/ umpak badé
> minggah/ ompak badé minggah/ pangkat dhawah
>
> minggah kendhang/ munggah kendhang
>
> ciblon/ irama III
>
> seseg/ sesegan
>
> suwuk/ suwukan
>
> minggah/ munggah/ inggah/ unggah/ dhawah/ ndhawah

awis/ arang

bubaran/ bibaran

3. The terms *lancaran* and *ladrang* are not always used consistently. In Surakarta, *Singa Nebah* is called a lancaran, while *Sembung Gilang* is called a ladrang. In Yogyakarta, both would be called bibaran.

The source of the notation of each gendhing is indicated by a number corresponding to the following list.

(1)   A handwritten copy of a book of gendhing possessed by the Jaksanegara family of Surakarta compiled from information supplied by Pak Bei Pradjapangrawit and Prawiropangrawit, 1970.

(2)   R. Ng. S. Probohardjono (compiler). *Gendhing-gendhing Ingkang Kanggé Nabuhi Wajangan Purwa.* 5th edition. Jogjakarta: Puspa Rahaju, 1964.

(3)   Sulaiman Gitosapradja (compiler). *Titilaras Gendhing Djawi.* Malang, 1971. (Handwritten)

(4)   Djakoeb and Wignjaroemeksa (compilers). *Serat Enoet Gendhing Slendro.* Batavia: Lansdrukkerij, 1919.

(5)   Ki Wedono Larassumbogo (compiler). *Titi Laras Gending Ageng. Vol. 1, Slendro Patet.* R. Murtedjo, Adisoendjojo, Djakarta: Noordhoff-Kolff N.V., 1953.

(6)   G. P. H. Prabuwinata, son of Paku Buwana X of Surakarta (compiler). *Serat Titlaras Gending Lantjaran.* Minasumarto, 1936.

(7)   Andrew Toth. *The Gamelan Sekati of Central Java.* Senior honors paper, Wesleyan University, Middletown, Conn., 1970.

(8)   R. L. Martopangrawit (compiler), assisted by Sumarsam. *Gérong Bedhayan.* Surakarta: Akademi Seni Karawitan Indonesia, 1971.

(9)   K. R. T. Wasitodipura (compiler). *Gerong.* Yogyakarta, 1971.

(10)   R. L. Martopangrawit. *Teori Karawitan.* Surakarta, n.d.

(11)   R. L.   Martopangrawit   (compiler).   *Titilaras   Kendangan.*
         Surakarta: Konservatori Karawitan Indonesia, 1972.

(12)   Sulaiman   Gitosapradja   (compiler),   from   material   from
         R. L. Wignjosusastro. *Titi Laras Rebab.* Malang, 1971.

(13)   Sumarsam (compiler), from his personal collection. Wesleyan
         University.

(14)   Kangjeng Radèn Mas Tumenggung Sumonagara. *Titi Swara.*
         Surakarta: Persatuan, 1936.

(15)   Judith Becker (compiler). Notebook of notation from information
         supplied by Sumardjo. Malang, 1971.

(16)   R. Sumijanto (compiler). *Naskah Gending-gending Wajangan.*
         Klatèn, c. 1968.

(17)   *Pergelaran Karawitan.*   Surakarta: Akademi Seni Karawitan
         Indonesia, 1971.

(18)   R. L. Martopangrawit. *Draai Book Sendratari Ramayana Festival
         Internasional.* 1971.

(19)   *Karawitan Wajang Gedog.* Kraton Surakarta, n.d.

(20)   Mantle Hood. *The Nuclear Theme as a Determinant of Pathet in
         Javanese Music.* Gröningen, Jakarta: J. B. Wolters, 1954.

(21)   Jaap Kunst. *Music in Java.* Vol. 2. The Hague: Martinus
         Nijhoff, 1973.

(22)   Hardja Susilo (compiler). Personal collection. University of
         Hawaii.

(23)   Ki Nartosabdho. *Tjondong Raos.* Semarang, 1971.

(24) R. C. Hardjasubrata. *Serat Tuntunan Aku Bisa Nembang.* Vol. 3. Jakarta: Ministry of Education and Culture, 1951.

(25) R. M. Ng. Tiknopranoto. *Titi Laras Gending Djawi Muljaning Agesang.* Surakarta: Trijasa, 1963.

(26) S. Mihardjo and J. S. Hadisoetrisno. *Pradonggosari (Noot Gendhing Raras Slendro).* Malang: Soenardi, 1939.

(27) *Rekaman Gending Klasik Gaja Surakarta.* Akademi Seni Karawitan Indonesia, 1971.

(28) R. Tedjohadisumarto. *Mbombong Manah 2.* Djakarta: Penerbit Djambatan, 1958.

(29) *Peladjaran Bawa Gerong.* Malang: Direktorat Djenderal Kebudajaan Djawa Timur, 1967.

(30) R. M. Soekanto Sastrodarsono. *Tuntunan Nabuh Gamelan.* Surakarta: Kemudawati, 1960.

(31) Kenang Darmoredjono. *Gending Djawi Sekarsari.* Solo: Djawatan Penerangan Kabupaten Wonogiri, 1968.

(32) R. Ng. S. Probohardjono. *Tuntunan Lagu Dolanan.* Surakarta: Budhi Laksana, 1953.

(33) Ki Nartosabdho. *Gendhing-gendhing Djawi Saha Dolanan Gagrak Enggal.* Semarang: Ngesti Pandawa, 1969.

(34) Kodiron. *Tuntunan Karawitan Gending Djawi.* Solo: Trijasa, 1964.

(35) Sastrapustaka (compiler). Personal collection. Yogyakarta, 1978.

(36) K. R. T. Wasitodipura. *Titilaras Gendhing-gendhing untuk Konsert Gamelan.* Yogyakarta, 1968.

(37) Sulaiman Gitosaprodjo. *Ichtisar Teori Karawitan dan Teknik Menabuh Gamelan.* Malang, 1970.

(38)   S. Mloyowidodo (compiler). *Gending-gending Jawa, Gaya Surakarta.* 3 vols. Surakarta: Akademi Seni Karawitan Indonesia, 1977.

(39)   R. L. Martopangrawit (compiler). *Gending-gending Santiswaran.* 2 Vols. Surakarta: Akademi Seni Karawitan Indonesia, 1977.

(40)   K. R. T. Kertanegara. *Pakem Wirama: Wileting Gendhing Berdangga* (version in the possession of B. Y. H. Sastrapustaka). 1899(?).

(41)   Paku Buwana X (sponsored by). *Noot Gendhing lan Tembang.* Solo: Toko Buku Sadubudi, ca. 1930.

(42)   K. R. T. Wasitodipura. Photocopy of gendhing-gendhing for *Sendratari Ramayana.* Yogyakarta, ca. 1970.

Notation could not be found for a number of gendhing mentioned in the texts. The titles of some gendhing probably have changed over time and these actually may be included in this appendix under a different name. Similar titles, which may represent the missing gendhing, are also listed. Other gendhing may simply have been lost through disuse.

Gendhing for Which Notation Has Not Been Found

Abu Sinta, Gendhing (possibly Madu Sita, Gendhing)
Among Raras, Ladrang (possibly Among-among, Ladrang)
Ayak-ayakan Umbul Donga
Barang Kinasih, Ladrang (possibly Barang, Lancaran)
Béndrong Gambang, Gendhing
Bentrok, Gendhing
Bujang Daleman, Gendhing
Dhendha Séwu, Gendhing
Dhenggung Banten, Gendhing
Gendari, Gendhing
Gipé, Ladrang
Glana, Ladrang
Glathik Glindhing, Jineman
Gonjang Miring, Gendhing
Grenteng, Ladrang

Hayuningrat, Gendhing
Jaka Lentho, Gendhing
Jalamprang/Jlamprang, Gendhing
Jaranan, Dolanan
Kagok, Gendhing
Kala Gothang, Gendhing
Kedhaton Radya, Ketawang
Kemajuan, Ladrang
Kembang Katès, gendhing terbang
Ketawang, Ladrang
Ketawang Ageng, Gendhing
Ketawang Alit Sumreg, Gendhing
Kudup Turi, gendhing terbang
Kusuma Asmara, Ladrang
Kuwi Apa Kuwi, Dolanan
Kuwung/Kuwung Mudha/Kuwung Bedhaya, Gendhing
Lajar, Gendhing
Lempang Gariyah, Gendhing
Lénggang, gendhing terbang
Lintang, Dolanan
Lung Kara, gendhing terbang
Manis Renggo Gobagpel, Ladrang (possibly Manis, Ladrang)
Mari Kangen, Gendhing Ketawang
Mas Kumambang, Ketawang
Mawur Balik, Gendhing
Merang Mawut, Gendhing
Narpa Siwi, Ketawang
Pajar, Gendhing
Pangawé, Gendhing
Panguwuh, gendhing terbang
Panji, Ketawang
Parentah Karaton, Ketawang
Patalwé/Talwi, Gendhing
Petis Manis, Dolanan
Priyambada, Gendhing Ketawang
Purwaka, Lancaran
Puspa Sari, Gendhing
Raja, Ladrang
Raja Putri, Ladrang
Raja Suka, Ladrang
Rangu Asmara, Ladrang
Raras Rum, Ladrang

Raras Tawang, Gendhing
Rèndèng, Ladrang
Salisir, Gendhing
Samarang, Ladrang
Sambul, Ladrang
Santi, Ketawang
Sara Truna, Gendhing
Sembung Gilang, gendhing terbang
Sinom, Ketawang
Sinom Suka Utama, Ketawang
Slasih, Gendhing
Slebogé, gendhing terbang
Soyung, gendhing terbang
Sri Nugraha, Ladrang
Sri Nugraha Paréntah Karaton, Ladrang
Suka Rena, Ladrang
Suka Utama/Suka Pratama, Gendhing
Suka Wirya, Ketawang
Swaraning Bala, Gendhing
Tebah Jaja, Ladrang
Thepleg, Ladrang
Titigung, Dolanan
Tunggal Raja, gendhing cara balèn
Wala Gita, Ketawang
Wangsalan, gendhing terbang

For their assistance in compiling this appendix, I wish to thank Martin Hatch, Hardja Susilo, R. Anderson Sutton, and Sumarsam.

Agul-agul/Gulagul, Gendhing, kethuk 8 kerep, minggah
kethuk 16, pélog pathet lima (1).

buka: 3.216 5.5. 3.216 5.5. .2.2 .2.2 .5.6 .1.2N/G

mérong:
```
        t           t           t           t
   [.... 2212 33.2 .161 22.. 2212 33.2 .161
    22.. 2212 33.2 .161 .51. 51.5 1.12 3123N
    .... 33.. 33.2 3123 1235 .... 5654 .521
    .561 .... 11.. 1156 11.2 3216 5612 .321N
    .... 1161 22.1 .161 22.1 .161 22.3 5676
    .... 66.. 6676 5352 66.. 5676 532. 1232N
    .... 2235 6532 1232 .... 2235 6765 4.24
    .521 ..24 .521 3212 ..23 5676 .53. 2353N/G


        t           t           t           t
    .... 3323 55.3 2356 .5.3 .523 55.3 2356
    .5.3 .523 56.3 2356 .567 .654 216. 5616N
    ..61 3216 .1.6 .656 11.2 3212 .1.6 .5.3
    ...3 6532 ..24 .521 .51. 51.5 1.12 3123N
    ...3 6521 65.6 1232 ..23 1232 1656 1232
    .... 2212 33.2 .161 22.1 3216 ..63 2132N
    .... 2212 33.2 .161 22.6 2321 ..16 2165 →
    .... 5561 .2.1 .656 12.3 5676 .535 3212N/G]


    → .... 5561 .2.1 5565 .... 55.. 5654 5245N/G
```

umpak minggah:
```
        t           t           t           t
    .... 55.. 5654 5245 ..54 6542 141.2 4565
    .... 5535 6676 5352 66.. 6654 216. 5616N
    ..61 .216 .1.6 .656 12.3 1232 1656 1232
    .... 2212 33.2 .161 22.1 3216 ..63 2162N
    .... 2212 33.2 .161 22.6 2321 ..16 2165
    .... 5561 .2.1 .656 .... 2321 .654 2454N
    .22. 2321 .654 2465 .22. 2321 .654 1121
    .111 5621 .111 5621 ..56 11.2 4565 4212N/G
```

minggah:
```
     t   t    t    t    t    t    t    t
   [4.45 4241 .412 4542 4.45 4241 .412 4542
    4.45 4241 .412 4542 66.. 6676 532. 1232N
    .... 2235 6532 1232 66.. 6676 542. 1216
    1516 1516 1516 2232 .... 2235 6532 1232N
    .... 2235 6532 1232 66.. 6676 542. 1216
    1516 1516 1516 1121 .... 2321 .654 2465N
    .22. 2321 .654 2465 .22. 2321 .654 1121
    .111 5621 .111 5621 ..56 11.2 4565 4212N/G]
```

Agun-agun, Ladrang, sléndro
      pathet manyura (3).

buka: .36. 3132 6123 6532G

```
          t     t N
    [ 5352  5352
      5352  5356
      156.  156.
      1523  6532G

          t     t N
      3563  5616
      3561  3216
      .36.  3212
      6123  6532G ]
```

Agun-agun, Ladrang, sléndro
      pathet nem (16).

(minggah to Gendhing Mandhul Pathi)

```
      t    t N           t    t N
   [.... 2232         .62. 6232
    565. 5623         6165 .32.
    565. 5623         6165 .323
    5616 5352G        5321 6532G]
```

Aja Lamis, Lagu, pélog
      pathet nem (23).

buka: 235 6216G
```
        3132  3635G  )
      31323 5613216G  }  x2
```

```
        N N   N N
     [2321  6523G
      1235  6321G
      2321  6523G
      1235  2126G
      2523  5253G
      5621  2645G
      2321  6523G
      1235  2126G]
```

Alas Kobong, Ladrang, sléndro pathet nem (1).

buka: 2 .356 .22. 2321 .2.6 .3.5N/G

t	t N	t	t N	t		t	N
.6.3	.6.5	.6.3	.6.5	$\overline{253}$ $\overline{253}$		$\overline{253}$ $\overline{253}$	
.6.3	.6.5	.6.3	.6.5	. 5 2 3		5 5 3 5	
.2.3	.5.3	..23	5565	. . 2 1		. . 2 1	
.2.1	.6.5G	.1.6	5323G	3 5 3 2		. 1 6 5G	

Alas Padhang, Gendhing [Ketawang], kethuk
   2 kerep, sléndro pathet manyura (1).

buka: 3.3. 2.32 1.1. 2.1. 6.26 5353N/G

mérong: t   t   N
       [523. 6532 5653 2165
        11.. 3216 2321 6523G

             t   t   N
        523. 6532 5653 2165
        11.. 3216 2321 6523G

             t   t   N
        66.. 6656 3561 6535
        11.. 3216 2321 6523G

             t   t   N
        66.. 6656 3561 6535
        11.. 3216 3561 6523G]

minggah: Ladrang Jong Kèri

Andhong-andhong, Gendhing, kethuk 2 kerep,
     minggah kethuk 4, pélog pathet lima (1).

buka: 3 .561 .13. 212. .165 1216N/G

mérong: t   t   N
       [33.. 6532 .165 1216
        55.. 5535 6653 2365
        .... 5535 6654 2126→
        33.. 6532 .165 1216G]

ompak minggah:
```
          t         t   N
  → .3.6 .3.2 .6.5 .1.6G
```
minggah:
```
         t    t    t    t N
   [.3.6 .3.2 .6.5 .1.6
    .3.5 .1.6 .5.3 .6.5
    .6.5 .3.6 .5.4 .1.6
    .3.6 .3.2 .6.5 .1.6G]
```

Andhong-andhong, Gendhing, kethuk 2 kerep,
    pélog pathet nem (1).

buka: 35 6111 3312 .165 1216G
mérong:
```
        t         t   N
  [ 33.. 6532 .165 1216
    55.. 5535 .653 2321
    55.. 5535 .654 2126
    33.. 6532 .165 1216G ]
```

ngelik:
```
        t         t   N
    11.. 3216 3565 3212
    11.. 3216 3565 3212
    55.. 5535 6654 2126
    33.. 6532 .165 1216G]-
```
```
        t         t   N
  [ 2321 3216 2321 3216
    ..6. 2321 3253 6532
    .5.3 .5.2 .5.3 .5.2
    .33. 3635 1612 3216G ]
```

Anglir Mendhung, Gendhing, pélog pathet barang
    (gendhing kemanak) (8).
buka celuk: $\overline{35}$ $\overline{53}$ $\overline{37}$ 7N/G

```
          t                    t           N
[. . .    . . . .   . . 2 7  . 6 5 6
  6 . .5   . . . .   . . . 67  . . 67.G
  7 . .672 . . . .   . . 3 2  . 7 5 6
  . . .    . . . .   . 7 6 .  565 353G
  . . 232  . . . .   . . . .  35 . . 35.G
  . . .    . . . .   . . 35   . . 35.G
  5 . . 6  . . . .   . . 7 7  . . 67.
  7 . . 6  . . . .   7 . 5 5  . 5 35.G
  5 . . .  . . . .   . . . .  . . . .
  . . .    . . . .   . . . 6  . . .75G
  . . 653  . . . .   . . 5 5  . 6 7 56
  . . 565  . 6 532   . . 3 3  . 2 .77G
  . . .    . . 675   . . 67   . . 656
  6 . .77  . . . .   35. . 5  . . 35.G
  5 . . 6  . . . .   . . . .  . . . .
  . . . 5  . . . .   7 . 5 6  . 5 353G
  . . 232  . . . .   . . 5 5  . 6 7 56
  . . 565  . 653235  . . . .  3 3 .235G →
  . . . .  . . . .   . . . .  . . . 3G
  . . . .  . . . .   . . 5 3  . 2 727
  7 . . .  . . 6     . . . 5  . . 353G
  . . . 2  . . . .   . . . .  35 . 5 35.G
  . . . .  . . . .   . . 7 7  . . 67.
  5 . . 6  . . . .   . .7 7   . . 67.
  7 . . 6  . . . .   7 .65 5  . . 35.G
  5 . . .  . . . .   . . . .  . . . .
  . . . .  . . . .   . 3 5 5  .33 .77G]
```

seseg:

```
          t                    t           N
→. . . .   . . . .   . . 7 .  7 7 6 7G
  . . . .  . . . .   . . . .  5 3 2 32
  7 . 7 2  3 . . .   . . . .  2 3 5 3G
  . . . .  3 2 . .   3 2 . .  2 3 5 3G
  . 2 7 2  . . . .   . . . .  7 7 6 7
  7 . . 23 . . 232   2 . 3 2  . 7 6 7G
  7 . . .  . . . 2   . . 3 2  . 1 5 6
  . . 5 6  7 . . .   . 2 7 .  7 7 6 7G
  7 . . .  . . . .   . . . .  . . . .
  . . . .  . . . .   . . 2 .  3 . 2 3G
```

64

```
      t                 t           N
. 2 7 2   7 7 . .   7 7 2 7   2 7 6 5
5 . 3 5   6 . 7 5   . . 6 5   . . 3 3G
. . 5 3   . . 2̄3̄2   2 . 7 7   . 2 3 2
2 . . .   7 7 6 5   5 . 7 6   . 5 3̄5̄3G
. . . 7   . . .̣ .   . . 2 7   2 7 6 5
5 . 3 5   6 . 6̄7̄5   . . 6 5   . . .̄6̄2G
. . . .   . . . .   . . . .   . . . .
. . . .   .̣_. . .   . . 2 .   3 . 2 3G
. 2 7 2   3̄5̄2 . .   3 2 7 .   2 7 6 5
. 6 2_3   5 5 6 2   . 3 5 5   3 6 5 3G
. . 2̄3̄2   . . . 3   . . . . .   . . 2 1
. 2 5 5   . 5 . .   5 . 6 6   . . 7 5G
```

seseg badhé [will] suwuk:

```
      t                 t           N
. . . .   . . . .   . . . .   . . . .
. . . .   . . . .   . . 2 .   3 . 2 3G
. 2 7 2_  7 7 . .   7 7 2_7   2_7 6 5
5 . 3 5̄6̄ . 6 7 5   . . 5̄6̄5   .̄3̄5 .̄6̄2G
```

Angkruk, Gendhing, pélog pathet nem (1).

buka: 6 6532 6123 6532G

    [6356 2365G

```
          N
1216 5323
6532 3123
6532 3123
566. 6532
6123 6532G ]
```

Arjuna Mangsah, Ladrang,
     pélog pathet barang (38).

buka: .55. 3235 6727 6535G

```
       t    t N
 [ .555 3235
   .555 6765
   .555 3235
   6727 6535G
```

ngelik:
       t   t N
   77.. 7656
   7576 7576
   .5.3 .5.2
   .523 6532G

```
       t    t N
   ..23 5676
   3567 6532
   .352 .352
   7767 6535G ]
```

Asmarandana, Ladrang, sléndro
     pathet manyura (2).

buka: .3.2 .3.2 3132 .126N/G

```
        t    t N
   [2126 2123
    5321 3231
    6321 3216
    5321 3216G]
```

irama III:
```
         t      t    N
   [.2.1 .2.6 .2.1 6123
    6132 6321 3532 5321
    3632 5321 3532 3126
    5353 6521 3532 3126G]
```

Asmarandana, Ladrang, pélog
pathet barang (38).

```
    t    t N
[2726 2723
 5327 3237
 6327 3276
 5327 3276G]
```

irama III:
```
     t               t       ___  N
[2 3 2 7  3 2 7 6  2 3 2 7̄6̄  7̄2̄3̄5̄6̄5̄3
 6 7 3 2  6 3 2 7  . 3 . 2  5 3 2 7
 6 7 3 2  6 3 2 7  . 3 . 2  . 7 . 6
 5 3 5 3  2 3 2 7  . 3 . 2  . 7 5 6G]
```


Asmarandana, Ladrang, sléndro
pathet manyura (3).

buka: .3.2 .3.2 3312 .126N/G

```
    t    t N
[2126 2123
 5321 3231
 6321 3216
 5321 3216G]
```

irama III:
```
     t               t       ___  N
[2 3 2 1  3 2 1 6  2 3 2 1̄6̄  1̄2̄3̄5̄6̄5̄3
 6 1 2 3  6 3 2 1  3 5 3 2  5 3 2 1
 6 1 2 3  6 3 2 1  3 5 3 2  5 6 1 6
 5 3 5 3  1 6 2 1  . 3 . 2  . 1 . 6G]
```


Asri Katon, Gendhing, kethuk 2 kerep, minggah
kethuk 4, pélog pathet barang (10).

buka: 667 6535 66.7 6532 7732 .756N/G

mérong:
```
         t         t    N
[..67 5676 ..67 2327
 ..32 .767 2343 2767
 ..32 .756 3567 6523 →
 ..35 6532 7732 .756G
```

```
ngelik:    t          t    N
        77.. 7765 .676 5323
        77.. 7765 .676 5323
        ..32 .756 3567 6523
        ..35 6532 7732 .756G]
```

umpak minggah:
```
          t          t    N
       →.5.6 .3.2 .3.2 .7.6G
```

minggah:
```
          t    t    t    t N
       [.7.6 .2.7 .2.3 .2.7
        .3.2 .3.7 .2.3 .2.7
        .3.2 .7.6 .2.7 .5.3
        .5.6 .3.2 .3.2 .7.6G]
```

Ayak-ayakan, sléndro pathet manyura (3).

buka kendhang: 2N/G

```
        N N   N N   N N   N N
       .3.2P .3.2P .5.3P .2.1G
```

```
        N N   N N   N N   N N
      [2321P 2321P 3532G
       3532P 5356G
       5356P 5356P 5323P 6532G
       3532P 3532P 5323P 2121G]
```

suwuk:
```
        N N   N N
       2321  3216G
```

68

Ayak-ayakan/Ayak-ayakan Alas-alasan/Ayak-ayakan
    Wantah, sléndro pathet sanga (2).

buka kendhang: 1N/G

```
    N N   N N   N N   N N
    .2.1P .2.1P .3.2P .6.5G
    1656P 5356P 5356P 3235G
   [3235P 3235P 1656P 5321G
    2321P 2321P 3532P 5356G
    5356P 5356P(2321G)      (omit for Ayak-ayakan
    2321P 3235G                      Alas-alasan)
    3235P 3235P 3212P 3565G]
```

Ayak-ayakan/Ayak-ayakan Babak Unjal,
    sléndro pathet nem (2).

buka kendhang: 6N/G

```
    N N   N N   N N   N N   N N
    .5.6P .5.6P .2.1P .3.2P .6.5G
   [3235P 1656P 5356P 3532G
    5653P 5653P 2126P 2123G
    5653P 2132P 6535G
    3235P 3235P 2353P 5235G]
```
suwuk:
```
    N N   N N
    5656P 3216G
```

Ayak-ayakan Gadhung Mlathi, sléndro pathet sanga (39).

buka kendhang: 1N/G

```
    N N   N N   N N   N N
    .2.1P .2.1P .3.2P .6.5G
    1656P 5356P 5356P 3565G
    3235P 3235P 1656P 5321G
```

irama III:

```
 N N    N N    N N    N N
6521P  6521P  3212P  5356G
2516P  2516P  2321G
6521P  3265G
3265P  3256P  5621P  3265G
```

```
         N                 N                  N                    N
‾6‾ ‾6‾  .   ‾2‾  ‾3‾ ‾2‾  1P      ‾6‾ ‾6‾   .   ‾2‾  ‾3‾ ‾2‾  1P  .  ‾1‾
6̿ 1̿ 5̿ 6̿ 1   . 1̿ 6̿ 1̿ 5̿ 6̿ 1P  . 1̿ 6̿ 1̿ 5̿ 3̿ 2       ‾3‾ ‾5‾  6P
```

```
3       2       6       5G
3       2       3       5P       3        2      3      ‾5‾P‾ . ‾5‾
6̿ 1̿ . 1̿ 2̿ 5̿ . 5̿ 6̿ 1̿ . 1̿ 2P .5̿6̿1̿2̿..5̿6̿1̿2̿ 3 1   6    5    3    5G
```

Ayak-ayakan Kadhatonan,
       sléndro pathet nem (16).

buka kendhang: 5N/G

```
 N N    N N    N N    N N
.6.5P  .6.5P  .1.6P  .5.6P
.2.1P  .3.2P  .6.5G
[3235P  1656P  5356P  3532G
5653P  5653P  2126P  2123G
5653P  2132P  6535G
3235P  3235P  2353P  6535G]
```

Ayak-ayakan Kumuda, pélog
    pathet lima (19).

buka kendhang: 5N/G

```
 N N    N N    N N    N N
1515P  1515P  5561P  6545G
6356P  5323P  2121P  6545G
4245P  4245P  3212P  1645G
```

```
 N N    N N    N N    N N    N N
[1515P  1515P  3323P  2121P  6545G
 4245P  4245P  3212P  1645G]
```

suwuk: N N   N N
               1515P 3265G

Ayak-ayakan Kumuda, pélog
    pathet nem (6).

buka kendhang: 6N/G

```
 N N    N N    N N    N N    N N
1616P  1616P  5612P  5321P  6545G
6165P  6165P  3356P  3532G
5653P  5653P  6545P  4245P  4245P
3212P  5356G
```

```
 N N    N N    N N    N N    N N
[1616P  1616P  3323P  2121P  6545G
 4245P  4245P  3212P  5356G]
```

suwuk: N N   N N
               1616P 3216G

Ayak-ayakan Pamungkas, sléndro
    pathet manyura (3).

buka kendhang: 2N/G

```
 N N   N N   N N   N N
[.3.2P .3.2P .5.3P .2.1G
 2321P 2321P 3532G
```

```
       N   N
   312. 6123G
   ..65 3212G
   312. 6123G
   ..65 3212G
   66.. 2321G
   3263 6532G
   ..23 2121G
   6123 5616G
   ..61 2321G
   3263 6532G]
```

suwuk:
```
   N N   N N
   2321P 3216G
```

Ayak-ayakan Panjang Mas,
    sléndro pathet nem (11).

buka kendhang: 5N/G

```
 N N   N N   N N
.6.5P .6.5P .1.6
.2.1P .3.2P 6535G
[3235P 1656P 5356P 3532G
 5653P 5653P 2126P 2123G
 5653P 2132P 6535G
 3235P 3235P 2353P 5235G]
```

```
   N   N    N   N    N   N    N   N    N   N
.66. 6535P .22. 6535P .22. 6535P .35. 2126P .2.1 .6.5P
.66. 6535P .22. 6535P .22. 6535P .35. 2126P .2.1 .6.5G
.33. 1126P 2653 6532G

      N          N          N          N          N          N
[.32. 2356 .365 .3.2P .32. 2356 .365 .3.2P .6.6 .2.1 .3.2 .1.6P
 .3.3 .... .6.5 .3.2G

             N                    N
.563 .563 ..21 .216 .6.1 .2.3 ...1 .232P
.563 .563 ..21 .216 .6.1 .2.3 ...1 .232P

      N      N
.5.6 .5.3 .2.1 .6.5G
.65. 5612 .621 6535P
.65. 5612 .621 6535P
.33. 6532 .356 .5.3G
.11. 3312 .621 6523P
.11. 3312 .621 6523P
.6.6 .2.1 .6.5 .3.5G
.65. 5612 .621 6535P
.33. 1126 2653 6532G]
```

Ayak-ayakan Rangu-rangu,
    pélog pathet barang (6).

buka kendhang: 7N/G

```
   N N   N N
[2727P 2727P
 2353P 5653P
 5653P 6765P
 3237G]
```

suwuk:
```
   N N   N N
2727P 2627G
```

Ayak-ayakan Tlutur, sléndro
pathet sanga (2).

buka kendhang: 1N/G

```
    N N   N N   N N   N N
[ 6161P 6535P 1656P 5323G
  6161P 6535P 2321G
  3565P 3565P 3212P 6535G
  3235P 3235P 1656P 2353G ]
```

suwuk: N N   N N
          2321P 3235G

Ayun-ayun, Ladrang, pélog
pathet nem (3).

(minggah to Gendhing
Randhu Kintir)

```
    t     t N
[ 2321 3532
  5321 3532
  5356 2165
  3632 3126G ]
```

irama III:

```
    t        t    N
[ 56.. 2321 21.. 3532
  12.. 2321 21.. 3532
  12.. 2356 ..21 6545
  .356 .532 5316 2126G ]
```

Babar Layar, Ladrang, pélog pathet bem (15).

```
  t    t N     t    t N      t    t N     t    t N
6563 6563    6563 6563    .4.4 .4.1    6546 4561
6563 6532    6563 6532    .1.1 .1.5    6546 4561
6526 5265    6526 5265    .1.5 .1.5    6546 4561
2523 5653G   2523 5654G   4.4. 4561G   2321 6563G
```

Babar Layar, Ladrang, sléndro pathet sanga (1).

buka: 3.2 16.3 .561 .265N/G

```
       t    t N        t    t N        t    t N
    [..56 1121      ..56 1121      ..12 3323
     .2.2 .356      ..12 3565      .321 6123
     .653 2356      ..56 1653      .321 6563
     2321 6535G     6535 1121G     .561 .265G ]
```

Babar Layar (Bedhaya), Gendhing, kethuk 4 kerep, minggah kethuk 8,
    pélog pathet lima (1).

buka: [5.53 .3.. 1235 .5..] x2 .3.3 .321 6546 4561N/G
mérong:

```
      t   _____   _____   _____               t               t         N
[. . . 1  .654561  .654561  .654561  2 3 1 2  . 1 6 5  2 2 . .  5 6 1 2
 . . . 2  3 5 3 2  3 5 3 2  323 21.6 .5.4.2.4 .24 6 5  2 2 . .  5 6 1 2
 . . . 2  3 5 3 2  3 5 3 2  323 21.6 .5.4.2.4 .24 6 5  3 3 . .  2 1 2 3
 . . . 3  6 5 421  5 5 . .  5 5 . 6  1 1 . .  1 1 6 54 54545454 545 6 1G

      t   _____   _____   _____               t               t         N
 . . . 1  .654561  .654561  .654561  2 3 . .  6 5 3 2  3 2 1 6  5 3 2 3
 . . . 3  1 2 3 3  1 2 3 3  6 5 3 5  6 6 5 3  6 5 3 5  . 5 3 2  5 6 5 3→
 . . . 3  1 2 3 3  1 2 3 3  6 5 3 5  6 6 5 3  6 5 3 5  . 5 3 2  5 6 5 3
 . 4 . 2  4 5 2 1  4 1 . 2  3 5 6 5  . . 5 6  7 6 5 4  2 1 6 54 545 6 1G]
```

umpak minggah:

```
      t               t               t               t         N
→. . . 3  1 2 3 3  1 2 3 3  6 5 3 5  6 6 5 3  6 5 3 5  . 5 3 2  5 6 5 4
 . 4 . 4  . 4 . 1  . 1 . 1  . 1 . 5  . 1 . 5  . 1 . 5  . 4 4 6  4 5 6 1G
```

minggah:

```
 t    t    t    t    t    t    t    t N
[.233 .121 .233 .121 55.. 55.4 2456 .1.6
..21 .621 6544 2121 55.. 55.4 2456 .1.6
..21 .621 6544 2121 23.. 6532 3216 2165
421. 1245 421. .245 61.. 1165 4245 4241G
```

```
 t    t    t    t    t    t    t    t N
.233 .121 .233 .121 55.. 55.6 1216 5323
.356 5356 4424 2121 55.. 55.6 1216 5323
.356 5356 4424 2121 23.. 6532 3216 2165
421. 1245 421. 1245⁺61.. 1165 4245 4241G]
```

sesegan:
```
               t    t    t    t N
            ⁺61.5 .1.5 .446 4561G
```

```
 t    t    t    t    t    t    t    t N
[6546 4561 6546 4561 6546 4561 2523 5653
6563 6563 6563 6532 5325 3253 2523 5653
6563 6563 6563 6532 5325 3253 2523 5654
.4.4 .4.1 .1.1 .1.5⁺.1.5 .1.5 .446 4561G]
```

suwukan:
```
              t    t    t    t N
           ⁺..23 55.3 6532 .3.5G
```

Babat, Gendhing, kethuk 2 kerep, minggah kethuk 4,
    sléndro pathet nem (1).

buka: 2 .356 .6.3 .6.3 .6.5 .3.2N/G
mérong:
```
   t         t    N
[..35 .... 2356 .532
..35 .... 2356 .532
66.. 6656 3561 6523
.333 5653 2353 2126G
```

```
   t         t    N
3532 ..23 5653 2126
3532 ..23 5653 2126
3532 ..23 5653 2165 ⁺
33.6 3561 3265 .3.2G]
```

umpak minggah:

```
     t        t   N
→ .3.6 .2.1 .6.5 .3.2G
```

minggah:

```
   t    t    t    t N
[.3.5 .6.5 .1.6 .3.2
 .3.5 .6.5 .1.6 .3.2
 .5.6 .5.6 .2.1 .5.3
 .5.6 .5.3 .2.3 .1.6G

   t    t    t    t N
 .3.2 .3.2 .5.3 .1.6
 .3.2 .3.2 .5.3 .1.6
 .3.2 .3.2 .5.3 .6.5
 .3.6 .2.1 .6.5 .3.2G]
```

Babat Kenceng, Ladrang, sléndro pathet sanga (2).

buka: 2 5352 6365N/G

```
  t    t N        t    t N        t    t N
[.3.6 .3.5      .5.3 .5.2      .1.6 .3.5
 .3.6 .3.5      .5.3 .5.2      .1.6 .3.5
 .2.3 .5.3      .5.3 .5.2      .2.3 .5.3
 .6.5 .3.5G     .6.3 .6.5G     .6.5 .3.2G ]
```

Babon Angrem, Gendhing, kethuk 4 kerep,
    pélog pathet nem (1).

buka: 6653 1123 2126N/G
mérong:

```
       t                    t
[. 6 6 .  6 1 2 3  .53 .53  . 5 . 3
 . 6 6 .  6 1 2 3  .53 .53  . 5 . 3N
 . 6 6 .  6 1 2 3  .53 .53  . 5 . 3
 . . . 2  . 2 . 6  . 1 . 2  . 3 . 2N
 . . . 3  . . . 2  . . . 1  . . . 6
 . . . 2  . . . 1  . . . 5  . . . 3N
 . . . 1  . . . 6  . . . 3  . . . 2
 . . . 1  . . . 2  . . . 1  . . . 6N/G
```

Badranaya, Ladrang, sléndro
   pathet manyura (1).

buka: 2 2352 5356 5352N/G

```
   t    t N        t     t N
[ 5356 5352      1653 2356
  5356 5352      1653 2356
  66.. 6656      22.. 2352
  1653 2356G     5356 5352G ]
```

Balabak, Ladrang, pélog
   pathet lima (23).

```
  t    t N
3231 3235
3231 3235
..76 5421
3231 3235G
```

Bali-balèn, Ladrang (11).

(from gangsaran)

```
            N
[ ...2 .2.5
  ..16 ..15
  ..16 ..15
  161. 2165G ]
```

Bandhil Ori, Gendhing, kethuk 2 kerep, minggah
    kethuk 4, pélog pathet barang (3).

buka: 5 .5.5 3567 .7.7 .6.5 .7.6 .532N/G
mérong:
          t   t   N
    [.352 .352 5653 2767
     .3.2 .765 ..56 7232→
     35.. 55.. 5565 3567
     .3.2 .765 7656 3532N/G]

umpak minggah:

          t   t   N
    →.3.5 .6.5 .6.5 .6.7
     .3.2 .6.5 .7.6 .3.2G

minggah:

      t   t   t   t N
    [.3.2 .3.2 .5.3 .2.7
     .3.2 .6.5 .6.5 .3.2
     .3.5 .6.5 .6.5 .6.7
     .3.2 .6.5 .7.6 .3.2G]

Bang-bang Wétan, Gendhing, kethuk 2
    kerep, minggah kethuk 4, sléndro
    pathet manyura (2).

buka: 3 561. 1.2. 1656 56.5 1653N/G

mérong: N
    [..36 3561 ..12 1656
     .56. 3561 ..12 1656
     .56. 3561 ..12 1656
     55.. 5565 1656 5323G →

          t   t   N
     .13. 1235 .1.6 5323
     .13. 1235 .1.6 5323
     .13. 1235 .1.6 5323
     11.. 11.. 5516 5323G]

```
minggah: t    t    t    t N
      →[.5.3 .6.5 .1.6 .5.3
       .5.3 .6.5 .1.6 .5.3
       .5.3 .6.5 .1.6 .5.3
       .6.1 .6.1 .5.6 .5.3G

        t    t    t    t N
       .5.3 .6.1 .5.3 .5.6
       .5.6 .1.2 .5.3 .5.6
       .5.6 .1.2 .5.3 .5.6
       .3.5 .6.5 .1.6 .5.3G]
```

Bango Maté/Bangun Mati, Gendhing,
   minggah kethuk 4, sléndro
   pathet sanga (17).

(minggah to Gendhing Kalunta)

```
    t    t    t    t N
 [ .2.1 .2.1 .3.2 .6.5
   .2.1 .2.1 .3.2 .6.5
   .6.5 .6.5 .1.6 .3.2
   .3.1 .3.2 .3.2 .6.5G ]
```

Banthèng Warèng/Banthèng Lorèng,
   Gendhing, kethuk 2 kerep,
   sléndro pathet manyura (38).

buka: 661 6523 .661 6532 12.6 1232N/G

```
mérong:    t         t    N
      [[ .62. 62.6 2123 5653
         2132 .62. 62.3 5653
         2132 .126 3561 6523
         .661 6532 12.6 1232G ]
```

```
ngelik:    t         t    N
         66.. 6656 3561 6523
         11.. 3216 3561 6523
         2132 .126 3561 6523
         .661 6532 12.6 1232G ]
```

minggah: Èsèg-èsèg

Banyak Nglangi, Ladrang, pélog pathet lima (1).

```
  t    t N        t    t N        t    t N
[ .123 5123      22.. 6545      .612 1645
  .123 5123      22.. 6545      .612 1645
  .123 5123      .254 .254      .612 1645
  11.. 6545G     .254 2165G     33.. 2123G ]
```

Barang Miring, Ladrang,
    pélog pathet barang (7).

```
   t    t N
 [6765 7653
  6535 6532
  5323 5356
  3565 3567G

   t    t N
  6765 7653
  6535 6532
  5323 5356
  3565 3235G

   t    t N
  3656 5653
  5656 3532
  5323 5356
  3565 3235G

   t    t N
  3656 5653
  5656 3532
  5323 5356
  3565 3567G]
```

Bawa Raga, Gendhing, kethuk 4 kerep, minggah
kethuk 8, sléndro pathet sanga (25).

buka: 2 .2.6 .2.1 .1.3 .212 .121 6535N/G

mérong:
```
      t          t          t          t      N
   .555 2235 2353 2121 ..12 3532 5321 6535
  [.555 2235 2353 2121 ..12 3532 5321 6535
   .555 2235 2353 2121 ..12 3532 5321 6535 →
   66.. 6656 3565 3212 .35. 235. 2353 2121G

      t          t          t          t      N
   3532 .165 2356 3532 .123 .123 .123 1121
   3532 .165 2356 3532 .123 .123 .123 1121
   3532 .165 2356 3532 ..23 6532 66.. 3356
   .... 66.. 3565 3212 .35. 235. 2353 2121G

      t          t          t          t      N
   .... 1121 3212 .165 ..56 1653 2321 6535]
```

umpak:
```
      t          t          t          t      N
  →.3.6 .5.6 .3.5 .3.2 .3.5 .3.2 .3.2 .6.5G
```

minggah:
```
    t    t    t    t    t    t    t    t  N
  [.6.5 .6.5 .6.5 .3.2 .3.2 .3.2 .5.6 .3.5
   .6.5 .6.5 .6.5 .3.2 .3.2 .3.2 .5.6 .3.5
   .6.5 .6.5 .6.5 .3.2 .3.2 .3.2 .5.6 .3.5
   .3.6 .5.6 .3.5 .3.2 .3.5 .3.2 .3.2 .6.5G

    t    t    t    t    t    t    t    t  N
   .6.5 .6.5 .2.3 .2.1 .2.1 .3.2 .3.1 .6.5
   .6.5 .6.5 .2.3 .2.1 .2.1 .3.2 .3.1 .6.5
   .6.5 .6.5 .2.3 .2.1 .2.1 .3.2 .3.1 .6.5
   .3.6 .5.6 .3.5 .3.2 .3.5 .3.2 .3.2 .6.5G]
```

Bayem Tur, Ladrang, pélog
    pathet lima (3).

buka: .33. 3635 3635 3132N/G

```
       t     t N
[ .356 3532  ⎫
  .356 3532  ⎬  x2
  .33. 3635  ⎪
  3635 3132G ⎭

       t     t N
  .444 2126  ⎫
  .444 2126  ⎬  x2
  .33. 3635  ⎪
  3635 3132G ⎭  ]
```

Bayem Tur, Ladrang, pélog
    pathet nem (7).

buka:
```
  t           t    N
...2 ...4 .5.6 .5.4
.6.5 .2.4 .5.6 .5.4
.6.5 .2.1 .3.2 .6.5
.3.3 .5.3 .2.1 .2.1G

   t           t    N
[.3.2 .6.5 .3.5 .6.1
 .3.5 .3.2 .1.6 .3.5
 ...5 55.6 .7.6 .5.4
 .2.1 .6.1 .2.3 .2.1G

   t           t    N
.2.3 .5.2 .3.5 .6.5
.6.7 .3.2 .6.3 .5.6
.7.6 .5.3 .5.2 .3.5
.6.5 .3.2 .1.2 .3.2G

   t           t    N
.3.2 .1.6 .5.6 .1.2
.3.2 .1.6 .5.6 .1.2
.3.5 ...6 .7.6 .5.4
.2.1 .3.2 .1.6 .3.5G

   t           t    N
.6.7 ...5 .6.7 .6.7
.5.6 .7.2 ...7 .6.5
...5 55.6 .7.6 .3.2
.3.5 .6.5 .3.2 .1.2G]
```

sesegan:
```
       t           t    N
[.3.2  .1.6  .5.6  .1.2
 .3.2  .1.6  .5.6  .1.2
 .3.5  ...3  .6.5  .3.2
 .3.3  .2.1  .6.5  .3.5G

       t           t    N
 .2.2  ...3  .1.2  .3.2
 .5.6  .5.3  .1.2  .3.2
 .5.6  .5.4  .2.1  .6.5
 .6.1  .2.1  .6.5  .3.5G

       t           t    N
 .2.2  ...4  .5.6  .5.4
 .6.5  .2.4  .5.6  .5.4
 .6.5  .2.1  .3.2  .6.5
 .3.3  .5.3  .2.1  .2.1G]
```

Bedhat, Ladrang, pélog
    pathet nem (38).

buka: 2 .5.3 .5.2 .356 .5.3N/G
```
    t     t N
[.111  2321
 2123  5321
 2123  5321
 33.5  63ᵣᶜᶜ

    t          t    N
 3 3 6 5   2 1 2 6
 3 3 6 5   2 1 2 6
 3 3 6 5   2 1 2 6
 .7.6.7.6  .5.3523G

     t            t    N
 .5.3.5.3   .5.3562
 .5.3.5.3   .5.3562
 .5.3.5.3   .5.3562
 523 5 6   7 6 5 3G]
```

84

Bedhat, Ladrang, sléndro
    pathet nem (2).

buka: 532 .5.3 .52. 2356 .5.3N/G

```
    t    t N
[ .111 2321
  561. 2321
  561. 2321
  3212 .126G

    t    t N
  .123 2126
  .123 2126
  .123 2126
  1165 1653G

    t        t    N
  .356 .356 .356 .532
  .356 .356 .356 .532
  .356 .356 .356 .532
  .5.5 .... .1.6 .5.3G ]

    t    t N
  .323 5653
  .323 5653
  .561 .561
  .563 5616G

    t    t N
  .535 6156
  .535 6156
  .561 .561
  .516 5323G
```

Bedhaya, Gendhing, kethuk 4 arang, minggah
   kethuk 8, pélog pathet barang (27).

buka: .576 .532 ..7. 6.7. 6.73 .532N/G

mérong:

```
         t                    t
[..23 2767 .2.7 6535 .... 55.. 5576 .532
 ..23 55.. 5576 .532 ..7. 6.7. 6.73 .532N
 ..23 2767 .2.7 6535 .6.3 5635 ..65 3567
 ..2. 7.23 4323 2756 .... 6656 .2.3 5676N
 .... 6656 .653 2356 .653 2356 .567 .653
 235. 55.. 55.. 6356 ..35 6732 723. 3532N
 ..23 2767 .2.7 6535 .65. 5672 .3.2 .765 →
 .... 55.. 5576 .532 ..7. 6.7. 6.73 .532N/G]
```

ompak inggah:

```
       t                    t
→..3. 2.72 ..3. 2.72 ..3. 2.7. 6.67 6535N/G
```

inggah:

```
   t    t    t    t    t    t    t    t N
[..3. 2.7. 6.67 6535 234. 234. 3.42 .4.3
 ..2. 7.2. 7.67 6535 234. 234. 3.42 .4.3
 ..2. 7.2. 7.67 6535 ..23 5576 .532 7232
 ..3. 2.72 ..3. 2.72 ..3. 2.7. 6.67 6535G]
```

Bèdru, Ladrang, sléndro
   pathet sanga (38).

buka: 612 1635 323. 3635N/G

```
    t    t N
[1612 1635
 1612 1635
 1612 1635
 1621 6561G
```

```
    t        t   N
 .2.1.2.1 .2.1256
 .2.1.2.1 .2.1256
 .2.1.2.1 .2.1265
 3 2 3 .  3 6 3 5G]
```

Bèlèk, Gendhing, kethuk 4 arang, minggah
kethuk 8, pélog pathet barang (1).

buka: .6.6 .765 63.5 67.7 .5.6 35.3N/G

mérong:
```
       t                t
[.356 .356 .356 .356 5653 2756 33.. 6532
 5653 2756 33.. 6532 5653 2767 .3.2 .756N
 3567 6563 77.. 5676 3567 6563 ..36 3567
 22.. 22.. 22.3 2767 ..32 .767 2343 2756N
 3567 6563 77.. 5676 3567 6563 ..36 3567
 22.. 22.. 22.3 2767 ..32 .767 2343 2756N
 22.. 2327 232. 6563 ..36 3567 2327 6563
 22.. 22.3 56.7 6523 ..35 67.. 7656 .5.3N/G]
```

ompak:
```
       t                t        N
 77.. 7767 ..72 3353 6765 3276 .7.6 .5.3
 77.. 7767 ..72 3353 6765 3276 .7.6 .5.3
 77.. 7767 55.. 7653 6765 3276 .7.6 .5.3
 .5.3 .7.6 .5.3 .7.6 .5.3 .7.6 .7.6 .5.3G
```

minggah:
```
   t    t    t    t    t    t    t    t N
[.5.3 .7.6 .5.3 .7.6 .5.3 .7.6 .7.6 .5.3
 .2.7 .2.7 .5.6 .5.3 .6.5 .7.6 .7.6 .5.3
 .2.7 .2.7 .5.6 .5.3 .6.5 .7.6 .7.6 .5.3
 .5.3 .7.6 .5.3 .7.6 .5.3 .7.6 .7.6 .5.3G]
```

Bendrong, Lancaran, pélog
pathet nem (3).

buka: .5.2 .5.2 .5.3N/G

```
 t tN t tN t tN t tN
[.5.3 .5.2 .5.2 .5.3G
 .5.3 .5.2 .5.2 .5.6G
 .4.2 .4.5 .2.4 .5.6G
 .4.2 .4.5 .2.4 .5.6G
 .2.3 .2.1 .6.5 .2.3G]
```

87

Béndrong, Lancaran, sléndro
    pathet manyura (2).

buka: 5.2 .5.2 .5.3N/G

    [.5.3 .5.2 .5.2 .5.3G
     .5.3 .5.2 .5.2 .5.6G
     .1.6 .1.5 .1.5 .1.6G
     .1.6 .1.5 .1.5 .1.6G
     .2.3 .2.1 .6.5 .2.3G]

Bima Kurda, Ladrang, pélog
    pathet barang (1).

buka: ...5 .235 .35. 6765N/G

        t   t N ⎞
    [...5 .235   ⎟
     ...5 .235   ⎬ x2
     ...5 .235   ⎟
     .35. 6765G ⎠

ngelik:
        t   t N ⎞
     .77. 7656   ⎟
     567. 7656   ⎬ x2
     567. 7656   ⎟
     .53. 2365G ⎠

        t   t N ⎞
     .22. 2327   ⎟
     672. 2327   ⎬ x2
     6732 .756   ⎟
     .53. 2365G ⎠]

Bima Kurda, Ladrang, pélog
pathet barang (22).

buka: (from Gangsaran)

```
    t   t N  ⎞
[.5.5 .2.5  ⎟
 .5.5 .2.5  ⎬ x2
 .5.5 .2.5  ⎟
 .25. 6765G ⎠

    t   t N  ⎞
 ..57 5676  ⎟
 7576 7576  ⎬ x2
 756. 6725  ⎟
 .25. 6765G ⎠

    t   t N
 ..57 5676
 7232 .765
 ..57 5676
 7232 .765G

    t   t N   ⎞
 6352 3565   ⎟
 7656 3532   ⎬ x2
 6567 6532   ⎟
 1216 5365G ⎠]
```

Bindri, Lancaran, sléndro
pathet sanga (2).

buka: $\overline{5}1\overline{65}\overline{35}1$ 2165N/G

```
    N  N  N  N
[61 21 21 65G
 61 21 21 65G
 16 53 52 35G→
 16 53 52 35G]

    N    N    N    N
→1 6  5 3  5 23  561G
```

(transition to Bindri, Ladrang)

Bindri, Ladrang, sléndro pathet sanga (16).

```
    t   t N      t   t N      t   t N      t   t N
[ .165 3561   .165 3561   ..52 3565   ..52 3565
  .165 3561   .165 3561   1656 5321   1656 5321
  .165 3561   .165 3561   5616 5321   5616 5321
  55.2 3561G  55.2 3565G  55.2 3565G  55.2 3561G ]
```


Bolang-bolang, Gendhing, kethuk 4
    kerep, sléndro pathet manyura (1).

buka: .661 6535 .22. 2356 .365 3212N/G

mérong:
```
    t    t    t    t    N
[ .123 .123 .123 6123 ..35 6535 2353 2126
  .561 .516 .561 6523 ..35 6535 2353 2126
  .561 .516 .561 6523 66.. 6656 3561 6523
  .516 .... 3561 6535 .22. 2356 .365 3212G ]
```


Bondhan Kinanthi, Gendhing, kethuk 4 kerep,
    minggah kethuk 4, pélog pathet nem (3).

buka: 3 .561 .1.3 .212 .126N/G

mérong:
```
    t      t      t      t      N
[ ..61 2165 3561 3216 .... 6656 2321 6535
  ..56 1654 2.44 2126 .... 6656 2321 6535
  ..56 1654 2.44 2126 33.. 3353 6535 3231→
  6563 .... 33.6 3561 .... 1121 3212 .126G]
```

umpak minggah:
```
    t      t      t      t      N
→ .5.3 .5.3 .5.3 .2.1 .2.1 .2.3 .1.2 .1.6G
```

minggah:
```
   t    t    t    t N
[.1.6 .1.6 .2.1 .3.2
 .3.1 .2.6 .2.1 .3.2
 .3.1 .2.6 .3.2 .3.1
 .2.1 .2.1 .3.2 .1.6G]
```

Bondhèt, Gendhing, kethuk 8 kerep, minggah
kethuk 16, pélog pathet barang (1).

buka: 3.27 2766 .6.. 3.27 2766 .6.. .6.6 .6.6 .7.6 5323N/G

mérong:
```
        t           t           t           t
  [...3 6532 .7.6 5323 ...3 6532 .7.6 5323
   ...3 6532 .7.6 5323 21.2 .165 ..52 3565N
   ..57 .656 .5.3 .7.6 .5.3 .7.6 .532 .4.3
   .4327 6576 ..67 5676 33.. 3327 .765 3576N
   33.. 6532.3267 5676 33.. 6532 .4.3 2765
   63.6 356. 63.6 356. 6756 .532 ..35 3272N
   ..35 3272 ..35 3272 356. 6532 .4.3 2765→
   .7.6 .532 ..23 5676 .... 66.. 6676 5323N/G]
```

umpak minggah:
```
       t           t           t           t
  → .7.6 .532 .2.2 .235 ..57 5672 .653 2365N/G
```

minggah:
```
     t    t    t    t    t    t    t    t
  [..57 5672 .653 2365 ..57 5672 .653 2365
   ..57 5672 .653 2365 7.76 5323 44.. 2343N
   .33. 3327 .667 2342 .33. 3327 .653 2365
   .11. 1231 .653 2365 7.76 5323 44.. 2344N
   .33. 3327 .667 2342 .33. 3327 .653 2365
   .11. 1231 .653 2365 7.76 5323 44.. 2344N
   234. 4327 ..72 3434 234. 4323 .333 2765
   .22. 2765 .22. 2765 .77. 7632 .653 2365N/G

     t    t    t    t    t    t    t    t
   .77. 7632 .653 2365 .77. 7632 .653 2365
   .77. 7632 .653 2365 7.76 5323 44.. 2343N
   33.. 3327 .667 2343 .33. 3327 .653 2365
   .77. 7632 .653 2365 7.76 5323 44.. 2343N
   .33. 3327 .667 2343 .33. 3327 .653 2365
   .77. 7632 .653 2365 7.76 5323 4434 2344N
   234. 4327 ..72 3434 234. 4323 .333 2765
   .22. 2765 .22. 2765 ..57 5672 .653 2365N/G]
```

Bondhèt, Gendhing, kethuk 2 kerep, minggah kethuk 4,
slèndro pathet sanga, pélog pathet nem (3).

buka: .661 2355 6656 2612 2165N/G

mérong:
```
      t        t    N
..53 6535 22.3 5635
[..53 6535 22.3 5616→
..6. 6656 2321 6523
.333 5654 2454 2165G

      t        t    N
22.. 22.3 5654 2165]
```

umpak minggah:
```
      t        t    N
→.5.6 .5.6 .2.1 .5.3
.5.6 .5.3 .2.4 .6.5G
```

minggah:
```
   t    t    t    t N
[.6.5 .3.2 .3.2 .6.5
.6.5 .3.2 .3.2 .6.5
.1.6 .1.6 .2.1 .5.3
.5.6 .5.3 .2.4 .6.5G ]
```

Bondhèt/Bundhèt, Gendhing, kethuk 2 kerep,
dhawah kethuk 4, slèndro pathet sanga (5).

buka: 353 5653 2132 55.5N/G

lamba:
```
      t        t    N
.3.2 .3.5 .6.3 .6.5
.3.5 .6.5 .2.3 .5.6
.1.6 .1.2 .3.1 .5.3
5353 1653 2132 1635G
```

dados:
```
      t        t    N
[3512 .365 1653 2165
3565 3235 2523 5616
2126 .132 5321 6523
5353 1653 2132 1635G]
```

pangkat ndhawah:
```
      t        t    N
   3512 .365 1653 2165
   3565 3235 2523 5616
   2126 .132 5321 6523
   .5.3 .5.3 .1.2 .6.5G
```

dhawah:
```
      t    t    t    t N
  [.6.5 .3.2 .3.2 .6.5
   .6.5 .3.2 .3.2 .1.6
   .1.6 .3.2 .3.1 .5.3
   .5.3 .5.3 .1.2 .6.5G]
```

Bontit, Gendhing, kethuk 4 kerep, minggah
kethuk 8, sléndro pathet sanga (2).

buka: 352 .6.5 .2.3 .5.1 .5.6N/G

mérong:
```
      t           t           t           t     N
  [..61 6535 .352 .356 .352 ..23 5653 2165
   .612 .165 1653 2356 11.. 1121 3212 .165
   .612 .165 1653 2356 11.. 1121 3212 .165 →
   2356 3532 ..25 2356 ..61 6535 11.. 3216G]
```

umpak minggah:
```
        t           t           t           t     N
  → .2.3 .5.2 .5.3 .5.2 .5.3 .5.2 .6.3 .6.5G
```

minggah:
```
      t    t    t    t    t    t    t    t N
  [.2.1 .2.6 .3.6 .3.2 .6.5 .3.2 .6.5 .1.6
   .3.2 .1.6 .3.6 .3.2 .6.5 .3.2 .6.5 .1.6
   .3.2 .1.6 .3.6 .3.2 .6.5 .3.2 .6.5 .1.6
   .2.3 .5.2 .5.3 .5.2 .5.3 .5.2 .6.3 .6.5G]
```

Boyong, Gendhing [Ketawang], kethuk 2
    kerep, pélog pathet barang (16).

buka: 3. 3.27 672. 2327 .6.5 .3.2N/G

mérong:
```
            t         t    N
      [.6.5 .6.3 .6.5 .3.2 →
       .6.5 .6.3 .6.5 .3.2G
```

ngelik:
```
            t         t    N
       66.. 66.. 6765 3356
       .765 33.5 6756 .523

            t         t    N
       .567 .... 7656 .523
       66.. 6532 7232 .756

            t         t    N
       33.. 3356 3532 .756
       22.. 2327 3265 3532G]
```

umpak:
```
            t         t    N
       →.6.3 .6.5 .6.3 2356G
```

dhawah: Ladrang Boyong

Boyong, Ladrang, pélog pathet barang (16).

(dhawah to Gendhing Boyong)
```
   t    t N          irama III:  t     t N
 [.7.6 .7.6                    [.7.6 .7.6
  .7.6 .5.3                     .2.7 .5.3
  .6.5 .6.5                     .2.7 .5.6
  .3.2 .7.6G]                   .3.2 .7.6G]
```

Boyong Basuki, Ketawang, pélog
    pathet barang (3).

buka: ..67 2327 3265 .3.2N/G
umpak:
         t   t N t   t N
    [[.6.5 .6.3 .6.5 .3.2G]
ngelik:
         t   t N t   t N
      66.. 66.. 6765 3356G
      .765 33.5 6756 .523G
      66.. 6532 7232 .756G
      .2.3 .2.7 3265 .3.2G]

Boyong Basuki, Ladrang,
    pélog pathet barang (16).

      t   t N
    [.7.6 .7.6
     .2.7 .5.3
     .2.7 .3.2
     .3.7 .5.6G]

Bremara, Gendhing, kethuk 2 kerep,
   pélog pathet lima (1).

buka: 1.23 5.31 .235 .5.2 .5.2 4521N/G

```
    t         t    N
[...1 2321 2321 3565
 ..56 7653 .333 1235
 ..56 7653 .333 1235
 ...5 2232 .444 65421̄G

    t         t    N
 ...1 23.5 2312 3565
 ..56 7653 .333 1235
 ..56 7653 .333 1235
 ...3 1121 .312 3565G

    t         t    N
 ..5. 35.. 6727 6535
 7656 5356 7653 2123
 1235 6756 .653 2123
 1235 6565 .532 5653G

    t              t       N
. . 3 .  3 2 5 6  7 6 5 3  2 1 2̲ 3
1 2 3 5  6 7̲ 5̲ 6  5 4 . 2  5 4 4̄2̄1
5 4 2 1  5 4̄2̄1̄2̄4  . 4 4 4  6 5 4̄2̄1
6 6 . .  6 6 5 4  2 4 . 2  4 5 4̄2̄1G

    t         t    N
 ...1 23.1 23.1 2321
 55.. 5532 3216 2165
 33.. 6532 3216 2165
 .6.3 .6.3 .6.5 .6.3G]

    t         t    N
 .6.5 .6.3 .655 .532
 5325 3253 6555 3532
 5325 3353 655. 3532
 5325 3254 .444 65421̄G

    t         t    N
 22.. 2216 3565 5522
 5325 3253 6555 5532
 5325 3253 655. 5532
 5325 3254 .444 65421̄G

    t         t    N
 66.. 6612 3216 5612
 33.. 6532 3216 2165
 33.. 6532 3216 2165
 1.16 1.15 1.16 1.15G
```

```
         t        t    N
1.16  1.15  1.16  1.15
33..  6532  3216  2165
33..  6532  3216  2165
33..  33..  555.  5523G

         t        t    N
.655  .552  2.65  5532
5325  3253  635.  5532
5325  3253  655.  5532
5325  3254  444.  65421G

         t        t    N
66..  6612  3216  5616
32..  6532  3216  2165
33..  6532  3216  2165
1.16  1.15  1.16  1.15G]
```

seseg:
```
         t        t    N
[1216  1215  1216  1215
3323  6532  3216  2165
3323  6532  3216  2165
1216  1215  1216  1215G]
```

Bribil, Ketawang, sléndro
    pathet sanga (1).

buka: 11. 1612 .6.2 .6.1N/G

```
   t    t N  t    t N
[ 6162  6261  6162  3235G
  3235  3235  2163  1321G ]
```

Bubaran Nyutra, Lancaran,
    sléndro pathet sanga (2).

buka: 2 .3.5 .6.1 .6.5N/G

```
   N     N    N     N
[.6.3  .5.3  .5.2  .3.5G
 .3.2  .3.2  .3.2  .6.5G
 .2.1  .2.1  .2.1  .6.5G ]
```

Budheng-budheng, Gendhing, kethuk 2 awis,
   minggah kethuk 4, pélog pathet nem (1).

buka: 3 .5.6 .565 .5.6 .5.4 .2.4 2121N/G

mérong:
```
         t                    t         N
[..12 3565 ..56 .532 ..13 .21. 6.21 6535
 .6.3 5635 33.. 1232 ..13 .21. 6.21 6535
 .6.3 5635 33.. 1232 ..13 .21. 6.21 6535 →
 33.. 33.. 3356 .535 ..56 .5.4 .2.4 2121G]
```

umpak:
```
         t                    t         N
→ 33.. 33.. 3356 .535 .2.4 .5.4 .1.2 .5.3G
```

minggah:
```
   t    t    t    t N
[.5.6 .5.6 .5.3 .1.2
 .5.6 .5.6 .5.3 .1.2
 .5.3 .5.6 .2.1 .6.5
 .2.4 .5.4 .1.2 .5.3G]
```


Cacadingrat, Gendhing, kethuk 4 kerep, minggah
   kethuk 8, pélog pathet barang (1).

mérong:
```
    t         t         t         t      N
[.3.3 .567 .2.7 6535 7656 5323 ...3 6723
 ...3 6723 ...3 6723 .53. 5327 .2.7 6563
 21.. 11.. 11.2 3565 ..57 .656 .532 .765
 33.6 3567 .2.7 6535 33.6 3567 .2.7 6535G
```

ngelik:
```
    t         t         t         t      N
.... 55.. 55.6 .535 ..56 5323 ..35 6767
...7 .567 .567 2765 32.3 5676 .535 3272
..23 6532 52.3 5676 ..67 5676 53.. 6723 →
...3 6723 ...3 6723 .53. 5356 7653 6723G]
```

ompak:
```
    t         t         t         t      N
→ ...3 6723 ...3 6723 55.. 7653 ..35 6767G
 ...3 6723 ...3 6723 55.. 55.. 55.6 .535
 7653277.. 77.2 3434 .... 44.. 4323 2767
 ...7 .567 .567 .567 55.. 55.. 7656 3565
 .532 7232 3276 5672 672. 2723 4327 6535G
```

inggah:
```
   t    t    t    t    t    t    t    t N
[33.6 3567 2327 6535 7656 5323 .333 2723
 .333 2723 .333 2723 .53. 5327 2327 6563
 21.. 11.. 11.2 3565 ..57 .656 .532 .765
 33.6 3567 2327 6535 66.3 3567 2327 6535G]
```

Candra, Gendhing, kethuk 2 kerep, minggah
    kethuk 4, sléndro pathet sanga (2).

buka: 2 .356 .6.1 .2.1 .2.6 .3.5N/G

mérong:
```
     t         t    N
[..53 6532 ..23 5635
 ..53 6532 ..23 5635
 ..53 6532 ..23 1232
 ..23 5321 2321 6535G

     t         t    N
 ..56 1653 2321 6535
 ..56 1653 2321 6535
 22.. 5321 .111 6535
 ..53 6532 ..23 5635G

     t         t    N
 ..53 6532 ..23 5635
 ..53 6532 ..23 5616 →
 .... 2321 55.6 1653
 22.3 5321 2321 6535G]
```

umpak minggah:
```
       t         t    N
 → .5.6 .2.1 .5.6 .3.2
   .3.5 .2.1 .2.1 .6.5G
```

minggah:
```
    t    t    t    t N
[.6.5 .3.2 .3.2 .6.5
 .6.5 .3.2 .3.2 .5.6
 .5.6 .2.1 .5.6 .3.2
 .3.5 .2.1 .2.1 .6.5G

    t    t    t    t N
 .2.5 .2.1 .2.1 .6.5
 .2.5 .2.1 .2.1 .6.5
 .2.6 .2.1 .2.1 .6.5
 .6.5 .3.2 .3.2 .6.5G]
```

99

Candra Nata, Gendhing, kethuk 2
    kerep, pélog pathet lima (3).

buka: 3. 2165 .5.3 2165 .65. 5612 1312 .165N/G

mérong:
            t   t   N
      [.65. 5612 1312 .165
       33.. 3353 6535 3212
       .316 .3.2 .316 .3.2
       16.. 6653 .532 .356G

            t   t   N
       ..6. 6653 .532 .356
       ..6. 6653 .532 .356
       55.. 55.6 7656 5421
       561. 5612 1312 .165G]

Candra Sari, Gendhing, kethuk 4 kerep,
    pélog pathet lima (1).

buka: 465 .421 .21. 1245 4645 .421N/G

mérong:
     t   t   t   t   N
[.21. 1245 4645 .421 23.. 33.. 6535 3212
 .316 .312 .316 .312 16.. 6653 .532 .356
 ..6. 6653 .532 .356 ..6. 6653 .532 .356
 44.. 44.. 4465 .421 .21. 1245 4645 .421G]

Candra Upa/Candra Hupaya, Ladrang,
    sléndro pathet sanga (2).

buka: 556 3565 6621 3265N/G

```
   t     t N
[ ..56 1232
  .216 5612
  ..23 5.65
  6621 3265G
```

```
  t  __     t   N
2 2 .356 1 615 6
2 2 .356 1 615 6
2 2 .356 1 6 1 5
2 3 2 1 . 5 6 1G
```

```
  t     t N
..32 .165
1656 5312
66.1 6535
6621 3265G ]
```

Cangket, Gendhing, kethuk 4 awis, minggah
    kethuk 8, pélog pathet barang (38).

buka: 2 .2.2 .723 .3.2 .723 .272 .756N/G

mérong:
```
            t                  t            N
[.3.3 .532 .327 .3.2 76.. 66.. 3567 6535
 .23. 33.5 67.6 5356 3567 6532 723. 3532N
 76.. 3532 .327 .3.2 76.. 66.. 3567 6535
 .23. 33.5 67.6 5356 3567 6532 723. 3532N
 76.. 3532 .327 .3.2 76.. 66.. 3567 6535
 .23. 33.5 67.6 5356 3567 6532 7232 .756N →
 22.. 2327 2327 6563 ..36 3567 2327 6563
 22.. 22.3 56.7 6523 272. 2723 6532 .756N/G]
```

umpak:
```
      t         t         t         t
→.2.7 .5.3 .5.6 .5.3 .5.2 .4.3 .4.3 .7.6N/G
```

minggah:
```
  t    t    t    t    t    t    t    t N
[.7.6 .2.3 .4.3 .2.3 .4.3 .2.3 .4.3 .7.6
 .7.6 .2.3 .4.3 .2.3 .4.3 .2.3 .4.3 .7.6
 .7.6 .2.3 .4.3 .2.3 .4.3 .2.3 .4.3 .7.6
 .2.7 .5.3 .5.6 .5.3 .5.2 .4.3 .4.3 .7.6G]
```

Cangklek, Ladrang, sléndro
pathet manyura (15).

```
   t    t N
[ 5653 5652
  5653 2126
  2321 3216
  3356 5352G ]
```

Capang, Gendhing, kethuk 2 kerep, minggah
kethuk 4, sléndro pathet manyura (2).

buka: 2 .356 .6.6 .5.3 .5.2 .1.6N/G

mérong:
```
       t      t    N
[..12 1653 6532 .356
 ..12 1653 6532 .356 →
 ..12 1653 6532 .356
 .... 6165 3352 3565G

       t      t    N
 1656 5323 6532 3565
 1656 5323 6535 3212
 5653 2123 ..35 2352
 66.1 6532 .165 1216G]
```

umpak minggah:
```
       t      t    N
→..12 1653 6532 .3.2
 .3.2 .5.6 .1.6 .3.2G
```

minggah:
```
       t    t    t    t N
[.3.2 .5.6 .1.6 .3.2
 .3.2 .5.6 .1.6 .3.2
 .5.3 .2.3 .5.6 .5.3
 .5.6 .3.2 .6.5 .1.6G

       t    t    t    t N
 .3.2 .5.3 .5.2 .5.6
 .3.2 .5.3 .5.2 .5.6
 .3.2 .5.3 .5.2 .3.2
 .3.2 .5.6 .1.6 .3.2G]
```

Carang Gantung, Gendhing, kethuk 2
kerep, sléndro pathet manyura (1).

```
    t        t   N
.123 ..61 2356 5352
.123 ..61 2356 5352
.126 ..6. 3561 6523
561. 1653 6521 3216G
```

Cèlèng Mogok, Ladrang, sléndro
pathet manyura (20).

buka: 1312 1516 5323 6532N/G

```
   t    t N        t     t N
[ 5356 5352      1312 1516
  5356 5352      1312 1516
  5356 5352      1312 1516
  5323 5616G     5323 6532G ]
```

Cempa Rowa, Dolanan, sléndro
pathet sanga (28).

```
                       [ 61  5
.2  35  2  .6     61  21  61  5
.2  35  2  .      2   6   2   1
2   6   2  .      2   6   2   1
2   6   2  .      .   5   23  5
22  22  56  15    15  22  22  11
21  61  21  11    21  61  21  11
21  61  21  1 ]
```

Céré Méndé, Ladrang, pélog
    pathet nem (1).

buka: 33. 2132 6123 6532N/G

```
  t   t N        t    t N
.22. 2123      ..23 2161
.33. 6563      ..23 2161
.33. 6563      .33. 3132
6535 6121G     3123 6532G
```

Clunthang, Ladrang, sléndro
    pathet sanga (3).

buka: .555 6165 2232 1121N/G
```
  t   t N
5616 5321
5616 5656
5656 3535
.2.1 .6.5N/G
```

irama II & III:
```
   t   t N
[.1.6 .3.5
 .1.6 .3.5
 .1.6 .3.5
 .2.3 .2.1G

   t   t N
 .5.6 .2.1
 .5.6 .5.6
 .5.6 .3.5
 .2.1 .6.5G]
```

Clunthang, Ladrang, pélog
   pathet nem (3).

buka: 555 6165 2232 1121N/G

t t N		t t N	
.5.6	.2.1	.1.6	.3.5
.5.6	.5.6	.1.6	.3.5
.5.6	.3.5	.1.6	.3.5
.2.1	.6.5G	.2.4	.2.1G

Clunthang/Lala Grantung, Ladrang,
   sléndro pathet sanga (16).

(minggah to Gendhing Sumedhang)

t t N		t t N	
.5.6	.2.1	.1.6	.3.5
.5.6	.5.6	.1.6	.3.5
.5.6	.3.5	.1.6	.3.5
.2.1	.6.5G	.2.3	.2.1G

Cublak-cublak Suweng, Dolanan,
   sléndro pathet sanga (30).

buka celuk: 1N/G

t t N	
[.5.3	.2.1
.5.3	.2.1
.5.6	.2.1
.5.6	.2.1
.5.6	.2.1
.2.1	.2.1
.2.1	.2.1G]

Cucur Bawuk, Gendhing, kethuk 2
  kerep, sléndro pathet manyura (3).

buka: .222 3322 3132 .126N/G

mérong:
```
          t        t    N
        .6.6  .6.6 3561 6535
       [.23.  33.5 6561 6535
        .23.  33.5 61.6 5356
        3561  6532 1232 .126G

          t        t    N
        22..  2321 2321 6523
        ..36  3561 2321 6523 →
        22..  22.3 56.1 6523
        212.  2123 6532 .126G
```

ngelik:
```
          t        t    N
        ..6.  6656 3561 6535]
```

umpak:
```
          t        t    N
      →.1.2 .5.6 .2.1 .5.3
       .2.1 .2.3 .1.2 .1.6G
```
minggah: Paré Anom, kethuk 4

Damar Kèli, Gendhing, kethuk 4 kerep, minggah
  kethuk 8, sléndro pathet manyura (2).

buka: 3 .561 .1.1 .2.3 .212 .126N/G

mérong:
```
        t         t         t         t    N
      [..65 3356 2321 6532 ..23 6532 5323 5616
       ..65 3356 2321 6532 ..23 6532 5323 5616
       ..65 3356 2321 6532 ..23 6532 5323 5616 →
       33.. 33.. 3361 2321 .... 1123 6532 .126G

        t         t         t         t    N
       .... 66.. 3561 6523 ..35 6532 1216 3532
       5653 2126 3561 6523 ..35 6532 1216 3532
       5653 2126 3561 6523 ..35 6532 1216 3532
       5653 2165 33.6 3561 .... 1123 6532 .126G]
```

umpak minggah:
```
     t         t         t         t    N
→.5.3 .5.3 .5.3 .2.1 .2.3 .2.1 .2.1 .5.3G
```
minggah:
```
   t   t   t   t   t   t   t   t N
[.5.3 .2.1 .2.3 .2.1 .2.3 .2.1 .2.1 .5.3
 .5.3 .2.1 .2.3 .2.1 .2.3 .2.1 .2.1 .5.3
 .5.6 .2.1 .5.3 .2.1 .2.1 .2.6 .5.6 .5.3
 .6.5 .2.1 .5.6 .5.3 .6.5 .2.1 .2.1 .5.3G]
```

Dana Raja, Gendhing, kethuk 4 awis, minggah
    kethuk 8, sléndro pathet sanga (38).

buka: .352 .6.6 .2.3 .5.6 .1.6N/G

mérong:
```
        t                 .        t
 .1.1 .1.1 .3.2 .165 .356 3532 66.1 6535
[.356 3532 66.1 6535 2356 5321 6132 .165N
 .61. 1216 532. 2365 .61. 1216 532. 2365
 11.. 11.2 3516 3532 5653 2121 3532 .165N
 .61. 1216 532. 2365 .61. 1216 532. 2365
 11.. 11.2 3516 3532 5653 2121 3532 .165N→
 11.. 3216 3565 2232 ..25 2356 3565 2232
 66.. 66.. 661. 5616 ..23 55.. 55.6 1656N/G
```
```
        t                      t
 .561 .561 5612 .165 .356 3532 66.1 6535]
```
umpak:

```
→.2.3 .5.2 .5.3 .5.2 .5.3 .5.2 .6.3 .6.5N/G
```
minggah:
```
   t   t   t   t   t   t   t   t N
[.2.1 .2.6 .3.6 .3.2 .6.5 .3.2 .6.5 .1.6
 .3.2 .1.6 .3.6 .3.2 .6.5 .3.2 .6.5 .1.6
 .3.2 .1.6 .3.6 .3.2 .6.5 .3.2 .6.5 .1.6
 .2.3 .5.2 .5.3 .5.2 .5.3 .5.2 .6.3 .6.5G]
```

Dara Dasih, Gendhing, [Ketawang], kethuk 4 kerep,
    minggah kethuk 8, pélog pathet lima (1).

buka: 123. 2165 123. 2165 .3.3 .321 1412 4565N/G

mérong:

```
      t              t              t              t          N
[. . . .  5 6 5 4  2 4 5 .  5 6 5 4  2 4 5 .  5 4 5 6  . 6 5 4  2 1 2 1
 5 6 1 .  1 3 1 2  5 6 1 .  1 3 1 2  5 6 1 .  1 1 . 2  4 5 6 5  4 2 1 2G

      t              t                 t                 t       N
. 2 2 2  4 5 4 2  4 5 4 2  323 216  5 5 . .  5 6 1 2  323 216  2 1 6 5
 1 5 . .  5 6 1 2  323 216  2 1 6 5  3 3 . .  3 3 5 3  6 5 3 2  2 1 2 6G

    t          t              t                 t        N
356 356  356 216  6 6 . .  2 1 5 2  . . . .  3 3 5 6  621 621  621 5 3
 . . . .  3 3 5 6  621 621  621 5 4  2 4 . 2  4 5 421  7 7 . .  5 6 7 6G

      t              t              t              t          N
. 7 6 .  6 7 6 5  2 4 5 4  6 5 421  4 1 . 2  4 5 421  4 1 . 2  4 5 421
 4 1 . 2  4 5 421  4 1 . 2  4 5 421  . . . .  . . . .  5 6 5 4  5 2 4 5G

      t              t              t              t          N
. . . .  5 6 5 4  2 4 5 .  5 6 5 4  2 4 5 .  5 4 5 6  . 6 5 4  2 1 2 1
 5 6 1 .  1 3 1 2  5 6 1 .  1 3 1 2  5 6 1 .  1 1 . 2  4 5 6 5  4 2 1 2G

      t              t              t              t          N
. 2 2 2  4 5 4 2  4 5 4 2  1 6 5 4  . 4 4 .  4 4 5 6  1 6 5 4  2 4 6 5
 6 2 1 .  6 5 4 4  6 5 6 1  6 5 4 4  6 5 4 6  5 4 6 5  4 6 4 5  6 1 2 1G]
```

minggah:

```
  t    t    t    t    t    t    t    t N
[.233 .121 .233 .121 ..56 11.2 3323 2121
 .111 5621 .111 5621 ..56 11.2 4565 4212G

  t    t    t    t    t    t    t    t N
.222 4542 4542 1654 .44. 4456 1652 2465
.621 6544 6561 6544 6546 5465 4645 6121G]
```

Dara Dasih, Gendhing [pamijèn], kethuk 4 awis:
1st kenong, kethuk 2; when gong, kethuk 3;
sléndro pathet sanga (4).

buka: 2 .2.6 .2.1 .3.2 .165 32.3 5635N/G
mérong:
        t   t
  [612. 2165 1653 2356 11.. 1121 3212 .165N
  .612 .165 1653 2356 11.. 1121 3212 .165
  11.. 3216 3565 2232 66.. 66.. 3561 6535N
  .35. 5356 ..16 5352 .321 6132 66.. 6535
  2356 3532 66.. 6653 .... 3356 5323 2126N
  .16. 6123 5653 2126 33.. 3353 6535 3212 →
  5653 2165 32.3 5635N/G]

umpak:
       t
→.5.3 .6.5 .3.2 .6.5N/G

minggah: Ladrang Uluk-uluk

Dara Dasih, Ketawang, sléndro
pathet manyura (1).

buka celuk:

  t   t N t   t N
..33 3353 .635 6121G
..12 3265 3312 5321G
55.. 1653 .2.1 .216G

  t   t N t   t N
[2123 2126 2123 2126G
..6. 6165 335. 1653G
..61 2353 5565 3565G
33.. 3353 6165 1653G
55.. 5565 .6.5 1616G
.... 6632 312. 5321G
55.. 1653 .2.1 .216G]

Dempo, Dolanan, sléndro
pathet sanga (30).

```
  t tN t tN t tN t tN
[ ...5 2221 6165 2321
  55.6 1216 2321 6165G
  5555P ]
```

Dhalang Karahinan, Gendhing, kethuk 2 kerep,
minggah kethuk 4, sléndro pathet manyura (1).

buka: 2 .3.2 .5.3 .55. 6653 2356 2126N/G

mérong:
```
          t      t    N
   [..12 1653 6532 .356
    ..12 1653 6532 .356
    22.. 22.3 55.6 5323
    ..35 6535 2353 2126G
```

ngelik:
```
          t      t    N
    ..12 1653 6532 .356
    .... 6656 11.. 5616
    22.3 5356 22.3 5356
    22.. 2235 2356 3532G

          t      t    N
    .... 2235 2356 3532
    .... 2235 2356 3532
    33.. 6535 .22. 6535
    22.. 22.3 5653 2126G]
```

minggah:
```
      t    t    t    t N
   [.3.2 .5.3 .5.2 .1.6
    .3.2 .5.3 .5.2 .1.6
    .3.2 .3.2 .5.6 .5.3
    .5.6 .5.3 .2.3 .1.6G]
```

Dhandhang Gula Kéntar/Dhandhang
   Gula Mas Kéntar, Ladrang,
   sléndro pathet sanga (35).

buka: 235 2321 5612 1111N/G

```
   t    t N        t    t N
[.2.1 .2.1      2621 5321
 .2.1 5635      3532 1635
 .612 1635      2235 2321
 2621 2635G     5612 5321G]
```

Dhandhang Gula Mas Kéntar, Ladrang,
   pélog pathet lima (38).

buka: 556 .165 2232 1121N/G

```
    t    t N
[.5.6 .2.1
 .5.6 .5.6
 .3.2 .1.6
 .2.1 .6.5G
```

```
   t          t   N
.  .1̄2̄1̄6̄2  1̄5̄2 1 6̄3
3  .6̄5̄3̄2    3̄2̄1̄6̄5̄3̄5̄2
2  1̄3̄2̄1̄6̄2  3̄2̄1̄6̄5̄3̄5̄2
2  .5̄6̄5̄4̄6  5̄3̄3̄2̄1̄2̄1G]
```

Dhandhun, Gendḥing, kethuk 2 kerep,
  minggah kethuk 4, sléndro pathet nem (2).

buka: 3 .561 .1.3 .212 .126 .5.3N/G

mérong:
```
            t         t    N
    [.23.  3235  .616 5323
     .23.  3235  .616 5323
     .23.  3235  6123 ..23
     ....  3356  3565 2232G

            t         t    N
     5653  2126  33.. 6532
     5653  2126  33.. 6532
     5653  2165  33.6 3561 →
     ..13  .212  .126 .523G]
```

umpak minggah:
```
            t         t    N
     →.2.3 .1.2  .1.6 .5.3G
```

minggah:
```
      t    t    t    t N
    [.2.3 .6.5 .1.6 .5.3
     .2.3 .6.5 .1.6 .5.3
     .2.3 .6.5 .2.3 .5.3
     .5.3 .5.3 .6.5 .3.2G

      t    t    t    t N
     .5.3 .1.6 .3.6 .3.2
     .5.3 .1.6 .3.6 .3.2
     .5.3 .6.5 .3.5 .6.1
     .2.1 .3.2 .1.6 .5.3G]
```

Dhempel, Gendhing [Ketawang], kethuk 2
  kerep, sléndro pathet sanga (5).

buka: 1 1615 61.. 1656 12.6 1232 11.1N/G
mérong:

```
        t        t      N
     2656  12.. 2253 2121
  [21656  12.6 12.3 5635G

      t        t      N
   21656  12.. 2253 2121
   21656  12.6 12.3 5635G

      t        t      N
   1653  22.3 5621 6535
   1653  22.. 22.3 5635G

      t        t      N
   1653  22.3 5621 6535
   2356  1651 5616 5321G →

      t        t      N
   21656  12.. 2253 2121]
```

pangkat dhawah:

```
        t        t      N
  → 21656  12.. 2253 2121
    21656  12.. 2253 2121G

      t        t      N
   21656  12.. 2253 2121
   2656  12.6 12.3 5635G
```

dhawah: Ladrang Dhempel

Dhempel, Ladrang,
  sléndro pathet sanga (5).

(dhawah to Gendhing Dhempel)

```
 t    t N
6326 2165
6326 2165
2312 1216
2321 6535G

 t    t N
22.3 5635
1216 5321
‾‾‾‾
21656 12.6
12.3 5635G

 t    t N
6326 2165
6326 2165
2356 1651
5616 5321G

 t    t N
612. 5321
612. 5321
.12. 1.2.
6621 2635G

 t    t N
66.6 2321
3216 2321
‾‾‾‾
21656 12.6
12.3 5635G

 t    t N
6326 2165
6326 2165
2312 1216
2321 2635G
```

Dhempel, Ladrang, sléndro
    pathet sanga (1).

```
t     t N
.323 5635
.323 5635
2356 1656
5323 2121G

t     t N
612. 2321
612. 2321
..2. 1.2.
6.21 6535G

t     t N
66.. 2321
3216 2321
2656 12.6
12.3 5235G

t     t N
.323 5635
.323 5635
22.. 22..
2321 6535G

t     t N
22.3 5235
1656 5321
2656 12.6
12.3 5235G
```

Dhempo Talu Tameng, Dolanan,
    sléndro pathet nem (32).

buka celuk:

```
      N         N
[ . . 3 6   6 5 3 2G
  2 3 5 3   6 5 3 2G
  3 3 3 3   3 6 6 5G
  5 3 6 5   5 3 3 2G
  . . . .   2 2 2 6G
  6 5 5 2   3 5 3 5G
  . . 6 6   12.6535G
  6 . 122   1 6 165G ]
```

Dhendha Gedhé, Gendhing [Ketawang], kethuk
    2 kerep, sléndro pathet sanga (38).

buka: .532 .2.3 .235N/G
mérong:
```
         t        t    N
    [..53 2356 .2.1 .6.5
     1216 .532 ..23 5635G →

         t        t    N
     ..53 2356 .2.1 .6.5
     1216 .532 66.1 6535G

         t        t    N
     .352 ..23 5653 2165
     2312 ..23 5653 2165G

         t        t    N
     22.. 22.3 5653 2165
     1216 .532 ..23 5635G]
```
→ minggah: Ladrang Dhendha Gedhé.

Dhendha Gedhé, Ketawang,
    pélog pathet nem (38).

buka: 2 .2.3 .235G
```
        t    t N  t    t N
    [ .532 ..23 5654 2165G
      2312 ..23 5654 2165G →
      1216 3532 ..23 5635G
      .532 6656 ..61 2165G ]
```
    suwuk:
```
        t    t N  t    t N
    →1216 3532 11.. 32.6G
```

116

Dhendha Gedhé, Ketawang,
    sléndro pathet sanga (2).

buka: 2 .2.3 23.5N/G

      t   t N t   t N
[..53 2356 .2.1 .6.5G →
 1216 .532 ..23 5635G

ngelik:
      t   t N t   t N
 .352 ..23 5653 2165G
 2312 ..23 5653 2165G
 1216 .532 ..23 5635G]

suwuk:
      t   t N t   t N
→1216 .532 66.1 6535G

Dhendha Gedhé, Ladrang,
    sléndro pathet sanga (38).

(minggah to Gendhing Dhendha Gedhé)
      t   t N   t   t N   t   t N
 .6.5 .1.6   .6.5 .1.6   .2.1 .2.1
 .2.1 .6.5   .2.1 .6.5   .3.2 .6.5
 .6.5 .3.2   .6.5 .3.2   .1.6 .3.2
 .3.2 .6.5G   .3.2 .3.1G   .3.2 .6.5G

Dhendha Santi, Ketawang,
    sléndro pathet sanga (16)

buka: 51 6532 .11. 561. 5612 .165G

```
      t    t N  t    t N
  [.61. 561. 5612 .165G
   22.3 5.65 1656 .532G
   ..23 5.65 1656 .532G
   .11. 561. 5612 .165G
   .61. 561. 5612 .165G
   11.. 1121 22.1 6535G
   ..23 5565 1656 .532G
   2.23 5565 1656 .532G
   .11. 561. 5612 .165G
   22.. 2232 6123 6532G
   ..23 5565 1656 .532G
   11.. 561. 5612 .165G]
```

seseg:
```
      t    t N  t    t N
  [.61. 561. 5612 .165G]
```

Dhendha Sari/Dhendha Sri (?),
    Ketawang, sléndro pathet sanga (35).

buka: 225 2356 6161 5555N/G

lamba:
```
      t        t    N
   . 3 . 2 . 1 . 6
   . 2 . 1 . 6 . 5G

      t        t    N
   2 3 5 2 5 3 5 6
   2 3 2 1 65.2 3565G
```

dados:

```
        t         t    N
 [3353 6532 .523 5616 →
  2321 2321 65.2 3565G

        t         t    N
  61.1 3216 3565 3232
  356. 6656 1561 6532G

        t         t    N
  22.3 6532 .523 5635
  1656 5321 3532 1635G]
```

pangkat seseg:

```
        t         t    N
 →.2.3 .2.1 .3.2 .6.5G
```

seseg:

```
   t    t N  t    t N
 [.3.2 .1.6 .2.1 .6.5G]
```

Dhenggung Asmaradana/Dhenggung Semaradana,
    Gendhing, kethuk 4 kerep, minggah kethuk
    8, pélog pathet lima (1).

buka: adangiah, .3.6 7653 .232 5321N/G

mérong:

```
      t         t         t         t    N
 [.5.1 .5.1 .5.1 .233 123. 123. 5323 2121
  ...1 .561 .561 .233 123. 123. 5323 2121
  ...1 .561 .561 .233 123. 123. 5323 2121
  55.. 55.. 55.6 7653 123. 123. 5323 2121G]
```

minggah:

```
    t    t    t    t    t    t    t    t N
 [3231 3235 6765 3235 6765 3235 6765 3231
  3231 3235 6765 3235 6765 3235 6765 3231
  3231 3235 6765 3235 6765 3235 6765 3231
  5676 5421 5676 5421 3213 2165 3235 3231G]
```

Dhenggung Gong, Gendhing, kethuk 4
   kerep, pélog pathet lima (1).

buka: [5.53 .3.. 1235 .5..]x2   .323 1235 .323 2121N/G

mérong:
```
       t         t         t         t    N
 [.5.1 .5.1 .5.1 .232 35.. 3231 235. .1.5
 ..12 35.. 3231 235. 323. 5..1 235. .1.5
 ..12 35.. 3231 235. 323. 5..1 235. .1.5
 .3.2 .165 .3.2 .165 ..12 35.. ..53 2121G]
```

minggah: Ladrang Dhenggung Gong

Dhenggung Gong, Ladrang,
   pélog pathet lima (1).

(minggah to Gendhing Dhenggung Gong)
```
    t    t N
  3231 3235
  6365 3235
  6365 3235
  6365 3231G
```

Dhenggung Laras, Gendhing, kethuk 2 kerep,
   minggah kethuk 4, pélog pathet lima (1).

buka: [5.53 .3.. 1235 .5..]x2   .6.6 .5.3 ..25 .321N/G

mérong:
```
        t         t    N
  [...1 .561 ..12 .321
  ...1 .561 ..12 .321
  ...1 .561 ..12 .321
  .3.2 3216 ..61 2321G
```

ngelik:
```
        t         t    N
  55.. 5535 ..56 .765
  ...5 .235 ..56 .765
  ...5 .235 ..56 .765
  .7.6 7653 ..23 .321G]
```

minggah:
```
      t    t    t    t N
   [3231 3235 6365 3231
   .2.3 .5.3 .6.5 .2.1
   .2.3 .5.3 .6.5 .2.1
   3231 3235 6365 3231G]
```

Dhenggung Sulur Kangkung, Gendhing, kethuk 4 kerep,
    minggah kethuk 8, pélog pathet lima (1).

buka: adangiah; .33. 3235 .323 2121N/G

mérong:
```
      t         t         t         t    N
   [.5.1 .5.1 .5.1 .233 123. 1235 ..61 2165
   .... 55.6 1216 5323 123. 1235 ..61 2165
   .... 55.6 1216 5323 123. 1235 ..61 2165
   .3.2 .165 .3.2 .165 .33. 3235 .323 2121G]
```

minggah:
```
    t         t         t         t         t         t         t         t N
 [3 2 3 1  3 2 3 5  3 6 3 5  3 2 3 5  3 6 3 5  3 2 3 5  3 6 3 5  3 2 3 1
 . . . 1  . 2 3 53 6 .36 5  .3.23 5  .3.36 5  .3.23 53 6 .36 5  3 2 3 1
 . . . 1  . 2 3 53 6 .36 5  .3.23 53 6 .36 5  .3.23 53 6 .36 5  3 2 3 1
 . 1 1 1  6 1 2 3  6 5 2 1  6 1 2 3  6 5 2 1  3 2 6 5  3 2 6 5  3 2 3 1G]
```

seseg:
```
      t    t    t    t    t    t    t    t N
   [3231 3235 3635 3235 3635 3235 3635 3231
   3231 3235 3635 3235 3635 3235 3635 3231
   3231 3235 3635 3235 3635 3235 3635 3231
   .111 6123 6521 6123 6521 3265 3265 3231G]
```

Dhenggung Turu Laré, Gendhing, kethuk 2 kerep,
     minggah kethuk 4, pélog pathet lima (1).

buka: [5.53. 1235]x2   .35. .325 535. 35.1N/G

mérong:
```
        t        t    N
    [.... 1235 .535 35.1
     .... 1121 3212 .165
     15.6 1.21 3212 .165 →
     .33. 3235 .535 35.1G]
```

umpak:
```
        t        t    N
    →33.. 3235 3635 3231G
```

minggah:
```
     t    t    t    t N
    [3231 3235 3635 3231
     .2.3 .5.3 .6.5 .2.1
     .5.3 .6.5 .653 .2.1
     .66. 2165 3235 3231G]
```


Dhengklung/[Dhengklung Sari?],
     Ladrang, pélog pathet bem (18).

buka: .245 4241 5612 1645N/G
```
      t    t N
    [.612 1645
     4245 4241
     4245 4241
     5612 1645G]
```

Dhudha Gathuk, Gendhing, kethuk 2 kerep,
    minggah kethuk 4, sléndro pathet manyura (1).

buka: 3 .3.2 3123 ..56 5352 5653 2126N/G

mérong:

```
          t         t    N
    [..61 3216  ..61 2.32
     ..21 3216  ..61 2353
     ..35 1653  ..35 6356
     .... 1653  22.3 5.65G

          t         t    N
     .... 5535  6616 5352
     .... 2356  3565 3212
     33.. 33..  33.2 3123→
     ..56 5352  5653 2126G]
```

umpak:

```
          t         t    N
    →.5.6 .3.2  .5.3 .1.6G
```

minggah:

```
      t    t    t    t N
    [.1.6 .1.6 .1.6 .3.2
     .3.2 .1.6 .1.6 .5.3
     .5.3 .5.3 .5.3 .5.6
     .5.6 .5.3 .2.3 .6.5G

      t    t    t    t N
     .6.5 .1.6 .3.5 .3.2
     .3.2 .5.6 .3.5 .3.2
     .5.3 .5.3 .5.6 .5.3
     .5.6 .3.2 .5.3 .1.6G]
```

Dirata Meta, Ladrang, sléndro
   pathet nem (3).

buka: .561 2165 1111 3216N/G

    t   t N
   .66. 6656
   1653 2232
   6365 6362
   6365 6362G

    t   t N
  [6365 6362
   6365 6362
   6365 235.
   2353 2126G

    t   t N
   3365 2126
   3365 2126
   3365 2126
   3365 3212G

   t   t   N
 . . $\overline{235}$ $\overline{61}.\overline{6156}$
 1 2 $\overline{.35}$ $\overline{61}.\overline{6156}$
 1 2 $\overline{.35}$ $\overline{61}.\overline{6561}$
 $\overline{656}$ 1 2 . 3 5 6G

   t   t   N
 $\overline{516}$ $\overline{516}$ $\overline{516}$ $\overline{516}$
 1 6 5 3 2 2 3 2
 6 3 6 5 6 3 6 2
 6 3 6 5 6 3 6 2G]

sesegan:
     t   t N
   [6365 6362
    6365 6362
    6365 6362
    6365 6362G]

Dolo Dolo, Lancaran,
    sléndro pathet sanga (2).

buka: 6 .2.1 .2.6 .3.5N/G

    t tN t tN t tN t tN
[.3.6 .3.2 .3.6 .3.5G
  .3.6 .3.2 .3.6 .3.5G
  .2.6 .2.1 .2.6 .3.5G
  .2.6 .2.1 .2.6 .3.5G]

Éla-éla, Gendhing, kethuk 2 kerep,
    minggah kethuk 4, pélog pathet nem (38).

buka: 556 4565 .561 6532 1132 .165N/G

mérong: t   t   N
        [.... 55.6 12.3 5653
         2132 ..56 12.3 5653
         2132 .165 ..56 4565
         .561 6532 1132 .165G

ngelik: t   t   N
         11.. 1121 3212 .165
         ..56 1121 3216 .532
         .365 .... 556. 4565
         .561 6532 1132 .165G]

minggah: t   t   t   t N
        [.2.1 .2.1 .3.2 .6.5
         .2.1 .2.1 .3.2 .6.5
         .6.5 .1.6 .5.6 .3.2
         .3.1 .3.2 .3.2 .6.5G]

125 ·

Ela-ela, Gendhing [Ketawang], kethuk
2 kerep, sléndro pathet sanga (2).

buka: 2 .2.1 .3.2 .2.1 6123 .6.5 3212N/G
mérong:

```
        t       t    N
   .... 22.. 22.1 .3.2
   ..21 6123 .6.5 3232G

        t       t    N
   55.. 5653 2321 6535
   .22. 2356 .2.1 .6.5G

        t       t    N
   ...5 2165[2321 6535 →
   .22. 2356 22.3 1232G

        t       t    N
   .126 .... 2321 3216
   22.. 2321 55.2 3565G

        t       t    N
   ...5 2165 2321 6535
   66.. 6656 2321 6535G

        t       t    N
   11.. 1216 5323 2121
   55.. 5653 6523 2121G

        t       t    N
   ...1 2321 5653 2121
   22.. 2232 6165 3212G

        t
   .165 ...5]
```

umpak minggah:

```
        t       t    N
   →.22. 2356 .2.3 .2.1G
```

minggah: Ladrang Ela-ela.

Ela-ela, Ladrang, sléndro
pathet sanga (2).

(minggah to Gendhing Ela-ela)

```
  t    t N     t    t N      t    t N
[ .2.1 .2.1   .2.1 .6.5    .5.6 .2.1
  .2.1 .6.5   .2.1 .6.5    .2.1 .6.5
  .6.5 .6.5   .2.1 .2.6    .6.5 .1.6
  .2.1 .6.5G  .2.3 .2.1G   .2.3 .2.1G ]
```

Ela-ela Kali Bèbèr, Gendhing [Ketawang], kethuk 2
kerep, minggah kethuk 4, sléndro pathet sanga (38).

buka: .5.5 3523 5.53 2356 .2.1 .6.5N/G

mérong:

```
          t                t           N
   . . . . 5 5 . .  5 5 . 3  5 2 3 5
   . . 5 3 2 3 5 6  . 2 . 1  6 5 3 5G

          t                t           N
[ . . . 5 2 1 6 5  2 3 2 1  6 5 3 5
  . 2 2 . 2 3 5 6̄3̄ 3 .3̄3̄5̄2̄1̄ 6̄5̄6̄1̄2̄3̄2G

          t                t           N
 3̄2̄.3̄2̄1̄2̄1̄ 6̄5̄6̄1̄2̄1̄6̄ . . 6 2  . 3 5 6
  2 2 . . 2 1 6 5  6̄1̄2 1̄6̄1̄6̄ 5̄3̄2̄3̄5̄6̄5G

          t        ̄ ̄ ̄ ̄     t           N
 6̄5̄.6̄5̄3̄5̄3̄ 2̄1̄2̄3̄5̄3̄2̄ 6 6 . 1  6 5 3 5→
  1 1 . . 1 2 1 6̄3̄ 3 .3̄3̄ .3̄ 3̄5̄2 3 5G

          t                t           N
   . . 5 6 3 5 6 5  1 6 5 6  5 3 2 1
   . 6 5 . 5 6 1 2̄6̄ 6 .6̄6̄1̄5̄3̄ 2̄1̄2̄3̄5̄3̄2G

      ̄ ̄ ̄ t ̄ ̄ ̄ ̄ ̄ ̄ ̄           t           N
 .2̄ 3̄5̄6̄1̄6̄5̄3̄6̄ 5̄2̄3̄6̄5̄3̄5̄ . 2 . 1  . 6 . 5
  . 2 2 . 2 3 5 6  . 2 . 1  6 5 3 5G]
```

umpak minggah:

```
          t        ̄ ̄ ̄   t  ̄ ̄        N
 →1 1 . . 3 2 1 6̄3̄ 3 .3̄3̄ .3̄ 3̄5̄2 3 5ɢ6
                                        G
```

minggah:

```
              t              t              N
[3 223656 .3 22356   516 5322 356 3 56
 3 223656  3 22356   516 5322 356 3 51
 1 .11 .1  1 .11612  2 .22162 1536532
2 3561.61.5 2 32121  55.5365 365 2 1G

    t       t         t       t   N
. 2 . 1 . 3 . 2 . 6 . 5 . 2 . 1
. 2 . 1 . 3 . 2 . 6 . 5 . 2 . 1
. 6 . 5 . 6 . 5 . 1 . 2 . 1 . 6
. 5 . 6 . 5 . 63 3 .33 .3 352 3 5 6 ]
                                  G
```

Éling-éling, Ladrang,
    pélog pathet lima (12).

buka: 5 5235 3231 12165G

```
   t   t N
[6532 1235
 6532 1235
 11.. 1235
 3231 3235G]
```

irama III:

```
   t       t    N
[.6.5 .2.1 .3.2 .6.5
 .6.5 .2.1 .3.2 .6.5
 .2.1 .2.1 .3.2 .6.5
 .3.2 .3.1 .3.2 .6.5G]
```

Éling-éling, Ladrang, sléndro
    pathet sanga (1).

buka: 5 5235 .321 .235N/G

```
   t    t N
[6532 1235
 6532 1235
 11.. 1235
 3231 3235G]
```

```
irama III:
        t       t   N
  [.6.5 .2.1 .3.2 .6.5
   .6.5 .2.1 .3.2 .6.5
   .2.1 .2.1 .3.2 .6.5
   .3.2 .3.1 .3.2 .6.5G]
```

Éling-éling, Ladrang, sléndro
    pathet sanga (15).

```
   t    t N
  3216 5612
  3216 5612
  5235 1632
  1635 1632G
```

Éling-éling Badranaya, Ladrang,
    sléndro pathet manyura (16).

buka: 123. 123. 6563 2126N/G

```
   t    t N      t    t N
  ..6. 3216     .3.3 6123
  3561 6532     22.. 6123
  5653 6532     .123 .123
  6123 5653G    6563 2126G
```

Éling-éling Kasmaran, Ladrang,
    sléndro pathet sanga (3).

buka: 2 2612 2165 5612N/G

        t   t N
        3216 5612
        3216 5612
        55.. 1632
        1615 1612G

        t   t N
        .6.5 .3.2
        .6.5 .3.2
        .6.5 .3.2
        .6.5 .3.2G

        t   t N
        3265 1612
        3265 1632
        5565 1632
        1615 1632G

        t   t N
        3265 1632
        3265 1632
        5565 1632
        1615 .621G

Éling-éling Suralaya, Ladrang,
    sléndro pathet manyura (22).

buka: 6 6356 6532 2356N/G

          t   t N
          1653 2356
          1653 2356
          22.. 2356
          5352 5356G

Embat-embat Penjalin, Ladrang,
   sléndro pathet sanga (2).

buka kendhang: 5N/G

```
    t    t N
[ .55. 5565
  6365 6365
  6365 6365
  32.3 5616G

    t    t N
  .66. 6616
  1516 1516
  1516 1516
  5323 5635G ]

    t        t   N
[. 5 5 .  5 5 6 5
  2 1 2 .  2 1 6 5
  2 1 2 .  2 1 6 53
  2 32.323 5653212G

    t        t   N
  . . 2 3  1 2 3 2
  33356535 32321212
  35616565 32321212
  35.65353 2123565G]
```

Éndhol-èndhol, Gendhing, kethuk 2 kerep,
   minggah kethuk 4, pélog pathet barang (38).

buka: .3 .3.4 2343 .66. 6765 327. 6727N/G
mérong:

```
        t        t   N
  [..32 .756 ..67 2327
   ..32 .756 ..67 2343
   .... 3323 44.. 2343→
   .66. 6765 327. 6727G]
```

```
ngelik:       t         t    N
        .... 7765 ..56 7567
        ..32 .765 ..52 3565
        .... 55.. 556. 3565
        .... 55.. 6727 6535G

              t         t    N
        .... 55.. 6727 6535
        66.. 66.. 6676 5323
        .... 3323 44.. 2343
        .66. 6765 327. 6727G]

umpak minggah:
              t         t    N
      → .66. 6765 3276 .2.7G

minggah:
        t    t    t    t N
      [.6.5 .6.5 .6.3 .2.7
       .6.5 .6.5 .6.3 .2.7
       .6.5 .6.5 .6.3 .5.3
       .5.3 .6.5 .7.6 .2.7G]
```

Engkok, Ladrang (1).

buka: 22. 2165 3352 .126N/G

```
           N
      ..15 .356
      ..15 .356
      .22. 2165
      3352 .126G
```

Érang-érang/Érang-érang Kembang (?),
    Ladrang, sléndro pathet nem (2).

buka: .2.3 6532 ..23 5635N/G

```
  t    t N    t    t N    t    t N    t    t N
[ .6.3 .6.5   .1.6 .3.2   .3.5 .2.1   .5.6 .3.2
  .6.3 .6.5   .1.6 .3.2   .2.6 .3.2   .5.6 .3.2
  .6.3 .6.5   .1.6 .5.6   .5.5 .5.6   .5.6 .3.5
  .1.6 .3.2G  .2.1 .2.6G  .1.6 .3.2G  .6.3 .6.5G ]
```

Érang-érang/Ngérang-ngérang, Gendhing,
    kethuk 2 kerep, sléndro pathet nem (38).

buka: .561 .561 5612 .165N/G

mérong:
           t   t   N
    [..61 .561 5612 .165
    ..61 .561 5612 .165
    ..61 .561 5612 .165
    22.. 22.3 5653 2126G

           t   t   N
    3532 ..23 5653 2132
    1612 ..23 5653 2132
    1612 ..23 5653 2132
    11.. 3216 3565 3212G

           t   t   N
    11.. 3216 3565 3212
    11.. 3216 3565 3212
    11.. 3216 3565 3212
    55.. 5523 5653 2165G]

minggah: Ladrang Érang-érang

Érang-érang Pagelèn/Érang-érang Bagelèn, Gendhing,
    kethuk 2 kerep, pélog pathet nem (1).

buka: 6 .6.6 .563 .5.6 .532 1132 .165N/G

mérong:
              t   t   N
    1656 5421 3212 .165
    .65. 5612 1312 .165
    11.. 1121 3212 .126
    ..61 2165 3352 3565G

Èsèk-èsèk/Èsèg-èsèg, Gendhing, minggah
    kethuk 4, sléndro pathet manyura (1).

(minggah to Gendhing Banthèng Warèng, Gendhing
    Pucung, Gendhing Kembang Dara, Gendhing
    Rembun, and Méga Mendhung, kethuk 2 arang)

```
 t    t    t    t N
.3.2 .3.1 .2.6 .3.2
.3.2 .3.1 .2.6 .3.2
.5.3 .2.1 .2.1 .2.6
.5.6 .3.5 .1.6 .3.2G
```

Gadhung Mlathi, Ladrang, sléndro pathet
    sanga/pélog pathet nem (3).

buka: .2.1 .2.1 2211 .6.5N/G

umpak:
```
    t              t         N
. . . 2   . . . 1   . . . 6   . . . 5
. . . 2   . . . 1   . . . 6   . . . 5
1 1 . .   1 1 . .   1 1 3 2   1 6 5 3
.2352352  3562165   . 2 . 1   . 6 . 5G suwuk
```

ngelik:
```
      t                          t              N
. . . 2   . . . 1   . . . 6   . . . 5
. . . 2   . . . 1   . . . 5   . . . 6
. 2 1 2 6  . 2  1 2 6 5 6 1 2 . . . 2  1 . 6 . 5
. 5 6 1 . 1 2 5  . 5 6 1 . 1 2 .5 612 .5612 3 1  6 5 3 5G
```

Gajah Éndra, Ladrang, sléndro
    pathet manyura (1).

buka: 565. 5623 5616 5352N/G

```
  t    t N          t    t N
.62. 6232 )        ..2. 2232
565. 5623 } x2     6165 .32.
565. 5623 )        6165 .323
5616 5352G         5321 6532G
```

Gala Gothang, Gendhing, kethuk 4 kerep,
   minggah kethuk 8, sléndro pathet sanga (1).

buka: 3 .561 .2.1 .2.1 6532 .5.3N/G
mérong:
```
        t           t           t           t    N
   [.561 .561 .561 .561 .561 .561 3212 .165
    .612 .165 22.3 5.65 ..56 1656 5323 2121
    .216 .2.1 5616 5321 66.. 6656 3561 6535 →
    1656 5321 .111 2321 .111 2321 6532 5653G]
```

umpak minggah:
```
        t           t           t           t    N
 →.1.6 .2.1 .2.3 .2.1 .2.1 .2.1 .3.2 .5.3G
```

minggah:
```
     t    t    t    t    t    t    t    t N
  [.5.3 .2.1 .2.3 .2.1 .2.3 .2.1 .2.1 .6.5
   .6.5 .6.5 .3.2 .3.5 .6.5 .1.6 .2.3 .2.1
   .2.3 .2.1 .2.3 .2.1 .2.3 .2.1 .2.1 .6.5
   .2.3 .2.1 .2.3 .2.1 .2.3 .2.1 .3.2 .5.3G]
```


Gambang Suling/Swara Suling, Dolanan,
   pélog pathet nem (33).

buka: ...2 ...1 ...2 ...1N/G

```
[ . . . . 5 6 5 1 . . 5 6 5 4 3 2
  . . . . 1 3 1 2 . . 5 6 5 3 2 1
  . . . .6 545 6 1 . . 3 2 . 1 6 5
  . 4 . . 4 5 6 5 . 3 . . 3 5 3 2
  . 4 . . 4 5 6 5 . . 5 6 5 3 2 1G
```

umpak:
```
     ...1 ...5 ...6....2
     ...2 .454 ..65 4321G ]
```

Gambir Sawit, Gendhing, kethuk 2 kerep,
    minggah kethuk 4, sléndro pathet sanga (3).

buka: 5612 .2.1 .2.1 2612 .165N/G

mérong: t
        .352 .356⇀   t   N
    [[...5 2356⇀22.. 2321
      ..32 .126 22.. 2321⇀
      ..32 .165 ..56 1653
      22.3 5321 3532 .165G
               ...6G

ngelik: t   t   N
      66.. 66.. 22.. 2321
      ..32 .126 22.. 2321
      ..32 .165 ..56 1653
      22.3 5321 3532 .165G]

umpak minggah:
          t   t   N
   ⇀ .2.1 .6.5 .6.5 .3.2
     .3.5 .2.1 .2.1 .6.5G

minggah: t   t   t   t N
    [.6.5 .1.6 .1.6 .2.1
     .2.1 .2.6 .1.6 .2.1
     .2.1 .6.5 .1.6 .3.2
     .6.5 .2.1 .2.1 .6.5G]

Gambir Sawit Pancerana, Gendhing, kethuk 2
    kerep, minggah kethuk 4, pélog pathet nem (3).

buka: 5 .612 .2.2 .121 3212 .165N/G

mérong:
        t
      .352 .356⇀ t   N
    [[...5 2356⇀22.. 2321
      ..32 .126 22.. 2321⇀
      ..32 .165 ..56 1654
      22.3 5321 3532 .165G]

ngelik: t   t   N
      66.. 66.. 22.. 2321
      ..32 .126 22.. 2321
      ..32 .165 ..56 1654
      22.3 5321 3532 .165G]

umpak:
```
     t               t        N
→. 2 . 1  . 6 . 5  . 6 . 5  . 3 . 2
 . 3 . 5  . 2 . 1  66.65424 5652165G
```

minggah irama III:
```
   t         t         t         t      N
[6162  6165  6162  6165  6162  6165  2.23  2.21
 6162  6165  6162  6165  6162  6165  2.23  2.21
 3.32  3.31  3.36  3.35  3.31  3.36  3.35  3.32
 3.36  3.35  3.32  3.31  .66.  6542  4565  2165G]
```

Gambir Sawit Sembung Gilang, Gendhing, kethuk 2
    kerep, minggah kethuk 4, sléndro pathet sanga (1).

buka: same as Gendhing Gambir Sawit

mérong: same as Gendhing Gambir Sawit

umpak minggah:
```
         t          t      N
     .2.1  .6.5  .6.5  .3.2
     .6.5  .2.1  .2.1  .6.5G
```

minggah:
```
    t          t          t          t       N
[ .6.3 ...2  .2.3 .6.5  .6.3 .5.2  .2.3 .6.5
  11.. 3216  2152 5321  .6.3 ...2  .2.3 .6.5
  .6.3 ...2  .2.3 .6.5  11.. 3216  2152 5321
  66.. 66..  2321 3216  22.. 5321  5561 2165G ]
```

Gambuh, Ketawang, sléndro pathet
    manyura/sléndro pathet nem (1).

buka: 2 2132 6123 6532N/G

umpak:
```
       t          t
     . . 2 1  6 1 3 2
     6 1 2 3  6 5 3 2G
```

ngelik:
```
     t        t   N
  .6.6.... .1.2.6.5
  6356.3.2 .1.2.6.5G

     t        t   N
  6356.... .2.1.3.2
  .5.6.5.3 .2.1.6.5G

     t        t   N
  .2.2.... .3.5.3.2
  .6.1.2.3 .6.5.3.2G
```

Ganda Kusuma, Gendhing [Ketawang],
    kethuk 2 kerep, sléndro pathet sanga (2).

buka: 2 .356 .6.1 .2.1 .2.6 .3.5N/G

mérong:
```
         t        t   N
    [.2.3 .5.6 .2.1 .6.5
     .2.3 .5.6 .2.1 .6.5G

         t        t   N
     .2.1 .2.6 .2.1 .6.5
     .2.1 .2.6 .2.1 .6.5G
```
ngelik:
```
         t        t   N
     ..56 1653 2321 6535
     ..56 1653 2321 5321G


  . . 3 2 . 1 6 5 . 2 . 1 . 6 . 5
  2 2.356 1 . 615 . 2 . 1 . 6 . 5G

         t                 t        N
  2 2.356 1 . 615 . 2 . 1 . 6 . 5→
  . 2 2 . 2 3 5 6 . 2 . 1 . 6 . 5G]
```
umpak minggah:
```
         t        t   N
  →.2.3 .5.6 .2.3 .2.1G
```

Ganda Mastuti, Ketawang,
    pélog pathet nem (34).

buka: 6123 1132 .156N/G

umpak:
```
 t    t N  t    t N
.2.3 .2.1 .3.2 .1.6G
```

ngelik:
```
 t    t N  t    t N
..21 6532 5321 3216G
..21 6532 5321 3216G
7576 5421 3532 .156G
```


Ganda Riya/Gondra Riya/Gondorio
    Ladrang, pélog pathet nem (38).

buka: 335 2353 .226 1232N/G

```
  t    t N
[6162 6356
 3563 6523
 2353 6523
 2216 1232G ]
```


Ganda Suli, Ladrang,
    sléndro pathet sanga (1).

```
 t    t N    t    t N    t    t N
.5.6 .2.1  .3.2 .6.5  .1.2 .6.5
.5.6 .5.6  .1.6 .5.6  .1.6 .3.2
.5.6 .3.5  .5.6 .3.5  .3.2 .3.2
.2.1 .2.1G .6.1 .6.5G .3.1 .6.5G
```

Gandrung, Gendhing, kethuk 2 kerep, minggah
    kethuk 4, sléndro pathet sanga (1).

buka: 213 .213 2165 .1.6N/G

mérong:
                t   t   N
        [11.. 11.. 11.2 3532
         5653 2121 ..12 3532
         5653 2121 235. 6535
         ..56 1653 2321 6535G

                t   t   N
         2356 .... 3565 2232
         ..23 1232 .165 .612
         ..23 1232 .165 .612 →
         5653 5653 2165 1216G]

umpak minggah:
                t   t   N
        →.5.3 .5.3 .6.5 .1.6G

minggah:
            t   t   t   t N
        [.5.3 .5.3 .5.2 .1.6
         .5.3 .5.3 .5.2 .1.6
         .5.3 .5.3 .5.2 .3.2
         .3.2 .5.3 .6.5 .1.6G]

Gandrung Mangu, Gendhing, kethuk 2 awis,
    minggah kethuk 4, sléndro pathet manyura (2).

buka: 3 .3.2 .321 ..12 3216 .2.1 6523N/G

mérong: t   t   N
         ..35 1653 ..32 5321 ..12 3216 3561 6523
        [..35 1653 ..32 5321 ..12 3216 3561 6523
         ..35 1653 ..32 5321 ..12 3216 3561 6523
         .... 33.5 6635 6165 1635 6165 1632 5321G

                 t   t   N
         ..12 5321 55.. 1653 ..35 6165 1632 5321
         ..12 5321 55.. 1653 ..35 6165 1632 5321
         ..12 5321 55.. 1653 ..35 6165 1632 5321→
         33.. 33.5 6356 1651 6321 6531 1..1 3216G

                 t   t   N
         ..61 5616 ..61 2321 ..12 3216 3561 6523]

140

umpak minggah:
```
            t                    t       N
→.2.3 .5.3 .5.6 .3.5 .6.3 .6.5 .1.6 .2.1G
```

minggah:
```
      t    t    t    t N
    [.6.5 .6.5 .6.3 .2.1
     .6.5 .6.5 .6.3 .2.1
     .6.5 .6.5 .6.3 .5.3
     .5.3 .6.5 .1.6 .2.1G]
```

Gandrung Mangung Kung/Gandrung Winangun,
    Gendhing, kethuk 2 kerep, minggah
    kethuk 4, pélog pathet nem (38).

buka: 213 .213 2165 1216N/G

mérong:
```
          t         t    N
    [11.. 11.. 11.2 3532
     5654 2121 ..12 3532
     5654 2121 235. 6535
     ..56 1656 5421 6535G

          t         t    N
     2356 .... 3565 2232
     ..23 1232 .165 2232
     ..23 1232 .165 2232→
     .123 .123 2165 1216G]
```

umpak:
```
          t         t    N
    →.3.2 .5.4 .6.5 .1.6G
```

minggah:
```
      t    t    t    t N
    [.5.3 .5.3 .5.2 .1.6
     .5.3 .5.3 .5.2 .1.6
     .5.3 .5.3 .5.2 .3.2
     .3.2 .5.4 .6.5 .1.6G]
```

Gandrung Manis, Gendhing, kethuk 2 kerep,
minggah kethuk 4, sléndro pathet manyura (2).

buka: 6 6561 6532 .5.3N/G

mérong:
```
       t        t    N
[.561 .... 6165 3356
 3561 6535 61.6 5356
 3561 6535 61.6 5356
 3561 6532 1656 3532G

       t        t    N
.156 .123 5653 2156
.16. 6123 5653 2156
.16. 6123 5653 2156 →
.... 6561 6532 5653G]
```

umpak minggah:
```
      t        t    N
→.5.6 .2.1 .3.2 .5.3G
```

minggah:
```
     t    t    t    t N
[.2.1 .2.1 .2.6 .5.3
 .2.1 .2.1 .2.6 .5.3
 .2.1 .2.1 .2.6 .5.6
 .5.6 .2.1 .3.2 .5.3G]
```

Gandrung Manis, Gendhing, kethuk 2 kerep,
minggah kethuk 4, pélog pathet barang (1).

buka: 6 6567 6532 2353N/G

mérong:
```
       t        t    N
[.576 .... 6765 3356
 3567 6535 67.6 5356
 3567 6535 67.6 5356
 3567 6535 7675 3532G

       t        t    N
.756 .723 5653 2756
.76. 6723 5653 2756
.76. 6723 5653 2756 →
.... 6567 6532 5653G]
```

umpak:
```
      t        t    N
→.5.6 .2.7 .3.2 .5.3G
```

```
minggah:  t    t    t    t N
        [.2.7 .2.7 .2.6 .5.3
         .2.7 .2.7 .2.6 .5.3
         .2.7 .2.7 .2.6 .5.6
         .5.6 .2.7 .3.2 .5.3G]
```

Ganggong/Miyanggong, Gendhing, kethuk 4 kerep,
   minggah kethuk 8, sléndro pathet sanga (4).

buka: 2 .2.6 .2.1 .1.3 .212 .121 6535N/G

mérong:
```
        t         t         t         t    N
    [.555 2235 2353 2121 ..12 3532 5321 6535
     .555 2235 2353 2121 ..12 3532 5321 6535
     .555 2235 2353 2121 ..12 3532 5321 6535
     1656 5321 5616 5321 .65. 5612 5321 6535G

        t         t         t         t    N
     66.. 6561 5323 2121 66.. 6561 5323 2121
     ..12 5321 55.. 1653 ..35 6165 1632 5321
     ..12 5321 55.6 1653 ..35 6165 1632 5321 →
     3532 .165 .612 .165 .65. 5612 1312 .165G]
```

umpak minggah:
```
        t         t         t         t    N
    →.3.2 .6.5 .1.2 .6.5 .6.5 .1.2 .3.2 .6.5G
```

minggah:
```
     t    t    t    t    t    t    t    t N
   [.6.5 .6.5 .2.3 .2.1 .2.1 .3.2 .3.1 .6.5
    .6.5 .6.5 .2.3 .2.1 .2.1 .3.2 .3.1 .6.5
    .6.5 .6.5 .2.3 .2.1 .2.1 .3.2 .3.1 .6.5
    .1.6 .2.1 .5.6 .2.1 .6.5 .3.2 .3.2 .6.5G]
```

Ganggong Tirta, Ladrang,
   pélog pathet nem (38).

buka: 66. 6365 6532 3565N/G

```
    t          t    N
.555  6356  .666  5365
.555  6356  .666  5365
..32  1612  ..32  1612
.66.  6365  6532  3565G
```

Gangsaran, Lancaran (11)

buka kendhang: 2N/G

bonang: $\dfrac{2}{5}$ $\dfrac{1}{6}$ $\dfrac{2}{5}$ $\dfrac{1}{6}$ $\dfrac{2}{5}$ $\dfrac{1}{6}$ $\dfrac{2}{5}$ G

with N above the 1st, 3rd, 5th, 7th fractions.

Ganjur, Ketawang, sléndro
   pathet manyura (38).

buka: same as Suba Kastawa

```
  N          N
.2.1  .2.6  .3.1  .3.6G
```

Ganjur, Ketawang,
    sléndro pathet sanga (35).

buka: 1166 1155 1166 5555G

```
       t        t    N
[[.1.6 .1.2 .1.6 .1.5
  .1.6 .1.2 ⇥.1.6 .1.5G]
            → 11.5 6161G

       t        t    N
 ..1. 11.. 1165 3561
 55.. 55.6 11.5 6161

       t        t    N
 5612 .165 ..52 3565
 1656 5321 66.3 5616G

       t        t    N
 1561 6653 22.3 5635
 1656 5321 3532 1635G

       t        t    N
 22.3 5615 .615 2321
 2353 2321 3532 1635G]
```

Gantal Wedhar, Gendhing, kethuk 4 kerep, minggah
    kethuk 8, sléndro pathet nem (2).

buka: 2. 356. 12.3 2166 36.5 .3.2N/G

mérong:
```
       t         t         t         t    N
  ..23 6532 ..25 2353 ..35 2353 66.1 6535
 [.555 2235 2353 2126 ..61 2353 5653 2126
  .555 2235 2353 2126 ..61 2353 5653 2165 →
  2356 .532 ..25 2356 .12. 3216 6365 2232G

       t         t         t         t    N
  66.. 66.. 3561 6535 ..56 1653 2353 2165]
```

umpak minggah:
```
       t         t         t         t    N
 →.3.6 .3.2 .5.3 .5.6 .3.2 .1.6 .1.6 .3.2G
```

minggah:
```
    t    t    t    t    t    t    t    t N
 [.3.2 .1.6 .3.2 .1.6 .3.2 .1.6 .1.6 .3.2
  .3.2 .1.6 .3.2 .1.6 .3.2 .1.6 .1.6 .3.2
  .5.6 .2.1 .5.6 .3.2 .5.3 .1.6 .1.6 .3.2
  .1.6 .5.3 .1.6 .3.2 .5.3 .1.6 .1.6 .3.2G]
```

Gé́gér Sakutha, Ladrang,
sléndro pathet manyura (2).

buka: 352 .352 1121 6535N/G

```
   t   t N        t    t N       t    t N
[ 6561 2165      .6.. 5326      3235 6532
  6561 2165      .6.. 5326      3235 6532
  1615 1615      .6.. 5326      5352 5352
  66.. 5326G     3365 3212G     11.. 6535G ]
```

Gègèr Soré, Gendhing, kethuk 4 kerep, minggah
kethuk 8, slendro pathet sanga (2).

buka: 2 .2.6 .2.1 .2.2 .165 22.. 5321N/G

mérong:
```
      t       t       t       t     N
  ..32 .165 .352 .356 ..65 3356 3565 2232
  ..25 2356 3565 2232 .35. 235. 2353 2126
 [3532 ..23 5653 2132 1612 ..23 5653 2132 →
  1612 ..23 5653 2121 3532 1635 22.. 5321G

      t       t       t       t     N
  ..32 .165 .352 .356 .... 66.. 3561 6532
  11.. 3216 3565 3212 .35. 235. 2353 2126G]
```

umpak minggah:
```
       t       t       t       t     N
  →.3.2 .3.2 .5.3 .2.1 .3.2 .6.5 .2.3 .2.1G
```

minggah:
```
    t    t    t    t    t    t    t    t N
 [.3.2 .6.5 .3.2 .5.6 .5.3 .5.6 .3.5 .3.2
  .5.3 .5.6 .3.5 .3.2 .3.5 .3.5 .2.3 .1.6
  .3.2 .3.2 .5.3 .1.2 .3.2 .3.2 .5.3 .1.2
  .3.2 .3.2 .5.3 .2.1 .3.2 .6.5 .2.3 .2.1G]
```

145

Gégot, Ladrang, pélog
pathet nem (3).

buka: ...5 5654 2456 2165N/G

```
       t         t    N
12.3 .5.6 .2.1 .6.5
1651 5612 3232 5321
2121 2132 3232 5321
.55. 5654 2456 2165G
```

Gendhiyeng, Gendhing, kethuk 2 kerep, minggah
kethuk 4, pélog pathet nem (1).

buka: [123.216.6]x2 .3.3 .561 .3.2 .1.6N/G

mérong:
```
        t         t    N
[..61 3216 33.. 6532
 5654 2126 33.. 6532
 55.. 55.. 5356 5421
 6123 2165 3561 3216G
```

ngelik:
```
        t         t    N
11.. 3216 3565 3212
11.. 3216 3565 3212
55.. 55.. 5356 5421 →
6123 2165 3561 3216G]
```

umpak:
```
       t         t    N
→.3.2 .6.5 .2.1 .2.6G
```

minggah:
```
       t    t    t    t N
[.1.6 .1.6 .3.6 .3.2
 .5.4 .1.6 .3.6 .3.2
 .3.5 .6.5 .3.6 .2.1
 .3.2 .6.5 .2.1 .2.6G]
```

Gendhu, Gendhing, kethuk 2 kerep, minggah
  kethuk 4, sléndro pathet nem (2).

buka: 2 2165 .1.1 .2.6 .532 .356N/G

mérong:
```
         t        t    N
    [..12 .62. 62.1 6123
    .... 33.5 66.5 .653
    ..65 .323 5653 2165 →
    11.. 3216 .532 .356G]
```

umpak minggah:
```
         t        t    N
    →.2.1 .2.6 .3.2 .5.6
```

minggah:
```
      t    t    t    t N
    [.1.2 .3.2 .3.2 .5.3
    .5.3 .5.6 .5.6 .5.3
    .6.5 .2.1 .3.2 .6.5
    .2.1 .2.6 .3.2 .5.6G]
```


Gendrèh, Gendhing, kethuk 4 kerep, minggah
  kethuk 8, sléndro pathet manyura (16).

buka: 6. 36.3 6561 .216N/G

mérong:
```
       t        t        t        t       N
    [.2.1 .2.6 .2.1 .2.6 .... 66.. 3561 6532
    .352 .352 5653 2126 ..61 3216 3561 6532
    .352 .352 5653 2126 ..65 3356 33.. 6532 →
    5653 2121 653. 3516 356. 3561 3212 .126G]
```

umpak:
```
       t        t        t        t     N
    →.5.3 .2.1 .5.3 .1.6 .5.6 .2.1 .3.2 .1.6G
```

minggah:
```
      t    t    t    t    t    t    t    t N
    [.2.1 .2.6 .2.1 .2.3 .5.3 .5.6 .5.6 .3.2
    .3.2 .3.2 .3.2 .5.3 .5.3 .5.6 .5.6 .3.2
    .3.2 .3.2 .5.3 .1.6 .1.6 .1.6 .3.5 .3.2
    .5.3 .2.1 .5.3 .1.6 .5.6 .2.1 .3.2 .1.6G]
```

148

Gendrèh Kemasan, Gendhing; kenong 1, kethuk 4 kerep;
    kenong 2 & 3, kethuk 4 arang; gong, kethuk 3 arang;
    minggah kethuk 8; sléndro pathet sanga (16).

buka: 2 .2.6 .2.1 .3.2 .165 32.3 5635N/G
mérong:
```
        t        t        t        t
   [.612 .165 1653 2356 11.. 1121 3212 .165N

        t                 t
    .612 .165 1653 2356 11.. 1121 3212 .165
    11.. 3216 3565 2232 66.. 6616 3561 6535N
    .35. 5356 ..16 5323 ..35 2353 66.1 6535
    .35. 5356 ..16 5321 6123 5653 5653 2126N
    .16. 6123 5653 2126 33.. 33.. 6535 3212 →
                             5653 2165 32.3 5635N/G]
```
umpak:

       →.5.3 .6.5 .3.2 .6.5N/G

minggah:
```
        t    t    t    t    t    t    t    t N
   [.6.5 .6.5 .6.5 .1.6 .1.6 .2.3 .5.3 .6.5
    .6.5 .6.5 .6.5 .1.6 .1.6 .2.3 .5.3 .6.5
    .3.6 .5.6 .2.1 .2.6 .3.5 .6.3 .2.3 .1.2
    .3.2 .1.6 .2.3 .1.6 .1.6 .1.6 .3.2 .6.5G]
```

Genès, Gendhing, kethuk 2 kerep, minggah
    kethuk 4, sléndro pathet manyura (16).

buka: 661 6535 .1.1 .2.6 .3.5 3212N/G
mérong:
```
        t         t    N
   [55.. 5523 5653 2126
    .16. 6123 5653 2126 →
    .... 66.. 3561 6535
    11.. 3216 3565 3212G]
```
umpak:
```
        t         t    N
   →.5.6 .1.6 .2.1 .6.5
    .2.1 .2.6 .3.5 .3.2G
```

minggah:
```
      t    t    t    t N
[.3.5 .3.5 .2.3 .1.6
 .1.6 .2.3 .5.3 .1.6
 .5.6 .5.6 .2.1 .6.5
 .2.1 .2.6 .3.5 .3.2G]
```

Génjong, Gendhing, kethuk 2 kerep, minggah
kethuk 4, sléndro pathet sanga (2).

buka: .5.6 12.2 .212 1.61 2165N/G

mérong:
```
        t         t    N
11.. 1121 3212 .165
[.235 .621 5616 5312
 .132 .365 1216 5312
 11.. 3532 3532 .165G

      t         t    N
 ..56 1121 3212 .165]
```
minggah:
```
      t    t    t    t N
[.6.5 .3.2 .3.2 .5.1
 .2.1 .2.1 .3.2 .6.5
 .6.5 .2.1 .2.3 .2.1
 .2.1 .3.2 .3.2 .6.5G]
```

Génjong Goling, Gendhing, kethuk 2 kerep, minggah
kethuk 4, sléndro pathet sanga (25).

buka: 5612 .2.2 .1.6 3312 .165N/G

mérong:
```
          t         t    N
[22.. 2216 3532 .165
 .... 5535 6635 .312
 66.. 6535 1216 5312 →
 .35. 23.5 2126 3532 .165G]
```

150

```
umpak minggah:
        t       t   N
    →.2.1 .2.6 .3.2 .6.5G
minggah:
        t   t   t   t N
    [.1.2 .1.6 .3.2 .6.5
     .3.5 .1.6 .3.5 .3.2
     .5.6 .3.5 .1.6 .3.2
     .3.5 .1.6 .3.2 .6.5G]
```

Ginonjing, Ladrang, sléndro
    pathet manyura (2).

buka: 126 3356 5352N/G

```
    t    t N
  [ 5653 5652
    5653 5156
    5251 5356
    5356 5352G

    t    t N
    5653 5652
    5653 5156
    5251 5256
    5156 5352G ]
```

Giyak-giyak, Ladrang,
    sléndro pathet sanga (2).

buka: 2121 2211 .6.5N/G

```
      t       t   N
  [ . 2 . 1 . 6 . 5
    . 2 . 5 . 2 . 1
    . 2 . 1 . 6 . 5
    .6.5.6.5 .6.56 1G

      t       t   N
    . 2 . 1 . 5 . 6
    . 5 . 6 . 3 . 2
    .2356 5 . 2 . 1
    . 2 . 1 . 6 . 5G ]
```

Glagah Kanginan,
Lancaran (11).

```
     N
[ ..21
  6521
  6561
  2165G ]
```

Glathik Bélong, Gendhing (Santiswaran),
pélog pathet nem (39).

```
. 1 3   . 1 2   . 3 5   56532

. 2 3   . 1 2   . 3 5   56532

.   .   .   .   . 2 3 5 5 6 6

.   .   7   6   . 5 3   3 2 1

. 6 6   . 6 6   . 6 3 5 5 6 5

6 5 6 5   653 2 .13 .21G
```

Glathik Èncèng-èncèng. Gendhing, pélog pathet nem (19).

```
    t       t    N
.312 3532 .312 3532
.22. 2356 ..76 5352
.66. 6365 6532 1321G
```

Glélé, Gendhing (Santiswaran),
    sléndro pathet manyura (39).

```
.    . 3 5 3 2 3   . 3 3   35321
6 1 2   6   233   3 353   35321
6 1 2   6   5 2   5 6 6   1261653
.    . 1 2 1 6   . 253   1 216
.    . 1 2 1 6   . 253   1 216
. 3 3   . 3 3   . 3 3   . 3 23
. 3 3   6   5   6 253 .21 216G
```

Glendhèh, Gendhing, kethuk 4 kerep, minggah
    kethuk 8, pélog pathet lima (1).

buka: .356 4565 ..4. 2.4. 2465 .421N/G

mérong:
```
      t         t         t         t    N
[561. 1312 561. 1312 561. 1312 5654 2121
 561. 1312 561. 1312 561. 1312 5654 2121
 561. 1312 561. 1312 561. 1312 5654 2121
 55.. 55.. 556. 4565 ..4. 2.4. 2465 .421G]
```

ompak minggah:
```
      t         t         t         t    N
.6.5 .6.5 .4.6 .4.5 .4.2 .4.2 .4.5 .2.1G
```

minggah:
```
   t    t    t    t    t    t    t    t N
[.2.1 .3.2 .3.1 .3.2 .3.1 .3.2 .5.4 .2.1
 .2.1 .3.2 .3.1 .3.2 .3.1 .3.2 .5.4 .2.1
 .2.1 .3.2 .3.1 .3.2 .3.1 .3.2 .5.4 .2.1
 .6.5 .6.5 .4.6 .4.5 .4.2 .4.2 .4.5 .2.1G]
```

Glendheng, Gendhing, kethuk 4 arang, minggah
   kethuk 8, pélog pathet lima (1).

buka: odangiah: .6.6 .5.4 .24. 124. 5424 2121N/G

mérong:
      t   t
[.2.. 12.1 66.. 6654 .2.4 .2.1 66.. 6654
.2.4 .2.1 66.. 6654 .24. 124. 5424 2121N
23.. 33.. 3321 6123 .321 63.. 2321 6123
.321 63.. 3.32 .165 .... 55.. 44.. 2245N
..24 25.. 5.54 .245 ..24 25.. 5.54 .245
..24 25.. 5.54 2456 ..77 .654 ..24 2121N
.6.. 6621 .621 6545 245. 5621 .621 6545
2456 .... 6676 .654 .24. 124. 5424 2121N/G]

ompak:
      t   t
2 4 2 5 2 4 5 6 6 6 7 6 5 4 2 1N
. 5 5 5 1 2 4 5 . 5 5 5 1 2 4 5
.6545 .6 545 6 1 62.61 62 .61 6 5N/G

minggah:

[.4545454 545 6 1 62.61 62 .61 6 5
.4545454 545 6 1 62.61 62 .61 6 5N
.4545454 545 6 1 62.61 62 .61 6 5
4 2 4 5 2 1 2 1 2 3 5 3 2 1 2 3N
5 6 5 3 2 1 2 3 5 6 5 3 2 1 2 3
2 2 . . 2 2 . . 4 4 4 4 2 1 6 5N
.454545 1 2 4 5 .454545 1 2 4 5
.4545454 545 6 1 62.61 62 .61 6 5N/G]

Gléwang Gonjing/Gonjing Gléwang, Gendhing,
   kethuk 2 kerep, minggah kethuk 4,
   sléndro pathet manyura (4).

buka: 6 .1.2 .3.2 .1.6 .3.3 .5.6 .5.3 .5.2N/G

mérong:
        t   t   N
[.6.5 .6.3 .6.5 .3.2
.6.5 .6.3 .532 .126
.563 .561 3532 .126
33.. 3356 3565 3212G]

Gléyong (Sekatèn)/Gléyong (Mataram),
    Ladrang, pélog pathet nem (7).

buka:
```
     t     t N
    .113  3132
    .5321 2353
    5235  2321
    321.  1235G

     t     t N
    2321  6535
    2321  6535
    .225  2356
    5424  2126G

     t     t N      ⎞
   [2321  6535      ⎟
    2321  6535      ⎬ x2
    2523  5676      ⎟
    5424  2126G     ⎠

     t     t N      ⎞
    5756  5323      ⎟
    5676  5323      ⎬ x2
    2523  5676      ⎟
    5424  2126G]    ⎠
```

Gléyong, Ladrang, pélog
    pathet nem (1).

buka: 2 2356 7654 2126N/G

```
     t     t N
    2321  6535
    2321  6535
    22..  2356
    7654  2126G
```

ngelik:
```
     t     t N
    .666  5323
    .356  7653
    6532  .356
    7654  2126G
```

Gléyor/Ora Aring, Ladrang,
   pélog pathet nem (7).

bubuka:
```
    t         t    N
...1 .1.3 .3.1 .3.2
...5 .321 .2.3 .5.3
.5.2 .3.5 .2.3 .2.1
.3.2 .1.2 .3.5 .2.3G

    t         t    N
...3 .3.. .3.5 .7.6
...5 .3.7 .3.2 .7.6
...3 .3.. .6.5 .3.2
.3.1 .3.2 .3.1 .2.6G
```

dados:
```
     t         t     N
.33. 6532 3132 3126
.33̄3̄3̄576 .537 3276
.33̄3̄3̄576 .537 3276
.33. 6532 3132 3126G
```

sesegan:
```
   t     t    N
...5 ...2 ...1 ...6
...5 ...6 ...7 ...6
...5 ...6 ...7 ...6
...5 ...2 ...1 ...6G
```

Gliyung, Gendhing, kethuk 2 kerep, minggah
   kethuk 4, sléndro pathet manyura (2).

buka: 2 .356 .6.6 .5.3 .5.2 .1.6N/G

mérong:
```
       t         t    N
[..12 1653 6532 .356
55.. 55.6 1656 5323
6535 3212 66.. 3356
3561 6523 6532 .126G]
```

umpak minggah:
```
     t         t    N
.5.6 .5.3 .5.2 .1.6G
```

minggah:
```
     t    t    t    t N
[.3.2 .5.3 .5.2 .5.6
.3.5 .3.5 .1.6 .5.3
.6.5 .3.2 .5.3 .5.6
.5.6 .5.3 .5.2 .1.6G]
```

Glompong, Gendhing, kethuk 4 kerep, minggah
   kethuk 8, sléndro pathet sanga (25).

buka: 5 .5.6 5321 2132 .6.5N/G

mérong:
```
        t         t         t         t    N
   .555 2235 2353 2126 ..21 .653 22.3 5635
  [.555 2235 2353 2126 ..21 .653 22.3 5635
   .555 2235 2353 2126 ..21 .653 22.3 5635
   .... 55.6 1656 5312 ..23 5321 2321 6535G→

        t         t         t         t    N
   11.. 1121 3212 .165 ..56 1653 2321 6535]
```

badhé minggah:
```
        t         t         t         t    N
 →66.. 3356 ..61 2.32 5653 2165 3565 2232
  66.. 3356 ..61 2.32 5653 2165 3565 2232
  66.. 3356 33.. 6532 5653 2165 3565 2232
  .3.2 .6.5 .3.2 .6.5 .3.2 .3.1 .6.5 .3.2G
```

minggah:
```
      t    t    t    t    t    t    t    t N
  [.3.2 .6.5 .3.2 .6.5 .3.2 .3.1 .6.5 .3.2
   .3.6 .5.6 .3.5 .3.2 .5.3 .6.5 .3.5 .3.2
   .3.6 .5.6 .3.5 .3.2 .5.3 .6.5 .3.5 .3.2
   .3.2 .6.5 .3.2 .6.5 .3.2 .3.1 .6.5 .3.2G

      t    t    t    t    t    t    t    t N
   .3.2 .6.5 .3.2 .6.5 .3.2 .3.1 .6.5 .3.2
   .5.3 .5.3 .6.5 .3.2 .5.3 .6.5 .3.5 .3.2
   .5.3 .5.3 .6.5 .3.2 .5.3 .6.5 .3.5 .3.2
   .3.2 .6.5 .3.2 .6.5 .3.2 .3.1 .6.5 .3.2G

      t    t    t    t    t    t    t    t N
   .3.2 .6.5 .3.2 .6.5 .3.2 .3.1 .6.5 .3.2
   .5.6 .5.6 .3.6 .3.2 .5.3 .6.5 .3.5 .3.2
   .5.6 .5.6 .3.6 .3.2 .5.3 .6.5 .3.5 .3.2
   .3.2 .6.5 .3.2 .6.5 .3.2 .3.1 .6.5 .3.2G]
```

157

Glondhong Pring, Gendhing, kethuk 2
    kerep, sléndro pathet nem (38).

buka: 2 .2.1 .3.2 .2.3 .6.5 .3.5 .3.2N/G

mérong: t   t   N
        [.... 22.3 5616 5323
         6535 .323 5616 5323
         6535 2232 .321 6132 →
         5653 2165 3365 2232G

               t   t   N
         .... 22.3 5616 5323
         6535 .323 5616 5323
         6535 2232 .321 6123
         .... 3353 6535 3212G

ngelik: t   t   N
         66.. 6656 3561 6523
         6535 .323 5616 5323
         6535 3212 .321 6132
         5653 2165 3365 2232G]

umpak minggah:
               t   t   N
        →.5.3 .6.5 .6.5 .3.2G

minggah: Ladrang Glondhong Pring

Glondhong Pring, Ladrang,
     sléndro pathet nem (38).

(minggah to Gendhing Glondhong Pring)

    t   t N   t   t N
  .5.6 .3.5   .5.6 .2.1
  .1.6 .3.5   .5.6 .2.1
  .2.3 .5.2   .2.3 .5.2
  .6.5 .3.2G   .6.5 .3.2G

158

Gobet/Gobed, Gendhing, kethuk 4 kerep, minggah
kethuk 8, pélog pathet nem (10).

buka: [...3 ..63 .216] x2   .2 .16 12353 .6.5 3212N/G
mérong:
```
        t         t          t          t    N
    [..23 1232 ..24 .521  ..12 3216 ..61 2353
    ..35 .653 6542 4521  ..12 3216 ..61 2353
    ..35 .653 6542 4521  ..12 3216 ..65 6356
    .... 66.. 6676 5421  612. 2212 33.. 1232G

        t         t          t          t    N
    ..23 1232 ..23 5653  .523 5654 2.44 2165
    .... 5535 66.. 1653  22.1 3216 ..63 2132 →
    .444 2126 .444 2123  .... 33.. 33.2 3521
    .6.3 2132 3123 2123  .... 3353 6535 3212G]
```
umpak minggah:
```
        t         t          t          t    N
   →.444 2126 .444 2165  .5.5 .266 ..76 5421
    .111 2321 .111 6124  .44. 4456 5424 2165G
```
minggah:
```
      t    t    t    t    t    t    t    t N
  [..6. 5.63 ..35 6532 3235 6535 4216 5612
   3216 5323 ..35 6532 3235 6535 4216 5612
   3216 5323 ..35 2.26 2.26 2.26 2123 2165 →
   .55. 5532 .55. 5532 .62. 62.3 5654 2165G]
```
umpak-umpakan:
```
      t    t    t    t    t    t    t    t N
  →3635 3632 3635 3632 3535 3632 3532 3635G
```
sesegan:
```
      t    t    t    t    t    t    t    t N
  [3635 3635 3635 2232 3216 5352 5323 5653
   6563 6563 6563 2232 3216 5352 5323 5653
   6563 6563 6563 2.26 2.26 2.26 2123 2165
   3635 3632 3635 3632 3635 3632 3632 3635G]
```

Godheg, Gendhing, kethuk 4 awis, minggah
    kethuk 8, sléndro pathet nem (25).

buka: 2.2. 3.1. 6..6 1216 5336 53.2N/G

mérong: t   t
    [66.. 6656 ..65 3561 22.. 2321 3212 .126
    ..61 3216 33.. 6532 5653 2165 3365 2232N
    ..25 2353 6535 2232 66.. 66.. 3561 6532
    .... 2235 2356 3532 5653 2165 3365 2232N
    ..25 2353 6535 2232 66.. 66.. 3561 6532
    .... 2235 2356 3532 5653 2165 3365 2232N →
    .... 22.3 5653 2126 3532 ..23 5653 2126
    33.. 33.. 6535 3212 5653 2165 3365 2232N/G]

umpak minggah:
     t   t   t   t   N
→.5.3 .5.6 .5.3 .5.6 .3.6 .3.2 .6.5 .3.2G

minggah:
    t   t   t   t   t   t   t   t N
    [.5.6 .1.2 .6.5 .1.6 .3.6 .3.2 .6.5 .3.2
    .5.3 .5.6 .3.6 .3.2 .3.5 .3.2 .6.5 .3.2
    .5.3 .5.6 .3.6 .3.2 .3.5 .3.2 .6.5 .3.2
    .5.3 .5.6 .5.3 .5.6 .3.6 .3.2 .6.5 .3.2G]

Godhong Nangka, Ladrang,
    pélog pathet nem (19).

buka celuk: 5N/G

   t   t N   t   t N
[.63. 3635   .123 .132
  .63. 3356   .123 .132
  3561 6532   66.. 2321
  1123 6532G   3265 4245G]

Golong, Gendhing, kethuk 2 kerep, dhawah
kethuk 4, sléndro pathet nem (5).

buka: 356 3532 35.6 1653 2132 55.5N/G

lamba:
```
        t         t   N
    .6.2 .3.2 .3.2 .6.5
    .6.2 .3.2 .3.2 .6.5
    .3.6 .3.2 .3.6 .3.2
    35.6 1653 2132 1635G
```

dados:
```
        t         t   N
   [.612 .312 .312 1635
    .612 .312 .312 1635
    2356 3532 5356 3532
    66.. 6623 55.2 3565G

        t         t   N
    121. 1216 5323 5635
    121. 1216 5323 5635
    2356 3532 5356 3532
    35.6 1653 2132 1635G]
```

pangkat dhawah:
```
        t         t   N
    .612 .312 .312 1635
    .612 .312 .312 1635
    2356 3532 5356 3532
    .6.5 .6.3 .1.2 .6.5G
```

dhawah:
```
     t    t    t    t N
   [.6.2 .3.2 .3.2 .6.5
    .6.2 .3.2 .3.2 .6.5
    .3.6 .3.2 .3.6 .3.2
    .1.6 .1.6 .3.2 .6.5G

     t    t    t    t N
    .2.1 .2.6 .3.2 .6.5
    .2.1 .2.6 .3.2 .6.5
    .3.6 .3.2 .3.6 .3.2
    .6.5 .6.3 .1.2 .6.5G]
```

Gondhel, Gendhing, kethuk 2 kerep,
    sléndro pathet manyura (1).

buka: 661 6523 .12. 2123 6532 .126N/G

mérong:
            t   t   N
    [..61 3216 ..61 2.32
    .... 2212 3312 .321
    3212 .126 3561 6523
    .12. 2123 6532 .126G

            t   t   N
    66.. 6656 3561 6523
    11.. 3216 3561 6523
    .516 .... 3561 6523
    .12. 2123 6532 .126G]

umpak: t   t   N
    .2.1 .2.3 .1.2 .1.6G

minggah: Paré Anom

Gondrong, Gendhing, kethuk 4 arang, minggah
    kethuk 8, pélog pathet lima (1).

buka: odangiah; ..56 7656 .654 24.2 4565 2421N/G

mérong: t   t
    [.2.. 12.1 ..12 3323 .253 .2.1 ..12 3323
    .253 .2.1 ..12 3323 .253 .2.1 ..6. 2165N
    .6.4 5645 22.. 2321 ..32 .165 22.. 2321
    ..32 .165 22.. 2321 ..32 .165 4524 5645N
    .6.4 5645 22.. 2321 ..32 .165 22.. 2321
    ..32 .165 22.. 2321 ..32 .165 4524 5645N →
    .... 55.. 2454 2121 ...4 1245 .424 2121
    55.. 55.. 55.6 7656 .657 24.2 4565 2421N/G]

umpak:
        t   t   t   t   N
    →.612 .165 .612 .165 .33. 3132 3132 1645G

minggah:
```
      t    t    t    t    t    t    t    t N
[.33. 3132 3132 1645 .33. 3132 3132 1645
 .33. 3132 3132 1645 .612 1656 .666 5356
 .556 7653 22.3 5.65 2325 2356 6676 5421
 3.32 1645 3.32 1645 .33. 3132 3132 1645G]
```

Gondrong (Bonangan), Gendhing, kethuk 4 awis,
   minggah kethuk 8, pélog pathet barang (11).

buka: .2.2 72765 .5.. .2.2 72765 .2.7 6723
        ..65 .32. 7.67 6535N/G

mérong:
```
            t              t
[.6.3 5635 22.. 2327 .6.7 .6.5 22.. 2327
 .6.7 .6.5 22.. 2327 .627 .65. 3.65 3232N
 77.. 2327 .627 .656 77.. 2327 .627 .656
 77.. 2327 .627 .65. .627 .65. 3.65 3232N
 ..23 5676 .535 3272 767. 7656 .535 3272
 ..67 2.67 2.27 6723 ..65 .32. 7.67 6535N →
 .67. 5676 .535 3232 767. 7656 .535 3232
 ..67 2.67 2.27 6723 ..65 .32. 7.67 6535N/G]
```

umpak:
```
       t          t          t          t
→ 7.76 5352 7.76 5352 66.. 6765 3352 .356N/G
```

minggah:
```
      t    t    t    t    t    t    t    t N
[.76. 6765 3352 .356 .76. 6765 3352 .356
 .76. 6765 3352 .356 5325 3253 .333 6723
 .22. 2327 .667 2372 672. 2723 5653 2765
 7.76 5352 7.76 5352 7576 7576 2356 5352G

      t    t    t    t    t    t    t    t N
 .352 .356 7576 5352 .352 .356 7576 5352
 .352 .356 7576 5352 5356 5323 .333 6723
 .22. 2327 .667 2372 672. 2723 5653 2765
 7.76 5352 7.76 5352 66.. 6765 3352 .356G]
```

Gondrong (Rebab), Gendhing, kethuk 4 awis,
minggah kethuk 8, pélog pathet lima (38).

buka: 556 7656 .654 24.2 4565 2421N/G

mérong:
```
          t                    t
[.2.6 1261 ..21 6123 55.. 5421 ..21 6123
 55.. 55.. 55.6 7656 .654 24.2 4565 2421N
 .2.6 1261 ..21 6123 55.. 5421 ..21 6123
 .... 33.. 3356 5421 66.. 6656 .2.3 5676N→
 .... 6653 .532 .356 .... 6653 .532 .356
 44.. 44.. 4465 .421 .... 11.. 1121 6123N
 ...3 6521 ..21 6123 55.. 5421 ..21 6123
 55.. 55.. 55.6 7656 .654 24.2 4565 2421N/G]
```

umpak:
```
          t                    t          N
.556 7653 22.3 5.65 2325 2356 6676 5421
3.32 1645 3.32 1645 22.. 2321 .654 2465G
```

minggah:
```
     t    t    t    t    t    t    t N
[.22. 2321 .654 2465 .22. 2321 .654 2465
 .22. 2321 .654 2465 .612 1656 .666 5356
 .556 7653 22.3 5.65 2325 2356 6676 5421
 3.32 1645 3.32 1645 22.. 2321 .654 2465G]
```


Gondrong Pengasih, Gendhing, kethuk 4 awis,
pélog pathet lima (38).

buka: 556 4565 .7.6 .532 .5.4 .521N/G

mérong:
```
          t                    t
.2.6 1261 ..21 6123 ...3 6521 ..21 6123
...3 6521 ..21 6123 ...3 6521 77.. 5676N
.... 6653 .... 5235 .... 5621 ..21 6123
...3 6521 ..21 6123 ...3 6521 77.. 5676N
.... 6653 .... 5235 .... 5621 ..21 6123
...3 6521 ..21 6123 ...3 6521 77.. 5676N
.76. 5421 ..21 6123 55.. 5421 ..21 6123
55.. 55.. 556. 4565 .7.6 .532 .5.4 .521N/G
```
minggah: Ladrang Rèndhèng

164

Gonjang, Ladrang, sléndro
   pathet manyura (2).

buka: .3.2 .3.2 3322 .1.6N/G

```
   t   t N        t   t N         t    t N
[.3.2 .1.6      .3.2 .1.6       .3.3 .5.6
 .3.6 .3.2      .3.1 .2.1       .5.3 .5.6
 .3.2 .3.2      .5.6 .2.1       .3.2 .3.1
 .3.2 .1.6G     .2.6 .5.3G      .3.2 .1.6G]
```

Gonjang Anom, Gendhing, kethuk 2 kerep,
   minggah kethuk 4, sléndro pathet manyura (4).

buka: 612 3216 .3.3 .5.6 .5.2 .5.3N/G

```
mérong:
             t          t   N
    [ ..3.  6532  ..23 5653
      ..3.  6532  ..23 5653
      ..3.  6532  66.5 3356
      3567  6532  1132 .126G

             t          t   N
      ..6.  3532  3532 .126
      ..6.  3532  3532 .126
      ..6.  3532  33.2 1123
      1121  3216  3532 5653G ]
```

minggah:
```
      t     t     t    t N
[ .1.6 .3.2 .3.2 .1.6
  .1.6 .3.2 .3.2 .1.6
  .1.6 .3.2 .5.3 .2.3
  .2.1 .2.6 .3.2 .5.3G

      t     t     t    t N
  .5.3 .5.2 .3.2 .5.3
  .5.3 .5.2 .3.2 .5.3
  .5.3 .5.2 .5.3 .5.6
  .2.1 .3.2 .1.2 .1.6G ]
```

Gonjang Anom Bedhaya, Gendhing [Ketawang],
    kethuk 8 kerep, minggah kethuk 16,
    pélog pathet lima (1).

buka: [.$\overline{123}$.$\overline{2}$ 16.6] x2 2161 2356 .7.6 .532 .5.3N/G

mérong:
```
          t              t              t              t
   [ .1.2 .3.5 .7.6 5323 .1.2 .3.5 .7.6 5323
     .1.2 .3.5 .7.6 5323 56.5 3212 ..23 56.5N
     44.. 44.. 44.5 6456 .567 .656 .535 3212
     ..23 6532 6535 2353 55.. 5653 2356 3565N/G

          t              t              t              t
     ..54 .5.4 .5.6 .535 32.3 5676 54.2 4521
     ..12 3216 ..61 2353 55.6 7654 2.44 2126N →
     .12. 2212 33.1 3216 .12. 2212 33.1 3216
     ..63 2132 3123 2161 2356 .7.6 .532 .5.3N/G ]
```

umpak:
```
        t    t    t    t    t    t    t    t
   → .12. 2212 33.1 3265 .5.5 .2.6 ..76 5421
     .111 2321 .111 6124 .44. 4456 5424 2165G
```

minggah:
```
        t    t    t    t    t    t    t    t
   [ ..6. 5.63 .635 6165 ..6. 5.63 .635 6165
     ..6. 5.63 .635 6165 6123 .123 6532 3565N
     ..56 7653 22.3 5.65 2325 2356 6676 5421
     .111 2321 .111 6124 .44. 4456 5424 2165N/G

        t    t    t    t    t    t    t    t
     ..54 2456 5424 2165 ..54 2456 5424 2165
     ..54 2456 5424 2165 6123 .123 6532 3565N
     ..56 7653 22.3 5.65 2325 2356 6676 5421
     .111 2321 .111 6124 .44. 4456 5424 2165N/G ]
```


Gonjang Anom Gendhing, Gendhing [Ketawang],
    kethuk 8 kerep, minggah kethuk 16,
    pélog pathet lima (1).   •

buka: [.$\overline{123}$.$\overline{2}$ 16.6] x2 2161 2356 .7.6 .532 .5.3N/G

mérong:
```
          t              t              t              t
   [.1.2 .3.5 .7.6 5323 .1.2 .3.5 .7.6 5323
    .1.2 .3.5 .7.6 5323 56.5 3212 ..23 56.5N
    44.. 44.. 44.5 6456 .567 .656 .535 3212
    ..23 .532 6535 .323 55.. 5653 2356 .535N/G
```

```
     t          t          t          t
..54 .5.4  .5.6 .535 32.3 5676 54.2 4521
..12 3216  ..61 2353 55.6 7654 2.44 2126N
.12. 2212 33.1 3216 .12. 2212 33.1 3216
..63 2132 3123 2123 .... 3353 .6.1 2353N/G

     t          t          t          t
.... 3353 55.3 2356 .5.3 .523 55.3 2356
.5.3 .523 55.3 2356 .535 3212 ..23 56.5N
44.. 44.. 44.5 6456 .567 .656 .535 3212
..23 .532 6535 .323 55.. 5653 2356 .535N/G

     t          t          t          t
.254 .5.4 .5.6 .535 32.3 5676 54.2 4521
..12 3216 ..61 2353 55.6 7654 2.44 2126N
.... 6653 .532 .356 .... 6653 .532 .356 →
..63 2132 3123 .2161 2356 .7.6 .532 .5.3N/G]
```

umpak:
```
       t          t          t          t
→..63 2132 3123 2121 .... 1165 ..56 1.21N/G

     t          t          t          t
..13 .212 .165 6121 ..13 .212 .165 6121
..13 .212 .165 6121 6123 .123 6532 3565N
..56 7653 22.3 5.65 2325 2356 6676 5421
.111 2321 .111 6124 .44. 4456 5424 2165N/G
```

minggah:
```
    t    t    t    t    t    t    t    t
[..6. 5.65 .635 6165 ..6. 5.65 .635 6165
..6. 5.65 .635 6165 6123 .123 6532 3565N
..56 7653 22.3 5.65 2325 2356 6676 5421
.111 2321 .111 6124 .44. 4456 5424 2165N/G

   t    t    t    t    t    t    t    t
..54 24.2 4254 2165 ..54 24.2 4254 2164
..54 24.2 4254 2165 6123 .123 6532 3565N
..56 7653 22.3 5.65 2325 2356 6676 5421
6676 5421 6676 5421 6123 55.. 55.6 7656N/G

    t    t    t    t    t    t    t    t
.654 24.2 4245 2165 6123 55.. 55.6 7656
.654 24.2 4245 2165 6123 .123 6532 3565N
..56 7653 22.3 5.65 2325 2356 6676 5421
.3.2 .165 .3.2 .165 ..21 65.1 55.6 12.3N/G
```

```
 t   t    t    t    t    t    t    t
.321 6563 .635 6123 .321 6563 .635 6123
.321 6563 .635 6123 .63. 63.6 3532 3565N
..56 7653 22.3 5.65 2325 2356 6676 5421
.111 2321 .111 6124 .44. 4456 5424 2165N/G

 t   t    t    t    t    t    t    t
66.. 6654 .545 2421 66.. 6654 .545 2421
66.. 6654 .545 2421 6123 .123 6532 3565N
..56 7653 22.3 5.65 2325 2356 6676 5421
.111 2321 .111 6124 .44. 4456 5424 2165N/G

 t   t    t    t    t    t    t    t
..67 27.3 2132 .165 ..67 27.3 2132 .165
..67 27.3 2132 .165 6123 .123 6532 3565N
..56 7653 22.3 5.65 2325 2356 6676 5421
.111 2321 .111 6124 .44. 4456 5424 2165N/G

 t   t    t    t    t    t    t    t
.22. 2352 5654 2165 .22. 2352 5654 2165
.22. 2352 5654 2165 6123 .123 6532 3565N
..56 7653 22.3 5.65 2325 2356 6676 5421
.111 2321 .111 6124 .44. 4456 5424 2165N/G

 t   t    t    t    t    t    t    t
6365 2356 .123 2165 6365 2356 .123 2165
6365 2356 .123 2165 6123 .123 6532 3565N
..56 7653 22.3 5.65 2325 2356 6676 5421
.111 2321 .111 6124 .44. 4456 5424 2165N/G

 t   t    t    t    t    t    t    t
61.2 .165 61.2 .165 61.2 .165 61.2 .165
61.2 .165 61.2 .165 6123 .123 6532 3565N
..56 7653 22.3 5.65 2325 2356 6676 5421 →
.111 2321 .111 6124 .44. 4456 5424 2165N/G]
```

suwukan:
```
   t    t    t    t    t    t    t    t
→ 61.6 2165 61.6 2165 ..54 24.2 4254 2165N/G
```

Gonjang Ganjing, Ladrang,
    sléndro pathet sanga (2).

buka: .2.1 .2.1 2211 .6.5N/G

```
        t    t N
  [ [ .2.1 .6.5
       .2.5 .2.1
       .2.1 .2.1
       .2.1 .6.5G ]

        t    t N
       .2.1 .6.5
       .2.5 .2.1
       .2.1 .2.1
       .2.1 .621G
```

ngelik:
```
        t    t N
       .3.2 .6.5
       .1.6 .5.6
       .5.6 .3.5
       .2.1 .6.5G ]
```

Gonjang Sèrèt, Ladrang, sléndro
    pathet manyura (2).

buka: .3.2 .3.2 3322 .1.6N/G

    [. 3 . 2 . 1 . 6
       . 3 . 6 . 3 . 2
      23.3 2121 23.3 2121
      23.3 21.6 35.6 35.6G

        t   t   N
      1262 1262 1262 1263
      .3.3 .356 1653 21.2
      23.3 2121 23.3 2121
      23.3 21.6 35.6 35.6G

        t   t   N
      1262 1262 1262 1263
      .3.3 .356 .165 3565
      61.1 6565 61.1 6565
      61.1 65.3 12.3 1236G

        t   t   N
      5636 5636 5636 5636
      .6.6 1651 6321 2321
      23.3 2121 23.3 2121
      23.3 21.6 35.6 35.6G]

Gonjing Miring, Ladrang,
    pélog pathet nem (3).

buka: .33. 3635 1621 3216N/G

        t   t   N
      .2.1 .2.6 .2.1 .2.6
      ..6. 2321 3263 6532
      .5.3 .5.2 .5.3 .5.2
      .33. 3635 1621 3216G

170

Goyang, Gendhing, kethuk 2 kerep, minggah
  kethuk 4, pélog pathet lima (38).

buka: .556 4565 .44. 2245 4645 .421N/G

mérong:
        t   t   N
    [.233 .121 .233 .121
     33.. 3353 6535 3212
     .... 22.3 5653 2132
     11.. 1312 1312 .165G

        t   t   N
     .65. 5612 1312 .165
     11.. 1121 3212 .165
     ..56 11.. 1132 .165 →
     44.. 4245 4645 .421G]

umpak:
        t   t
  →.2.4 .6.5 .6.5 .2.1G

minggah:
    t   t   t   t N
    [.2.3 .2.1 .2.3 .2.1
     .2.3 .5.3 .6.5 .3.2
     .3.2 .3.2 .5.3 .1.2
     .3.1 .3.2 .3.2 .6.5G

     t   t   t   t
     .6.5 .3.2 .3.2 .6.5
     .2.1 .2.1 .3.2 .6.5
     .2.1 .2.1 .3.2 .6.5
     .2.4 .6.5 .6.5 .2.1G]

Grompol, Ladrang, pélog
  pathet nem (1).

buka: 2321 3216 3565N/G

    t   t N
   623. 6235
   623. 6235
   .66. 2321
   3216 2365G

Grompol Mataram, Ladrang,
   sléndro pathet sanga (15).

```
      t    t N
 [ 6253 6165
   6253 6165
   6356 2321
   3216 2365G ]
```

Gudha Sih, Ladrang, sléndro
   pathet nem (3).

```
  t    t N        t    t N
.3.6 .3.5       .5.6 .2.1
.1.6 .3.5       .5.6 .2.1
.2.3 .5.2       .2.3 .5.2
.6.5 .3.2G      .6.5 .3.2G
```

Gudhawa, Ladrang, pélog
   pathet nem (1).

buka: 253 .253 5561 2312N/G

```
  t    t N        t    t N
.321 6132       66.. 6656
.321 6132       3565 3212
.253 .253       .321 6123
5561 2312G      6535 3212G
```

Guntur, Gendhing, kethuk 2 kerep, minggah
kethuk 4, sléndro pathet nem (2).

buka: 2 .356 .1.6 .1.6 .5.3 2356N/G
mérong:
```
           t         t    N
    [..1.  6.1.  6.53 2356
     ..1.  6.1.  6.53 2356
     ..1.  6.1.  6.53 2353
     ....  3356  3565 2232G

           t         t    N
     ....  2212  3312 .126
     ..12  ..12  3312 .126
     ..12  ..12  33.2 1121
     ....  1121  3212 .126G

           t         t    N
     ....  66..  3561 6532
     5653  2126  3561 6532
     5653  2126  3561 6532
     5321  2321  6532 .356G

           t         t    N
     2321  .2.1  6532 .356
     2321  .2.1  6532 .356
     2321  .2.1  6535 3323 →
     ....  3356  3565 2232G]

     → .5.3 .5.6 .3.5 .3.2
```
minggah:
```
           t     t     t     t N
    [.3.2 .5.3  .1.2  .1.6
     .3.2 .5.3  .1.2  .1.6
     .3.2 .5.3  .1.2  .3.1
     .2.1 .2.1  .3.2  .1.6G

           t     t     t     t N
     .5.6 .5.6  .2.1  .3.2
     .5.3 .1.6  .2.1  .3.2
     .5.3 .1.6  .2.1  .3.2
     .3.1 .2.1  .3.2  .1.6G

           t     t     t     t N
     .2.1 .2.1  .3.2  .5.6
     .2.1 .2.1  .3.2  .5.6
     .2.1 .2.1  .3.2  .5.3
     .5.3 .5.3  .6.5  .3.2G]
```

Gunung Sari, Ketawang,
   pélog pathet barang (22).

buka: 6723 3272 2732 66.6N/G

dados:
```
          t         t    N
   [..67 2353 6532 7567
    55.5 7653 6527 3276G

          t         t    N
    ..67 2353 6532 7567
    55.5 7653 77.5 6767G

         t          t    N
   .777777767 3532 .765
    33.3333.5 67.5 6767G

         t          t    N
   .777777767 3532 .765
    33.3333.5 66.3 5676G

          t         t    N
    55.2 3565 7656 5323
    27.6 2723 5653 2756G]
```

Ibu Pertiwi, Ketawang,
   pélog pathet nem (3).

buka: 22.. 5561 3212 .165N/G

```
    t       t  N    t       t  N
 [2 2 . . 5 5 6 1 . 3 1 2 . 1 6 5G
  2 2 . . 5 5 6 1 . 1 6 5 . 2 . 1G
  . .33123 5612165 .1654212 456 .45G
  6 .4561 6241245 2 2 . . 5 5 6 1G
  2 .21652 4565421 6 .5612 . 1 6 5G]
```

Ilir-ilir, Dolanan,
   pélog pathet nem (3).

           N
   ..61 6365
   3365 3316
   .123 2126
   .123 2126
   6165 2126G

Ima Winénda, Gendhing, kethuk 4 awis, minggah
   kethuk 8, sléndro pathet nem (1).

buka: 5 .61. 2165 1111 3216N/G

mérong:
          t   t
   [.... 6656 .653 2356 .... 6656 .653 2356
    356. 356. 3565 2232 .... 2253 6521 6132N
    .... 2232 .216 5612 .... 2232 .216 5612
    612. 612. 6123 6532 5653 2165 22.3 1232N
    .... 2232 3216 3353 ..35 2353 561. 1653
    6521 6123 5616 5321 .... 1121 3212 .165N →
    11.. 3216 3565 2232 ..25 2356 3565 2232
    11.. 11.. 1132 .165 .612 .165 11.. 3216N/G]

umpak minggah:

   →.1.6 .5.3 .5.6 .5.3 .5.3 .5.3 .5.2 .6.5G
minggah:
     t   t   t   t   t   t   t   t N
   [.6.5 .6.5 .6.5 .3.2 .3.2 .3.2 .5.3 .6.5
    .6.5 .6.5 .6.5 .3.2 .3.2 .3.2 .5.3 .6.5
    .3.6 .5.6 .2.1 .2.6 .3.5 .6.3 .2.3 .6.5
    .1.6 .5.3 .5.6 .5.3 .5.3 .5.3 .5.3 .6.5G]

sabetan:
    t   t   t   t   t   t   t   t N
   [3635 3632 3532 3635 3635 3632 3532 3635
    3635 3632 3532 3635 2356 532. 6656 2356
    5153 5156 5153 5156 356. 356. 3532 3635
    3635 3632 3635 3632 3635 3632 3532 3635G]

Inum/[Minum?], Ladrang,
   sléndro pathet sanga (35).

```
   t    t N
[.6.5 .6.5
 .1.2 .1.6
 .5.3 .5.3
 .6.5 .6.5G

   t    t N
 .6.5 .6.5
 .1.2 .1.6
 .5.3 .5.3
 .6.5 .3.2G

   t    t N
 .3.2 .3.2
 .5.6 .5.3
 .5.2 .1.6
 .3.5 .3.2G

   t    t N
 .3.2 .3.2
 .5.6 .5.3
 .5.2 .1.6
 .3.5 .3.2G]
```

Irim-irim, Gendhing, kethuk 2 kerep, minggah
   kethuk 4, sléndro pathet manyura (16).

buka: 661 6523 212. 2123 6532 .126N/G

```
mérong:    t         t    N
      [..61 22.. 2235 3231
       ..61 22.. 2235 3231
       ..32 .126 ..61 6523 →
       212. 2123 6532 .126G]
```

```
umpak:     t         t    N
       .2.1 .2.3 .1.2 .1.6G
```

```
minggah: t    t    t    t N
      [.3.2 .3.2 .5.3 .2.1
       .3.2 .3.2 .5.3 .2.1
       .3.2 .1.6 .2.1 .5.3
       .2.1 .2.3 .1.2 .1.6G]
```

Jagoan, Dolanan, sléndro
pathet sanga (3).

```
                    G
     [6565 2356 5321
           2121 2121
           2561 6535
2325 2325 6153 2532
1312 1312 5651 5321]
```

Jagung-jagung/Tunggu Jagung/
[Balung Jagung?], Ladrang,
sléndro [pathet nem] (35).

buka: 3.1 2312 .6.3 .6.5 .6.3 2.22N/G

```
irama I:   t    t N
        [6365 6362
         6365 6362
         6365 6362
         6365 6362G]
```

```
irama II:
           t         t    N
     [.6.3 .6.5 .6.3 .6.2
      .6.3 .6.5 .6.3 .6.2
      5653 2126 .123 2126
      156. 5.3. 2.53 2126G

           t         t    N
      156. 5.3. 2.53 2126
      156. 5.3. 2.53 2126
      .3.1 .3.2 .3.1 .3.2
      .6.3 .6.5 .6.3 .6.2G]
```

Jaka Lala, Gendhing, kethuk 2 kerep, minggah
kethuk 4, sléndro pathet manyura (1).

buka: .661 6523 .35. 5321 6612 .126N/G

mérong:
```
            t         t    N
     [..61 22.. 22.3 1232
      .126 ..61 23.6 3561
      .... 1653 22.3 5656
      .... 6653 22.. 5653G

            t         t    N
      ..35 6.16 .165 3212
      ..23 5616 .165 3212
      .126 .... 3561 6523 →
      .35. 5321 6612 .126G]
```

umpak:
```
          t         t
    →.5.3 .2.1 .3.2 .1.6G
```

minggah:
```
       t    t    t    t N
     [.3.2 .3.2 .3.1 .3.2
      .1.6 .1.6 .3.5 .2.1
      .2.1 .6.5 .3.6 .1.6
      .5.6 .5.3 .2.3 .5.3G

       t    t    t    t N
      .5.6 .5.6 .5.3 .1.2
      .5.6 .5.6 .3.2 .1.2
      .1.6 .5.6 .2.1 .5.3
      .5.3 .2.1 .3.2 .1.6G]
```

178

Jalaga, Gendhing [Ketawang], kethuk 8 kerep,
minggah kethuk 16, pélog pathet lima (1).

buka: adangiah; .3.3 .321 .312 3565N/G

mérong:
```
        t              t              t              t
  [.... 5356 .5.3 .523 55.. 5356 .5.3 .523
   55.. 5356 .5.3 .523 66.. 5676 532. 1232N
   .... 2235 6532 1232 .... 2235 6765 4.24
   .521 ..24 .521 3212 ..23 5676 .53. 2353N/G

        t              t              t              t
   ...3 6521 66.. 2165 ..53 6532 .216 2165
   ..53 6532 .216 5612 35.3 6532 .216 5456N
   456. 3.32 .216 5456 456. 3.32 .444 2165
   .... 5561 2165 7767 .... 7765 35.2 3565N/G

        t              t              t              t
   .... 5567 .653 .523 55.. 5567 .653 .523
   55.. 5567 .653 6532 66.. 5567 .653 .523N
   .... 2235 6532 1232 .... 2235 6765 4.24
   .521 ..24 .521 3212 ..23 5676 .53. 2353N/G

        t              t              t              t
   ...3 6521 66.. 2165 ..53 6532 .216 2165
   ..53 6532 .216 5613 35.3 6532 .216 5456N
   456. 3.32 .216 5456 456. 3.32 .444 2165 →
   .... 5561 2165 3323 .... 3321 .312 3565N/G]
```

umpak:
```
        t              t              t              t
  → 33.. 6532 66.. 66.1 22.. 2321 .653 2365N/G

        t              t              t              t
   ..53 6532 ..26 5365 ..53 6532 ..26 5365
   ..53 6532 ..26 5365 2356 532. 6656 2356N
   .124 .124 .124 .126 .123 .123 .333 2165
   .55. 5532 .55. 5523 55.. 5356 5563 6535N/G
```

minggah:
```
      t    t    t    t    t    t    t    t
  [.22. 2356 5535 6535 .22. 2356 5563 6535
   .22. 2356 5563 6535 .356 532. 6656 2356N
   .124 .126 .124 .126 .124 .123 .333 2165
   .55. 5532 .55. 5523 55.. 5356 .216 5323N/G

      t    t    t    t    t    t    t    t
   .35. 2356 1216 5322 .35. 2356 1216 5322
   .35. 2356 1216 5322. 356 .532 6656 2356N →
   .124 .126 .124 .126 .124 .123 .333 2165
   .55. 5532 .55. 5523 55.. 5356 5563 6535N/G]
```

umpak-umpakan:
```
     t    t    t    t    t    t    t    t
→.124 .126 .124 .126 .124 .123 5653 2165
 3635 3632 3635 3632 3635 3632 3132 3635N/G
```

sesegan:
```
      t    t    t    t    t    t    t    t
[3635 3632 3132 3635 3635 3632 3132 3635
 3635 3632 3132 3635 2356 532. 6656 2356N
 .124 .126 .124 .126 .124 .123 5653 2165→
 3635 3632 3635 3632 3635 3632 3132 3635N/G]
```

suwukan:
```
     t    t    t    t    t    t    t    t
...5 5532 ..23 5535 ..23 55.3 6532 .3.5N/G
```

Jamba, Gendhing, kethuk 4 kerep, minggah
    kethuk 8, sléndro pathet nem (1).

buka: 352 .2.3 5612 .2.1 .216N/G

mérong:
```
        t         t         t         t    N
[ ..65 3356 2321 6535 ..53 6532 ..23 5616
  ..65 3356 2321 6535 ..53 6532 .321 6132
  .321 6132 66.1 6523 6532 ..23 5653 2165
  .22. 6535 .22. 6535 22.. 22.3 5653 2126G

        t         t         t         t    N
  ..65 3356 2321 6535 ..53 6532 ..23 5616
  ..65 3356 2321 6535 ..53 6532 .321 6132
  .321 6132 66.1 6523 6532 ..23 5653 2165
  .22. 6535 .22. 6535 33.. 6532 5653 2126G

        t         t         t         t    N
  .... 66.. 3561 6535 ..56 1653 5653 2126
  ..61 3216 3561 6535 ..53 6532 .321 6132
  .321 6132 66.1 6523 6532 ..23 5653 2165
  .22. 6535 .22. 6535 22.. 22.3 5653 2126G ]
```

minggah:
```
     t    t    t    t    t    t    t N
[ .1.6 .1.6 .2.1 .6.5 .6.5 .3.2 .3.2 .1.6
  .1.6 .1.6 .2.1 .6.5 .6.5 .3.2 .3.1 .3.2
  .3.1 .3.2 .5.6 .5.3 .5.2 .3.2 .5.3 .6.5
  .2.3 .5.2 .5.3 .5.2 .3.3 .5.2 .3.2 .1.6G ]
```

Jamba, Gendhing, kethuk 4 kerep, minggah
kethuk 8, sléndro pathet nem (16).

buka: 532. 5232 612. .2.1 .216N/G

mérong:
```
    t         t         t         t     N
..65 3356 2321 6535 ..53 6532 ..23 5616
..65 3356 2321 6535 ..53 6532 .312 6132
[..21 6132 66.1 6523 6532 ..23 5653 2165 →
.22. 6535 .22. 6535 22.. 22.3 5653 2126G

    t         t         t         t     N
..65 3356 2321 6535 ..53 6532 ..23 5616
..65 3356 2321 6535 ..35 6535 .321 6132
..21 6132 66.1 6532 6532 ..23 5653 2165
.22. 6535 .22. 6535 33.. 6532 5653 2126G

    t         t         t         t     N
.... 66.. 3561 6535 ..56 1653 2353 2126
..61 3216 3561 6535 ..53 6532 .321 6132]
```

umpak:
```
    t         t         t         t     N
→.2.3 .5.2 .5.3 .5.2 .5.3 .5.3 .3.2 .1.6G
```

minggah:
```
[.1.6 .1.6 .2.1 .6.5 .3.5 .3.2 .3.2 .1.6
 .1.6 .1.6 .2.1 .6.5 .3.5 .3.2 .3.1 .3.2
 .3.1 .3.2 .5.6 .5.3 .5.2 .3.2 .5.3 .6.5
 .2.3 .5.2 .5.2 .5.3 .5.3 .5.2 .3.2 .1.6G]
```

Jambé Thukul, Dolanan,
    pélog pathet nem (32).

buka celuk:
```
                                    N
[ . . 3 5  3 5 6 1  . . 1 2  3 1 2̲1̲6
  . . 3 5  3 5 6 1  . . 1 2  3 1 2̲1̲6
  . . 3 5  3 5 6 1  . . 1 2  3 1 2̲3̲3
  . 3 3 3  3 1 3 2  6 1̲2̲6 3  6 5 3 2G
  6 1 2 3  6 1 3 2  6 1 2 3  6 1 3 2G
  . . 6 6  1 2 6̲5̲3̲5̲ . 6 2̲5̲3  . 2 2̲3̲2̲1̲6G]
```

Jamuran, Dolanan, sléndro
   pathet sanga (28).

[. 6 $\overline{6}$15 $\overline{.232}\overline{322}$
  $\overline{6121}\overline{615}$ $\overline{.232}\overline{322}$
  2 6 2 1 2 6 $\underline{2\ 1}$
  5 5 $\overline{323}$ $\overline{51216}\overline{165}$
  5 5 2 3 1 2 3 5]

Jangga Lana, Ladrang,
   pélog pathet nem (1).

  6245 6245 6245 6165
  11.. 3216 2152 5621
  55.6 1216 2152 5621
  .66. 6542 4561 2165G

Jangkrik Génggong, Ladrang,
   sléndro pathet sanga (2).

buka: 165. 2165 32.3 5635N/G

lancaran: t tN
      [3235
       6165
       6165 →
       3235G]

       →3212G

   t   t N   t   t N
[..23 1232   ..52 3565
 5616 5321   212. 2165
 5616 5321   212. 2165
 6632 .165G   22.3 1232G]

Jangkung Kuning, Gendhing, kethuk 2 kerep,
   minggah kethuk 4, pélog pathet barang (3).

buka: .667 5676 .767 .653 65̄2̄3̄4̄2N/G

mérong:

```
        t              t        N
[. 3 5 6  . . 6 .  3 5 6 7  6 5 3 5
 . . 5 3  2 3 5 6  3 5 6 7  6 5 3 5
 7 6 5 6  5 3 2 3  6 5 3 2  3 5 6 5
 7 7 . .  7 6 5 6  7̄6̄7 6̄5̄3  6 5̄2̄3̄4̄2G]
```

minggah:

```
      t            t           t          t    N
[.7356756  27356756  ..672.32  73727675
 .7356756  27356756  ..672.32  73727675
 .2343243  42343243  ..356532  ..235665
 35673567  35675676  .767.653  .6.52342G]
```


Jati Kondhang, Gendhing, kethuk 2 kerep,
   minggah kethuk 4, pélog pathet lima (1).

buka: [.3.2165.5] x2   .1 5.56 12.3N/G

mérong:

```
      t         t     N
[...3 6521  ..21 6123
 ...3 6521  3212 .165
 ....  5561  3212 .165 →
 ..21 65.1  5.56 12.3G
```

```
      t         t     N
 ...3 6521  ..21 6123
 ...3 6521  77.. 5676
 .76. 676.  6567 6535
 ..23 55..  55.6 7656G
```

```
      t         t     N
 .76. 5421  ..21 6123
 ...3 6521  3212 .165
 ....  5561  3212 .165
 ..21 65.1  5.56 12.3G]
```

umpak minggah:

```
      t         t     N
→.2.1 .2.1 .2.6 .5.3G
```

minggah:
```
      t     t     t    t N
[.2.1 .2.1 .2.6 .5.3
 .2.1 .2.1 .2.6 .5.3
 .5.6 .5.6 .2.1 .6.5
 .2.3 .5.3 .1.6 .5.3G]
```

Jélé Drésé, Gendhing (Santiswaran),
   sléndro pathet sanga (39).

```
.   . 5 5 5 5     . 2 5 6 6 1 6
. 6 1   5   3 2   . 3 5   1 3 2
.   . 2 2 2 2     . 5 3   231 6 5
.   . 5 612 2     . 611 2 6 165G
.   . 5 5 5 5     . 2 5 6 6 1 6
. 6 1   5   3 2   . 3 5   1 3 2
.   . 2 2 2 2     . 5 3   231 6 5
.   . 5 612 2     . 611 2 6 165G
```

Jenthar, Gendhing, kethuk 4 awis, minggah
   kethuk 8, pélog pathet barang (38).

buka: 2 .2.2 .723 .3.2 .723 .272 .756N/G

mérong:
```
            t                    t
[..67 5676 ..67 2353 6765 3272 ..27 6723
 56.. 6656 3567 6523 ..35 6532 7232 .756N
 ..67 5676 ..67 2353 6765 3272 ..27 6723
 56.. 6656 3567 6523 ..35 6532 7232 .756N
 77.. 7767 .3.2 .765 .676 5323 77.. 7765
 .676 5323 77.. 7765 .676 .532 723. 3532N →
 ..23 2765 33.6 3567 22.. 2765 33.6 3567
 22.. 22.3 56.7 6523 272. 2723 6532 .756N/G]
```

umpak:
```
 →.4.3 .7.6 .2.3 .7.6 .3.2 .4.3 .4.3 .7.6N/G
```

184

minggah:
```
     t    t    t    t    t    t    t    t N
 [.7.6 .2.3 .4.3 .2.3 .4.3 .2.3 .4.3 .7.2
  .3.2 .3.2 .3.2 .4.3 .4.3 .2.3 .4.3 .7.2
  .3.2 .3.2 .3.2 .7.6 .5.6 .2.7 .5.6 .5.3
  .5.3 .7.6 .2.3 .7.6 .3.2 .4.3 .4.3 .7.6G]
```

Jongka/Jongkang, Gendhing [Ketawang], kethuk
   2 kerep, sléndro pathet sanga (2).

buka: 5235 32.3 5635N/G

mérong:
```
           t         t    N
     [..32 .165 .612 .165 →
      11.. 1216 1216 5323G

           t         t    N
     .... 5235 .616 5323
     .... 5235 32.3 5635G

           t         t    N
     .... 1121 ..12 3565
     ..56 1653 6165 2321G]
```
umpak: t   t   N
       →.2.1 .2.6 .1.6 .5.3G
minggah: Ladrang Jongka/Jongkang

Jongka/Jongkang, Ladrang,
     sléndro pathet sanga (1).

(minggah to Gendhing Jongka/Jongkang)
```
  t    t N     t    t N      t    t N
.5.3 .6.5    .2.1 .2.1     .3.2 .6.5
.1.6 .5.3    .2.1 .3.5     .3.2 .6.5
.5.3 .6.5    .1.6 .5.3     .2.1 .2.6
.3.2 .3.5G   .6.5 .2.1G    .1.6 .5.3G
```

Jong Kèri, Ladrang, sléndro
pathet manyura (1).

buka: 6.12 3.66 .2.1 .2.3 .5.3N/G

```
      t    t N
   [5253 5253
    6561 6532
    3132 3132
    6561 6523G]
```

ciblon:
```
     t          t   N
   [6532 5653 6532 5653
    66.. 2321 3263 6532
    5321 3532 5321 3532
    66.. 2321 3265 1653G]
```

Jong Layar, Ladrang,
sléndro pathet nem (38).

buka: 2 .356 .6.3 .6.3 .6.5 .3.2N/G

```
  t    t N     t    t N     t    t N     t    t N
.3.5 .3.2    .3.5 .3.2    .5.3 .5.6    .5.3 .5.6
.3.5 .3.2    .3.5 .3.2    .5.3 .5.6    .5.3 .5.6
.3.5 .6.5    .3.5 .6.5    .3.5 .6.5    .3.5 .6.5
.3.5 .3.2G   .2.3 .1.6G   .2.3 .1.6G   .6.5 .3.2G
```

Jong Mèru, Gendhing, kethuk 2 kerep, dhawah
kethuk 4, sléndro pathet manyura (5).

buka: 3561 3216 .356 .356 22.2 11.1N/G

lamba:
```
       t          t    N
     .5.5 .6.3 .2.3 .2.1
     .5.5 .6.3 .2.3 .2.1
     .6.5 .6.3 .6.5 .2.1
     212. 2165 3561 6523G
```

dados:

```
      t          t    N
[1121  ..12  3532  1653
 6536  3561  5616  5323
 1121  3216  5616  5323
 6165  6165  2353  2121G

   t          t    N
 5635  1653  6165  2321
 5635  1653  6165  2321
 5635  1653  6165  2321
 212.  2165  3561  6523G]
```

pangkat dhawah:

```
   t          t    N
 1121  ..12  3532  1653
 6536  3561  5616  5323
 1121  3216  5616  5323
 .6.5  .6.5  .2.3  .2.1G
```

dhawah:

```
   t     t     t    t N
[.6.5  .6.5  .6.5  .2.1
 .6.5  .6.5  .6.5  .2.1
 .6.5  .6.5  .6.5  .2.1
 .2.1  .6.5  .2.1  .5.3G

   t     t     t    t N
 .2.1  .6.5  .2.1  .5.3
 .2.1  .6.5  .2.1  .5.3
 .2.1  .2.6  .1.6  .5.3
 .6.5  .6.5  .2.3  .2.1G]
```

Jong Mèru Bah Gong, Gendhing, kethuk 2 awis,
umpak minggah kethuk 1 arang, minggah
kethuk 4, pélog pathet barang (11).

buka: 3 .3.2 .327 .66. 6727 .2.6 .5.3N/G

mérong:
```
            t                 t          N
 [..35 7653 77.. 3532 ..23 2756 3567 6563
  ..35 7653 77.. 3532 ..23 2756 3567 6563
  ..35 7653 77.. 3532 ..23 2756 3567 6563 →
  .... 33.5 6635 6765 7635 6765 7632 5327G

            t                 t          N
  ..72 .327 55.. 7656 ..67 6523 6765 3237
  ..72 .327 55.. 7656 ..67 6523 6765 3237
  ..72 .327 55.. 7656 ..67 6523 6765 3237
  66.. 66.7 22.3 2767 ..32 .756 3567 6523G]
```

umpak minggah:
```
                  t          N
       →.5.3 .5.3 .7.6 .2.7G
```

minggah:
```
       t    t    t    t N
    [.2.7 .2.3 .7.6 .2.7
     .2.7 .2.3 .7.6 .5.3
     .5.3 .5.6 .3.5 .7.6
     .7.6 .2.7 .5.6 .5.3G

     t    t    t    t N
     .5.3 .7.6 .2.7 .5.3
     .5.3 .7.6 .2.7 .5.3
     .5.3 .7.6 .2.7 .2.3
     .5.3 .5.3 .7.6 .5.3G]
```

Jong Mèru Kudus, Gendhing, kethuk 2 kerep,
minggah kethuk 4, slèndro pathet manyura (38).

buka: 3 .651 .5.5 .6.3 .6.5 3231N/G

mérong:
```
          t         t    N
     [55.. 1653 6165 3231
      55.. 1653 6165 3231
      55.. 1653 6165 3231 →
      .... 1165 3561 6563G

          t         t    N
      11.. 1165 3561 6563
      11.. 1165 3561 6563
      11.. 1165 3561 6563
      .516 3516 3561 2321G

          t         t    N
      .... 1123 .216 .523
      ..36 3561 2321 6563
      11.. 1161 22.1 6535
      33.5 6165 1635 5321G]
```

umpak:
```
          t         t    N
      →.2.1 .6.5 .1.6 .5.3G
```

minggah:
```
       t    t    t    t N
     [.2.1 .6.5 .1.6 .5.3
      .2.1 .6.5 .1.6 .5.3
      .2.1 .6.5 .1.6 .5.3
      .5.6 .5.6 .2.3 .2.1G

       t    t    t    t N
      .3.5 .6.3 .6.5 .2.1
      .3.5 .6.3 .6.5 .2.1
      .3.5 .6.3 .6.5 .2.1
      .2.1 .6.5 .1.6 .5.3G]
```

Kabor, Gendhing, kethuk 2 kerep,
    sléndro pathet nem (3)

buka: 6 $\overline{612}6.\overline{6}$ .232 6532 2223 5616N/G

mérong:

```
        12.2 .2.3 561. 5616
        55.. 5653 5653 2165G

          t         t    N
     [[.555 2235 2356 3565 →
        33.. 3353 6535 3212G

          t         t    N
        .5.3 .5.2 .5.3 .5.2
        55.. 5653 5653 2165G]
```

ngelik:

```
        →66.. 6656 11.. 3216

          t         t    N
        ..12 ..23 561. 5616
        55.. 5653 5653 2165G]
```

minggah: Ladrang Karawitan

Kaduk, Ladrang, pélog pathet nem (1).

```
 t    t N     t    t N     t    t N     t    t N
.3.2 .5.6    .6.3 .6.5    .3.5 .6.5    .3.5 .6.5
.5.6 .5.3    .6.3 .6.5    .1.2 .1.6    .1.2 .1.6
.2.1 .2.3    .3.2 .5.3    .5.3 .5.3    .5.3 .5.3
.2.1 .6.5G   .6.5 .3.2G   .6.5 .3.2G   .6.5 .3.2G
```

Kaduk Manis, Gendhing, kethuk 4 kerep,
minggah kethuk 8, sléndro pathet nem (2).

buka: 66.1 .6.5 .6.3 .5.6 .3.5 .3.2N/G

mérong:
```
         t          t          t          t    N
[..23 .532 66.1 6535 .653 5616 3565 3212
 ..23 .532 66.1 6535 .653 5616 3565 3212
 ..23 .532 66.1 6535 .653 5616 3565 3212
 33.. 3353 6521 6132 5653 2121 3265 3235G

      t          t          t          t    N
.555 2235 33.. 6532 5653 2121 3265 3235
.555 2235 33.. 6532 5653 2121 3265 3235
.555 2235 33.. 6532 5653 2121 3265 3235 →
 66.. 6656 3561 6535 .653 5616 3565 3212G]
```

umpak:
```
            t          t          t          t    N
→.3.6 .5.6 .2.1 .6.5 .6.3 .5.6 .3.5 .3.2G
```

minggah:
```
   t    t    t    t    t    t    t    t N
[.3.2 .6.5 .3.2 .6.5 .3.2 .6.5 .3.5 .3.2
 .1.6 .1.6 .3.6 .3.2 .5.3 .6.5 .3.5 .3.2
 .1.6 .1.6 .3.6 .3.2 .5.3 .6.5 .3.5 .3.2
 .3.2 .6.5 .3.2 .6.5 .3.2 .6.5 .6.5 .3.2G

   t    t    t    t    t    t    t    t N
.3.2 .6.5 .3.2 .6.5 .3.2 .6.5 .6.5 .3.2
.5.6 .5.6 .2.1 .2.6 .5.6 .3.5 .6.5 .3.2
.5.6 .5.6 .2.1 .2.6 .5.6 .3.5 .6.5 .3.2
.3.2 .6.5 .3.2 .6.5 .3.2 .6.5 .3.5 .3.2G]
```

Kagok, Ladrang, pélog pathet lima (1).

buka: 5 5612 1645 11.5 6121N/G

```
   t    t N       t    t N       t    t N
.111 5621      55.. 5535      7656 5421
.111 5612      ..56 7656      3212 .165
..24 5.65      .653 2232      .612 .165
6654 2121G     ..24 5.65G     11.5 6121G
```

Kagok Laras, Gendhing, kethuk 2 kerep,
minggah kethuk 4, pélog pathet lima (1).

buka: [3.21 65.5] x2 .2.2 .2.2 .5.6 .1.2N/G

mérong:
```
        t       t    N
 [....  2212  33.2  .161
  22..  22.4  5654  .521
  .561  ....  1132  .165
  .15.  15.6  123.  1232G

        t       t    N
 55..  55..  55.6  .535
 ..56  5323  ..35  6767
 ...7  .567  .567  .765
 33..  3356  7653  2123G

        t       t    N
 ....  3356  7653  2123
 1235  ....  5654  .521
 .561  ....  1132  .165 ⇀
 .15.  15.6  123.  1232G]
```

umpak:
```
        t       t    N
 ⇀..56  7654  2.44  2165G

        t       t    N
 ....  5561  .2.1  .656
 11..  2321  .654  1121
 .111  5621  .111  5621
 ..56  11.2  4565  4212G
```

minggah:
```
  t     t     t    t N
 [4.45  4241  .412  4542
 66..  5676  5421  3216
 1516  1516  1516  1121
 ..56  11.2  4565  4212G

  t     t     t    t N
 4.45  4241  .412  4542
 66..  5676  5421  3216
 1516  1516  1516  2232
 ..61  22.4  5654  2165G
  t     t     t    t N
 .22.  2352  5654  2165
 .22.  2352  5654  2121
 .111  5621  .111  5621
 ..56  11.2  4565  4212G]
```

192

Kagok Madura, Ladrang,
    sléndro pathet sanga (2).

buka: 5 323. 3635 1612 1615N/G

```
      t    t N
 [ [1612 1615
   1612 1615
   1612 1615
   323. 3635G ]
```

ngelik:
```
      t    t N
   11.. 1121
   3212 .165
   1632 5616
   3561 6535G

      t    t N
   1656 5321
   5616 5321
   5616 5321
   6632 .165G

      t    t N
   323. 3635
   323. 3635
   323. 3635
   1612 1615G ]
```

Kaki-kaki Tunggu Jagung, Ladrang,
    sléndro pathet nem (1).

buka: 3.1 2312 .6.3 .6.5 .6.3 .6.2N/G

```
      t    t N
   6365 6362
   6365 6362
   6365 6362
   6365 6362G

      t         t    N
 .6.3 .6.5 .6.3 .6.2
 .6.3 .6.5 .6.3 .6.2
 .253 2126 .123 2126
 ..66 5533 2213 2126G

      t         t    N
 ..66 5533 2253 2126
 ..66 5533 2253 2126
 .3.1 2312 .3.1 2312
 .6.3 .6.5 .6.3 .6.2G
```

Kala Ganjur/Kala Panganjur/Nala Ganjur (22).

buka: 2N/G

```
    N N
    3232G
    3232G
```

Kalongking, Ladrang, pélog
    pathet nem (1).

buka: 235 3235 6661 3216N/G

```
    t    t N
    .56. 3356
    .56. 2123
    .235 3253
    66.1 3216G
```

Kandha/Kandha Manyura, Ladrang,
    sléndro pathet manyura (2).

buka: 3.5 6321 .12. 2321 .216 .5.3N/G

```
    t    t N       t    t N       t    t N
[.5.6 .5.3       .5.6 .5.6       .5.3 .1.6
 .5.3 .2.1       .2.1 .6.5       .5.3 .1.6
 .2.3 .2.1       .6.3 .2.1       .3.2 .5.3
 .2.6 .5.3G      .2.6 .5.3G      .1.6 .5.3G]
```

Kambang Katès, Ladrang,
pélog pathet (?) (1).

buka: 6612 1653 6123 6532N/G

```
     t    t N
 [5653 6532
  5653 6532
  6612 1653
  6123 6532G]
```

irama ciblon:
```
      t           t     N
 [.52. 2523 5356 3532
  .52. 2523 5356 3532
  .356 6612 3216 5323
  216. 6123 5356 3532G]
```

Kanyut, Gendhing, kethuk 4 kerep, minggah
kethuk 8, sléndro pathet nem (2).

buka: 2 .5.3 .5.2 .6.3 .6.5N/G

mérong:
```
  t          t          t          t    N
 [.1.6 .532 11.. 3216 .... 6653 5653 2165
  .555 2235 2353 2126 ..61 2353 5653 2165
  .555 2235 2353 2126 ..61 2353 5653 2165 →
  22.. 22.3 55.6 5323 ..35 6532 .6.3 .6.5G]
```

umpak minggah:
```
  t          t          t          t     N
 →.2.3 .5.2 .5.3 .5.2 .5.3 .5.2 .6.3 .6.5
```

minggah:
```
  t    t    t    t    t    t    t    t N
 [.2.1 .2.6 .2.1 .2.6 .2.1 .2.3 .5.3 .6.5
  .2.1 .2.6 .2.1 .2.6 .2.1 .2.3 .5.3 .6.5
  .2.1 .2.6 .2.1 .2.6 .2.1 .2.3 .5.3 .6.5
  .2.3 .5.2 .5.3 .5.2 .5.3 .5.2 .6.3 .6.5G]
```

Kapang-kapang, Ladrang, pélog pathet nem (1).

buka: 612 3612 .126N/G

t	t N	t	t N	t	t N
.3.2	.1.6	.3.5	.1.6	.3.5	.3.2
.3.2	.1.6	.3.5	.1.6	.6.5	.3.2
.3.2	.3.5	.5.6	.5.6	.3.2	.3.5
.6.4	.1.6G	.2.3	.5.6G	.6.4	.1.6G

Kapi Dhondhong, Ladrang,
     pélog pathet nem (3).

buka: .556 1216 2152 5321N/G

irama II & III:

t		t	N
.3.2	.3.5	.2.3	.2.1
.3.2	.3.5	.3.6	.3.2
5316	2312	5316	2312
55.1	.216	2152	5321G

Karawitan, Gendhing [Ketawang], kethuk
4 kerep, sléndro pathet nem (3).

buka: 3 3561 .1.1 .2.1 3212 .126N/G

mérong:
```
        t        t        t        t    N
.3.3 .3.3 .3.2 .321 .11. 1121 3212 .126
.... 66.. 6616 5323 5653 2165 3561 3216

   t        t        t        t    N
3565 2232 5653 2126 .666 3356 3532 .356
3565 2232 5653 2165 22.. 22.3 5653 2165G

   t        t        t        t    N
.555 2235 2356 3353 ..35 6532 5653 2165
11.. 3216 3532 .356 22.. 2321 3265 2232G

   t        t        t        t    N
..23 6532 ..21 3216[.666 3356 3532 .356
11.. 1121 3265 3561 .... 1123 6532 .126G

   t        t        t        t    N
33.. 33.5 6165 3231 .... 1123 6532 .126
.... 66.. 6616 5323 5653 2165 3561 3216G

   t        t
3565 2232 5653 2126]
```

umpak minggah:
```
                        t        t    N
   t        t      .36. 3561 .3.2 .1.6
.2.1 .2.6 .2.1 .2.6 .2.1 .2.6 .3.2 .5.6G
```

Karawitan, Ladrang, sléndro
  pathet nem (3).

(minggah to Gendhing Kabor &
  to Gendhing Karawitan)

```
 t    t N
.5.3 .5.6   (first gongan
.5.3 .5.6    used only for
.5.6 .5.6    Gendhing Karawitan)
.2.1 .2.6G

 t    t N
[.3.5 .6.5
.3.6 .5.3
.5.2 .3.2
.6.5 .3.2

 t    t N
.3.5 .6.3
.1.6 .5.3
.1.6 .5.3
.2.3 .6.5G

 t    t N
.3.2 .6.5
.3.2 .3.2
.3.2 .3.2
.5.3 .6.5G suwuk

 t    t N
.3.2 .6.5
.2.1 .2.6
.5.6 .5.6
.2.1 .2.6G]
```

Kasatriyan, Ketawang,
    sléndro pathet sanga (38).

buka: .2.1 .2.1 .3.2 .6.5N/G

```
 t    t N  t    t N
1216 3265 1216 2165G
```

ngelik:
```
 t         t  N    t         t  N
6 5 2 1  3 2 6 5  . .1652  1 6 3 5G
6 5 2 1  3 2 6 5  . .1652  1 6 3 5G
1 1 2 1  3 2 1 6  3 5 3 2  1 6 3 5G
```

Kasmaran/Éling-éling Kasmaran,
    Ladrang, sléndro pathet sanga (16).

(dhawah from Gendhing Renyep)

```
    t    t N
    3216 5612
    3216 5612
    55.. 5612
    1615 1612G
```

irama ciblon:

```
     t         t    N
[.3.2 .6.5 .1.6 .3.2
 .3.2 .6.5 .1.6 .3.2
 .3.2 .6.5 .1.6 .3.2
 .1.6 .1.5 .1.6 .3.2G]
```


Katé-katé, Ladrang, sléndro
    pathet manyura (38).

buka: 661 6532 1261 3216N/G

```
   t    t N
[2126 2126
 3561 6532
 6561 6532
 1261 3216G]
```

irama ciblon:

```
    t         t    N
[...1 ...6 ...1 ...6
 ..6. 3532 1216 3532
 66.. 2321 3263 6532
 1261 3532 5653 2126G]
```

199

Kaum Dhawuk, Ketawang,
    pélog pathet barang (8).
buka celuk: 6N/G

```
     t    t N  t    t N
[[.2.3 .2.7 .2.3 .7.6G]x2
.... 7576 3567 6532G
.352 .352 5653 2756G
.2.3 .2.7 .2.3 .7.6G]
```

Kawit, Gendhing [Ketawang], kethuk
    2 kerep, sléndro pathet nem (3).
buka: 6 6123 .3.3 .5.3 .6.1 2353N/G
mérong:
```
         t       t    N
    [...3 .123 .123 .123
     22.. 2232 3565 3212G

         t       t    N
    ..2. 2232 3565 3212
    33.. 3353 .6.1 2353G]
```
minggah: Ladrang Kawit

Kawit, Ladrang, sléndro
    pathet nem (3).
(minggah to Gendhing Kawit)
```
    t    t N    t    t N
5356 1653    3235 6532
5356 1653    3235 6532
22.. 2232    33.. 3353
3565 3212G   5616 5323G
```

Kayun, Gendhing, kethuk 4 kerep, minggah
kethuk 8, pélog pathet barang (38).

buka: .576 .532 .7.7 .2.3 7732 .756N/G

mérong:
```
       t          t          t          t      N
[..67 5676 22.. 2327 ..32 .327 33.. 6532
 ..23 2756 .765 3567 2372 .756 33.. 6532
 5653 2765 3567 3276 .... 6656 3567 6535 →
 .635 66.. 3567 6532 77.. 6723 6532 .756G]
```

umpak:
```
      t          t          t          t      N
→.6.5 .7.6 .2.7 .3.2 .7.6 .3.2 .3.2 .7.6G
```

minggah:
```
     t    t    t    t    t    t    t    t N
[.7.6 .7.6 .2.3 .2.7 .3.2 .7.6 .2.7 .3.2
 .7.6 .3.2 .5.3 .2.7 .3.2 .7.6 .2.7 .3.2
 .7.6 .3.2 .5.3 .6.5 .6.5 .7.6 .2.7 .6.5
 .6.5 .7.6 .2.7 .3.2 .7.6 .3.2 .3.2 .7.6G]
```

Kebo Giro, Lancaran,
    sléndro sanga/pélog nem (6).

buka: 5612 1312 1615N/G

```
N N   N N
6532 3265G
6532 3265G
6521 2165G
6521 2165G
1632 3265G
```

Kebo Giro/Maésa Giro, Lancaran,
    pélog pathet barang (1).

buka: 5672 7372 7675N/G

```
t tN t tN t tN t tN
.6.5 .3.2 .3.2 .6.5G
.6.5 .3.2 .3.2 .6.5G
.6.5 .6.7 .6.7 .6.5G
.6.5 .6.7 .6.7 .6.5G
.7.6 .3.2 .3.2 .6.5G
```

Kebo Giro Gambir Sawit, Lancaran,
sléndro pathet sanga (2).

buka: .2.1 .2.1 .6.5N/G

```
   t tN t tN t tN t tN
[ .6.5 .1.6 .1.6 .2.1G
  .2.1 .2.6 .2.6 .2.1G
  .2.1 .3.5 .6.5 .3.2G
  .5.6 .2.1 .3.2 .3.5G ]
```

Kebo Giro Kedhu, Lancaran,
sléndro pathet sanga (2).

buka: .6.3 .6.3 .6.5N/G

```
   t tN t tN t tN t tN
[ .6.5 .6.3 .6.3 .6.5G
  .6.5 .6.2 .6.2 .6.1G
  .6.1 .6.2 .6.2 .6.1G
  .6.1 .6.3 .6.3 .6.5G ]
```

Kedhaton Bentar, Gendhing, kethuk 2 kerep,
minggah kethuk 4, sléndro pathet nem (2).

buka: 5 .6.3 .6.5 .352 .5.3N/G

mérong:
```
            t         t    N
     [..36 3565 2356 3565
      1653 6535 2356 3565
      1653 6535 2232 1232
      .... 22.3 5653 2126G

        t         t    N
      3532 ..23 5653 2126
      .... 6656 3561 6535
      1653 1121 3212 .165
      1653 6535 22.3 5653G

        t         t    N
      ..36 3565 2356 3565
      1653 6535 2356 3565
      1653 6535 22.. 1121
      .... 1121 3212 .126G

        t         t    N
      ..62 ..23 5653 2126
      3532 1121 3212 .165
      1653 1121 3212 .165→
      1653 6535 22.2 5653G]
```

umpak minggah:
```
              t         t    N
      → .6.3 .6.5 .3.2 .5.3G
```

minggah:
```
          t    t    t    t N
     [.5.3 .6.5 .3.6 .3.5
      .6.3 .6.5 .3.6 .3.5
      .6.3 .6.5 .3.2 .3.2
      .3.2 .3.2 .5.3 .1.6G

        t    t    t    t N
      .3.2 .3.2 .5.3 .1.6
      .3.2 .3.1 .3.2 .6.5
      .6.3 .2.1 .3.2 .6.5
      .6.3 .6.5 .3.2 .5.3G]
```

Kembang Dara, Gendhing, kethuk 2
kerep, pélog pathet nem (1).

buka: 6 .6.1 6523 .52. 2365 2161 2312N/G

mérong:
```
          t         t   N
         .52. 2523 6535 3212
         .52. 2523 6521 6535
         ..56 5323 123. 6535
         .35. 5352 6123 6532G
```

Kembang Gadhung, Ladrang,
sléndro pathet nem (16).

buka: 22 165. 5612 .1.6N/G
```
  t    t N      t    t N
 .1.6 .3.2     .5.6 .5.6
 .1.6 .3.2     .2.1 .6.5
 .3.2 .6.5     .3.2 .6.5
 .2.3 .1.6G    .2.3 .1.6G
```

Kembang Gayam/Karang Gayam, Gendhing,   ·unan,
kethuk 2 kerep, minggah kethuk 4,
pelog pathet nem (3)

buka: 332 3123 .661 6532 1123 2126N/G

mérong:
```
         t          t    N
      [..61 3216 3561 6532
       5654 2126 3561 6532
       5654 2123 ..32 1123 →
       .661 6532 1123 2126G]
```

umpak minggah:
```
    t                    t        N
 →. 6 6 1  6 5 3 2 11..1231 12161312G
```

204

minggah:
```
     t                      t
[2352126  6121653  6 5 3 2  6121653
 6 5 3 2  3 1 2 3  1 2 1 6  1 3 1 2N
 2352126  6121653  6 5 3 2  6121653
 6 5 3 2  3 1 2 3  1 2 1 6  1 3 1 2N
 . 5 . 3  . 5 . 2  .˙5 . 1  . 5 . 6
 . 5 . 2  . 5 . 1  . 5 . 6  . 5 . 3N
 . 5 . 6  . 5 . 6  . 5 . 3  . 5 . 2
 1 1 . .  1 2 3 1  1 2 1 6  1 3 1 2N/G]
```

Kembang Gempol, Gendhing, kethuk 2
    kerep, pélog pathet lima (1).

buka: odangiah: .33. 3532 3132 .126N/G

mérong:
```
        t         t      N
  [.33.  3532  3132  .126
   .33.  3576  .567  .356
   .33.  3576  .567  .356 →
   .33.  3532  3132  .126G]
```
umpak:
```
        t         t      N
  →.33.  3635  3635  3132G
```
minggah: Ladrang Bayem Tur

Kembang Kapas, Gendhing, kethuk 2 kerep,
    ndhawah kethuk 4, sléndro pathet manyura (5).

buka: 661 6532 1121 3216 3565 22.2N/G

lamba:
```
        t         t      N
   .1.1  .2.6  .3.6  .3.2
   .1.1  .2.6  .3.6  .5.3
   .3.6  .3.2  .3.6  .3.2
   1121  3216  3565  3232G
```
dados:
```
        t         t      N
  [1121  3216  .356  .352
   1121  3216  .356  .353
   5356  3532  5356  3532 →
   1121  3216  3565  3232G]
```

```
pangkat dhawah:
          t         t   N
      →.3.1 .2.6 .3.5 .3.2G

dhawah: t    t    t    t N
      [.3.1 .2.6 .3.6 .3.2
       .3.1 .2.6 .3.6 .5.3
       .5.6 .3.2 .3.6 .3.2
       .3.1 .2.6 .3.5 .3.2G]
```

Kembang Layar, Ladrang, pélog
    pathet barang (38).

```
t    t N       t    t N
.2.7 .2.6     .5.3 .5.6
.2.7 .2.6     .2.7 .3.2
.2.7 .2.6     .3.7 .3.2
.3.2 .5.3G    .3.2 .7.6G
```

Kembang Mara, Gendhing, kethuk 2 kerep,
    minggah kethuk 4, pélog pathet lima (1).

buka: [3.21 65.5]x2 .3.3 .321 .1.5 6121N/G

mérong: t
      [...1 .561 .561 .561
       .3.2 .165 15.6 1.21
       ...1 .561 .561 3216
       ..61 .216 .1.2 .321G

         t   t   N
       ...1 .561 .561 .561
       .3.2 .165 15.6 1.21
       ...1 .561 .561 3216
       .... 6656 .2.3 5676G

         t   t   N
       .... 6656 .2.3 5676
       .765 33.. 33.5 6767
       .765 33.. 3532 3123
       .53. 5356 7653 2123G
```
```

```
        t    ,    t    N
   .... 3356 7653 2123
   1235 .... 5654 2456
   .654 65̲4̲2141.. 6656
   .... 6654 24.2 45̲4̲21G

        t         t    N
   41.2 45̲4̲21.444 65̲4̲21
   41.. 6656 ..65 6356
   .765 4216 55.. 5535 →
   ..56 7654 2.44 2121G]
```

umpak:
```
        t         t    N
 →..56 7654 216. 5616

        t         t    N
   ..61 2212 33.1 3216
   .... 66.. 6535 3212
   .444 5654 2.44 2165
   .22. 3216 5654 2465G
```

minggah:
```
       t    t    t    t N
   [11.. 1232 3216 5616
   33.. 3356 5321 3216
   33.. 3356 5321 3216
   11.. 1232 3216 5616G

       t    t    t    t N
   .76. 676. 6535 3212
   676. 676. 6535 3212
   .444 5654 2.44 2165
   .22. 3216 5654 2465G]
```

Kembang Pépé, Ladrang,
    sléndro pathet manyura (2).

buka: 2 2.63 1132 .1.6N/G

```
   t    t N      t    t N  ⎫
 .5.3 .1.6     .1.6 .5.3   ⎪
 .5.3 .1.6     .5.2 .5.3   ⎬ x2
 .5.2 .5.3     .5.2 .5.3   ⎪
 .1.2 .1.6G    .1.2 .1.6G  ⎭
```

Kembang Peté, Gendhing,
    sléndro pathet manyura (5).

buka: .661 6533 5616 5321 6123 66.6G

```
        t        t    N
     .1.6 .5.3 .2.3 .2.1
     .3.2 .6.1 .2.3 .2.1
     .3.2 .1.6 .2.1 .5.3
     5616 5321 6123 2126G
```

```
        t        t    N
  [ .16. 1653 2353 2121
    3523 .161 2353 2121
    3523 .126 3561 6523
    5616 5321 6123 2126G ]
```

pangkat dhawah:
```
        t        t    N
     .16. 1653 2353 2121
     3523 .161 2353 2121
     3523 .1.6 .2.1 .5.3
     .5.6 .2.1 .5.3 .1.6G
```

dhawah:
```
     t    t    t    t N
  [ .1.6 .1.6 .2.3 .2.1
    .2.1 .2.1 .2.3 .2.1
    .3.2 .1.6 .2.1 .5.3
    .5.6 .2.1 .5.3 .1.6G ]
```

Kembang Tanjung, Ladrang,
    sléndro pathet sanga (3).

buka: .2.1 .2.1 2211 .6.5N/G

umpak:
```
      t    t N
   [.2.3 .2.1
    .2.6 .2.1
    .2.6 .2.1
    .2.1 .6.5G
```

```
    t    t N
   .2.3 .2.1
   .2.6 .2.1
   .2.6 .2.1
   .2.1 .5.6G
```

ngelik:
```
    t    t N
   .5.6 .2.1
   .2.6 .2.1
   .2.6 .2.1
   .2.1 .6.5G]
```

Kembang Tiba, Gendhing, kethuk 4 kerep, minggah
kethuk 8, sléndro pathet nem (2).

buka: 3.3 .2.1 .66. 6121 .3.2 .1.6N/G

mérong:
```
       t           t           t           t    N
[.3.2 .1.6 .3.2 .1.6 22.. 22.3 5653 2121
 3265 3235 .352 .356 ..32 .126 22.. 2321
 3265 3235 .352 .356 ..32 .126 22.. 2321 →
 .261 2353 .521 6123 6521 6656 3532 .126G
```

ngelik:
```
       t           t           t           t    N
 .3.2 .1.6 .3.2 .1.6 .... 66.. 3561 6535
 .653 2165 .352 .356 .... 66.. 3561 6535
 .653 2165 .352 .356 ..32 .126 22.. 5321
 .261 2353 .521 6123 6521 6656 3532 .126G]
```

umpak minggah:
```
       t           t           t           t    N
→.2.1 .2.3 .2.1 .2.1 .2.1 .2.6 .3.2 .1.6G
```

minggah:
```
  t    t    t    t    t    t    t    t N
[.3.2 .1.6 .3.2 .1.6 .3.2 .3.2 .5.3 .2.1
 .6.5 .3.5 .3.2 .5.6 .3.2 .1.6 .2.3 .2.1
 .6.5 .3.5 .3.2 .5.6 .3.2 .1.6 .2.3 .2.1
 .2.6 .2.3 .2.1 .2.3 .2.1 .2.6 .3.2 .1.6G]
```

Kembang Saré, Gendhing, kethuk 4
kerep, sléndro pathet sanga (40).

buka: 23 .121 .3.2 .165 32.2 11.1N/G

lamba:
```
       t           t           t           t    N
 .3.2 .6.5 .5.1 .5.6 .6.1 .5.6 .3.5 .3.2
 .2.3 .5.6 .3.5 .3.2 .35. 235. 2356 1216
 .2.2 .2.3 .5.3 .1.2 .2.2 .2.3 .5.3 .1.2
 .2.2 .2.3 5653 2121 3532 1635 2353 2121G
```

dados:
```
     t          t          t          t     N
[ 3532 1635 ..51 5616 ..61 5616 3565 3232
 ..25 2356 3565 3232 .35. 235. 2356 1216
 62.2 22.3 5653 2132 1612 ..23 5653 2132 →
 1612 ..23 5653 2121 3532 1635 2353 2121G ]
```

pangkat dhawah:

→ 1612 .3.2 .5.3 .2.1 .3.2 .6.5 .2.3 .2.1G

dhawah:

[.3.2 .6.5 .6.5 .1.6 .1.6 .5.6 .3.5 .3.2

[source incomplete]

Kenceng, Gendhing, kethuk 2 kerep, minggah
kethuk 4, sléndro pathet sanga (38).

buka: 3 .5.2 .6.6 .2.3 .5.6 .1.6N/G

mérong:
```
           t         t     N
    [..61 6535 ..56 1656
     ..61 6535 ..56 1656
     .... 1653 22.3 5.65
     1656 5312 1312 .165G

           t         t     N
     .65. 5612 1312 .165
     .65. 5612 1312 .165
     .... 55.6 11.. 5616 →
     ..23 55.. 55.6 1656G]
```

umpak:
```
           t         t     N
     →.5.6 .3.5 .6.5 .1.6G
```

minggah:
```
         t    t    t    t N
   [.5.6 .3.5 .6.5 .1.6
    .5.6 .3.5 .6.5 .1.6
    .1.6 .5.3 .2.3 .6.5
    .1.6 .3.2 .3.2 .6.5G

         t    t    t    t N
    .6.5 .3.2 .3.2 .6.5
    .6.5 .3.2 .3.2 .6.5
    .6.5 .6.5 .1.2 .1.6
    .5.6 .3.5 .6.5 .1.6G]
```

Kenceng, Ladrang, sléndro
pathet manyura (15).

```
   t    t N
1516 1523
1516 1523
6356 2165
3632 3123G
```

Kencèng Barong, Gendhing, kethuk 2 kerep,
    minggah kethuk 4, sléndro pathet sanga (2).

buka: 2 .2.6 .2.1 .3.2 .165 32.3 5635N/G

mérong:
```
          t          t     N
   [.612 .1.6  .532  .365
    .612 .1.6  .532  .312
    .365 ..56  1656  5321
    3532 .165  32.3  5635G

          t          t     N
   61261261216 .532  .365
   61261261216 .3.2  .356
    .... 2321  3212  .165
    .... 5561  3212  .165G

          t          t     N
    .... 5561  3212  .165
    .... 5561  3216  5312
    .365 ..56  1656  5321 →
    3532 .165  32.3  5635G]
```

umpak minggah:
```
            t       t    N
   → .3.2  .6.5  .3.2  .3.5G
```

minggah:
```
           t     t     t     t N
   [ .1.2  .1.6  .3.2  .6.5
     .1.2  .1.6  .3.2  .3.2
     .3.5  .3.5  .1.6  .2.1
     .3.2  .6.5  .3.2  .3.5G ]
```

Kidung-kidung, Gendhing (Santiswaran),
   pélog pathet barang (39).

```
.  6 6 6756.   . 7 2    23276
.    . 2 7 2 3    4 2 7 3 2 7 6
. 2 7 2 3 423 2   3 2 2 7 2 327
2 6 7 2 342 3 2   3 2 7 3 2 7 6G
.    . 6 6 6756.   . 7 2    23276
.    . 2 7 2 3    4 2 7 3 2 7 6
.    . 6 7 2 3    . 6 7 2 2 327
.    . 6 7 2 3    . 732   23276G
```

Kinanthi, Gendhing, minggah kethuk 4,
   sléndro pathet manyura (8).

buka celuk: 6N/G

```
   t     t     t     t N
[ .1.6  .1.6  .2.1  .3.2
  .3.1  .2.6  .2.1  .3.2
  .3.1  .2.6  .3.2  .3.1
  .2.1  .2.3  .1.2  .1.6G ]
```

212

Kinanthi, Ketawang, pélog
    pathet nem (1).

buka: 6123 .2.1 2321 5616N/G

umpak: t   t N   t   t N
         [[2123 2126 2123 2126G] x2

ngelik: t   t N   t   t N
         11.. 6612 1123 2126G
         .123 6321 2132 5321G
         33.. 6532 5654 2126G]

Kinanthi Dura Dasih (Bedhayan),
    Ketawang, sléndro pathet manyura (8).

buka celuk: 5N/G

    t   t N   t   t N
    33.. 3353 .635 6121G
    .... 1265 3312 5321G

    t   t N   t   t N
    [55.. 1653 2123 2126G
    2123 2126 2123 2126G
    22.. 2232 .3.2 .126G
    .... 6165 3312 5321G
    55.. 1653 .2.1 .2.6G
    2123 2126 2123 2126G
    22.. 2232 .3.2 .126G suwuk
    .... 6165 335. 1653G
    ..61 2353 5565 3565
    33.. 3353 6165 1653G
    55.. 5565 .6.5 .616G
    .... 6632 312. 5321G]

213

Kinanthi Ludira, Gendhing, minggah
  kethuk 4, pélog pathet barang (1).

(minggah to Gendhing Ludira Madura)

```
    t    t    t    t N
  .7.6 .7.6 .2.7 .3.2
  .3.7 .5.6 .2.7 .3.2
  .3.7 .5.6 .3.5 .2.7
  .2.7 .2.3 .7.2 .7.6G
```

Kinjeng Trung, Gendhing,
  pélog pathet barang (1).

buka: 6. 6.75 6.76 .22. 22.3 5567 6535N/G

```
         N
  [6365 7576
   5365 7576
   5365 7576
   5323 5635G]
```

ciblon: N
```
  [7 6532365  .575676
   7 6532365  .575676
   7 6532365  .575676
   . 22.22 35 5676535G]
```

Kiswa, Gendhing (Santiswaran),
pélog pathet nem (39).

```
  .  . 6 1 2 3      . 3 2 .15 .32
1 . 6 1 2 3 5    6 123 .21 216
  .  . 6 1 2 3      . 3 2 .15 .32
1 . 6 1 2 3 5    6 1 2 .31 216
  .  . 6 3 5 6      . 1 2 .31 216
. 3 5   5 .235.    . 565 .44 565
  .  . 5 6 1 2    3 6 5   5 653
. 6 1 2312165    6 123 .21 216
. 125   2 .31    . 125   2 .31
. 3 2 .31 216    6 545 621 216G
```

Klenthung, Gendhing, kethuk 4 awis, minggah
    kethuk 8, pélog pathet lima (1).

buka: [53.1235]x2 44. 2245 .456 .2.1 6123 2121N/G

mérong:
```
              t                      t
     [..32 .161 245. 5421 ..32 .161 245. 5421
     .23. 123. 123. 1216 ..1. 6.5. 4.24 5645N
     .456 5452 ..24 .245 .456 5452 ..24 .245
     ..24 5.24 5.24 2121 77.. 77.. 7765 4565N
     .456 5452 ..24 .245 .456 5452 ..24 .245
     44.. 44.. 44.. 2245 .456 .2.1 6123 2121N
     ..32 .161 245. 5421⁺..32 .161 245. 5421
     44.. 44.. 44.. 2245 .456 .2.1 6123 2121N/G]
```

umpak:
```
                              t
         t                 →2425 2456 6676 5421
     .245 2421 .245 2421 .22. 216545454545454561N/G
```

minggah:
```
        t            t            t            t
     [2 1 2 .   2 1 6 54  54545454  545 6 1
      2 1 2 .   2 1 6 54  54545454  545 6 1N
      2 1 2 .   2 1 6 54  54545454  545 6 1
      2 3 1 2   . 1 6 5   . 4 . 2   . 4 . 5N
      . 4 . 2   . 4 . 5   . 4 . 2   . 4 . 5
      2 4 2 5   2 4 5 6   6 6 7 6   5 4 2 1N
      . 2 4 5   2 4 2 1   . 2 4 5   2 4 2 1
      2 2 . .   2 1 6 54  54545454  545 6 1N/G]
```

Klenthung, Ladrang, sléndro
   pathet sanga (1).

(minggah to Gendhing Klenthung)

```
 t    t N
323. 3635
323. 3635
323. 3635
6616 5323G

 t    t N
6521 6123
6521 6123
56.. 6656
3565 3212G

 t    t N
.33. 3635
323. 3635
323. 3565
22.3 5635G

 t    t N
.55. 5565
.2.3 5635
.356 3565
22.3 5616G
```

Klentung/Klenthung, Gendhing, kethuk
   4 arang, slendro pathet sanga (1).

buka: 5 .5.5 3561 .1.2 .6.5 35.2 3565N/G

mérong:

```
           t                     t
[.55. 5565 .2.3 5635 .356 3565 22.3 5616
.... 6656 11.. 5616 ..6. 1653 22.6 1232N
.... 2232 165. 5612 .... 2232 165. 5612
612. 612. 6123 6532 5653 2121 3265 3235N
.61. 1653 22.3 5635 .61. 1653 22.3 5635
11.. 11.2 35.6 5312 5653 2121 3265 3235N
11.. 3216 3565 2232 5325 2356 3565 2232
55.. 55.. 5565 3561 ..32 .165 35.2 3565N/G]
```

minggah: Ladrang Klenthung

Klèwèr, Gendhing, kethuk 2 kerep, dhawah
kethuk 4, sléndro pathet manyura (5).

buka: 661 6533 212. 2165 33.5 11.1N/G

lamba:
```
         t           t    N
    .3.2  .6.5  .3.5  .6.1
    .5.3  .5.6  .2.1  .5.3
    .1.2  .1.6  .5.1  .5.3
    212.  2165  33.5  6121G
```

dados:
```
         t           t    N
    [3532  .165  33.5  6121
    3532  .516  3561  6523
    2232  .356  3561  6523
    212.  2165  33.5  6121G

         t           t    N
    3532  .165  33.5  6121
    ....  1161  2321  6535
    ....  5535  6616  5323
    535.  5356  1656  5323G

         t           t    N
    535.  5356  1656  5323
    5616  ..65  3561  6523
    2232  .356  3561  6523
    212.  2165  33.5  6121G]
```

pangkat dhawah:
```
         t           t    N
    3532  .165  33.5  6121
    3523  .516  3561  6523
    .3.2  .1.6  .2.1  .5.3
    .2.1  .2.3  .5.3  .2.1G
```

dhawah:
```
      t    t    t    t N
    [.3.2  .5.3  .5.3  .2.1
    .5.3  .1.6  .2.1  .5.3
    .1.2  .1.6  .2.1  .5.3
    .2.1  .2.3  .5.3  .2.1G

      t    t    t    t N
    .3.2  .5.3  .5.3  .2.1
    .2.1  .2.1  .2.1  .6.5
    .6.5  .6.5  .1.6  .5.3
    .5.3  .5.6  .1.6  .5.3G

      t    t    t    t N
    .5.3  .5.6  .1.6  .5.3
    .1.6  .1.6  .2.1  .5.3
    .1.2  .1.6  .2.1  .5.3
    .2.1  .2.3  .5.3  .2.1G]
```

Klumpuk, Gendhing (cara balèn), pélog pathet barang (36).

```
      N
   ...6
   2.76
   2.76
   2.76G
```

Klumpuk, Lancaran, sléndro (13).

```
      N
   ...5
   2.65
   2.65
   2.65G
```

Kocak, Gendhing, kethuk 4 kerep, minggah
   kethuk 16, sléndro pathet nem (16).

buka: 2 .356 .6.3 6532 ..23 6532N/G

mérong:
```
   t          t          t          t    N
[..23 6532 ..25 2356 ..61 2353 5653 2165
 .555 2235 ..56 1232 .352 .352 5653 2165
 .555 2235 ..56 1232 .352 .352 5653 2165 →
 2356 .532 ..25 2356 ..63 6532 ..23 6532G]
```

umpak:
```
    t          t          t          t    N
→.2.3 .5.6 .5.3 .5.6 .1.6 .3.2 .6.5 .1.6G
```

minggah:
```
  t    t    t    t    t    t    t    t N
[.1.6 .3.2 .1.6 .3.2 .1.6 .3.2 .5.3 .6.5
 .6.5 .3.2 .1.6 .3.2 .1.6 .3.2 .5.3 .6.5
 .6.5 .3.2 .1.6 .3.2 .5.6 .3.5 .6.3 .6.5
 .2.3 .5.6 .5.3 .5.6 .1.6 .3.2 .6.5 .1.6G]
```

Kodhokan, Gendhing, kethuk 4 kerep,
   pélog pathet lima (1).

buka: odangiah; ..56 7767 .656 7767 .653 2365N/G

mérong:
```
          t        t        t        t    N
      ..56 7767 .656 7767 .656 7767 .653 2365
      ..56 2165 15.6 1.21 .... 1121 3212 .165
      ..56 2165 15.6 1.21 .... 1121 3212 .165 ⇥
      ..56 7767 .656 7767 .656 7767 .653 2365G
```

umpak minggah:
```
          t        t        t        t    N
   ⇥..56 7767 .656 7767 .656 7767 .6.5 .3.2G
```

minggah: Ladrang Kodhokan

Kodhokan, Ladrang, pélog
   pathet lima (1).

(minggah to Gendhing Kodhokan)
```
      t    t N
   [.6.3 .5.2
    .6.3 .5.2
    .6.3 .5.2
    .6.5 .3.2G

      t    t N
    ..32 5612
    .132 5612
    .132 5612
    .6.5 .3.2G

      t    t N
    ..3. .523
    523. 3523
    523. 3523
    .6.5 .3.2G

      t    t N
    .7.7 .6.5
    .4.2 .4.1
    .4.2 .4.1
    .4.6 .4.5G

      t    t N
    ..56 7767
    .656 7767
    .656 7767
    .6.5 .3.2G]
```

sesegan
```
    t    t N
 [.4.6 .4.5
  .4.2 .4.1
  .4.2 .4.1
  .4.6 .4.5G]
```

Kodhok Ngorèk, Ketawang (15).

buka kendhang: 5N/G
```
          N         N/S
 [ 6 .  6 5  6 .  6 5
  .352 3565 6325 2356 (saron)

          N         N/G
   6 .  6 5  6 .  6 5
  .563 5616 1561 6535 ] (saron)
```

Kombang Mara, Gendhing, kethuk 2 kerep,
    minggah kethuk 4, pélog pathet lima (3).

buka: 53.2 1652 .5.5 .5.5 .5.6 .165N/G

mérong:
```
         t         t    N
 [...5 2165 2156 2165
  15.6 1.21 3212 .165
  15.6 1.21 3216 .165
  ..56 1654 2456 2165G

         t         t    N
  ...5 2165 2156 2165
  15.6 1.21 3212 .165
  15.6 1.21 3212 .165
  33.. 3353 6532 3123G

         t         t    N
  ..3. 3356 7653 2123
  1235 ..5. 5654 .521
  .561 ..1. 11.. 1156
  11.2 3216 5612 3212G
```

```
            t        t    N
      ..2.  22.4  5654  2165
      15.6  1.21  3212  .165
      15.6  1.21  3212  .165
      66..  6656  .1.6  5323G]
```

umpak:
```
            t        t    N
      ...3  .123  .123  .123
      .6.5  .421  ..12  4565
      6542  1245  6542  1654
      .44.  4456  1654  2121G
```

minggah:
```
        t     t     t    t N
      [22..  2216  1216  5323
      .333  6532  6616  5323
      .333  6532  6616  5424
      .44.  4456  1654  2121G
```

```
        t     t     t    t N
      66..  6612  3216  5616
      33..  6532  3216  5616
      33..  6532  3216  5616
      11..  11.2  3323  2121G
```

```
        t     t     t    t N
      .312  35.4  2.32  1656
      33..  6521  ..21  4565
      6542  1245  6542  1654
      .44.  4456  1654  2121G]
```

Koncang/Kuncang, Ladrang,
    sléndro pathet sanga (20).

buka: 3.3 6532 3521 5555N/G

```
        t        t    N
      ...3  ...2  ...6  ...5
      ...3  ...2  ...1  ...6
      .5.3  .5.2  .5.3  .5.6
      .3.3  6532  3521  6535G
```

```
        t        t    N
      [3353  6532  3521  6535
      3353  6532  3521  6356
      1653  22..  2523  5616
      3353  6532  3521  6535G
```

```
   t        t    N
3353 6532 3521 6535
3353 6532 3521 6356
1653 22.. 2523 5616
3353 6532 35.2 3565G

   t        t    N
6561 2561 2561 6535
6561 2561 2561 6535
61.. 1121 3532 6356
3353 6532 35.2 3565G

   t        t    N
6561 2561 2561 6535
6561 2561 2561 6535
61.. 1121 3532 6356
3353 6532 3521 6535G]
```

Kondha, Ladrang, sléndro
    pathet nem (38).

buka: 2 .356 .12 1216 6365 .3.2N/G

```
   t    t N
.3.5 .3.2
.6.1 .3.2
.3.2 .3.2
.6.5 .3.2G
```

ngelik:
```
   t    t N
.3.5 .3.2
.3.2 .1.6
.3.2 .1.6
.3.5 .3.2G

   t    t N
.3.5 .3.2
.5.6 .3.5
.6.5 .6.5
.1.6 .3.2

   t    t N
.3.5 .3.2
.5.3 .1.6
.3.2 .1.6
.3.5 .3.2G
```

Kopyah Ilang, Ladrang, pélog
    pathet nem (3).
buka: 5 5235 2356 5312N/G

```
  t    t N
3132 3132
3132 3132
.355 2355
2356 5312G

  t    t N
7576 7576
7576 7576
.356 2353
2356 5312G
```

Kuwung-kuwung, Gendhing, kethuk 2 kerep,
    minggah kethuk 4, pélog pathet barang (3).
buka: 3567 .7.3 .232 .726 .723N/G
mérong:
```
     t       t     N
[...3 6532 .756 .523
 ...3 6532 .756 .523
 ...3 6532 .756 .523
 56.. 6656 3567 6535G

     t       t     N
.635 66.. 6567 6535
.635 66.5 33.5 6.27
..7. 3276 3565 3272
.327 .2.7 66.5 3272G

     t       t     N
.327 .2.7 .2.3 .532
.327 .2.7 .2.3 .5.3 →
.576 ..6. 3565 3237
 33.. 6532 .756 .523G]
```
umpak:
```
     t       t     N
.5.6 .5.6 .3.5 .2.7
.2.7 .2.3 .7.6 .2.7G
```
minggah:
```
 t    t    t    t N
[.2.7 .2.3 .7.6 .2.7
 .2.7 .2.3 .7.6 .5.3
 .5.3 .5.6 .3.5 .2.7
 .2.7 .2.3 .7.6 .2.7G]
```

Kuwung-kuwung, Ladrang,
  pélog pathet barang (1).

```
t     t N
.... 7567
.756 .523
..5. 3.5.
3.52 .5.3G
```

ngelik:
```
t     t N
..35 6756
3567 6532
..67 2353
.3.2 .756G
```

```
t     t N
.567 .3.2
..67 .3.2
..67 2353
6532 .756G
```

Lagu, Gendhing, kethuk 4 kerep, minggah
  kethuk 8, sléndro pathet manyura (4).

buka: 3 .3.2 3123 .1.1 .2.3 .3.2 .126N/G
mérong:
```
t         t         t         t    N
.3.3 .3.3 .6.5 3212 .126 .... 3561 6532
[.126 .... 3561 6523 ..35 6656 3561 6532
..23 6532 5323 5653 66.. 66.. 3561 6532
55.. 1653 ..32 1123 11.. 1123 6532 .126G
```

```
t         t         t         t    N
33.. 33.5 6165 3212 .126 .... 3561 6532
.126 55.. 55.6 1653 ..32 5321 2321 6563
.516 ..35 66.1 2353 ..32 5321 2321 6532
..23 6532 5323 5653 11.. 1123 6532 .126G
```

```
t         t         t         t    N
3532 3532 3532 1653 ..35 1653 11.. 3216
3532 3532 3532 1653 ..35 1653 11.. 3216
3532 3532 3532 1653 ..35 1653 11.. 3216→
22.. 2321 .111 2321 33.. 6532 1232 .126G
```

```
     t        t        t        t    N
.... 66.. 3561 6532 .126 .... 3561 6532]
```
umpak minggah:
```
      t        t        t        t    N
→.2.3 .2.1 .2.3 .2.1 .2.3 .2.1 .2.1 .5.3G
```
minggah:
```
   t    t    t    t    t    t    t    t N
[.5.3 .2.1 .2.3 .2.1 .2.3 .2.1 .2.1 .5.3
 .5.3 .2.1 .2.3 .2.1 .2.3 .2.1 .2.1 .5 3
 .5.6 .2.1 .5.3 .2.1 .5.3 .2.1 .2.1 .5.3
 .2.1 .6.5 .2.1 .2.3 .6.5 .2.1 .2.1 .5.3G]
```

Lagu, Ladrang, pélog
     pathet nem (1).

buka: ..3. 212. 2321 3216 .5.3N/G

```
   t    t N
6563 6563
6563 .2.1
.2.3 .2.1
3216 .5.3G
```

Lagu Dhempel, Gendhing [Ketawang], kethuk
     2 kerep, sléndro pathet sanga (16).

buka: 1 .1.6 5621 ..16 5612 .612 1121N/G

mérong:

```
[..16 5612 .612 1121
 ..16 5612 .612 1121G

    t         t    N
 ..16 5612 .612 1121
 ..16 5612 ..23 5.65G

    t         t    N
 .653 22.. 66.1 6535
 .653 22.. 22.3 5.65G

    t         t    N
 .653 22.. 66.1 6535
 2356 1656 5323 2121G]
```

dhawah: Ladrang Lagu Dhempel

Lagu Dhempel, Ladrang, sléndro
    pathet sanga (16).

(dhawah to Gendhing Lagu Dhempel)
```
     t    t N
[ .323 5635
  .323 5635
  22.. 3216
  2321 6535G

     t    t N
  22.3 5.65
  1656 5321
  .656 12.6
  12.3 5.65

     t    t N
  .323 5635
  .323 5635
  2356 1656
  5323 2121G

     t    t N
  .12. 2321
  .12. 2321
  ..2. 1.2.
  6.21 6535G ]
```

Laler Mengeng, Gendhing; kenong 1, 2, & 3, kethuk
    2 awis; gong, kethuk 2 kerep; minggah kethuk
    8, sléndro pathet sanga (16).

buka: 555 3561 .612 .165 22.3 5.65N/G

mérong: t   t   N
```
....: 5535 22.3 5616 .... 6656 33.1 2353
.... 3323 55.. 1121 .... 1121 3212 .165
.65. 5612 1312 .165 .... 55.. 5565 3561 →
     t    t    N
.3.2 .165 35.2 3565G
```

umpak: t   t   N
```
→.3.2 .6.5 .3.2 .6.5G
```

minggah:
```
 t   t   t   t   t   t   t   t N
.6.5 .6.5 .3.2 .5.6 .5.6 .3.2 .3.1 .2.3
.5.3 .6.5 .6.5 .2.1 .2.1 .3.2 .3.2 .6.5
.6.5 .3.2 .3.2 .6.5 .6.5 .6.5 .2.1 .6.1
.6.5 .3.2 .3.2 .6.5 .6.5 .6.5 .2.1 .6.1
               .3.2 .6.5 .3.2 .3.5G
```

Lambang Sari, Gendhing, kethuk 4 kerep,
   minggah kethuk 8, sléndro pathet manyura (2).

buka: 661 6523 6126 3132N/G

mérong:
```
    t          t          t          t      N
[..23 2165 33.5 6121 ..12 .321 33.5 6532
.321 .3.2 ..23 .2.1 ..12 .321 33.. 6532
.321 .3.2 ..23 .2.1 ..12 .321 33.. 6532 →
6621 6523 .561 6523 .2.1 .2.6 .2.1 .3.2G]
```

umpak minggah:
```
   t       t        t        t      N
→.6.1 .5.3 .6.1 .5.3 .2.1 .2.1 .2.6 .3.2
```

minggah:
```
 t   t   t   t   t   t   t   t N
[.3.2 .3.2 .3.2 .6.1 .2.1 .2.1 .5.6 .3.2
.3.2 .3.2 .3.2 .6.1 .2.1 .2.1 .5.6 .3.2
.3.2 .3.2 .3.2 .6.1 .2.1 .2.1 .5.6 .3.2
.6.1 .5.3 .2.1 .5.3 .2.1 .2.1 .5.6 .3.2G]
```

Lana, Gendhing, kethuk 2 kerep, minggah
   kethuk 4, sléndro pathet nem (2).

buka: 2 2165 .35. 235. 5612 .1.6N/G

mérong:
```
    t       t      N
[.365 .365 .365 .3.2
.126 .365 .365 .3.2
.126 ..6. 6616 5323
.333 5653 2353 2165G
```

```
         t         t    N
    16532  .523  ..35  6535
    16532  .523  ..35  6535
    16532  .523  ..35  6535→
     235.  235.  2353  2126G]
```

umpak minggah:
```
          t         t    N
    →.6.5  .6.5  .2.3  .1.6G
```

minggah:
```
        t     t     t    t N
    [.3.5  .3.5  .3.5  .3.2
     .1.6  .3.5  .3.5  .3.2
     .1.6  .5.6  .2.1  .5.3
     :5.6  .5.3  .2.3  .6.5G

        t     t     t    t N
     .3.2  .5.3  .5.6  .3.5
     .3.2  .5.3  .5.6  .3.5
     .3.2  .5.3  .5.6  .3.5
     .6.5  .6.5  .2.3  .1.6G]
```

Lana, Gendhing, kethuk 4 kerep, minggah
  kethuk 8, sléndro pathet nem (4).

buka: 2 .356 .532 .35. 235. 2356 1216N/G

mérong:
```
         t          t          t          t    N
    [.365  .365  .365  3212  .126  .365  .365  3212
     .126  ....  3561  6523  6532  ..23  5653  2165
     .555  2235  2353  2126  ..61  2353  5653  2165 →
     2356  5323  ..35  6532  .35.  235.  2356  1216G]
```

umpak minggah:
```
                                         N
    .1.6 .5.3 .5.6 .3.5 .6.5 .3.2 .5.3 .1.6G
```

minggah:
```
       t     t     t     t     t     t     t     t N
    [.3.5  .3.5  .3.5  .3.2  .1.6  .3.5  .3.5  .3.2
     .1.6  .5.6  .2.1  .5.3  .5.2  .3.2  .5.3  .6.5
     .6.5  .6.5  .2.3  .1.6  .1.6  .2.3  .5.3  .6.5
     .1.6  .5.3  .5.6  .3.5  .6.5  .3.2  .5.3  .1.6G]
```

Langen Branta, Ladrang,
    pélog pathet nem (1).

buka: 5 .61. 2165 .623 111.N/G

```
  t   t N
.1.1 6123
5653 2121
.55. 5612
3353 2121G

  t   t N
.1.1 6123
5653 2121
.55. 5612
3532 1635G

  t   t N
656. 6521
3532 1635
.442 4521
3532 1635G

  t   t N
656. 6521
3532 1635
.442 4521
3353 2121G
```

Langen Gita, Ketawang, sléndro
    pathet sanga (2).

buka: 2.1 .2.1 2211 .6.5N/G

```
  t    t N  t    t N
[[.2.1 .2.6 .3.2 .6.5G]
```

ngelik:
```
  t    t N  t    t N
..5. 6165 1216 5312G
66.. 6165 1216 5312G
11.. 3532 .621 6535G]
```

Langen Gita Sri Naréndra/Langen
   Gita Anglir Mendhung, Ketawang,
   pélog pathet barang (29).

buka: .22. 6723 7732 .756N/G

umpak: t   t N   t   t N
       [.2.3 .2.7 .2.3 .2.6G
        .2.3 .2.7 .2.3 .6.7G

ngelik: t   t N   t   t N
        77.. 7767 2327 6523G
        ..35 6756 3567 6523G
        22.. 6723 .732 .756G]

Lara Asmara, Gendhing, kethuk 2 awis, minggah
   kethuk 4, pélog pathet barang (1).

buka: 667 6535 .35. 5676 32.6 7232N/G

mérong: t   t   N
       [.32. 3276 .... 66.7 22.. 22.3 4434 3232
        .32. 3276 .... 66.7 22.. 22.3 4434 3232
        .32. 3276 .... 66.7 22.3 4327 6535 6756→
        .... 66.. 6567 6535 .35. 5676 32.6 7232G]

umpak:
       →.5.6 .5.6 .567 6532 .77. 7576 5356 5352G

minggah:
          t   t   t   t N
       [.352 .356 5756 5352
        .352 .356 5756 5352
        33.. 33.5 6767 6532
        77.. 7576 5356 5352G]

Lara Manglong, Gendhing (Santiswaran),
sléndro pathet sanga (39).

```
.   . 2 2 2 2    . 1 1 2 2 3 3
.   . 1 3 5 5    . 232 .13 .52
.   . 2 2 2 2    . 1 1 2 2 3 3
.   . 1 3 5 5    1 3 2 1 6 165
.   . 5 1 2 2    . 1 1 2 2 3 3 3
3 5 5   5 6 5    . 1 1 2 2 3 3 2
2 2 2 2 2 2 2    5 6 5 .32 321G
```

Lara Nangis, Gendhing, kethuk 2
kerep, sléndro pathet nem (2).

buka: 2 .2.1 .3.2 .2.3 .6.5 .3.5 .3.2N/G

mérong:
```
            t          t    N
[ ....   2235 2356 .532
  66..   66.1 2321 6523
  .561   22.. 2321 6132
  5653   2165 3365 2232G

            t          t    N
  ....   2235 2356 .532
  66..   66.. 3561 6523
  .561   .... 11.2 1616
  3561   6535 2356 3532

            t          t    N
  66..   6535 2356 3532
  .126   .... 3561 6523
  .561   .... 11.2 1616
  3561   6535 2356 3532G

            t          t    N
  66..   6535 2356 3532
  .126   ..61 2321 6523
  .561   22.. 2321 6123 →
  5653   2165 2565 2232G ]
```

umpak minggah:
```
            t          t    N
→.5.3   .6.5 .3.5 .3.2G
```

minggah: Ladrang Weling-weling

Lara-lara, Gendhing, kethuk 2 kerep,
sléndro pathet sanga (2).

buka: 5 .5.6 .1.6 .61. 1621 5323 2121N/G

mérong:
```
            t       t   N
[ [ 3265  ..23 5653 2121
    3265 1121 3212 .165
    .621 .... 3212 .126
    .61. 1621 5323 2121G ]
```

ngelik:
```
            t       t   N
    .... 1121 3212 .165
    .621 .... 3212 .165
    .621 .... 3212 .126
    .61. 1621 5323 2121G ]
```

Laranjala/Rara Jala, Gendhing, kethuk 2 awis,
minggah kethuk 4, pélog pathet lima (37).

buka: 5.56 5424 .24. 4565 21.5 6121N/G

mérong:
```
        t                   t       N
[.21. 2165 ..5. 55.6 11.. 11.2 3323 2121
 .21. 2165 ..5. 55.6 11.. 11.2 3323 2121
 .21. 2165 ..5. 55.6 11.2 3216 5424 5645→
 ..5. 55.. 5456 5424 .24. 4565 21.5 6121G]
```

umpak minggah:

→.4.5 .4.5 .456 5421 66.. 6465 4265 4241G

minggah:
```
        t    t    t    t N
    [.241 .245 4645 4241
     .241 .245 4645 4241
     22.. 22.4 5676 5421
     66.. 6465 4245 4241G]
```

232

Laras Ati, Gendhing, kethuk 2 kerep, minggah
kethuk 4, sléndro pathet nem (1).

buka: 2 .356 .6.1 2165 3365 .3.2N/G

mérong:
      t   t   N
  [..23 6532 ..25 2356
  ..61 2353 5653 2165
  2356 5323 ..56 5323→
  .... 3353 6535 2232G

ngelik:
      t   t   N
  66.. 6656 3561 6532
  11.. 3216 3561 6532
  11.. 3216 3561 6532
  .35. 235. 2353 2126G

      t   t   N
  33.. 6535 2353 2126
  22.. 22.3 5653 2165
  2356 5323 ..56 5323
  .... 3353 6535 2232G]

umpak:
      t   t   N
  →.5.3 .5.3 .6.5 .3.2G

minggah:
     t   t   t   t N
  [.3.2 .3.2 .5.3 .5.6
  .5.6 .5.3 .5.3 .6.5
  .1.6 .5.3 .5.6 .5.3
  .5.3 .5.3 .6.5 .3.2G

     t   t   t   t N
  .5.6 .5.6 .2.1 .3.2
  .3.1 .2.1 .6.5 .3.2
  .3.1 .2.1 .6.5 .3.2
  .3.5 .6.5 .2.3 .1.6G

     t   t   t   t N
  .5.3 .6.5 .2.3 .1.6
  .3.2 .3.2 .5.3 .6.5
  .1.6 .5.3 .5.6 .5.3
  .5.3 .5.3 .6.5 .3.2G]

Laras Maya, Ketawang, pélog
  pathet barang (3).

buka: .667 2327 5563 2.76N/G

umpak: t   t N t   t N
   [[.2.3 .2.7 5653 2756G]

ngelik: t   t N t   t N
     ..6. 6765 53.5 6356G
     55.. 7653 .2.7 .2.6G
     .2.3 .2.7 5653 2756G]

Laras Tawan, Ladrang, pélog
  pathet nem (1).

buka: 23. 363 522. 3565N/G

   t   t N
   .23. 3635
   .23. 3635
   .23. 3635
   22.3 5635G

   t   t N
   .23. 3635
   .23. 3635
   .23. 3635
   22.3 5676G

   t   t N
   .563 5676
   123. 3216
   123. 3216
   55.2 3565

   t   t N
   22.. 2232
   ..23 5535
   ..65 2126
   35.2 3565G

Laré Angon, Gendhing, kethuk 2 kerep, dhawah
   kethuk 4, sléndro pathet manyura (5).

buka: 6616 533. 212. 2165 5156 33.3N/G

lamba:
```
         t        t    N
    .5.6  .2.1  .1.2  .5.3
    .5.6  .2.1  .1.2  .5.3
    .5.6  .6.5  .6.1  .5.3
    1121  3265  .156  5323G
```

dados:
```
         t        t    N
   [5616  5321  ..12  3523
    5616  5321  ..12  3523
    5616  ..65  3561  6523→
    1121  3265  .156  5323G]
```

pangkat dhawah:
```
         t        t    N
   →.2.1  .6.5  .1.6  .5.3G
```

dhawah:
```
      t     t     t     t N
  [.1.6  .2.1  .2.1  .5.3
   .1.6  .2.1  .2.1  .5.3
   .1.6  .1.6  .2.1  .5.3
   .2.1  .6.5  .1.6  .5.3G]
```


Layar Banten, Gendhing, kethuk 4 kerep, minggah
   kethuk 8, pélog pathet barang (1).

buka: 576 .532 .11. 1612 .327 6535N/G

mérong:
```
    t          t            t           t     N
 [.65.  5672  .3.2  .765  22..  2327  .2.3  .532
  .327  .6.5  ..56  7567  ....  7767  22.7  6535
  ....  .55.  672.  7653  7656  .532  72.6  7232 →
  35..  55..  5576  .532  .11.  1612  .327  6535G]
```

umpak:
```
    t          t            t           t     N
 → 3276  5672  3276  5672  35..  7632  1132  1635G
```

minggah:
```
    t     t     t     t     t     t     t     t N
 [7675  7672  3532  7672  3532  7672  3532  7675
  .3.2  .3.5  .7.6  .3.2  .3.2  .3.5  .7.6  .3.2
  .3.2  .3.5  .7.6  .3.2  .3.2  .3.5  .7.6  .3.2
  3276  5672  3276  5672  35..  7632  3532  7675G]
```

Layar Tukung, Gendhing, kethuk 2
    kerep, pélog pathet barang (1).

buka: 576 .532 .77. 567. 5672 .765N/G

mérong: t   t   N
     [.67. 567. 5672 .765
      22.. 2235 7656 .532
      .... 2235 7656 .532
      .77. 567. 5672 .765G

ngelik: t   t   N
      77.. 7767 22.7 6535
      7656 .532 72.6 7232
      35.. 55.. 5576 .532
      .77. 5672 3532 .765G]

umpak: t   t   N
      .57. 567. 5672 .765
      22.. 2235 7656 .532
      .... 2235 7656 .532
      767. 5672 3532 .765G

minggah: Ladrang Layar Tukung

Layar Tukung, Ladrang, pélog
    pathet barang (1).

(minggah to Gendhing Layar Tukung)

     t   t   N
  7675 7672 3532 .765
  .3.2 .3.5 .7.6 .3.2
  .3.2 .3.5 .7.6 .3.2
  767. 5672 3532 7675G

Layu-layu, Gendhing, kethuk 2 kerep,
   minggah kethuk 4, pélog pathet nem (1).

buka: 2 2165 .65. 5612 1312 .165N/G

mérong: t   t   N
      [.65. 5612 1312 .165
       33.. 3353 6535 3212→
       .... 2212 3312 .165
       .65. 5612 1312 .165G

         t   t   N
       .65. 5612 1312 .165
       22.. 22.3 56.1 .216
       .... 6656 11.6 .532
       .... 2356 3565 3212G

         t   t   N
       .... 2356 3565 3212
       55.. 55.. 5356 .535
       1216 5421 3212 .165
       .65. 5612 1312 .165G]

ompak inggah:
         t   t   N
    → .3.2 .5.3 .1.2 .6.5
      .6.5 .3.2 .3.2 .6.5G

inggah: t   t   t   t N
      [.6.5 .3.2 .3.2 .6.5
      .2.3 .5.3 .6.5 .3.2
      .3.2 .5.3 .1.2 .1.6
      .6.5 .3.2 .3.2 .6.5G]

Lebda Sari, Ketawang,
    sléndro pathet manyura (1).

     t   t N
 [11.. 3532
   5321 3216G

     t   t N
   3356 3356
   1126 3532G

     t   t N
   6132 6132
   5653 2126G

```
  t    t N
 ..65 3561
 .232 6563G

  t    t N
 22.. 2123
 22.. 2123G

  t    t N
 6563 6563
 6521 3216G ]
```

Lempang, Ladrang, pélog pathet nem (1).

buka: .3.2 .3.2 .6.5N/G

```
 t    t N      t    t N      t    t N
.3.6 .3.5     .6.3 .6.5     .6.3 .6.5
.3.6 .3.5     .6.5 .6.5     .6.3 .6.5
.3.2 .3.2     .3.2 .3.2     .3.6 .5.6
.5.4 .6.5G    .5.4 .6.5G    .2.3 .6.5G
```

Lempang Jawi, Gendhing (Santiswaran),
     pélog pathet nem (39).

```
.   . 2 3 5 6      . 5 5 .635653
3 2 3 2 3 5 6      . 121  12165
.   . 2 3 5 6      . 5 5 .635653
3 2 3 2 3 5 6      . 121  12165
. 5 3 .25 .32     3 565  56532
.   . 6 1 2 3 2   3 6 5  5 653
5 2 3   5 2 3 6   6 6 6 5 6 7 5G
```

Lempang Pujang/Lempang Bujang, Gendhing
  (Santiswaran), pélog pathet barang (39).

```
[.    .    .    .      .   . 3 5 6 7 6
 7 675 .62   3      4 3 5 6 7 6 .
 7 3 2   23276      7 232   23276
 .   . 3 5 6 7 6   7 3 2   2 327
 . 3 3   . 3 3     . 3 3 2 2 342G
 . 5 6 7 5   7 65 3 675   65323 5
 . 3 6 .75   7 65 3   . 3 5 6 7 6
 7 3 2   23276      7 232   23276
 .   . 3 5 6 7 6   7 3 2   2 327 →
 . 3 3   . 3 3     . 3 5   6   7
 6   6   7   2     3   6 7 5 3 2 32
 7 ]
```

suwuk:

```
→ . 3 3   . 3 3      . 3 3 2 2 342G
```

Lempung Gunung, Gendhing, kethuk 2 kerep,
  minggah kethuk 4, pélog pathet barang (1).

buka: [.3.23 2726]x2   .6.6 .6.6 .6.7 .6.5N/G

mérong: t   t   N
        [.536 .536 .567 6535
         .536 .536 .567 6535
         .536 .536 .567 6535
         67.. 7656 532. 4323G

                 t   t   N
         .234 .234 .323 2767
         .234 .234 .323 2767
         .234 .234 .323 2767
         33.. 6532 7656 5356G]

minggah: t   t   t   t N
        [.2.3 .2.7 .5.6 .5.3
         .2.3 .2.7 .5.6 .5.3
         .2.3 .2.7 .5.6 .5.3
         .5.6 .2.7 .3.2 .4.3G]
```
```

Lendhi, Gendhing, kethuk 4 kerep,
   sléndro pathet manyura (4).

buka: 6 .123 .3.3 .5.3 .5.2 .5.3N/G

mérong:
```
      t        t         t         t    N
 [..35 1653 ..32 3565 .... 5535 6616 5323
  121. 1312 ..23 5565 .... 5535 6616 5323
  121. 1312 5653 2126 .... 6656 1156 .523→
  ..25 3.25 3.53 2121 6123 .... 3352 5653G]
```

umpak:
```
      t        t         t         t    N
→..25 3.25 3.53 2121 .55. 1653 2123 2126G
```

minggah: Ladrang Sawung Galing

Lenggang Jati, Gendhing, pélog pathet nem (19).

buka celuk:
```
 . 6 1 2   1 6 5 3   6 5 3 2   3 5 6 5G
 65.5635   65.5635   6 5 6 5   6 5 6 5G
 . .23566  1326532   1 1 2 3   365 532G
 . 2 2 .   3 1 2 3   . 3 3 .   2 3 1 2G
 . 2 2 .   3 1 2 3   . 3 3 .   2 3 1 2G
 32.2312   32.2312   3 2 3 2   3 2 3 2G
```

Lèngkèr, Ladrang, pélog
   pathet nem (1).

buka: 3 5612 6.35 6123 .321 6563N/G

   t   t N
   ..35 6126
   ..35 6126
   ..35 6126
   .321 6563G

   t   t N
   11.. 1121
   3212 .126
   ..35 ..65
   1216 5323G

   t   t N
   ..35 6356
   3561 3216
   .653 2123
   6532 .126G

   t   t N
   33.5 6356
   3561 3216
   .653 2123
   .321 6563G

Léré-léré, Ladrang, sléndro
   pathet manyura (2).

buka: .3.1 2312 11.. 3216 .366 .532N/G

      t   t   N
[11.. 3216 .356 .532
  11.. 3216 .356 .532
  ..53 2126 .123 2126
  33.. 3321 6123 2126G

      t   t   N
  33.. 3321 6123 2126
  33.. 3321 6123 2126
  .3.1 2312 .3.1 2312
  11.. 3216 .356 .532G]

Linko-linko, Ladrang,
   pélog pathet nem (1).

buka: 33. 3132 6123 2126N/G

```
   t    t N
 323. 3216
 323. 3216
 .33. 3131
 6123 2126G
```

Lipur Érang-érang, Gendhing, kethuk
   2 kerep, sléndro pathet nem (1).

buka: 6 .616 .565 .5.6 .532 1132 .165N/G
```
mérong:    t        t    N
       .65. 5612 1312 .165
       11.. 1121 3216 .165
       .... 55.6 1216 5312
       66.. 6532 1132 .165G
```

Lipur Sari, Ladrang, sléndro
   pathet manyura (2).

```
    t        t    N
[[...3 ...2 ...3 ...2
 33.. 33.. 1132 5321
 3265 3561 3265 3561
 23.. 3361 22.3 .1.2G
```
```
    t        t    N
 ...3 ...2 ...3 ...2
 33.. 33.. 1132 5356
 ..35 3516 ..35 3561
 .3.2 .6.5 .1.6 .5.3]
```

ngelik:
```
    t        t    N
 6165 1653 6165 1653
 66.. 6165 1632 5321
 3265 3561 3265 3561
 23.. 3361 22.3 .1.2G]
```

Liwung, Ladrang, sléndro
pathet manyura (2).

buka: 6 .1.2 .1.6 .365 .3.2N/G

```
  t    t N        t    t N
[ .5.6 .3.2      .653 2126
  .5.6 .3.2      .653 2126
  .5.6 .1.6      .3.5 .6.5
  .653 2126G     .6.5 .3.2G ]
```

Lobaningrat, Gendhing, kethuk 4 awis, minggah
kethuk 8, sléndro pathet nem (16).

buka: 2 .356 ..1. 6.1. 6.53 2356N/G

mérong:
```
           t                    t
[..1. 6.1. 6.53 2356 ..1. 6.1. 6.53 2353
 .... 3356 3565 2232 .... 22.3 5653 2165N
 ..1. 6.53 .... 5235 ..1. 6.53 .... 5235
 33.. 33.. 6535 3212 5653 2165 22.6 1232N
 ..23 .532 66.1 6535 ..56 1656 3565 3212
 ..23 .532 66.1 6535 ..56 1656 3565 3212N→
 5653 2126 3565 2232 ..25 2356 3565 2232
 .62. 62.6 2.23 2121 ..32 .165 32.3 5616N/G]
```

umpak:
```
   t    t    t    t   N
→.5.3 .1.6 .2.3 .1.6 .5.6 .5.3 .5.3 .1.6G
```

minggah:
```
  t    t    t    t    t    t    t    t N
[.2.1 .2.6 .2.1 .5.3 .5.3 .5.6 .2.1 .3.2
 .3.1 .3.2 .3.1 .5.3 .5.3 .5.6 .2.1 .3.2
 .3.1 .3.2 .3.1 .5.6 .5.6 .2.1 .2.6 .3.2
 .5.3 .1.6 .2.3 .1.6 .5.6 .5.3 .5.3 .1.6G]
```

Lobong, Gendhing, kethuk 2 kerep, minggah
    kethuk 4, sléndro pathet manyura (3).

buka: 3565 3216 12.. 2321 3235 3356N/G

mérong: t   t N
    [22.. 2321 3265 3356
    33.. 3356 3532 .126
    33.. 3356 3532 .126→
    22.. 2321 3265 3356G

ngelik: t   t N
    22.. 2321 3265 3356
    11.. 3216 3532 .126
    11.. 3216 3532 .126
    22.. 2321 3265 3356G]

umpak minggah:
    t   t N
  →.3.2 .3.2 .3.1 .2.6G

minggah:t t t t N
    [.1.6 .1.6 .2.1 .3.2
    .3.1 .2.6 .2.1 .3.2
    .3.1 .2.6 .3.2 .3.1
    .2.1 .2.1 .3.2 .1.6G]

Logondhang, Gendhing, kethuk 2
    kerep, pélog pathet lima (3).

buka: .556 4565 .33. 3231 5612 .165N/G

mérong: t   t N
    .65. 5612 312. 5321
    ..16 5612 312. 5321
    .235 ..5. 55.6 4565
    33.2 5321 5612 .165G

ngelik: t   t N
    11.. 1121 3212 .165
    .621 ..1. 3212 .165
    ..5. 55.. 55.6 4565
    33.2 5321 5612 .165G

Lokananta, Gendhing, kethuk 2 kerep, minggah
    kethuk 4, sléndro pathet nem (2).

buka: 2 2165 .1.1 .2.6 .532 .356N/G

mérong:
        [..12 1653 6532 .356
        ..12 1653 6532 .356
        22.. 22.3 356. 3356
        ..61 6535 2356 3532G

            t   t   N
        55.. 5523 5653 2126
        33.. 6535 2353 2126
        22.. 22.3 5653 2165→
        11.. 3216 .532 .356G]

umpak minggah:
            t   t   N
    →.2.1 .2.6 .3.2 .5.6G

minggah:
        t   t   t   t N
        [.3.2 .5.3 .5.2 .1.6
        .3.2 .5.3 .5.2 .5.6
        .3.2 .3.2 .5.3 .5.6
        .5.6 .3.5 .6.5 .3.2G

        t   t   t   t N
        .3.6 .3.5 .2.3 .1.6
        .2.3 .6.5 .2.3 .1.6
        .3.2 .3.2 .5.3 .6.5
        .2.1 .2.6 .3.2 .5.6G]

Lompong Kèli, Ladrang,
        sléndro pathet sanga (2).

buka: 5.6 .165 2222 1121N/G

    t   t N   t   t N
[.6.5 .2.1   .3.2 .6.5
  .6.5 .2.1   .3.2 .6.5
  .6.5 .3.2   .2.3 .2.1
  .6.1 .6.5G   .6.5 .2.1G]

Longgor/Longgor Lasem, Ladrang,
    pélog pathet barang (1).

(minggah to Gendhing Sembur Adas)

```
   t    t N
66..  6676
323.  3276
323.  3276
5653  2365G

   t    t N
.756  7276
.756  7276
.756  7276
5653  2365G (suwuk)

   t    t N
22..  2232
.32.  2327
232.  2327
6765  3567G

   t    t N
.767  6567
.765  2576
..35  6676
5327  3532G
```

Lonthang, Gendhing, kethuk 4 kerep,
    minggah kethuk 8, sléndro pathet nem (16).

buka: 235 .621 .66. 6532 .3.5N/G

mérong:

```
   t         t         t         t    N
[.1.6 .532 ..25 2353 ..35 2353 66.1 6535
 .555 2235 2353 2126 ..61 2353 5653 2165
 .555 2235 2353 2126 ..61 2353 5653 2165 →
 22.. 2235 .621 6165 1621 6656 3532 .365G]
```

umpak minggah:

```
    t         t         t         t    N
→.2.3 .1.6 .2.3 .1.6 .5.3 .5.3 .5.2 .6.5G
```

minggah:

```
   t    t    t    t    t    t    t    t N
[.6.5 .6.5 .6.5 .2.3 .5.3 .5.3 .5.2 .6.5
 .6.5 .6.5 .6.5 .2.3 .5.3 .5.3 .5.2 .6.5
 .6.5 .6.5 .6.5 .2.3 .5.3 .5.3 .5.2 .6.5
 .2.3 .1.6 .2.3 .1.6 .5.3 .5.3 .5.2 .6.5G]
```

Lonthang Kasmaran, Gendhing, kethuk 4 kerep,
minggah kethuk 8, sléndro pathet sanga (2).

buka: 6123 .3.3 .3.3 .6.1 .2.2N/G

mérong:
```
t          t          t          t    N
[...3 .123 .123 2212 ..21 3216 ..61 2353
 ...3 .123 .123 2212 ..21 3216 ..61 2.32
 .... 2212 3312 .212 3312 .212 3312 .126
 .165 3516 .165 3561 22.1 3216 33.. 6532G

 t          t          t          t    N
 5653 2126 3561 6532 11.. 11.2 3516 2165
 ..56 1653 6165 2165 33.. 6532 ..23 5616
 55.. 1653 6165 2165 33.. 6532 ..23 5616→
 22.. 22.. 2321 6123 .... 3353 .6.1 2353G]
```

ompak:
```
t          t          t          t    N
→.5.3 .5.2 .5.3 .5.2 .5.3 .5.2 .6.3 .6.5G
```

minggah:
```
t    t    t    t    t    t    t    t N
[.2.1 .2.1 .2.1 .3.2 .3.2 .3.2 .5.6 .5.3
 .5.3 .5.3 .5.6 .3.5 .6.3 .6.5 .3.2 .5.3
 .5.3 .6.5 .6.3 .6.5 .6.3 .6.5 .2.3 .6.5
 .2.3 .5.2 .5.3 .5.2 .5.3 .5.2 .6.3 .6.5G]
```

Loro-loro, Gendhing, pamijèn,
pélog pathet barang (3).

buka: 777 3265 3335 6356N/G

3567 6532N

NNNN
2276 3532N

NNNN
2223 5653

5253 6567

2621 3265N

3335 6356N/G

Loro-loro, Gendhing, pamijèn,
 sléndro pathet manyura (3).

buka: 111 3265 3335 6356N/G

   3561 6532N

   NNNN
   2216 3532N

   NNNN
   2223 5653

   5253 6561

   2621 3265N

   3335 6356G

ngelik:
        N
   .5.3 .5.6
   .5.3 .5.6
   .3.2 .5.3
   .1.2 .1.6G

umpak:
        N
   .3.2 .5.3
   .5.2 .5.3
   .5.2 .5.3
   .1.2 .1.6G

Loro-loro Géndhong, Gendhing, kethuk
 2 kerep, minggah kethuk 4,
 sléndro pathet manyura (25).

buka: 3 .3.2 3123 121. 1216 6653 2126N/G

mérong: t   t   N
   [.... 3321 653. 3516
   .... 3321 653. 3516
   33.. 33.. 33.5 6121
   .... 1265 33.5 6356G

      t   t   N
   .... 6653 22.6 1232
   66.. 6653 22.6 1232
   33.. 33.. 33.2 3123 →
   121. 1216 6653 2126G]

```
umpak:    t          t    N
     →.1.2 .1.6 .5.3 .1.2G
minggah:
      t    t    t    t N
   [.3.2 .3.1 .2.6 .1.2
    .3.2 .3.1 .2.6 .5.3
    .5.3 .2.1 .2.1 .2.6
    .5.6 .3.5 .1.6 .3.2G]
```

Loro-loro Topèng, Gendhing, pamijèn,
   sléndro pathet manyura (16).

buka: 111 3265 33.5 6356N/G

```
      t         t    N
   [3561 6532 2216 1312
    2223 5653 5253 2321
    2621 3265 33.5 6356G]
```

Loyo, Gendhing, kethuk 4 awis, minggah
   kethuk 8, sléndro pathet nem (1).

buka: 2231 6.61 2165 3365 .3.2N/G

mérong:
```
       t                   t
   [..23 6532 ..25 2356 ..63 6532 ..25 2353
    .... 33.. 33.. 5325 33.. 3353 6535 2232N
    ..23 6532 ..25 2356 ..63 6532 ..25 2353
    .... 33.. 33.. 5325 33.. 3353 6535 2232N
    ..23 6532 66.1 6535 2356 3532 66.1 6535
    2356 3532 66.1 6535 2356 5321 6132 .165N→
    11.. 3216 3565 2232 ..25 2356 3565 2232
    .... 22.. 2321 6132 5653 2165 3365 .3.2N/G]
```

umpak:
```
                                     N
   →.2.3 .5.2 .5.3 .5.2 .5.3 .5.2 .6.5 .3.2G
```

minggah:
```
    t    t    t    t    t    t    t    t N
   [.3.2 .3.2 .3.2 .5.3 .5.3 .5.6 .5.6 .3.2
    .3.2 .3.2 .3.2 .5.3 .5.3 .5.6 .5.6 .3.2
    .5.6 .5.6 .3.5 .3.2 .3.2 .3.2 .5.3 .6.5
    .2.3 .5.2 .5.3 .5.2 .5.3 .5.2 .6.5 .3.2G]
```

249

sabetan:
```
    t    t    t    t    t    t    t    t N
 [3132 3132 3132 3635 3635 3635 3635 2232
  5325 3253 2523 5653 6563 6563 6563 2232
  5325 3253 2523 5653 22.. 22.3 5653 2165
  1216 5352 5356 5352 5356 5352 3365 2232G]
```

Loyo, Ladrang, sléndro
    pathet manyura (1).

buka: gendèr
```
    t    t N
  .5.6 .3.2
  .5.6 .3.2
  .5.6 .1.6
  .5.6 .3.2G
```

gecul:
```
    N    N
  .62. 2356
  1653 6532G

    N    N
  .62. 2356
  1653 6532G

    N    N
  5653 2126
  2123 2126G

    N    N
  .22. 2356
  3356 5352G
```

Ludira, Gendhing, kethuk 4 kerep, minggah
kethuk 8, pélog pathet barang (38).

buka: 2.2 .2.7 65.2 .2.2 .765 .3.3 .2.7 .2.6 .5.3N/G

mérong:
```
          t          t          t          t     N
[...3 .563 .563 .567 .2.3 .2.7 .2.6 3567
 ...7 6563 ..36 3567 2372 .756 33.. 6532
 672. 2723 672. 2723 56.. 6765 7632 .756
 .765 3576 .765 3567 22.. 22.3 44.. 2343G

          t          t          t          t     N
 .... 3327 66.7 5676 .5.3 .7.6 .532 .756
 33.. 6532 .327 .3.2 3723 2765 ..52 3565
 ..57 .656 .5.3 .7.6 .5.3 .7.6 .532 .765
 ..56 7276 .756 7276 33.. 3327 .2.6 .5.3G]
```

ngelik, then umpak:
```
          t          t          t          t     N
 66.. 66.. 66.5 6356 ..65 7653 ..35 6767
 ...7 .567 .567 2766 32.3 4323 6765 3272
 ..23 6532 52.3 5676 ..67 5676 5365 3272
 ..23 6532 52.3 4323 .... 3343 .6.7 2343G

          t          t          t          t     N
 .... 3327 66.7 5676 .5.3 .7.6 .532 .756
 33.. 6532 .327 .3.2 3723 2765 ..52 3565
 ..57 .656 .5.3 .7.6 .5.3 .7.6 .532 .756
 ..56 7276 .756 7276 33.. 3327 2327 6563G
```

minggah:
```
     t    t    t    t    t    t    t    t N
[6563 6563 6563 6567 2.27 2.27 2.26 3567
 2.27 6563 6536 3567 2372 .756 33.. 6532
 672. 2723 672. 2723 56.. 6765 7632 .756
 .765 3576 .765 3567 22.. 22.3 44.. 2343G

     t    t    t    t    t    t    t    t N
 .... 3327 66.7 5676 .5.3 .7.6 .532 .756
 33.. 6532 .327 .3.2 3723 2765 ..52 3565
 ..57 .656 .5.3 .7.6 .5.3 .7.6 .532 .765
 ..56 7276 .756 7276 .756 7276 .532 .5.3G]
```

sesegan:
```
     t    t    t    t    t    t    t    t N
[6563 6563 6563 6567 2.27 2.27 2.26 3567
 2.27 6563 6536 3567 2372 .756 33.. 6532
 672. 2723 672. 2723 56.. 6765 7632 .765
 ..56 7276 .756 7276 .756 7276 .532 .5.3G]
```

Ludira Madu/Ludira Madura, Gendhing, kethuk
4 kerep, pélog pathet barang (8).

buka: 3 .27 276 ...3 .27276 .3.3 .567 .3.2 .7.6N/G

mérong:
```
     t         t         t         t    N
[ ..65 7653 ..36 3567 2.7. 3276 33.5 6756
  ..65 7653 ..36 3567 2.7. 3276 33.. 6532
  55.. 55.. 55.. 6356 ..35 6732 7232 .756
  .... 6656 3567 6535 66.7 6532 7656 3532G

     t         t         t         t    N
  ..23 2756 .... 6656 3567 6532 76.7 2372
  ..23 2756 ..67 2372 3723 2767 ...7 6567
  .... 77.. 77.. 2672 .765 .... 5565 3567
  .3.2 .765 7656 5323 272. 2765 3567 3276G ]
```

Ludira Madura, Ladrang,
    pélog pathet barang (1).

buka celuk:

```
    t    t N
[ .... 77..
  77.. 6672
  ..23 2756
  33.. 6532G

    t    t N
  .... 2232
  55.. 3356
  ..67 653.
  3323 2232G

    t    t N
  ..23 .2.7
  .2.3 6532
  3276 55..
  5565 3356G

    t    t N
  ..67 653.
  3356 .532
  3276 ....
  33.5 6767G ]
```

Lung Gadhung, Ladrang,
   pélog pathet barang (1).

buka: 6 .356 352 356 .7.6N/G

t	t N		t	t N
7673	7376		7273	7372
7673	7376		7276	7675
7673	7372		7576	7672
7273	7372G		7273	7376G

Lung Gadhung Pèl (Sekatèn),
   pélog pathet lima (7).

buka: N
   ...1 .1.3 .3.1 .3.2
   ...5 .321 .2.3 .5.3
   .5.2 .3.5 .2.3 .2.1
   .3.2 .1.2 .3.5 .2.3G

                           N
   ...3 ...3 .2.1 .3.2
   .5.6 .5.3 .2.1 .3.2
   .2.2 .1.1 .2.2 .1.1
   .3.3 .6.1 .2.3 .1.2G

       t   t   N
   [.5.6 .5.3 .5.1 .5.2
   .5.6 .5.3 .5.1 .5.2
   .5.3 .5.1 .5.2 .5.1
   .5.3 .5.1 .5.3 .5.2G]

sesegan: t   t N
       [5756 5756
       5357 5256
       5352 5352
       5753 5253G

        t   t N
       5653 5653
       1615 1615
       1651 5251
       5351 5352G]

Lungkèh, Gendhing, kethuk 4 awis, minggah
    kethuk 8, sléndro pathet nem (4).

buka: 2 .2.3 .126 .6.1 2165 3565 .3.2N/G

mérong:
```
        t                    t
[323. 323. 323. 3235 .616 3532 323. 3235
 612. 612. 6123 6532 5653 2165 3565 2232N
 323. 323. 323. 3235 .616 3532 323. 3235
 612. 612. 6123 6532 5653 2165 3565 2232N
 66.. 6656 2321 3216 2321 3216 ..61 6523
 6535 3212 66.1 6523 6535 .321 6132 .165N→
 11.. 3216 3565 2232 ..25 2356 3565 2232
 .... 22.. 2321 6132 5653 2165 3565 2232N/G]
```

umpak minggah:
```
     t         t         t         t    N
→.66. 6621 .55. 6621 .55. 6621 5153 6532G
```

minggah:
```
   t    t    t    t    t    t    t    t N
[3532 3635 3632 3635 3632 3635 3635 3132
 .1.6 .1.6 .3.6 .3.2 .5.3 .6.5 .3.5 .3.2
 .1.6 .1.6 .3.6 .3.2 .5.3 .6.5 .3.5 .3.2
 .66. 6621 .55. 6621 .55. 6621 5153 6532G]
```


Lunta/Kalunta, Gendhing, kethuk 2 kerep,
    sléndro pathet sanga (2).

buka: 516 .532 .11. 561. 5612 .126N/G

mérong:
```
       t                  t              N
[. . 2 1  . 6 5 .  5 6 1 2  . 1 6 5
 2 2 . .  2 2 . 3  5 6 . 1  5 6 1 6
 .56 .56  .56 1 6  1 1 3 2  . 1 6 5
 .35 .35  .65 3 2  1 1 . 2  3 2 1 2G
```
```
       t                  t              N
 .12 .12  .32 1 2  1 6 5 .  5 6 1 2
 .12 .12  .32 1 2  1 6 5 .  5 6 1 2
 . 3 6 5  . . . .  5 6 1 6  . 5 3 2→
 . 1 1 .  5 6 1 .  5 6 1 2  . 1 2 6G]
```

ompak minggah:
```
        t                  t             N
→. 3 . 1  . 3 . 2  . 3 . 2  . 6 . 5G
```

minggah: Bango Maté/Mangun Mati

Madu Brangta, Ladrang,
  sléndro pathet sanga (20).

buka: 212. 2165 2232 11.1N/G

```
    t       t    N
...2 ...1 ...2 ...1
...2 ...6 .2.1 .6.5
1656 5312 6561 6535
2353 2126 2321 6535G.

    t       t    N
[22.. 22.3 5621 6535
2353 2126 2321 6535
.1.6 .1.5 .156 1232
.1.2 2165 2353 2121G

    t       t    N
.3.2 .3.1 .3.2 .3.1
22.. 22.3 5621 6535
1656 5312 6561 6535
2353 2126 2321 6535G]
```

Madu Kochak, Gendhing, kethuk 4 kerep,
  minggah kethuk 8, sléndro pathet sanga (1).

buka: 356 5323 .55. 5612 1312 .165N/G

mérong:
```
   t        t        t        t    N
[.555 2235 1656 5312 6165 .312 1312 .165
.555 2235 1656 5312 6165 .312 1312 .165
.555 2235 1656 5312 6165 .312 1312 .165 →
2356 5323 ..56 5323 .55. 5612 1312 .165G]
```

umpak:
```
   t        t        t        t    N
→ .1.6 .5.3 .5.6 .5.3 .6.5 .3.2 .3.2 .6.5G
```

minggah:
```
  t   t   t   t   t   t   t   t N
[.6.5 .6.5 .1.6 .3.2 .6.5 .3.2 .3.2 .6.5
.6.5 .6.5 .1.6 .3.2 .6.5 .3.2 .3.2 .6.5
.6.5 .6.5 .1.6 .3.2 .6.5 .3.2 .3.2 .6.5
.1.6 .5.3 .5.6 .5.3 .6.5 .3.2 .3.2 .6.5G]
```

Majemuk, Gendhing Bonangan, kethuk 4 kerep,
   minggah kethuk 8, pélog pathet lima (1).

buka: [55.2 1235]x2 33. 3235.621 6123N/G

mérong:
    t   t   t   t   N
  [.23. 3235 .621 6123 .6.5 .421 .5.6 .2.1
   .77. 7656.567. 7656.567. 7656 .5.3 .6.5
   .77. 7656.567. 7656.567. 7656 .5.3 .6.5→
   .3.2 .165 .3.2 .165 .33. 3235 .621 6123G]

umpak:
    t   t   t   t   N
→.3.2 .165 .3.2 .165 .2.1 .2.1 .3.2 .6.5G

inggah:
  t   t   t   t   t   t   t   t N
  [.2.1 .2.1 .3.2 .6.5 .2.1 .2.1 3212 3532
   312. 2356 .22. 2321 .6.5 .6.5 .33. 1232
   312. 2356 .22. 2321 .6.5 .6.5 .33. 1232
   312. 2356 .22. 2356 .2.1 .2.1 .3.2 .6.5G]

Majemuk, Gendhing, kethuk 2 kerep, minggah
   kethuk 4, sléndro pathet nem (3).

buka: ..3. 212. 3212 6132N/G

mérong: t   t   N
  [..3. 212. 3212 6132
   3123 2126 ..61 2353
   ..3. 33.5 6156 .532 →
   5653 2126 .123 2126
   ..3. 212. 3212 6132G]

umpak minggah:
    t   t   N
→.5.3 .1.6 .2.3 .1.6
 .2.1 .2.1 .3.2 .1.6G

minggah irama III:
  t   t   t   t N
  [.2.1 .2.1 .3.2 .1.6
   .1.6 .1.6 .1.6 .5.3
   .5.3 .5.6 .2.1 .3.2
   .5.3 .1.6 .5.3 .1.6
   .2.1 .2.1 .3.2 .1.6G]

Malarsih, Gendhing, ketnuk 2 kerep, minggah
    kethuk 4, pélog pathet barang (1).

buka: 667 6563 272. 2723 6532 .756N/G

mérong: t   t   N
        [[.563 .567 33.. 6532
          5653 2767 33.. 6532
          .756 .... 3567 6523
          272. 7723 6532 .756G]

ngelik: t   t   N
          .... 6656 3567 6523
          77.. 7576 3567 6523
          2723 .776 3567 6523
          272. 2723 6532 .756G]

minggah: t   t   t   t N
        [.7.6 .2.7 .2.7 .3.2
         .3.2 .3.7 .2.7 .3.2
         .3.2 .7.6 .2.7 .5.3
         .2.7 .2.3 .7.2 .7.6G]

Mandhul, Gendhing, kethuk 4 kerep, minggah
    kethuk 8, sléndro pathet sanga (16).

buka: 1.1. 612. 1612 .126 .3.5N/G

mérong:
        t   t   t   t   N
        [.1.6 .1.5 .1.6 .1.5 ..56 1656 5323 2121
         .216 .2.1 .3.2 .165 ..56 1656 5323 2121
         .216 .2.1 .3.2 .165 ..56 1656 5323 2121→
         3532 .126 3532 .126 11.. 3212 .126 .3.5G]

umpak:
        t   t   t   t   N
     → .3.2 .1.6 .3.2 .1.6 .2.1 .3.2 .1.6 .3.5G

minggah:
        t   t   t   t   t   t   t   t N
        [.1.6 .1.5 .1.6 .1.5 .3.5 .3.5 .1.6 .2.1
         .2.6 .2.1 .3.2 .6.5 .3.5 .3.5 .1.6 .2.1
         .2.6 .2.1 .3.2 .6.5 .3.5 .3.5 .1.6 .2.1
         .3.2 .1.6 .3.2 .1.6 .2.1 .3.2 .1.6 .3.5G]

Mandhul Pati, Gendhing, kethuk 2
    kerep, sléndro pathet nem (16).

buka: 2.2. 3.12 6.66 .121 6535 2232N/G

mérong: t   t   N
    [.... 2235 2356 3532
    66.. 66.1 2321 6535
    .653 .6.5 .653 .6.5
    235. 235. 6535 2232G

        t   t   N
    .... 2235 2356 3532
    33.. 3353 6535 3212
    6165 .32. 6165 .323
    55.. 5653 6532 .126G

        t   t   N
    33.. 6535 2353 2126
    22.. 22.3 5653 2165
    .653 .6.5 .653 .6.5
    235. 235. 6535 2232G]

minggah: Ladrang Agun-agun

Mandra Guna, Ladrang,
    pélog pathet nem (18).

buka: ..66 6521 .11. 6123N/G

    t   t N
    5356 2165
    6356 3532
    .365 2356
    2321 6123G

Mangu, Ladrang, sléndro pathet nem (2).

buka: 6535 6123 5612 2365 .3.2N/G

t t N	t t N	t t N
[.5.6 .5.3	.5.6 .5.3	.5.3 .1.6
.5.6 .5.3	.1.6 .5.3	.2.1 .2.3
.5.6 .1.6	.5.6 .1.6	.5.6 .1.6
.3.5 .3.2G	.3.5 .3.2G	.3.5 .3.2G]

258

Manis, Ladrang, pélog pathet barang (1).

(minggah to Gendhing Lempung Gunung)

```
 t   t N      t   t N
.2.7 .5.3    .2.3 .2.7
.5.6 .5.3    .2.3 .2.7
.6.5 .7.6    .2.3 .5.3
.3.2 .7.6G   .5.2 .7.6G
```

Manis, Ladrang, sléndro pathet manyura (2).

buka: 1 3261 2353 6532 .126N/G

```
   t   t N      t   t N
[ .2.3 .2.1    .2.1 .5.3
  .2.3 .2.1    .5.6 .5.3
  .2.3 .5.3    .6.5 .1.6
  .5.2 .1.6G   .3.2 .1.6G ]
```

Manis Betawèn, Ladrang,
    pélog pathet barang (1).

buka: 2 .272 6723 5633 22.7 .5.6N/G

```
   t       t   N
.  2  . 3  . 2  . 7
.  2  . 3  . 2  . 7
55.. 55.. 5563 5676
567. 7627 .3.2 .7.6G

   t       t   N
[7632 4.43 6732 6327
 5672 4.43 6732 6327
 55.. 55.. 5563 5676
 567. 7627 .3.2 .7.6G

   t       t   N
...2 ...7 ...5 ...3
...5 ...6 ...5 ...3
77.. 77.. 77.6 5356
567. 7627 .3.2 .7.6G]
```

259

Manyar Sèwu, Lancaran,
    sléndro pathet nem (2).

buka: .1.6 .1.6 .5.3N/G

```
    t tN t tN t tN t tN
  [.5.3 .5.3 .5.3 .6.5G
   .6.5 .6.5 .6.5 .3.2G
   .3.2 .3.2 .3.2 .1.6G
   .1.6 .1.6 .1.6 .5.3G]
```

```
   t   tN   t    tN   t    tN   t    t N
 [.5.23523 .5.23523 .5.23523 .6.35635G
  .6.35635 .6.35635 .6.35635 .3.12312G
  .3.12312 .3.12312 .3.12312 .1.56156G
  .1.56156 .1.56156 .1.56156 .5.23523G]
```

Mara Sanja, Gendhing, kethuk 4 awis, minggah
    kethuk 8, sléndro pathet nem (1).

buka: 6.6 .35.2 .2.32 .3.5 .6.6 .3.2N/G

mérong:
```
          t                    t
 [.2.2 .3.5 2356 3532 .22. 2235 2356 3532
  33.. 3353 6535 3235 2356 5321 6132 .165N
  22.. 2232 5653 2121 3261 22.3 5653 2121
  3261 22.. 2321 6535 11.. 3216 3565 2222N
  66.. 3356 2321 6535 1653 66.. 2321 6535
  1635 66.. 2355 2232 .... 2253 6531 6132N
  66.1 6523 5653 2126 3561 6523 5653 2126→
  .... 6653 3561 6532 .... 2235 2356 3532N/G]
```

umpak:
```
        t              t         N
→.5.3 .1.6 .2.3 .1.6 .3.2 .6.5 .3.2 .5.6G
```

minggah:
```
    t    t    t    t    t    t    t    t N
 [.3.2 .6.5 .3.2 .5.6 .3.2 .6.5 .3.2 .5.6
  .3.2 .6.5 .3.2 .5.6 .5.3 .5.3 .5.1 .6.5
  .3.2 .6.5 .3.2 .6.5 .3.2 .3.2 .5.3 .1.6
  .2.3 .1.6 .2.3 .1.6 .3.2 .6.5 .3.2 .5.6G]
```

Maraséba, Gendhing, kethuk 4 awis, minggah
     kethuk 8, pélog pathet barang (11).

buka: 6 .6.7 6535 66.7 6532 7232 .756N/G

mérong:
          t   t
[..67 5676 ..67 2353 6765 3272 ..27 6723
 56.. 66.. 66.7 6535 66.7 6532 7232 .756N
 ..67 5676 ..67 2353 6765 3272 ..23 2767
 ..63 .532 .756 .523N
 ..35 7653 77.. 7756 .567 6563 77.. 7756 →
 .567 6563 77.. 7756 .567 6522 723. 3532N
 ..23 2765 33.6 3567 22.. 2765 33.6 3567
 22.. 22.3 56.7 6535 66.7 6532 7232 .756N/G]

umpak:
→.567 6563 77.. 7756 .567 6532 7232 .756N
 .2.3 .7.6 .2.3 .7.6 .5.6 .5.3 .5.3 .7.6N/G

minggah:
   t   t   t   t   t   t   t   t N
[.2.3 .7.6 .2.7 .2.3 .5.3 .5.3 .5.3 .2.7
 .2.7 .2.7 .2.7 .2.3 .5.3 .5.3 .5.3 .2.7
 .2.7 .2.7 .2.7 .5.6 .5.6 .2.7 .5.6 .5.3
 .5.6 .5.3 .5.6 .5.3 .2.7 .2.3 .7.2 .7.6G]

Mari Kangen, Jineman,
     sléndro pathet manyura (3).

buka celuk: 3N

 [6132 6321N
  2632G 5321N
  2632 6261N
  33.. 6532N
  5653 .216G
  2632N]suwuk

Marta Puran/Cendhani Raras, Ketawang,
pélog pathet nem (1).

buka: 123 1635 5212N/G

```
   t    t N  t     t N
.123 2126 3365 3212G
.123 2126 3365 3212G
.123 2126 22.6 1232G
.123 2126 3365 3212G
66.. 6656 2165 3212G
5654 2126 3365 3212G
```

Mas Kéntar, Ketawang,
pélog pathet nem (38).

buka: 333 2126 .122 6122 6123 5653N/G

```
   t    t N  t     t N
[..53 2165 .... 5565G
..56 5323 11.. 3265G
..53 2123 ..56 5323G
6521 6.56 2165 2232G
..61 2232 ..23 5653G]
```

Mas Kumambang, Gendhing, kethuk 4 awis,
minggah kethuk 8, sléndro pathet nem (2).

buka: 365 .321 6123 .365 .3.2N/G

mérong: t   t
```
[..23 .532 66.1 6523 6535 3212 66.1 6523
6535 3212 66.1 6523 6535 .321 6132 .165N
2356 5323 6535 3235 2356 5323 6535 2232
..25 2356 3565 2232 .... 22.3 5653 2165N
2356 5323 6535 3235 2356 5323 6535 2232
..25 2356 3565 2232 .... 22.3 5653 2165N →
11.. 3216 3565 2232 ..25 2356 3565 2232
33.. 33.. 6535 .321 6123 ...3 6535 3212N/G]
```

261

umpak minggah:
                              N
→.1.6 .3.2 .6.5 .3.2 .3.2 .6.5 .6.5 .3.2G

minggah:
  t   t   t   t   t   t   t   t N
[.6.5 .3.2 .6.5 .3.2 .3.2 .3.2 .5.3 .6.5
 .3.2 .6.5 .3.5 .3.2 .3.2 .3.2 .5.3 .6.5
 .3.2 .6.5 .3.5 .2.3 .5.3 .5.2 .5.3 .6.5
 .1.6 .3.2 .6.5 .3.2 .3.2 .6.5 .6.5 .3.2G]

Mawur, Gendhing, kethuk 4 awis, minggah
    kethuk 8, sléndro pathet sanga (1).

buka: 1 .1.1 .2.2 .2.1 .612 .2.1 26.5N/G

mérong:

[.2.2 .321 .216 .2.1 65.. 55.6 123. 1232
 .126 .... 6561 6535 1656 5321 .216 .2.1N
 65.. 2321 .216 .2.1 65.. 55.6 123. 1232
 .126 .... 6561 6535 1656 5321 .216 .2.1N
 65.. 2321 .216 .2.1 65.. 55.6 123. 1232
 .126 .... 6561 6535 1656 5321 .216 .2.1N→
 11.. 3216 3565 2232 5325 2356 3565 1232
 11.. 11.2 35.6 5312 161. 1312 5321 6535N/G]

umpak:
                              N
→ .1.2 .6.5 .1.6 .3.2 .3.1 .3.2 .3.2 .6.5G

minggah:
  t   t   t   t   t   t   t   t N
[.1.2 .6.5 .1.2 .3.2 .3.2 .6.5 .1.6 .2.1
 .2.1 .2.1 .2.1 .3.2 .3.2 .3.5 .1.6 .2.1
 .2.1 .2.1 .2.1 .3.2 .3.2 .3.5 .2.1 .6.5
 .1.6 .3.2 .5.6 .3.2 .3.1 .3.2 .3.2 .6.5G]

Mayang Mekar/Mayang Kara, Gendhing, kethuk
  2 kerep, pélog pathet lima (38).

buka: 5 3.21 65.5 .53. 2165 .5.5 .5.5
                     .5.6 .165N/G

```
mérong:     t       t    N
    [...5 2165 2156 2165
    15.6 1232 ..23 5656
    .... 6656 1132 .165
    ..56 5323 ..35 6535G

         t       t    N
    ..56 5323 ..35 6535
    11.. 1121 3212 .165
    15.6 1.21 3212 .165 →
    ..56 1654 2456 2165G]

umpak:      t       t    N
    →66.. 6656 .1.6 5323G

         t       t    N
    ...3 .123 .123 .123
    .6.5 .421 ..12 4565
    6542 1245 6542 1645
    .612 1645 33.. 2123G
```

minggah: Ladrang Banyak Nglangi

Mayang Sari, Gendhing, kethuk 2 kerep,
  minggah kethuk 4, pélog pathet lima (38).

buka: 5 3.21 65.5 .53. 2165
      .65. 6512 1312 .165N/G

```
mérong:     t       t    N
    [.65. 5612 1312 .165
    .... 55.6 1216 5421
    3212 .165 .612 .165→
    .65. 5612 1312 .165G

         t       t    N
    .65. 5612 1312 .165
    11.. 1121 3212 .165
    1216 5421 3212 .165
    .65. 5612 1312 .165G]
```

```
umpak:      t            t    N
          →.6.5 .3.2 .3.2 .6.5G

minggah:  t     t     t    t N
        [.6.5 .3.2 .3.2 .6.5
         .6.5 .6.5 .1.6 .2.1
         .3.2 .6.5 .3.2 .6.5
         .6.5 .3.2 .3.2 .6.5G

          t     t     t    t N
         .6.5 .3.2 .3.2 .6.5
         .2.1 .2.1 .3.2 .6.5
         .1.6 .2.1 .3.2 .6.5
         .6.5 .3.2 .3.2 .6.5G]
```

Mayar-mayar, Ketawang, sléndro
   pathet sanga (1).

buka: 666 2321 3216 2165N/G

```
      t    t N   t    t N
   [[.666 2321 3216 2165G]
```

ngelik:
```
      t    t N   t    t N
   .... 2356 2153 2356G
   .... 5561 5216 2321G
   66.. 3532 .621 6535G]
```

Médhang Miring/Kembang Tiba/Baciran,
   Ladrang, sléndro pathet nem (38).

buka: 2 .356 .2.2 .1.6 .3.2 .3.5N/G

```
      t    t N
     .3.2 .3.5
     .3.2 .3.5
     .1.2 .1.6
     2161 6535G
```

Méga Mendhung, Gendhing, kethuk 2
   arang, pélog pathet nem (10).

buka: 223 1232 .23. 3235 .632 1232N/G

mérong: t   t   N
   [..23 1232 ..23 5656 .... 2165 3365 2353
     2132 ..12 3312 .126 .... 2165 3365 2353
     2132 ..12 3312 .126 .... 6656 1126 5323
     .23. 323. 323. 1232 323. 3235 .632 1232G]

Méga Mendhung, Gendhing, kethuk 4
  .kerep, sléndro pathet nem (1).

buka: 2216 5.35 1235 1235 .235 2126N/G

mérong:t   t   t   t   N
   [..65 3356 3565 2232 .... 22.3 5653 2126
    ..61 2353 5653 2126 22.. 22.3 5653 2165
    .555 2235 2353 2126 ..61 2353 5653 2165
    .612 .165 .612 .165 .35. 235. 2356 1216G]

Menggah, Gendhing, kethuk 4 kerep,
   minggah kethuk 8, sléndro pathet nem (1).

buka: 6.12 6.5. 3.5. 3.5. 3.56 1232N/G

mérong:t   t   t   t   N
   [.352 .352 .352 .352 .352 .352 5653 2165
    .555 2235 ..56 1232 .352 5352 5653 2165
    .555 2235 ..56 1232 .352 .352 5653 2165→
    2356 3532 ..25 2353 ..5. 3.5. 3.56 1232G]

umpak: t   t   t   t   N
   →2356 3532 ..25 2353 .5.3 .5.3 .1.6 .3.2G

minggah:
    t   t   t   t   t   t   t   t N
   [.3.2 .3.2 .3.2 .3.2 .3.2 .3.2 .5.3 .6.5
    .6.5 .6.5 .6.5 .3.2 .3.2 .3.2 .5.3 .6.5
    .6.5 .6.5 .6.5 .3.2 .3.2 .3.2 .5.3 .6.5
    .1.6 .5.3 .1.6 .5.3 .5.3 .5.3 .1.6 .3.2G]

Menggak ͺLayar, Ladrang,
    sléndro pathet sanga (38).

[. 5 5 5   2 2 3 5
  2 3 5 3̲   2 1̲ 2 6
  2 2 . 3̲5̲   6̲1̲.6̲1̲ 5
  2 3 2 1   6 5 3 5G

      t   t   N
  . 5 5 5   2 2 3 5
  2 3 5 3̲   2 1̲ 2 6
  2 2 . 3̲5̲   6̲1̲.6̲1̲ 5
  2 3 2 1̲2̲   3̲5̲6̲1̲.2̲1̲G

ngelik:
      t   t   N
  . . . .   1 1 2 1
  3 2 1 2   . 1 6 5
  1 6 5 6   5 3 2 1
  2 3 2 1   6 5 3 5G]

Mènjeb/Kèjeb, Gendhing,
    kethuk 2 kerep, ndhawah kethuk
    4, sléndro pathet manyura (5).

buka: 661 6533 .356 5321 .2.6 22.2N/G

lamba: t
          .1.6 .5.3 .5.3 .2.1
          .3.2 .1.6 .5.1 .5.3
          .3.6 .1.6 .5.6 .5.3
          .356 .352 .523 5616G

dados: t   t   N
          [1561 23.1 3532 1216
          5565 33.5 61.5 6121
          3532 .126 3561 6523
          ..35 6532 12.6 1232G

          t   t   N
          1216 1523 5653 2121
          3532 .126 3561 6523
          .356 .356 1656 5323
          .356 .352 .523 5616G]

267

pangkat ndhawah:
```
       t        t    N
    1561  23.1 3532 1216
    5565  33.5 61.5 6121
    3532  .126 3561 6523
    .1.6  .3.2 .1.6 .3.2G
dhawah:  t    t    t    t N
      [.1.6 .5.3 .5.3 .2.1
       .3.2 .1.6 .2.1 .5.3
       .1.6 .1.6 .1.6 .5.3
       .1.6 .3.2 .5.3 .1.6G

        t    t    t    t N
      .2.1 .2.1 .3.2 .1.6
      .5.3 .5.3 .5.3 .2.1
      .3.2 .1.6 .2.1 .5.3
      .1.6 .3.2 .1.6 .3.2G]
```

Méntok-méntok/Méntog-méntog, Ladrang,
pelog pathet nem (3).

buka: 2 2132 6123 6532N/G

```
  t    t N        t    t N
5356 5352      2356 5365
5356 5352      2356 5365
66.. 6356      22.. 2356
2163 6535G     2163 6532G
```

Menyan Kobar, Gendhing, kethuk 4 kerep, minggah
kethuk 8, sléndro pathet sanga (2).

buka: 2 .356 5323 .52. 2356 .2.1 .6.5N/G

mérong:
```
      t        t         t          t     N
  [.1.6 .1.5 .1.6 5612 .... 2232 5323 2121
   .216 .2.1 ..16 5612 .... 2232 5323 2121
   .216 .2.1 ..16 5612 .... 2232 5323 2121→
   3532 1653 .52. 2523 .52. 2356 .2.1 .6.5G]
```

umpak minggah:
```
      t        t        t          t     N
 → .3.2 .5.3 .5.2 .5.3 .5.2 .5.6 .2.1 .6.5G
```

```
minggah:
      t     t     t     t     t     t     t     t N
  [.1.6  .1.5  .1.6  .1.2  .3.2  .3.2  .5.3  .2.1
   .2.6  .2.1  .2.6  .1.2  .3.2  .3.2  .5.3  .2.1
   .2.6  .2.1  .2.6  .1.2  .3.2  .3.2  .5.3  .2.1
   .3.2  .5.3  .5.2  .5.3  .5.2  .5.6  .2.1  .6.5G]
```

Menyan Séta, Gendhing, kethuk 2 kerep,
    minggah kethuk 4, sléndro pathet nem (2).

buka: 2 .356 .6.1 .2.1 .2.6 .3.5N/G

```
mérong:     t           t      N
       [..56 5323  ..36 3565
        ..56 5323  ..36 3565
        ..56 5323  66.. 3356 →
        ..61 6535  2356 3532G

            t           t      N
        55.. 5523  5653 2126
        33.. 6535  2353 2126
        33.. 6535  2353 2126
        22.. 2321  3265 3532G

            t           t      N
        11.. 1121  3212 .165 ]
```

umpak minggah:
```
            t      t      N
    → .5.6  .3.5  .6.5  .3.2G
```

```
minggah:  t     t     t     t N
     [.3.5  .3.5  .2.3  .1.6
      .2.3  .6.5  .2.3  .1.6
      .2.3  .6.5  .2.3  .1.6
      .3.2  .3.1  .6.5  .3.2G

       t     t     t     t N
      .3.1  .2.1  .3.2  .6.5
      .1.6  .5.3  .5.6  .3.5
      .1.6  .5.3  .5.6  .5.6
      .5.6  .3.5  .6.5  .3.2G]
```

Merak Kasimpir, Gendhing [Ketawang],
    kethuk 2 kerep, sléndro pathet manyura (1).

buka: 6 .123 .3.2 .2.1 .3.2 .1.6N/G

mérong: t   t   N
        [.165 33.. 33.5 6356
         3561 22.. 3132 .126G

ngelik: t   t   N
         .165 33.. 33.2 5321
         ..32 .165 33.5 6356G

             t   t   N
         .165 33.. 33.2 5321
         ..32 .165 33.5 6356G

             t   t   N
         .165 2321 2321 6132
         6123 .... 33.5 6356G

             t   t   N
         .632 11.. 1132 5321
         612. 2212 3212 .126G]

Mijil, Jineman, sléndro
    pathet manyura (3).

buka celuk: 6N

                 N
        [3621 5321
         2132 5321
         33.. 6532
         5653 2126G
         1632]suwuk

Mijil/Mijil Yogan, Ketawang [gendhing
    kemanak], sléndro pathet sanga (8).

buka celuk: 1N/G

```
        t                    t        N
[.   .   1   2      . 1 6 5 6 1 5 .3
  2   .   2 3 2      . 1 1   6 1 1G

        t                    t        N
  .   .   . .       . .   . .
  .   .   3 5 3      . 2 .   2 355G

        t                    t        N
  .   .   5   6      . 1 5 .32   .
  6 1 6 1 6 1 6 1 1   .   2 3 1G

        t                    t        N
  .   .   1 6 5      . .   . .
  .   .   6   6      1 2 2   1 1 1G

        t                    t        N
  .   .   . 232     .   6   1 2 1
  . 6 .   6 1 6 1 1   .   . 6 6G

        t                    t        N
  .   .   . .   . .   . .
  3   3   3 5 3      . 2 .   2 355G  suwuk

        t                    t        N
  .   .   5   6      . 1 5 .32   .
  2   2   2 3 2      . 1 1   6 1 1G

        t                    t        N
  .   .   . .   . .   . .
  .   .   2   5 6    .   6   5 6 1G6 .

        t                    t        N
  .   .   . .       1   6   . 5 6 1
  6   6   6 1 6      . 5 .   5 611G]
```

Mijil Lagu Dhempel, Ketawang,
   sléndro pathet sanga (8).

(from Gendhing Lagu Dhempel)

buka celuk:

```
  t    t N   t    t N
[..16 1653 2232 5321G
 .... 1121 3353 2235G
 ..56 15.3 2232 1121G
 612. 2321 612. 2321G
 3265 66.. 6616 5561G
 ..16 1553 2216 5321G
 .... 1121 22.3 5616G
 .165 .... 2232 1121G]
```

Mijil Lagu Dhempel/Mijil Lamun Sira,
   Ketawang, sléndro pathet sanga (1).

buka celuk:
```
  t    t N   t    t N
[1.16 1653 22.6 2321G
 .... 1121 3353 2235G
 .532 .... 6612 5321G
 612. 2321 6612 5321G
 3265 66.. 6616 5561G
 ..16 1653 22.6 2321G
 .... 1121 22.3 5656G
 .165 .... 2216 1121G
 ..16 1653 2216 2321G
 .... 1121 3353 2235G
 .652 22.. 6612 5321G
 612. 2321 6612 5321G
 3265 66.. 6616 5561G]
```

Mijil Ludira/Mijil Wastra Ngrangrang,
Ladrang, pélog pathet barang (8).

(from Gendhing Ludira Madu)

buka celuk:

```
 t    t N
..23 2756
3356 3532
.... 2232
5565 3356G

 t    t N
..67 653.
3323 2232
.... 2232
7723 2232G

 t    t N
..23 2767
2723 2232
3276 5676
5565 3356G

 t    t N
..67 653.
3356 3532
.... 2232
33.5 6767G

 t    t N
[ ... 2767
2767 6672
..23 2756
3356 3532G

 t    t N
.... 2232
5565 3356
..67 653.
3323 2232G

 t    t N
.... 2232
7723 2232
..23 2767
2723 2232G

 t    t N
3276 5676
5565 3356
..67 653. →
3356 3532G
```

```
  t    t N
 .... 2232
 7723 2232
 3276 5676
 33.5 6767G ]
```
→ suwuk:

```
 3327 3532G
```

Mijil Ludira/Mijil Wastra Ngrangrang,
      Ketawang, pélog pathet barang (8).

(from Ladrang Mijil Ludira)

```
  t    t N  t    t N
[.... 2767 2767 6672G
 ..23 2756 3356 3532G
 .... 2232 5565 3356G
 ..67 653. 3323 2232G
 .... 2232 7723 2232G
 ..23 2767 2723 2232G
 3276 5676 5565 3356G →
 ..67 653. 3356 3532G
 .... 2232 7723 2232G
 3276 5676 33.5 6767G]
```

suwuk:
```
  t    t N  t     t N
→..67 653. 3327 3532G
```

Mijil Sulastri, Ketawang,
     pélog pathet barang (3).

umpak:
```
 [.2.3 .2.7 .3.2 .7.6G
  .2.3 .2.7 33.. 3356G
```

ngelik:
```
  .... 7576 7732 .2.7G
  .2.3 .2.7 .2.3 .2.7G
  55.. 7653 5627 3276G]
```

Miling, Gendhing, kethuk 4 awis, minggah
    kethuk 8, sléndro pathet manyura (1).

buka: 236 ..23 55.. 6356 .532N/G

mérong:
```
             t                    t
[.253 .253 .253 2356 .... 6623 55.. 6356
 .... 6623 55.. 6356 33.. 3353 6521 6132N
 .123 2126 2321 6535 .555 2235 2353 2126
 .... 6656 3561 6535 .356 3563 6521 6132N
 .123 2126 2321 6535 .555 2235 2353 2126
 .... 6656 3561 6535 .356 3563 6521 6132N
 5653 2126 3565 2232 5325 3356 3565 2232
 11.. 1121 3212 .356 ..23 55.. 6356 .532N/G]
```

minggah:
```
    t    t    t    t    t    t    t    t N
[.5.3 .5.2 .5.3 .5.6 .2.1 .5.6 .2.1 .5.3
 .2.1 .2.3 .1.2 .1.6 .1.6 .1.6 .2.1 .5.3
 .2.1 .2.3 .1.2 .6.5 .6.5 .1.6 .1.6 .2.1
 .3.2 .1.6 .3.2 .1.6 .3.2 .3.2 .3.1 .3.2G]
```


Miyang Gong, Gendhing, kethuk 2 awis, minggah
    kethuk 4, pélog pathet nem (11).

buka: 6 .6.6 .565 ..56 .532 .2.3 .6.5N/G

mérong:
```
       t                  t           N
[..53 2365 ..53 2356 ..76 5326 ..76 5312
 ..35 3212 165. 5612 ..35 3212 165. 5612
```
```
            t          t    N
          .126 .... 66.. 5535 →
          ..53 6532 ..23 5.65G]
```

umpak minggah:
```
                t        t    N
          → .6.5 .3.2 .3.2 .6.5G
```

minggah:
```
             t    t    t    t N
          [.6.5 .1.6 .3.2 .6.5
           .6.5 .1.6 .3.2 .3.2
           .3.2 .3.2 .3.2 .5.6
           .5.6 .5.6 .3.2 .6.5G]
```

Moncèr, Ladrang, pélog
    pathet barang (3).

buka: .235 6532 7653 5676N/G

umpak: t   t N
    [5376 5376
     33.. 6532
     3235 6532
     7653 5676G

ngelik: t   t N
     ..63 5676
     7767 6532
     3235 6532
     7653 5676G]

Moncèr, Ladrang, sléndro
    pathet manyura (3).

buka: .235 6532 1653 5616N/G

umpak: t   t N
    [5316 5316
     3323 6532
     3235 6532
     1653 5616G

         t   t N
     ..63 5616
     1161 6532
     3235 6532
     1653 5616G]

Monggang, Gendhing (11).

buka kendhang: 5N/G

     N   N
  [1615 1615G]

276

Mongkok/[Menggok?], Gendhing, kethuk 4 kerep,
minggah kethuk 8, pélog pathet nem (1).

buka: [123.216.6.]x2 13 .5.3 .6.5 3212N/G

mérong:
```
         t        t        t        t      N
[..23  1232  ..23  5653  .523  5654  2.44  2126
...6  .2.6  2.61  2353  6535  .421  6123  5.65
.... 55..  55.3  2356  .567  5676  .535  3212
..23  6532  6535  2353  .53.  5365  4512  3212G]
```

umpak:
```
         t        t        t        t      N
..23  1232  ..23  5653  .523  5654  2.44  2165
...5  .235  ..53  2356  ..61  2.32  5654  2165
...5  .235  ..53  2356  ..61  2.32  5654  2126
.3.2  .1.6  .3.2  .1.6  .22.  3216  33..  6532G
```

minggah:
```
     t    t    t    t    t    t    t    t N
[.321 3216 33.. 6532 33.. 3353 6532 3565
.532 3532 5654 2123 .... 3353 6532 3565
.532 3532 5654 2123 55.. 5356 6676 5421
6612 3216 3532 3216 22.. 2621 6535 2232G

     t    t    t    t    t    t    t    t N
..61 22.3 5676 5323 .53. 6521 6676 5323
.35. 6532 ..56 5323 .53. 6521 612. 3212
.35. 6532 .35. 6535 2325 2356 6676 5421
6612 3216 3532 3216 22.. 3216 33.. 6532G]
```

Mongkok Dhelik, Gendhing, kethuk 4
awis, sléndro pathet nem (4).

buka: 6 .6.1 .6.5 .63. 3532 .161 2312N/G

mérong:
```
         t                       t
[..23 .532 66.1 6523 6535 3212 66.1 6523
6535 3212 66.1 6523 6535 .321 6132 .165N
.61. 1653 .223 5635 .61. 1653 .223 5635
33.. 33.. 6535 3212 5653 2121 3265 3235N
.61. 1653 .223 5635 .61. 1653 .223 5635
33.. 33.. 6535 3212 5653 2121 3265 3235N →
11.. 3216 3565 2232 ..25 2356 3565 2232
66.. 66.. 3561 6535 .63. 3532 .161 2312N/G]
```

umpak minggah:
```
      t         t         t         t      N
→.66. 6621 .55. 6621 .55. 6621 5153 6532G
```

minggah: Rondha Maya

Montro, Gendhing, kethuk 2 kerep, minggah
  kethuk 4, sléndro pathet manyura (3).

buka: .661 6523 .12. 2321 3216 .5.3N/G

mérong: t   t   N
    [.132 .132 5653 2126
     .132 .132 5653 2126
     33.. 3356 3561 6523 →
     ..61 2321 3216 .5.3G]

umpak minggah:
          t   t   N
     →.2.1 .2.6 .3.2 .1.6G

minggah:t   t   t   t N
    [.2.1 .2.1 .2.3 .1.6
     .2.1 .2.1 .2.3 .1.6
     .5.3 .5.6 .2.1 .5.3
     .2.1 .5.6 .3.2 .5.6G]

Montro Kendho, Gendhing, kethuk 2 awis,
  minggah kethuk 4, sléndro pathet manyura (4).

buka: 6616 5321 ..23 2126 .653 2126N/G

mérong: t   t   N
    [.... 3532 5321 3532 5321 3532 6123 2126
     .... 3532 5321 3532 5321 3532 6123 2126
     33.. 33.5 61.6 5356 .... 6653 22.3 5635 →
     .... 5535 6616 5321 6123 2126 .653 2126G]

umpak minggah:
          t   t   N
    →.3.5 .3.6 .1.6 .2.1 .2.3 .1.6 .5.3 .1.6G

minggah: t   t   t   t N
    [.2.1 .2.1 .2.3 .1.6
     .2.1 .2.1 .2.3 .1.6
     .5.3 .5.6 .2.1 .5.3
     .2.1 .2.6 .3.2 .1.6G]

Montro Kendho, Gendhing, kethuk 4 kerep,
    minggah kethuk 4, sléndro pathet manyura (1).

buka: .661 6523 .12. 2126 6653 2126N/G

mérong:
```
        t           t           t           t      N
[.... 3532 5321 3532 5321 3532 6123 2126
 .... 3532 5321 3532 5321 3532 6123 2126
 33.. 33.. 33.5 6356 .... 1653 22.3 5.65
 .... 5535 6616 5323 212. 2126 6653 2126G]
```

minggah:
```
          t
[.2.1 .2.1 .2.3 .1.6
 .2.1 .2.1 .2.3 .1.6
 .5.3 .5.6 .2.1 .5.3
 .2.1 .2.6 .3.2 .1.6G]
```

Montro Madura, Gendhing; kenong 1 & 2, kethuk
    4 kerep; kenong 3 & 4, kethuk 2 kerep;
    minggah, kenong 1 & 2, kethuk 8; kenong
    3 & 4, kethuk 4; sléndro pathet manyura (16).

buka: .3.3 .2.3 21.2 .1.2 .126 .6.5 .653N/G

mérong:
```
      t           t           t           t      N
[..35 1653 ..35 6121 ..12 3216 3561 6523
 ..35 1653 ..35 6121 ..12 3216 3561 6523
                     66.. 6635 6165 3212
                     5321 2353 6532 .126G

      t           t           t           t      N
 .666 3532 5321 3532 5321 2353 6532 .126
 .666 3532 5321 3532 5321 2353 6532 .126
                     33.. 3361 2253 2121 →
                     ..12 3216 3561 6523G]
```

umpak:
```
        t           t
→.3.2 .1.6 .2.1 .5.3G
```

minggah:
```
 t    t    t    t    t    t    t    t N
[.5.3 .5.3 .5.3 .2.1 .2.1 .2.6 .5.6 .5.3
 .5.3 .5.3 .5.3 .2.1 .2.1 .2.6 .5.6 .5.3
                     .5.6 .5.3 .5.3 .3.2
                     .3.1 .2.3 .1.2 .1.6G

 t    t    t    t    t    t    t    t N
 .1.6 .3.2 .3.1 .3.2 .3.1 .2.3 .1.2 .1.6
 .1.6 .3.2 .3.1 .3.2 .3.1 .2.3 .1.2 .1.6
                     .5.3 .5.3 .2.3 .2.1
                     .2.1 .2.6 .2.1 .5.3G]
```

Mudhatama, Gendhing, kethuk 2 kerep,
   sléndro pathet sanga (3).

buka: ...5 5616 ..61 6532 1612 1121N/G

mérong: t   t   N
   [[2621 2312 5616 5321
     2621 2312 5616 5321
     5235 .535 6132 6165
     6561 6532 1612 1121G]

ngelik: t   t   N
   ...1 1121 3212 .165
   .621 ..1. 3212 .165
   1656 5321 165. 5612
   66.1 6532 1612 1121G]

minggah: Ladrang Mudhatama

280

Mudhatama, Ladrang, sléndro
pathet sanga (3).

buka: 5235 1652 5321N/G

umpak: t   t N
       6562 6561
       6562 6561
       2321 5235
       1652 5321G suwuk

ngelik:t   t N
       5235 6165
       6132 6165
       6561 6532
       1612 5321G

Mugi Rahayu, Ladrang, sléndro
pathet manyura (2).

buka: 66. 6165 1653 6132N/G

      t   t N
   [361. 3612
     361. 3612
     33.. 6165
     1653 6132G]

Muncar, Gendhing, kethuk 2 kerep, dhawah
kethuk 4, pélog pathet barang (22).

buka: 235. 2356 7756 22.2N/G

dados: t   t   N
   [.365 ..56 7756 3532
    6567 6532 .3.2 .765
    7675 7672 3532 .765 →
    235. 2356 7756 3532G]

pangkat dhawah:
        t   t   N
   →.6.5 .3.6 .7.6 .3.2G

```
ndhawah:
       t    t    t    t N
    [.6.5 .6.5 .7.6 .3.2
     .6.7 .3.2 .3.2 .6.5
     .6.5 .3.2 .3.2 .6.5
     .6.5 .3.6 .7.6 .3.2G]
```

Muncar, Gendhing, kethuk 2 kerep,
    pélog pathet barang (1).

buka: [2.272765.]x2 .235 2356 7756 .532N/G

```
mérong:    t         t    N
       [.365 .... 7656 .532
        6567 6532 7372 7675
        7675 7672 3532 7675
        235. 2356 7756 .532G]
```

minggah: Ladrang Sumyar

Mundhuk, Gendhing [Ketawang], kethuk 8 kerep,
    minggah kethuk 16, pélog pathet nem (13).

buka: odangiyah .6.6 .7.6 .535 3212N/G

```
mérong:

     .6.6 .535 .421 6123 .532 .6.5 .421 6123
     .532 .6.5 .4.2 4521 ..12 3216 ..65 3523N
    [..35 .653 .5.3 2356 .567 .656 .535 3212
     ..23 .532 6535 .323 55.. 5653 2356 .535N/G

       t         t         t         t
     .22. 6535 .421 6123 .532 .6.5 .421 6123
     .532 .6.5 .4.2 4521 ..12 3216 ..65 3523N]→

ompak:

    →..35 .653 .5.3 2356 ..76 5326 ..76 5312
     .312 3532 .312 3532 .66. 6535 4216 5616N/G

minggah:
       t    t    t    t    t    t    t    t
    [.12. 2321 2123 2126 .12. 2321 2123 2126
     .12. 2321 2123 2126 .123 2126 ..65 3565N
     7653 6535 7653 6535 .22. 2356 6676 5312
     .312 3532 .312 3532 .66. 6535 4216 5616N/G]
```

282

Muntap, Gendhing, kethuk 4 kerep, minggah
kethuk 8, pélog pathet lima (1).

buka: [3 .2̄16 5.5.] x2 .3.2 3253 .561 2321N/G

mérong:
```
     t         t         t         t    N
[5616 .1.6  .1.2  .321  .3.2  .165  33.. 6535
 .654 22..  2254  .521  61.6  2165  33.. 6535
 .654 22..  2254  .521  61.6  2165  33.. 6535
 .676 5424  5654  2165  .3.2  3253  .561 2321G

     t         t         t         t    N
5616 .1.6   .1.2  .321  .3.2  .165  33.5 6356
.765 42..   2254  .521  65.6  1232  .321 6535
..56 2165   15.6  1232  ..23  1232  16.1 3216 →
..62 .123   .123  2165  .3.2  3253  .561 2321G]
```

umpak:
```
     t         t         t         t    N
→..62 .123  .123  2165  ....  55.. 5654 5245G

     t         t         t  ___    t    N
.... 55..   5654  5245  ..54 6542141.2 4565
..56 .532   ..23  2121  ..13 .212 .1.6 .5.3
...3 6532   ..24  .521  .... 11.. 11.2 3212
.216 5616   ..61  3216  33.. 6532 3216 5323G
```

minggah:
```
    t    t    t    t    t    t    t    t N
[.33. 3356 1216 .654 2465 .421 2353 2121
 .312 35.4 2.32 1654 .44. 4456 1654 2121
 66.. 6656 1216 5424 6546 4561 2321 6544
 6561 6544 6561 6544 6546 4561 2321 6544G

    t    t    t    t    t    t    t    t N
6546 4561 2321 6544 6561 6544 33.. 2121
.312 35.4 2.32 1654 .44. 4456 1654 2121
.... 11.. 11.2 3565 2325 2356 6676 5421
66.. 3216 ..61 3216 33.. 6532 3216 5323G]
```

Nawung Branta, Gendhing, pélog pathet nem (22).

buka: 126 ...6 66.3 .126 .67. 7656 3565 22.2G

lamba:

```
         t         t   N
   .2.2 .1.3 .5.2 .1.3
   .5.2 .5.4 .2.4 .1.6
   .6.6 .1.6 .1.6 .1.3
   .3.2 3521 6123 5676G
```

dados:

```
         t              t           N
 [ . 6̄6̄6̄ 6̄6̄ 6 7 6 5   3 3 . 5   6 7 6 7
   5 6 7 2 . 7 5 6   3 5 6 5   3 2 3 2
   6 1 2 3 6 5 3 2   6 5 3 5   2 3 5 3
   5 6 7 . 7 6 5 6   3 5 6 5   3 2 3 2G
```

```
       t              t           N
 . 2̄2̄2̄ 2   3 1 2 3   6 5 3 2   3 1 2 3
 6 5 3 2   5 6 5 3   2 4 5 4   2 1 2 6
 . 6̄6̄6̄ 6   2 1 2 6   2 1 2 6   2 1 2 3
 . 3̄3̄3̄ 2   5 6 2 1   6 1 2 3   5 6 7 6G ]
```

minggah lajeng ndhawah:

```
       t              t           N
 . 6̄6̄6̄ 3   2 1 3 2   3 1 2 3   2 1 6 5
 . 5 . 5   . 3 2 6   . 6 1 6   5 3 2 6
 . 6 5 3   2 3 5 6   1 6 5 3   2 3 5 6
           t          t         t
 2 2 . 2   3 2 1 6   3 5 6 5   3 2 3 2G
```

ndhawah:

```
     t          t          t          t    N
 [ .5.3 .2.5 .2.3 .5.3 .6.5 .6.3 .6.7 .6.5
   ...2 .2.5 .2.3 .5.3 .6.5 .6.3 .6.7 .6.5
   .6.3 .5.6 .5.3 .2.. .1.1 .2.1 .3.5 .3.2
   .6.5 .6.6 66.5 .4.5 .3.2 .1.6 .1.2 .1.6G
```

```
     t          t          t          t    N
   ...2 .2.. .3.1 .3.2 .5.6 .5.4 .2.1 .6.5
   ...2 .2.. .3.1 .3.2 .5.6 .5.4 .2.1 .6.5
   ...2 .2.. .3.1 .3.2 .5.6 .5.4 .2.1 .6.5
   .6.3 .5.6 .5.3 .2.. .1.1 .2.1 .3.5 .3.2G ]
```

suwuk:

```
     t          t          t          t
   ...5 .2.3 .5.5 ...3 .6.5 .3.2 .223 .6.5G
```

284

Okrak-okrak, Gendhing, kethuk 2 kerep, minggah
    kethuk 4, sléndro pathet manyura (38).

buka: 2 .356 .6.6 .5.3 .532 .365N/G

mérong: t   t   N
    [1656 5323 6532 3565
     1656 5323 6535 3212
     .62. 62.6 2.23 2121 →
     ..32 .126 3352 3565G]

umpak minggah:
        t   t   N
    →.3.2 .1.6 .3.2 .6.5G

minggah:
     t   t   t   t N
    [.6.5 .1.6 .3.2 .6.5
     .6.5 .1.6 .3.2 .3.2
     .3.2 .3.2 .3.2 .5.6
     .5.6 .5.6 .3.2 .6.5G]

Onang-onang, Gendhing, kethuk 2 kerep,
    minggah kethuk 4, pélog pathet nem (3).

buka: 6 6126 .6.1 .2.1 .2.6 .3.5N/G

mérong: t   t   N
    [..53 6532 ..23 5635
     11.. 1121 3212 .165 →
     ..5. 5535 66.5 3356
     2321 6535 2356 3532G

         t   t   N
     66.. 6535 2356 3532
     55.. 5523 5654 2121
     3212 .165 22.3 1232
     ..23 5321 3532 .165G]

umpak: t   t   N
    →.3.5 .3.6 .5.3 .5.6
     .2.1 .6.5 .6.5 .3.2G

285

```
minggah:  t     t     t     t N
      [.3.2  .6.5  .6.5  .3.2
       .3.2  .6.5  .6.5  .2.1
       .2.1  .6.5  .6.5  .3.2
       .3.5  .2.1  .2.1  .6.5G

        t     t     t     t N
       .6.5  .3.2  .3.2  .6.5
       .2.1  .2.1  .3.2  .6.5
       .6.5  .1.6  .5.3  .1.6
       .5.6  .3.5  .6.5  .3.2G]
```

Onang-onang, Gendhing, kethuk 2 kerep,
    dhawah, kethuk 4, sléndro pathet sanga (5).

buka: 5612 .2.2 5321 1216 55.5N/G

```
lamba:    t           t     N
       .5.3  .5.2  .2.3  .6.5
       .1.1  .1.2  .3.2  .6.5
       .5.5  .3.5  .6.3  .5.6
       1561  6535  3365  3232G

dados:    t           t     N
      [66.6  2165  3365  3232
       55..  5523  5653  2121
       3532  1635  22.3  1232
       ..23  5321  3532  1635G

        t           t     N
       ..53  6532  ..23  5635
       11..  1161  3532  .165
       ....  5535  6653  5616
       1561  6535  3365  3232G]
```

pangkat dhawah:
```
        t           t     N
       66.6  2165  3365  3232
       55..  5523  5653  2121
       3532  1635  22.3  1232
       .3.5  .2.1  .2.1  .6.5G
```

dhawah:
```
      t    t    t    t N
 [.6.5 .3.2 .3.2 .6.5
  .2.1 .2.1 .3.2 .6.5
  .6.5 .1.6 .5.6 .3.6
  .2.1 .6.5 .3.5 .3.2G

      t    t    t    t N
  .3.2 .6.5 .6.5 .3.2
  .3.2 .6.5 .6.5 .2.1
  .2.1 .6.5 .6.5 .3.2
  .3.5 .2.1 .2.1 .6.5G]
```

Opak Apem, Ladrang, pélog pathet nem (1).
(minggah to Gendhing Érang-érang Pagelèn)

```
     t                   t             N
.65. 5612 3265 2123 6523 ..56 .532 3565
.65. 5612 3265 2123 6523 ..56 .532 3565
.53. 5656 .6.5 .3.2 ...5 ...3 ...5 ...2
...3 .3.. .3.5 .1.6 .356 .35. .552 3565G
```

Pacar Banyu, Gendhing, kethuk 2 kerep,
    dhawah kethuk 4, sléndro pathet manyura (5).

buka: 661 6535 .35. 6532 5616 33.3N/G

lamba:
```
      t         t    N
  .3.5 .1.6 .1.5 .2.3
  .3.5 .1.6 .1.5 .2.3
  .6.3 .5.6 .2.1 .6.5
  .35. 6532 5616 5323G
```

dados:
```
      t         t    N
 [..35 6156 2165 3523
  ..35 6156 2165 3523
  56.3 5616 3561 6535
  .35. 6532 5616 5323G]
```

```
pangkat dhawah:
     t         t    N
 ..35 6156 2165 3523
 ..35 6156 2165 3523
 56.3 5616 3561 6535
 .6.3 .5.2 .5.6 .5.3G
```

```
dhawah:
     t    t    t    t N
 [.5.3 .1.6 .1.6 .5.3
  .5.3 .1.6 .1.6 .5.3
  .1.6 .1.6 .2.1 .6.5
  .6.3 .5.2 .5.6 .5.3G]
```

Pacar Cina, Ladrang, sléndro
pathet nem (20).

buka: 253 .253 5561 2312N/G

```
  t    t N
.321 6132
.321 6132
.253 .253
5561 2312G
```

```
  t     t N
[.321 6132
 .321 6123
 .253 .253
 ..52 5565G
```

```
  t     t N
.... 5535
..56 7767
..76 5323
35.2 3535G
```

```
  t     t N
.... 5535
..56 7656
..76 5323
.232 5321G
```

```
  t     t N
.111 2321
.111 2321
.21. 2165
..56 1232G]
```

Pacul Gowang, Ladrang,
pélog pathet barang (38).

(minggah to Gendhing Tunggul
and Gendhing Tunggul Kawung)

```
       t         t    N
[.5.7 .5.6 .5.2 .5.3
 .5.7 .5.6 .5.2 .5.3
 .5.7 .5.6 .5.7 .5.6
 .22. 2356 .5.2 .5.3G]
```

Padhang Bulan, Ketawang, sléndro
pathet manyura (9).

buka celuk: 6N/G

```
    t    t N    t    t N
[ .1.6 .1.6 .2.1 .3.2G
  .3.1 .2.6 .2.1 .3.2G
  .3.1 .2.6 .3.2 .3.1G
  .2.1 .2.3 .1.2 .1.6G ]
```

Pakumpulan, Ladrang, sléndro
pathet sanga (1).

buka: 66.. 6532 3561 2165N/G

umpak: t   t N
          [1561 5612
           3532 1615
           23.3 5653
           2321 6535G

ngelik:
          t   t   N
      2 2 . 3̄5̄ 6̄1̄.6̄1̄ 5
      6 3 . 2 2 3 6 5
      1 6 5 6 5 3 2 1
      .6̄.5̄.6̄.6̄ .5̄.6̄.5̄1

          t   t   N
   . . . 2 . . . 1   . . . 5   . . . 6
   . . 2 1̄ 2 6̄ . .2̄ 1̄2̄6̄5̄6̄1̄2̄ .̄2̄1 6 5̄5̄
  1̄5̄6̄1̄3̄1̄2̄5̄1̄5̄6̄1̄3̄1̄2̄   . . 2 1   . 6 . 5
   . 6 6 . 6 5 3 2   3 5 6 1   2 1 6 5G]
```
```

Palara-lara, Gendhing, kethuk 2 kerep,
    minggah kethuk 4, sléndro pathet sanga (1).

buka: 5.5. 6165 6.61 6565 3212N/G

mérong: t   t   N
    [3265 ..23 5653 2121
    3265 11.. 3212 .165
    .... 55.6 .656 1656 →
    .61. 1656 5323 2121G]

umpak: t   t   N
    →.5.6 .5.6 .2.3 .2.1G

inggah: t   t   t   t N
    [.6.5 .6.5 .2.3 .2.1
    .6.5 .2.1 .3.2 .6.5
    .6.5 .6.5 .1.2 .1.6
    .5.6 .5.6 .2.3 .2.1G]

Pancat Nyana, Gendhing, kethuk 2
    kerep, sléndro pathet sanga (1).

buka: 1.1. 1656 11.. 1312 .126 .1.5N/G

mérong: t   t   N
    .1.6 .1.5 .1.6 5612
    .... 22.3 5653 2121
    5616 5321 5616 5321
    .66. 5612 .621 6535G

Pangkur, Gendhing [Ketawang], sléndro
pathet manyura (gendhing kemanak) (8).

buka celuk: 2N/G

```
      t                        t        N
 .  .   1̄ 3̄ 1          . 1 1̄ .2̄2 3̄ 3
. 2 2   2̄ 1̄ 1          . 1 1̄ .2̄2 .3̄1 2.
                                      G
      t                        t        N
 .  .   2̄ 1̄ 6          .   .    .    .
. 1̄ 1   2̄ 1̄ 1          . 1 1̄ .2̄2 .3̄1 2.
                                      G
      t                        t        N
 .  .   2̄ 3̄ 1          . 2̄ 1̄ 2 6   5̄ 3
. 3̄ 3   3̄ 5̄3̄3         . 2 2 .1̄1 2 2G
      t                        t        N
 .  .3̄ 2̄ 1̄ 3         . 1 1̄ .2̄2 3̄ 2
. 1̄ 1 .2̄2 3̄ 3         . 2 2 .1̄1 2̄3̄2G
      t                        t        N
[.  .    .    .         .    .    .    .
. 1̄ 1 .2̄2 3̄ 3         . 2 2 .1̄3 5̄2̄1G
      t                        t        N
 .  .   2̄ 1̄ 6          .    .    .    .
. 1̄ 1   2̄ 1̄ 1          . 1 1̄ .2̄2 .3̄1 2.
                                      G
      t                        t        N
 .  .   2̄ 1̄ 6          .    .    .    .
. 1̄ 1   2̄ 1̄ 1          . 1 1̄ .2̄2 .3̄1 2.
                                      G
      t                        t        N
 .  .   2̄ 3̄ 1          . 2̄ 1̄ 2 6   5̄ 3
.   3   5̄ 3̄ 3         . 2 2   1̄ 2 2G
      t                        t        N
 .  .    .    .         .    .    .    .
. 1̄ 1 .2̄2 3̄ 3         . 2 2 .1̄1 2 2G
      t                        t        N
 .  .   2̄ 1̄ 6          .    .    .    .
. 1̄ 1   2̄ 1̄ 1          . 1 1̄ .2̄2 .3̄1 2
                                      G
      t                        t        N
 .  .   2̄ 3̄ 1          . 2̄ 1̄ 2 6   5̄ 3
. 3̄ 3   3̄ 5̄3̄3         . 2 2 .1̄1 2 2G
      t                        t        N
 . .3̄ 2̄ 1̄ 3          . 1 1̄ .2̄2 3̄ 2
. 1̄ 1 .2̄2 3̄ 3         . 2 2 .1̄1 2̄3̄2G]
```

Pangkur, Ladrang, pélog
  pathet barang (3).

buka: .3.2 .3.2 3732 .7.6N/G

```
    t    t N
 [ 3237 3276
   7632 5327
   3532 6532
   5327→3276G]
```

```
          N
 →.3.2 .7.6G
```

irama III:
```
    t         t    N
[[.3.2 .3.7 .3.2 .7.6
  77.. 6672 3263 .2.7
  ...3 ...2 3253 6532
  6732 6327→.3.2 .7.6G]
```

```
      →.3.2 .7.2G
```

ngelik:
```
    t         t    N
  ..2. 4323 ..35 6756
  22.. 4327 3265 7653
  ..35 7576 3567 6532
  6732 6327 .3.2 .7.6G]
```

Pangkur, Ladrang, sléndro
  pathet manyura (3).

buka: .3.2 .3.2 3132 .1.6N/G

```
    t    t N
   3231 3216
   1632 5321
   3532 6532
   5321 3216G
```

Pangkur, Ladrang, sléndro
pathet sanga (3).

buka: .2.1 .2.1 2211 .6.5N/G

```
      t    t N
   [2126 2165
    6521 3216
    2321 5321
    3216→2165G]
            N
   →...1 .6.5G
```

minggah:
```
      t         t    N
  [[.2.1 .2.6 .2.1 .6.5
    66.. 5561 2152 .1.6
    ...2 ...1 2132 5321
    5621 5216→.2.1 .6.5G]
           →.2.1 .6.1G
```

ngelik:
```
      t         t    N
    ..1. 3212 ..23 5635
    11.. 3216 2153 6532
    ..23 5635 2356 5321
    5621 5216 .2.1 .6.5G]
```

Pangkur Dhudha Kasmaran, Ketawang,
    sléndro pathet sanga (1).

buka: 666 2211 2216 2165N/G

umpak: t   t N t   t N
   [[66.. 2321 3216 2165G]

ngelik: t   t N t   t N
    22.. 2235 .565 3235G
    11.. 1165 .565 3212G
    ..2. 2232 3565 3212G
    11.. 1165 .612 .165G]

Pangkur Paripurna, Ketawang,
   [pélog pathet lima] (18).

umpak: t   t N t   t N
   [[..56 1121 2353 2121G]

ngelik:
   t   t N t   t N
  55.. 5653 .323 2121G
  ..12 3212 .165 2353G
  .... 3123 5676 5323G
  11.5 6121 2353 2121G]

Pangrembé, Ketawang, sléndro
   pathet manyura (1).

buka: 6 .123 .2.1 .3.2 .1.6N/G

umpak: t   t N t   t N
   [[.2.3 .2.1 .3.2 .1.6G] x2

ngelik: t   t N t   t N
  11.. 3216 3265 1653G
  22.. 6123 .132 .126G]

Pangrawit, Gendhing, kethuk 8 kerep, minggah
   kethuk 16, pélog pathet lima (1).

buka: [5.53.1235]x2 .6 .6.7 .6.5 .3.2 .5.3N/G

mérong: t   t   t   t
  [..31 .3.2 3.35 6532 .321 .3.2 3.35 6532
  .321 .3.2 3.35 6532 3.35 2321 ..12 3565N
  ..57 5676 776536523 55.7 5676 776536523
  55.7 5676 776536532 52.3 6532 .4.2 4521N
  ..13 .212 3.35 6532 .321 .3.2 3.35 6532
  .321 .3.2 3.35 6532 3.35 2321 66.. 2321N
  .216 .2.1 .216 .2.1 23.. 6532 3216 2165 →
  15.6 2165 15.6 2165 66.. 6676 .532 .5.3N/G]

umpak minggah
   t   t   t   t
→..56 7756 .756 7756 .756 7756 .532 .5.3N/G

294

minggah:
```
     t     t     t     t     t     t     t     t
[.635 6756 .532 .5.3 .635 6756 .532 .5.3
 .635 6756 .532 .5.3 .4.2 .4.1 ..12 3565N
 .3.6 .3.5 .3.6 .3.5 .3.6 .3.5 3213 1232
 3216 5365 323. 3235 323. 3235 6542 4521N
 323. 3235 6542 4521 323. 3235 6542 4521
 323. 3235 6542 4521 66.. 6656 7767 5676N
 5325 2352 5325 2356 5325 2356 7.76 5421
 656. 6521 656. 6521 ..56 .1.6 .1.6 5424N/G

     t     t     t     t     t     t     t     t
 6546 4561 2321 6544 6546 4561 2321 6544
 6546 4561 2321 6544 6561 6544 .3.2 .3.5N
 .3.6 .3.5 .3.6 .3.5 .3.6 .3.5 3213 1232
 3216 5365 323. 3235 323. 3235 6542 5421N
 323. 3235 6542 4521 323. 3235 6542 4521
 323. 3235 6542 4521 66.. 66.. 22.. 2321N
 .216 .2.1 .216 .2.1 23.. 6532 3216 2165
 ..56 7756 .756 7756 .756 7756 .532 .5.3N/G]
```

Paré Anom, Gendhing, kethuk 2 kerep, minggah
kethuk 4, sléndro pathet manyura (16).

buka: 661 6523 .561 .2.6 .3.5 .3.2N/G

mérong: t   t   N
```
[..23 5321 6123 2126
 22.. 22.3 5653 2121
 3212 .161 2353 2121
 33.. 6532 1232 .126G

      t          t     N
 ..61 2165 3561 3216
 33.. 33.5 61.6 5356 →
 3561 6535 61.6 5323
 11.. 3216 3565 3212G]
```

umpak: t   t   N
```
→.6.1 .6.5 .1.6 .5.3
 .2.1 .2.6 .3.5 .3.2G
```

minggah:
```
      t     t     t     t N
[.5.3 .5.3 .5.3 .1.2
:5.3 .5.3 .5.3 .1.2
 .3.2 .5.6 .2.1 .5.3
 .5.6 .3.2 .3.2 .1.6G]
```

Pari Gentang, Gendhing, kethuk 4 awis, minggah
kethuk 8, pélog pathet barang (1).

buka: [.2.272765.5..]x2 .276 ..7. 567.
6535 2232N/G

mérong: t   t
[..23 5535 .2.5 2356 .567 6535 .2.5 2356
..7. 567. 5676 5676 ..7. 567. 6535 2232N
..23 5535 .2.5 2356 .567 6535 .2.5 2356
72.. 22.. 22.7 6563 21.. 11.. 11.2 3565N
..36 .535 323. 3235 ..36 .535 323. 3235
67.. 77.. 77.6 5356 3567 6532 7232 .765N
.7.6 .532 .... 2235 .7.6 .532 2232
..35 3272 ..35 3272 ..3. 2.7. 6.67 6535N/G

     t   t
.7.6 .532 .... 2235 .7.6 .532 2232
..35 3272 ..35 3272 ..3. 2.7. 6.67 6535N
.7.6 .532 .... 2235 .7.6 .532 77.. 77.2
34.. 44.. 44.3 2765 6327 .... 7765 3565N
.2.5 2356 .7.6 .535 .2.5 2356 .7.6 .535→
67.. 77.. 77.6 5356 3567 6532 7232 .765N
.67. 5676 .535 3232 767. 7656 .535 3232
..3. 2.3. 2.3. 2.76 ..7. 567. 6535 2232N/G]

ompak: N
→67.. 77.. 77.6 5356 3567 6532 7232 .756
7653 2356 7653 2356 767. 7656 .535 2232G

inggah:
 t   t   t   t   t   t   t   t N
[767. 7656 .535 3232 767. 7656 .535 3232
767. 7656 .535 3232 33.. 33.. 5555 5567
234. 4327 234. 4327 234. 4323 .333 2765
.22. 2765 .22. 2765 .33. 6532 6732 .765G

 t   t   t   t   t   t   t   t N
.33. 6532 6732 .765 .33. 6532 6732 .765
.33. 6532 6732 .765 33.. 33.. 5555 5567
234. 4327 234. 4327 234. 4323 .333 2756
7653 2356 7653 2356 767. 7656 .535 2232G]

Pari Nom, Gendhing, kethuk 4 kerep, minggah
kethuk 8, sléndro pathet nem (1).

buka: 2 .2.1 .3.2 .2.3 .6.5 .3.5 .3.2N/G

mérong:
```
       t         t         t         t    N
[11.. 3216 .5.3 .1.6 .5.3 .1.6 2321 6535
 11.. 3216 .5.3 .1.6 .5.3 .1.6 2321 6535
 33.. 6532 .1.6 .3.2 .1.6 .3.2 5653 2126→
 22.. 22.3 5653 2165 1653 6535 2356 3532G]
```

umpak minggah:
```
      t         t         t         t    N
→ .3.2 .3.2 .5.3 .6.5 .6.3 .6.5 .1.6 .3.2G
```

minggah:
```
   t    t    t    t    t    t    t    t N
[.3.1 .2.6 .5.3 .1.6 .5.3 .1.6 .2.1 .6.5
 .2.1 .2.6 .5.3 .1.6 .5.3 .1.6 .2.1 .6.5
 .2.3 .5.2 .1.6 .3.2 .1.6 .3.2 .5.3 .1.6
 .3.2 .3.2 .5.3 .6.5 .6.3 .6.5 .1.6 .3.2G]
```

Pari Purna, Gendhing, kethuk 2 kerep,
sléndro pathet sanga (38).

buka: 1 .1.1 .612 .2.1 .612 .126 .1.5N/G

mérong:
```
          t         t    N
.1.6 .1.5 .1.6 .1.5
.... 55.6 1656 5312
66.1 6535 1656 5321
5621 5216 .2.1 .6.5G
```

minggah: Ladrang Pangkur

Pasang, Gendhing, kethuk 4 awis, minggah
    kethuk 8, pélog pathet lima (1).

buka: [3.2165.5.]x2   .3.3 .321 .1.5 6121N/G

mérong:
```
           t                      t
[..12 3323 .253 .2.1 ..12 3323 .253 .2.1
 22.. 22.. 22.3 5653 ..53 2126 12.6 1232N
 .... 2212 33.2 .161 22.. 2212 33.2 .161
 22.. 22.. 22.3 5653 ..53 2126 35.2 3565N
 .... 5565 612. 2165 612. 2165 .616 5323→
 .... 33.. 33.. 5235 .... 5565 .1.2 3565N
 .... 55.. 2454 2121 .41. 1245 2454 2121
 55.. 55.. 22.. 2321 ..32 .165 15.6 1.21N/G]
```

ompak:
```
                            N
                →.... 6356 ..76 5421
 66.1 3216 ..61 3216 33.. 6532 3216 5612G
```

minggah:
```
  t    t    t    t    t    t    t    t N
[33.. 6532 3216 5616 33.. 6532 3216 5616
 33.. 6532 3216 5616 11.. 11.. 11.2 3565
 .532 11.. 11.2 3565 2325 2356 6676 5421
 66.1 3216 ..61 3216 33.. 6532 3216 5616G]
```

Pasang Bandar, Ladrang,
    pélog pathet nem (1).

buka: .12. 2123 .61. 2312N/G
```
   t    t N
[.32. 2321
 .32. 2321
 .12. 2123
 ..61 2312G
```

ngelik:
```
   t    t N
 55.. 5535
 ..56 7767
 ..7. 7656
 53.6 5365G
```
```
   t    t N
 7654 2121
 3212 .165
 66.. 6656
 3567 6535G
```

```
      t   t N
    7656 5421
    3512 .165
    32.3 5676
    3565 3212G

      t   t N
    66.. 6656
    3567 6535
    ..23 55..
    55.6 7656G

      t   t N
    .654 2132
    .32. 2321
    .12. 2123
    ..61 2312G]
```

Pasang Wetan, Ladrang,
    pélog pathet nem (38).

buka: 32. 2321 .12. 2123
              ..61 2312N/G

```
      t   t N
   [.32. 2321
    .32. 2321
    .12. 2123
    ..61 2312G
```

ngelik:
```
      t   t N
    55.. 5535
    ..56 7767
    .... 7656
    53.6 5365G

      t   t N
    7654 2121
    3212 .126
    .... 6656
    .765 3565G

      t   t N
    7654 2121
    3212 .165
    32.. 2356
    1216 5312G
```

```
 t    t N
..3. 1232
.216 5323
..5. 3.56
1216 5312G

 t    t N
66.. 6656
.765 3565
..23 55..
55.6 7656G

 t    t N
.654 2132
.32. 2321
.12. 2123
..61 2312G]
```

Paséban, Gendhing, kethuk 8 kerep, minggah
    kethuk 16, pélog pathet lima (1).

buka:[.$\overline{123}$.$\overline{216}$.6]x2 ..2. 1261 .261 2353N/G

mérong:
```
  t       t        t        t
[..35 .653 ..32 5321 ..2. 1261 .261 2353
..35 .653 ..32 5321 612. 2212 33.1 3216N
..6. 66.. 66.5 6356 .567 .656 .532 3565
..5. 55.. 55.. 6356 .535 3212 ..23 5616N
..6. 66.. 66.5 6356 .567 .656 .532 3565
..5. 55.. 55.. 6356 .535 3212 ..23 5616N
..6. 66.. 66.5 6356 .7.6 5323 ..32 3521
.6.3 2132 3123 2121 ..2. 1261 .261 2353G]
```

umpak:
```
  t       t        t        t
..35 .653 ..32 5321 ..2. 1261 .261 2353
..35 .653 ..32 5321 612. 2212 3323 2121N
..1. 11.. 1121 6123 55.6 7654 2.44 2165
..5. 5535 66.. 1653 22.. 2321 6123 2126N
..63 2132 3123 2161 2356 7654 2.44 2165
..5. 5535 66.. 1653 23.3 .3.3 .532 3565N
..56 7653 22.3 5.65 2325 2356 6676 5421
.111 2321 .111 6124 .44. 4456 5422 2165N/G
```

300

unggah:
```
    t    t    t    t    t    t    t    t
[.555 2356 .123 2165 6365 2356 .123 2165
 6365 2356 .123 2165 6356 532. 2321 6132N
 .444 5654 .444 5654 .444 5654 2.44 2165
 6365 2356 .123 2165 6365 5323 6532 3565N
 .444 5654 .444 5654 .444 5654 2.44 2165
 6365 2356 .123 2165 6356 5323 6532 3565N
 ..56 7653 22.3 5.65 2325 2356 6676 5421
 .111 2321 .111 6124 .44. 4456 5424 2165N/G]
```

suwuk:
```
  t    t    t    t    t    t    t    t N
66.. 6532 ..25 2356 .56. 6561 2165 3235G
```

Patanya/[Tatanya ?], Gendhing (Santiswaran),
pélog pathet barang (39).

```
.   . 6 6 675 65 3 6 7 236 .53 .3
5 .73 6 7 3 2     . 2 7 .62 327 .7
2 .37 6 6 675 65 3 6 7 236 .53 .3
5 .73 6 7 3 2     . 2 7 .62 327 .7 →
2 .37 5 67653 5   6 2 3 .22 .76G
```

suwuk:
```
→ 2 .37 6 7 3 2 6 72365356232276G
```

Pawukir, Ketawang, sléndro
pathet manyura (2).

buka: 6 123. 2.1. 3312 .126N/G

umpak:
```
   t    t N t    t N
[[.2.3 .2.1 .3.2 .1.6G]
```

ngelik:
```
        t    t N t    t N
     3612 1312 6321 3532G
     3612 1312 6321 3532G
     11.. 5653 .132 .126G]
```

Pedaringan Kebak, Ladrang,
   sléndro pathet nem (source unknown).

buka: .2 .5.3 .5.2 .6.3 .6.5N/G

```
   t    t N  t    t N
 3.36 3.35 6.63 5.52G
 6.63 5.52 3.36 3.35G
```

Peksi Bayan, Gendhing, kethuk 4 kerep,
   minggah kethuk 8, sléndro pathet nem (1).

buka: 3 .561 .165 3561 .1.6 55.6 1656N/G

mérong:
```
    t         t         t         t    N
[.... 6656 3561 6523 6532 ..23 5653 2126
 ..61 3216 3561 6523 6532 ..23 5653 2126
 ..61 3216 3561 6523 6532 ..23 5653 2126
 22.. 22.3 5653 2165 1653 6535 2356 3532G

    t         t         t         t    N
 ..23 6532 66.1 6535 1653 6535 2356 3532
 ..23 6532 66.1 6535 1653 6535 2356 3532
 ..23 6532 66.1 6535 1653 6535 2356 3532 →
 66.. 2321 3216 2321 3216 2321 55.6 1656G]
```

umpak minggah:
```
    t         t         t         t    N
→.5.6 .2.1 .2.6 .2.1 .2.6 .2.1 .5.6 .1.6G
```

minggah:
```
   t    t    t    t    t    t    t    t N
[.5.6 .5.6 .2.1 .5.3 .5.2 .3.2 .5.3 .1.6
 .1.6 .1.6 .2.1 .5.3 .5.2 .3.2 .5.3. 1.6
 .1.6 .1.6 .2.1 .5.3 .5.2 .3.2 .5.3 .1.6
 .3.2 .3.2 .5.3 .6.5 .5.3 .6.5 .1.6 .3.2G

   t    t    t    t    t    t    t    t N
 .3.2 .3.2 .5.6 .3.5 .6.3 .6.5 .1.6 .3.2
 .3.2 .3.2 .5.6 .3.5 .6.3 .6.5 .1.6 .3.2
 .3.2 .3.2 .5.6 .3.5 .6.3 .6.5 .1.6 .3.2
 .5.6 .2.1 .2.6 .2.1 .2.6 .2.1 .5.6 .1.6G]
```

Peksi Kuwung/Peksi Kawung, Ladrang,
    sléndro pathet nem (16).

buka: .6.2 .6.2 .6.3 .6.5N/G

```
     t    t N
    .6.3 .6.5
    .6.3 .5.6
    .5.6 .5.6
    .2.3 .6.5G

     t    t N
  [.6.3 .6.5
    .6.3 .6.5
    .3.2 .3.2
    .5.3 .6.5G]
```

ngelik:
```
     t    t N
    .1.6 .3.5
    .1.6 .3.5
    .3.2 .3.2
    .5.3 .6.5G
```

Pengasih, Gendhing, kethuk 2 kerep, minggah
    kethuk 4, pélog pathet nem (1).

buka: 66. 565. 5.6. 5321 1132 .165N/G

mérong:
```
        t         t    N
   [..56 5323 ..35 6535
    ..56 5323 ..35 6535
    22.. 22.. 6535 3212
    ..35 3212 165. 5612G

        t         t    N
    ..35 3212 165. 5612
    ..35 3212 165. 5612 →
    .126 ..6. 66.. 5535
    ..56 .532 1132 .165G]
```

umpak minggah:
```
        t         t    N
   →.126 .3.6 .5.6 .3.5
    .3.5 .3.2 .3.2 .6.5G
```

minggah:

```
       t     t     t    t N
[.6.5 .6.3 .5.3 .6.5
 .6.5 .6.3 .5.3 .6.5
 .3.2 .3.2 .6.5 .3.2
 .3.5 .3.2 .6.5 .3.2G

       t     t     t    t N
 .3.5 .3.2 .6.5 .3.2
 .3.5 .3.2 .6.5 .3.2
 .1.6 .5.6 .5.6 .3.5
 .3.5 .3.2 .3.2 .6.5G]
```

Penganten Anyar, Ladrang,
   pélog pathet barang (35).

buka: 756. 3523 6535 66.6N/G

```
   t    t N
[756. 3576   ⎫
 756. 3576   ⎬ x2
 756. 3523   ⎪
 6535 6756G  ⎭

   t    t N
 3523 5653
 6765 3232
 5654 2121
 3216 7523G

   t    t N
 6563 6563
 6563 6532
 5654 2121
 3216 7523G

   t    t N
 56.3 5676
 3567 3276
 7653 2353
 6535 6756G]
```

Pengantèn Anyar/Maèsa Giro,
  Ladrang, pélog pathet nem (38).

buka: .352 .126 3532 .165N/G

```
  t    t N      t    t N       t    t N
[.612 .165    22.. 2232     66.. 6656
 .612 .165    ..23 5565     3567 6535
 22.. 22.3    .352 .126     .352 .126
 5654 2165G   3532 .165G    3532 .165G]
```

Pengawé, Gendhing, kethuk 4 awis, minggah
  kethuk 8, pelog pathet nem (1).

buka: 5 .5.6 4565 .4.4 .4.4 .5.6 .545N/G

```
mérong:  t                    t
[..56 .5.4 .254 2121 .2.6 1231 ..21 6123
 55.. 55.. 556. 4565 ..24 .... 4456 .545N
 ..56 .5.4 .254 2121 .2.6 1231 ..21 6123
 .... 33.. 3356 5421 66.. 6656 .2.3 5676N →
 .... 6653 .653 2356 .653 2356 .567 .653
 23.. 33.. 3356 .535 ..56 .5.4 .254 2121N
 .2.6 1231 ..21 6123 55.. 5421 ..21 6123
 55.. 55.. 556. 4565 ..24 .... 4456 .545N/G]
```

ompak inggah:

```
    t        t        t         t    N
→.556 7653 22.3 5.65 2325 2356 6676 5312
 .312 3532 .312 3532 11.. 11.2 4565 4212G
```

minggah:

```
  t    t    t    t    t    t    t    t N
[4.45 4241 .412 4542 4.45 4241 .412 4542
 4.45 4241 .412 4542 1612 1656 .666 5356
 .556 7653 22.3 5.65 2325 2356 6676 5312
 .312 3532 .312 3532 11.. 11.2 4565 4212G]
```

Perkutut Manggung/Kutut Manggung,
  Gendhing, kethuk 2 kerep,
  pélog pathet barang (3).

buka: .667 6563 272. 2765 33.5 6727N/G

mérong:
    .77. 7723 5653 2327
    .77. 7723 5653 2327
    3272 6356 3567 6523
    272. 2765 33.5 6727G

minggah: Ladrang Perkutut Manggung

Perkutut Manggung/Kutut Manggung,
  Gendhing, kethuk 2 kerep,
  sléndro pathet manyura (3).

buka: 661 6563 212. 2165 33.5 6121N/G

mérong:
    .11. 1123 5653 2121
    .11. 1123 5653 2121
    3212 .126 3561 6523
    212. 2165 33.5 6121G

minggah: Ladrang Perkutut Manggung

Perkutut Manggung/Kutut Manggung,
  Ladrang, pélog pathet barang (3).

(minggah to Gendhing Perkutut Manggung)

       t   t N
    [3253 6267
    3253 6267
    3276 5756
    3253 6267G]

irama III:
       t   t   N
    [3632 5653 6732 6327
    3632 5653 6732 5327
    3632 6356 3567 6576
    3232 5653 6732 6327G]

Perkutut Manggung/Kutut Manggung,
   Ladrang, sléndro pathet manyura (3).

(minggah to Gendhing Perkutut Manggung)

```
        t    t N
     [3253 6231
      3253 6231
      3216 5156
      3253 6261G]
```

irama III: t

```
     [3532 5653 6132 6321
      3532 5653 6132 6321
      3532 5356 3561 6516
      3232 5653 6132 6321G]
```

Petung Wulung, Gendhing, kethuk 2
   kerep, pélog pathet barang (38).

buka: 667 6563 272. 2765 33.5 6756N/G

mérong: t   t

```
     .666 6756 .... 2342N
     .... 2343 .... 3567N
     .3.2 .7.6 .756 .756N
     .567 6563 272. 2765
               3567 3276N/G
```

Pisan Bali/Pisahan Bali/Pisang Bali/
   Peli Pelèn/Bali Pelèn, Ketawang (11).

buka kendhang: 5N/G

```
      t    t N  t    t N
     .6.1 .6.5 .2.1 .6.5G
     [2621 2625 2621 2625G]
```

Pisan Bali/Pisahan Bali/Pisang Bali/
   Peli Pelèn/Bali Pelèn, Ketawang,
   pélog pathet barang (11).

buka kendhang: 6N/G

```
   t   t N  t    t N
[.7.2 .7.6 .3.2 .7.6G]
[..6. 7567 .3.2 .7.6G
..6. 7567 .3.2 .672G
..43 .756 .3.2 .7.6G]
```

Pisan Bali/Pisahan Bali/Pisang Bali/
   Peli Pelèn/Bali Pelèn, Ketawang,
   pélog pathet nem (3).

buka kendhang: 5N/G

```
umpak: t   t N  t    t N
      .6.1 .6.5 .2.1 .6.5

ngelik: t   t N  t    t N
      ..5. 6456 .2.1 .6.5G
      ..5. 6456 .2.1 .561G
      .3.2 .6.5 .2.1 .6.5G
```

Playon, Ketawang, pélog
   pathet barang (8).

buka: 7 .2.3 .2.7 .2.6 .2.7N/G

```
   t   t N  t    t N
 .767 2327 .767 2353G
 .356 7653 5327 6567G
[.767 6567 .765 3567G
 .765 .235 ..56 7567G
 .765 3232 66.. 5676G
 .635 6676 53.6 5365G
 22.. 2232 77.. 6567G
 .765 3323 .32. 2327G
 .767 2327 .767 2353G
 .356 7653 5327 6567G
 .767 2327 .767 2353G
 .356 7653 5327 6567G]
```

Playon, Ladrang, pélog
    pathet lima (8).

```
   t   t N
[ .542 1245
  .542 1245
  6542 1232
  66.7 5676G

   t   t N
  .654 2212
  ..24 5.65
  6542 1645
  .612 1645G

   t   t N
  .612 1646
  3365 3216
  5612 3212
  1654 2465G ]
```

Plupuh/Palupuh, Ladrang,
    sléndro pathet nem (16).

buka: 2 3532 6532N/G

```
   t   t N      t   t N      t   t N
[ .3.5 .3.2    .3.5 .3.2    .3.5 .1.6
  .3.5 .3.2    .3.5 .3.2    .3.5 .1.6
  .3.5 .3.2    .3.5 .1.6    .3.5 .3.2
  .6.5 .3.2G   .1.2 .1.6G   .6.5 .3.2G ]
```

Potong Sérong, Ladrang,
    pélog pathet nem (1).

buka: 33. 3516 2153 6532N/G

```
   t   t N
  1213 1312
  1213 1312
  .33. 3516
  2153 6532G
```

Prabu Anom, Ladrang, sléndro
  pathet manyura (1).

buka: 5.3 .2.1 .6.6 .3.3 .5.6
          .2.2 .2.2N/G

```
 t    t N
5356 1523        2123 2126
1216 1523        1632 5321
.356 2321        3532 3126
5653 2165G       3356 5352G
```


Pramugari, Gendhing, kethuk 2 kerep, minggah
  kethuk 4, pélog pathet barang (1).

buka: odangiah: .6.6 .6.6 .7.6 5323N/G

mérong:
```
      t        t    N
 21.1 .1.1 .1.2 3123
[.567 .... 7765 3565
 765̄3272.. 2327 6535
 ..56 7653 2356 3565G

    t         t    N
 765̄3272.. 22.3 5235
 765̄327265 ..56 7232 →
 ..23 4327 66.. 6656
 .... 66.. 6676 5323G

    t        t    N
 21.. 11.. 11.2 3123]
```

umpak:
```
      t        t    N
 →..23 4327 44.. 4434
 .... 44.. 4323 2767G

    t         t    N
 .234 .... 4323 2767
 55.. 55.. 7656 3565
 6532 7232 3276 5672
 672. 2723 4327 6535G
```

310

```
minggah:
      t    t    t    t N
  [.67. 567. 5672 3532
   .... 3276 5565 7232
   .22. 3276 5365 2232
   44.. 44.. 4323 2767G

      t    t    t    t N
   .234 .... 4323 2767
   55.. 55.. 7656 3565
   .532 7232 3276 5672
   672. 2327 4327 6535G]
```

Prawan Pupur, Gendhing, kethuk 2 kerep,
    minggah kethuk 4, pélog pathet barang (3).

buka: 667 6523 2723 6532 .756N/G

```
mérong:   t         t    N
     [.563 .567 33.. 6532
      5653 2767 33.. 6532 →
      .756 ..6. 3567 6523
      272. 2723 6532 .756G
```

```
ngelik:   t         t    N
      ..6. 6656 3567 6523
      77.. 3276 3567 6523
      2732 .756 3567 6523
      272. 2723 6532 .756G]
```

```
umpak minggah:
            t         t    N
   → .5.6 .5.6 .2.7 .5.3
     .2.7 .2.3 .7.2 .7.6G
```

```
minggah: t    t    t    t N
   [.7.6 .2.7 .2.7 .3.2
    .3.2 .3.7 .2.7 .3.2
    .3.2 .7.6 .2.7 .5.3
    .2.7 .2.3 .7.2 .7.6G]
```

Prihatin, Gendhing, kethuk 2 kerep, minggah
kethuk 4, sléndro pathet nem (2).

buka: 2 .356 .6.1 .2.1 .2.6 .3.5N/G

mérong:
```
          t        t    N
  [.3.3 .3.3 .6.5 .3.2
   .52. 2523 6535 3212
   .52. 2523 6535 3212
   .35. 235. 2321 6535G

          t        t    N
   22.. 2321 .216 .2.1
   65.. 2321 .216 .2.1
   65.. 2321 3265 3353 →
   .... 3356 3565 3212G]
```

umpak minggah:
```
          t        t    N
  → .5.3 .5.6 .3.5 .3.2G
```

minggah:
```
        t    t    t    t N
  [.3.2 .5.3 .6.5 .3.2
   .3.2 .5.3 .6.5 .3.2
   .3.2 .5.3 .6.5 .3.2
   .3.5 .3.5 .2.1 .6.5G

        t    t    t    t N
   .2.3 .2.1 .2.6 .2.1
   .2.3 .2.1 .2.6 .2.1
   .6.5 .2.1 .2.6 .5.3
   .5.3 .5.6 .3.5 .3.2G]
```

Prit Jowan, Gendhing, kethuk 2 kerep, minggah
kethuk 4, sléndro pathet manyura (1).

buka: 1 .2.2 .2.1 .6.3 .3.5 .6.1 5323N/G

mérong:
```
          t        t    N
  [.... 3356 1656 5323
   .... 3356 1656 5323
   .... 3356 1656 5323 →
   11.. 1123 6532 .126G

          t        t    N
   .165 1653 11.. 3216
   .165 1653 11.. 3216
   .165 1653 11.. 3216
   .... 3356 1656 5323G]
```

```
umpak:      t          t      N
       →.2.1  .2.3  .1.2  .1.6G

minggah: t    t     t    t N
       [.1.6  .5.3  .2.1  .2.6
        .1.6  .5.3  .2.1  .2.6
        .5.3  .5.3  .5.6  .5.3
        .5.3  .5.3  .1.6  .5.3G

         t    t     t    t N
        .5.3  .5.6  .1.6  .5.3
        .5.3  .5.6  .1.6  .5.3
        .5.3  .5.6  .1.6  .5.3
        .2.1  .2.3  .1.2  .1.6G]
```

Priyambada/Priyabada, Ladrang,
    pélog pathet barang (38).

buka: 235. 2356 7767 6535N/G

```
ngelik:  t     t N
       [.7.6  .2.7
        5672  .765
        .676  .532
        3565  3272G

         t     t N
        .672  .765
        22.7  6535
        3535  3565
        6727  6535G

         t     t N
        767.  7656
        ..67  2.32
        4343  2765
        .672  .765G

         t     t N
        .672  .672
        .672  .765
        .672  .672
        .672  .765G

         t     t N
        .672  .672
        .672  .765
        3535  3565
        6727  6535G]
```

Pucung, Gendhing, kethuk 2 kerep,
    sléndro pathet manyura (2).

buka: 6 .123 .3.3 .5.3 .216 1232N/G

mérong: t   t   N
   [..21 6132 ..21 6123
     ..36 3561 .216 .523
     .516 5321 3532 .126
     .16. 6123 .216 1232G]

minggah: Èsèk-èsèk

Pucung, Ketawang, sléndro
    pathet manyura (2).

buka: 6123 2216 3532N/G

 t   t N t   t N
[..21 6132 6123 6532G
  ..21 6132 ..21 6123G
  ..3. 33.5 6156 .523G
  .516 2321 3532 .126G
  .16. 6123 2216 3532G]

Pucung Rubuh, Ladrang, pélog pathet
    nem/sléndro pathet manyura (3).

    t   t   N
.235 .235 2356 5323
...6 ...5 ...3 ...2
...5 ...3 ...5 ...2
.35. 2356 1265 2353G

    t   t   N
.126 .126 1265 2353
...6 ...5 ...2 ...1
...3 ...2 .6.5 .3.2
.35. 2356 1265 2353G

314

Pujangga, Gendhing, kethuk 4 kerep, minggah
kethuk 8, sléndro pathet nem (1).

buka: 2 61.1 .3.2 .165 1216N/G

mérong:
```
       t              t              t              t    N
[.3.3 6532 .165 1216 .3.3 6532 .165 1216
 ..21 3216 3561 6523 6532 ..23 5653 2126
 ..21 3216 3561 6523 6532 ..23 5653 2126
 3565 2232 5325 2356 11.. 3212 .165 1216G]
```

minggah:
```
    t    t    t    t    t    t    t    t N
[.3.6 .3.2 .6.5 .1.6 .3.2 .6.5 .1.5 .1.6
 .1.6 .1.6 .2.1 .5.3 .5.2 .3.2 .5.3 .1.6
 .1.6 .1.6 .2.1 .5.3 .5.2 .3.2 .5.3 .1.6
 .3.5 .3.2 .5.3 .5.6 .2.1 .3.2 .6.5 .1.6G]
```

Pujangga Anom/[Pujangga Anom Madura ?],
Gendhing, kethuk 2 kerep, minggah
kethuk 4, sléndro pathet manyura (2).

buka: 6 .1.2 .3.2 .1.6 .3.3 .5.6 .532 .5.3N/G

mérong:
```
          t         t    N
[...3 6532 ..23 5653
 ...3 6532 ..23 5653
 ...3 6532 66.. 3356
 3561 6532 1232 .126G]
```

```
          t         t    N
 .666 3532 3532 .126
 .666 3532 3532 .126
 .666 3532 33.. 1123 →
 11.. 3216 3532 5653G]
```

umpak minggah:
```
          t         t    N
→.2.1 .2.6 .3.2 .5.3G
```

minggah:
```
       t     t     t     t N
 [.5.3 .5.2 .3.2 .5.3
  .5.3 .5.2 .3.2 .5.3
  .5.3 .5.2 .5.3 .5.6
  .2.1 .3.2 .3.2 .1.6G

       t     t     t     t N
  .1.6 .3.2 .3.2 .1.6
  .1.6 .3.2 .3.2 .1.6
  .1.6 .3.2 .5.3 .5.3
  .2.1 .2.6 .3.2 .5.3G]
```

Pujangga Gandrung, Gendhing, kethuk 4 kerep,
  minggah kethuk 8, sléndro pathet nem (1).

buka: 2 .356 .1.1 .3.2 .165 1216N/G

mérong:
```
      t     t      t       t     N
 [..61 3216 2321 3216 ..61 6523 6532 .126
  ..61 3216 2321 3216 .... 6656 3561 6523
  .516 .... 3561 6523 6532 ..23 5653 2165
  2356 3532 ..23 6532 11.. 3212 .165 1216G

      t     t      t       t     N
  .... 6656 3561 6535 .653 66.. 3561 6535
  .653 66.5 33.5 6121 .... 1216 .165 2353
  .516 .... 3561 6523 6532 ..23 5653 2165 →
  2356 3532 ..23 6532 11.. 3212 .165 1216G]
```

ompak:
```
      t       t        t       t      N
 →.1.6 .3.2 .1.6 .3.2 .3.1 .3.2 .6.5 .1.6G
```

minggah:
```
      t    t    t    t    t    t    t    t N
 [.1.6 .3.2 .6.5 .1.6 .1.6 .3.2 .6.5 .1.6
  .1.6 .3.2 .6.5 .1.6 .2.3 .5.3 .5.6 .5.3
  .5.3 .5.3 .6.5 .3.2 .3.2 .3.2 .5.3 .6.5
  .1.6 .3.2 .1.6 .3.2 .3.1 .3.2 .6.5 .1.6G]
```

sabetan:
```
      t    t    t    t    t    t    t    t N
 [5352 5356 5156 5352 5352 5356 5156 5352
  5352 5356 5156 5352 5356 5323 .333 5653
  .661 6532 3635 3632 3635 3632 5653 2165
  1216 5352 5356 5352 11.. 3216 5356 5352G]
```

Pujangga Tawang, Gendhing, kethuk 4 kerep,
minggah kethuk 8, sléndro pathet manyura (1).

buka: .6.1 .2.2 .2.1 .66. 6612 .3.2 .1.6N/G

mérong:
```
         t            t            t          t   N
[..61 3216 ..61 2.32 .... 2212 3312 .126
 ..61 3216 33.5 6.16 .... 6656 1156 .523
 ..35 1653 11.. 3216 .... 1653 22.3 1232
 .... 2212 3312 .126 .666 3532 3532 .126G]
```

minggah:
```
    t    t    t    t    t    t    t    t N
[.1.6 .1.6 .1.6 .3.2 .3.2 .5.3 .1.2 .1.6
 .1.6 .1.6 .5.3 .1.6 .5.6 .2.1 .1.6 .5.3
 .5.3 .5.3 .5.3 .2.1 .2.1 .2.6 .5.6 .3.2
 .3.2 .5.3 .1.2 .1.6 .1.6 .3.2 .3.2 .1.6G]
```

Puspa Giwang, Ketawang, sléndro
pathet manyura (2).

buka: 61 3212 3321 .216N/G

```
   t    t N  t    t N
[ 1561 3532 5321 3216G
  33.. 3356 1216 3532G
  6132 6132 6653 2126G ]
```

Puspanjala, Ketawang, pélog
pathet nem (3).

buka: .111 3312 3321 3216N/G

umpak:
```
    t    t N  t    t N
[[ 3216 3532 5321 3216G ]
```

ngelik:
```
    t    t N  t    t N
 ..6. 2321 3265 2353G
 3561 6523 3561 6523G
 22.. 3123 ..65 2126G ]
```

Puspa Warna, Ketawang,
pélog pathet nem (3).

buka: 6123 .2.1 3312 .126N/G

```
umpak:   t    t N   t    t N
      [[.2.3 .2.1 .3.2 .1.6G]
```

```
ngelik:  t    t N   t    t N
       ..6. 2321 3265 1653G
       ..32 5321 .3.2 .1.6G
       ..23 .2.1 .3.2 .1.6G]
```


Puspa Warna, Ketawang, sléndro
pathet manyura (2).

buka: 6 6123 .2.1 3312 .126N/G

```
umpak:   t    t N   t    t N
      [[.2.3 .2.1 .3.2 .1.6G]
```

```
ngelik:  t    t N   t    t N
       ..6. 2321 3265 1653G
       ..32 5321 .3.2 .1.6G
       .2.3 .2.1 .3.2 .1.6G]
```


Puspa Wedhar, Gendhing, kethuk 2 kerep,
   minggah kethuk 4, sléndro pathet nem (2).

buka: 3 .561 .1.3 .212 .1.6 .5.3N/G

```
mérong:    t         t    N
       [.23. 3235 .616 5323
        .23. 3235 .616 5323
        .23. 3235 ..52 3565
        ..56 5323 .635 6121G
```

```
           t         t    N
       ..32 .165 .653 .561
       .... 1216 .532 .126
       3532 .126 3532 .126 →
       33.. 3216 3561 6523G]
```

umpak minggah:
```
            t         t   N
      →.3.2 .1.6  .1.6 .5.3G
```

minggah:
```
          t    t    t    t N
      [.5.3 .6.5 .1.6 .5.3
       .5.3 .6.5 .1.6 .5.3
       .5.3 .6.5 .3.2 .3.5
       .6.5 .6.3 .5.3 .2.1G

          t    t    t    t N
       .3.2 .6.5 .6.3 .2.1
       .2.1 .2.6 .3.2 .1.6
       .3.2 .1.6 .3.2 .1.6
       .3.2 .1.6 .1.6 .5.3G]
```

Racikan (Sekatèn), pélog pathet nem (7).

bubuka [buka]:
```
                              N
. 3 . 5  . 3 3 6  ‾.35 ‾.36  5 3 3 6
. . . 3  . . . 6  . 5 3 2  . 3 . 5G

                              N
[. . . 5  5 3 3 6  ‾.35 ‾.36  5 3 3 6           ⎫
. . . 3  . . . 6  . 5 3 2  . 3 . 5             ⎬ x2
. . . 5  5 3 3 6  ‾.35 ‾.36  5 3 3 6           ⎭
. . . 3  . . . 6  . 5 3 2  . 3 . 5G

                              N
. . . 5  5 3 3 6  ‾.35 ‾.36  5 3 3 6
. . . 3  . . . 6  .5 3 2  .3 . 5
. . . 5  5 3 3 6  ‾.35 ‾.36  .36 5 3
. . . .  . 6 . 5  . . 3 2  . 3 . 2G

                              N
. . . 5  5 2 5 3  . ‾55‾352  . 2 5 3
. . . .  . 6 . 5  . . 3 2  . 3 . 2
. . . 5  5 2 5 3  . ‾55‾352  ‾442 4 1
. . . 1  . . . 2  3 3 . 2  . 1 . 6G

                              N
. . . 6  ‾563 . 6  ‾563 5 .  6 ‾635 6
. . . 3  . 6 . 5  . . 3 2  . 4 . 1
. . . 3  3 1 3 2  . ‾33‾231  ‾331 3 2
. . . 6  . . . 5  . . 3 2  . 5 . 3G
```

```
                                        N
. . . 5 . 3 . 6  .35 .36  5 3 . 2
. . . . . 6 . 5  . . 3 2  . 4 . 1
. . . 3 3 1 3 2  . 33231  665 6 4
. . . 6 . . . 4  . . . 6  . 53. 2G
                                        N
. . . 5 5 3 5 2  . 55352  552 5 3
. . . . . 6 . 5  . . 3 2  . 4 . 1
. . . 3 3 1 3 2  . 33231  331 3 2
. . . . . 6 . 5  . . 3 2  . 5 . 3G →
                                        N
. . . 5 . 3 . 6  .35 .36  5 3 5 3
. . . . . 6 . 5  . . 3 2  . 4 . 1
. . . 3 3 1 3 2  . 33231  331 1 6
. . . 3 . . . 6  . 5 3 2  . 3 . 5G]
pangkat ndhawah:
                                        N
→ . . . 5 . 3 . 6  .35 .36  .53 5 2
. . . . . 6 . 5  . . 3 2  . 4 . 1
. . . 3 3 1 3 2  . 33231  331 1 6
. 6 1 2 . . 3 .  5 . 2 .  3 3 2 1G
```

Racikaṇ Barang Miring (Sekatèn),
pélog pathet barang (7).

bubuka [buka]:
```
                                        N
. 3 . 5 . 3 3 6  .35 .36  5 3 3 6
. . . 3 . . . 6  . 5 3 2  . 3 . 5G
                                        N
. . . 5 5 3 3 6  .35 .36  5 3 3 6  ⎫
. . . 3 . . . 6  . 5 3 2  . 3 . 5   ⎬ x2
. . . 5 5 3 3 6  .35 .36  5 3 3 6  ⎪
. . . 3 . . . 6  . 5 3 2  . 3 . 5G ⎭
                                        N
. . . 5 5 3 3 6  .35 .36  5 3 3 6
. . . 3 . . . 6  . 5 3 2  . 3 . 5
. . . 5 5 3 3 6  .35 .36  .36 5 3
. . . . . 6 . 5  . . 3 2  . 3 . 2G
                                        N
. . . 5 5 2 5 3  . 55352  552 5 3
. . . . . 6 . 5  . . 3 2  . 3 . 2
. . . 5 5 2 5 3  55352 5  67756 7
. 7 . 7 . 6 . 5  5 5 5 7  . 5 . 6G
```

```
                                  N
[ . . 6 7  ‾.65 7 6   7 5 . 6   7 ‾756 7
 . 7 . 7   . 6 . 5    5 5 5 7   . 5 . 6
 . . . 5   . 6 . 3    . 6 . ‾56  ‾35535 2
 . . . 6   . . . 5    . . 3 2   . 5 . 3G

                                  N
 . . . 5   5 3 3 6   ‾.35 ‾.36   ‾.53 5 2
 . . . 6   . . . 5   . . 3 2    . 5 . 3
 . . . 5   5 3 3 6   ‾.35 ‾.36   5 3 3 6
 . . . 3   . . . 6   . 5 3 5    . 6 . 7G]
```

pangkat ndhawah:
```
                                  N
 . . . 5   5 ‾323 6   ‾.35 ‾.36   ‾.53 5 2
 . . . 6   . . . 5   . . 3 2    . 5 . 3
 . . . 5   5 3 3 6   ‾.35 ‾.36   5 3 3 6
 . . . 3   . . . 6   . 5 3 2    . 3 . 5G
```


Raja Manggala, Ladrang, pélog
    pathet bem (lima) (15).

```
   t     t N
[ 6563  6561
  2123  5321
  2123  5321
  6532  5653G

   t     t N
  6563  6561
  2123  5321
  2123  5321
  2216  2165G

   t     t N
  1612  1645
  1612  1645
  1612  1612
  1621  6561

   t     t N
  2165  1261
  2165  1261
  55.2  3565
  7654  2126G

   t     t N
  1561  5321
  2123  5321
  2123  5321
  6532  5653G ]
```

Raja Manggala, Ladrang,
    sléndro pathet nem (35).

buka: 1 .123 5321 6532 3333N/G

```
  t    t N
[ 6563 6561
  2123 5321
  2123 5321
  6532 5653G

  t    t N
  6563 6561
  2123 5321
  2123 5321
  2216 2165G

  t    t N
  1612 1615
  1612 1615
  1612 1615
  1621 6561G

  t    t N
  2165 6156
  2165 6156
  5523 5623
  1653 2126G

  t    t N
  1561 5321
  2123 5321
  2123 5321
  6532 5653G ]
```

Raja Swala, Ketawang,
    sléndro pathet sanga (2).

buka: 6 6221 .216 2165N/G

```
    t    t N  t    t N
[ 66.. 2321 3216 2165G
  66.. 2321 3216 2165G
  632. 2365 6.2. 6165G
  6.2. 2356 2152 5321G
  3216 2321 3216 2165G ]
```

322

Rambu (Sekatèn), Ladrang,
   pélog pathet lima (7).

buka:
```
t          t    N
...1 .1.3 .3.1 .3.2
...5 .321 .2.3 .5.3
.5.2 .3.5 .2.3 .2.1
.3.2 .1.2 .3.5 .2.3G

 t         t    N
...5 .3.6 .3.5 .3.2
...5 .2.4 .4.5 .2.1
...3 .3.. .3.2 .1.6
.6.6 .6.5 .3.2 .3.5G
```

dados:
```
 t         t    N
.3.6 .5.6 .5.6 .5.3
.5.6 .53. 653. 1232
5424 5456 542. 5421
23.2 3.12 3536 5323G

 t         t    N
[56.5 635. 653. 1232
5424 5456 542. 5421
23.2 3.12 3565 3216
.563 56.5 .23.23565G

 t         t    N
6756 .535 6756 3523
.576 .53. 653. 1232
5424 5456 542. 5421
23.2 3.12 3536 5323G]
```

pangkat seseg:
```
 t         t    N
56.5 635. 653. 1232
5424 5456 542. 5421
23.2 3.12 3565 3216
.563 56.5 .3.2 .3.5G
```

sesegan:
```
 t         t    N
[.3.6 .5.6 .5.6 .5.3
.5.6 .5.6 .3.1 .3.2
.5.4 .5.6 .2.4 .2.1
.3.2 .1.2 .3.5 .2.3G]
```

Rambu, Gendhing, kethuk 4 kerep, minggah
kethuk 8, pélog pathet nem (1).

buka:[3.2165.6] x2 .123 5654 2.44 2165N/G

mérong:
<pre>
        t   t   t   t   N
[.5.5 .5.5 61.2 .165 61.2 .165 33.. 2121
 ..21 6124 .444 5654 .444 5654 2.44 2165
 .65. 6563 .333 2123 ...3 6521 66.. 5535
 .676 5424 5654 2165 656. 656. 6561 2321G

        t   t   t   t   N
 ...1 6563 .567 .563 .567 .563 .333 1232
 ..23 56.5 4245 2165 .22. 2356 3565 2232
 .62. 62.6 2321 6123 ...3 6521 66.. 5535
 .676 5424 5654 2165 6123 5654 2.44 2165G

        t   t   t   t   N
 6123 55.. 55.6 .535 ..56 5323 ..35 6767
 ...7 .567 .567 2765 32.3 5676 .535 3212
 ..23 .532 52.3 5676 ..67 5676 5365 3212
 ..23 6532 6542 4521 ..2. 1261 .261 2353G

        t   t   t   t   N
 ...3 6521 66.. 5535 .254 2121 .261 2312
 ..23 56.5 4254 6727 .3.2 .765 33.. 1232
 .316 .3.2 3123 .123 .... 33.. 33.2 3521→
 .6.3 2132 3123 2161 2356 7654 2.44 2165G]
</pre>

ompak:
<pre>
        t   t   t   t   N
→.6.3 2132 3123 2123 .... 3353 .6.1 2353G

        t   t   t   t   B
 ..35 .653 ..32 3521 ..2. 1261 .261 2353
 ..35 .653 ..32 3521 612. 2212 33.. 1232
 .13. 2123 ..53 2161 23.. 6521 66.. 5535
 .676 5424 5654 2165 656. 656. 6561 2353G
</pre>

minggah:
<pre>
    t   t   t   t   t   t   t   t N
[.321 6563 .567 .563 .567 .563 .333 1232
 ..23 56.5 4254 2165 .22. 2356 3565 2232
 .62. 62.6 2321 6123 ...3 6521 66.. 5535
 .676 5424 5654 2165 6123 5654 2.44 2165G

    t   t   t   t   t   t   t   t N
 61.2 .165 61.2 .165 61.2 .165 33.. 2121
 ..21 6124 .444 5654 .444 5654 2.44 2165
 .65. 6563 .333 2123 ...3 6521 66.. 5535
 .676 5424 5654 2165 656. 656. 6561 2353G]
</pre>

Ramyang, Gendhing, kethuk 2 kerep, minggah
    kethuk 4, sléndro pathet manyura (2).

buka: 3 3216 .356 .356 3561 .216N/G

mérong:
```
            t         t    N
   [.356 .356 3561 .216
    .356 .356 3561 .216
    11.. 11.6 5536 5365
    ..5. 1656 1656 .523G

      t         t    N
    ..3. 2232 .126 .523
    ..3. 2232 .126 .523
    ..3. 2232 .126 .523
    .516 .516 3561 .126G]
```

minggah:
```
     t    t    t    t N
   [.5.3 .5.2 .1.6 .5.3
    .5.3 .5.2 .1.6 .5.3
    .5.3 .5.2 .1.6 .5.3
    .1.6 .1.6 .2.1 .2.6G

     t    t    t    t N
    .1.6 .1.6 .2.1 .2.6
    .1.6 .1.6 .2.1 .2.6
    .2.1 .6.1 .2.1 .3.5
    .6.5 .1.6 .1.6 .5.3G]
```

Randhat, Gendhing, kethuk 2 awis,
    sléndro pathet manyura (2).

buka: 2.2 .123 .3.2 .123 6121 6523N/G

mérong:
```
         t                  t              N
    ..35 1653 11.. 3212 ..23 2126 2321 6523
    22.. 22.3 55.6 5323 212. 2123 6121 6523
    ..35 1653 ..35 6656 .... 6653 22.3 2126→
    .... 66.. 3561 6523 212. 2123 6121 6523G
```

umpak minggah:
```
         t                  t              N
   →.... 66.. 3561 6523 .2.1 .2.3 .2.1 .5.3G
```

minggah: Ladrang Randhat

Randhat, Ladrang, sléndro
   pathet manyura (2).

(minggah to Gendhing Randhat)

t t N	t t N	t t N
.5.6 .5.3	.5.6 .5.3	.2.1 .5.6
.1.2 .5.3	.5.3 .6.5	.5.6 .5.3
.2.1 .2.3	.6.3 .6.5	.2.1 .2.3
.2.1 .5.3G	.2.3 .2.1G	.2.1 .5.3G

Randhu Kéntir, Gendhing, kethuk 2
   kerep, pélog pathet nem (3).

buka: 6656 .356 .35.36 .6532 1123 2126N/G

mérong: t   t   N
[. . 6 1 2 3 2 1 . . 1 2 3 5 3 2
 . 1 2 6 2 3 2 1 . . 1 2 3 5 3 2
 . 1 2 6 . . 6 . 2 3 2 1 3 2 1 6→
 .35 .36 .65 3 2 1 1 2 3 2 1 2 6G]
[umpak]: t   t   N
→ .35 .36 .65 3 2 5 3 1 6 2 1 2 6G

minggah: Ladrang Ayun-ayun

Rangkung, Ladrang, pélog
   pathet lima (7).

bubuka [buka]:

```
                N
...1 .1.3 .3.1 .3.2
.3.3 .2.1 .2.3 .5.3
.1.2 .3.5 .2.3 .2.1
.3.2 .1.. .1.2 .3.5G

                N
...5 .3.6 .532 .5.3
.6.5 .3.2 .235 5..5
...2 .2.2 .2.3 .5.6
.5.4 24.2 .565 2521G

  t         t   N
[2454 2124 5421 3212
3565 2321 2356 5323
1212 1235 2323 2321
2332 3212 3552 3565G

  t         t   N
2323 2356 5321 2353
6565 6532 3567 6535
2323 2323 2323 2356
7654 2442 4565 2421G

  t         t   N
2454 2124 5421 3212
3565 2321 2356 5323
1212 1235 2323 2321
23.2 321. 6.54 2454G

  t         t   N
5465 6446 6565 6564
5465 6446 6565 6523
5365 6226 6565 3212
3244 2442 4565 2421G]
```

suwuk:
```
  t         t   N
2454 2124 5421 3212
3565 2321 235. 3.23
.1.2 .3.5 .2.3 .2.1
.3.2 .1.6 .5.4 .2.4G
```

Rangsang Bali, Ladrang, pélog
    pathet nem (1).

buka: 352 .352 5654 2126N/G

```
  t    t N        t    t N
[.321 3216      .66. 5323
 .321 6132      6521 6123
 .352 .352      6532 .356
 5654 2126G     7654 2126G]
```

Rangsang Tuban, Ketawang,
    pélog pathet nem (38).

buka: 561. 2165 1111 3216N/G

```
  t    t N  t    t N
[.66. 6656 .653 2365G
 .532 1232 .216 5365G
 22.3 1232 .216 5365G
 33.. 3353 6521 6123G
 6521 6123 5676 5421G
 6123 5676 5424 2165G]
```

sesegan - suwukan:
```
  t    t N  t    t N
[612. 2165 612. 2165G
 612. 2165 11.. 3216G]
```

Rangu, Gendhing, kethuk 2 awis, minggah
    kethuk 4, pélog pathet nem (1).

buka: 2 .2.1 6123 .3.3 .5.6 .5.3 .6.5N/G

mérong:
```
        t                  t          N
[.632 1612 ..21 6123 .... 33.5 66.. 5535
 .632 1612 ..21 6123 .... 33.5 66.. 5535
 .632 1612 ..21 6123 .... 33.5 66.. 5535
 22.. 22.3 5654 2121 612. 2321 3265 3235G

        t                  t          N
 .555 2235 ..53 2356 ..61 2321 3265 3235
 .555 2235 ..53 2356 ..61 2321 3265 3235
 .555 2235 ..53 2356 ..61 2321 3265 3235
 22.. 22.1 22.1 6123 .... 3353 6532 3565G]
```

minggah:
```
         t    t    t    t N
    [.6.5 .1.6 .3.2 .6.5
     .6.5 .1.6 .3.2 .6.5
     .3.2 .3.2 .3.2 .6.5
     .5.6 .5.6 .3.2 .6.5G]
```

Ranu Manggala, Gendhing, kethuk 2
    kerep, pélog pathet nem (1).

buka: 5 .5.5 .356 1.1. 2.6. 5.16 .532N/G

mérong:
```
    [..23 2121 ..12 3532
     ..23 2121 ..12 3532
     .165 ..5. 5565 .165
     .612 .165 1216 3532G]
```

Rara Wudhu, Gendhing, kethuk 2
    kerep, sléndro pathet sanga (1).

buka: 5 5.61 65.6 .61. 1652 .612 1121N/G

mérong:
```
          t         t    N
    [2656 12.6 12.. 1121
     2656 12.6 12.. 1121
     .365 ..5. 55.6 1656
     561. 1652 .612 1121G
```

ngelik:
```
          t         t    N
    .... 1121 3212 .165
    .621 .... 3212 .165
    .... 55.. 55.6 1656
    .61. 1652 .612 1121G]
```

Rasa Madu/Dhandhang Gula, Gendhing,
   kethuk 2 kerep, minggah kethuk 4,
   pélog pathet lima (35).

buka: 5 .5.6 5421 67.5 6121N/G

mérong:
t		t	N
[.21.	2165	..56	1121
..16	5621	66.5	6356
..6.	6656	7767	5676
..6.	5561	3212	.165G

	t	t	N
..56	7656	5421	3216
33..	6532	3216	2165
22.1	3216	2321	6545 →
22.3	5654	6523	2121G]

umpak:
	t		t	N
→.3.1	.2.1	.6.5	.2.1G

minggah:
t	t	t	t N
[.2.1	.6.5	.1.6	.2.1
.2.1	.6.5	.1.6	.2.1
.2.3	.5.3	.6.5	.3.2
.3.1	.2.1	.6.5	.2.1G]

Rebeng, Gendhing, kethuk 4 kerep, minggah
   kethuk 8, pélog pathet nem (1).

buka: 3.2165. 3.21 6561 2356 5424 2121N/G

mérong:
t		t		t		t	N
[..12	35.6	532.	3216	3565	2232	..23	1.21
..12	35.6	532.	3216	3565	2232	..23	1.21
..12	35.6	532.	3216	3565	2232	66.5	6356
....	66..	6676	5421	6123	5654	2.44	5421G

t		t		t		t	N
41.2	4521	41.2	4521	41.2	4521	41.2	4521
....	55..	55.6	7656	.5.3	.523	553.	2312
35..	55..	55.6	7656	.5.3	.523	553.	2316 →
....	66..	6676	5421	612.	22..	22.3	5653G]

umpak minggah:
```
    t         t         t         t    N
→.... 66.. 6676 5421 612. 22.. 22.3 5653G

    t         t         t         t    N
.... 33.. 33.5 .323 55.. 5653 .2.3 .212
32.. 33.. 33.5 .323 55.. 5653 .2.3 .212
33.. 33.. 33.5 .2.6 ..76 5326 ..76 5312
.312 3532 .312 3532 .35. 6532 3216 5616G
```

minggah:
```
  t   t   t    t    t    t    t    t N
.16. 1653 .635 6126 .16. 1653 .635 6126
[.16. 1653 .635 6126 .123 .123 6532 3565
..56 7653 22.3 5.65 2325 2356 6676 5312
.312 3532 .321 3532 .35. 6532 3216 5616G

  t   t   t    t    t    t    t    t N
33.. 6532 3216 5616 33.. 6532 3216 5616]
```

Rembun, Gendhing, kethuk 4 kerep,
    sléndro pathet manyura (1).

buka: .22. 6123 .22. 6123 .216 3532N/G

mérong:
```
    t         t         t         t    N
[..23 6532 ..23 5653 .... 3353 .22. 2321
..32 .161 23.1 2353 .... 3353 .22. 2321
..32 .161 23.6 3561 .... 1265 33.5 6356
.... 6653 22.3 5653 .22. 6123 .216 3532G]
```

Remeng, Ladrang, sléndro
pathet nem (2).

buka: 561. 2165 1111 3216N/G

```
   t    t N
[.66.  6656
1653  2232
..61  2232
3216  5612G

   t    t N
3216  5612
3216  3353
.356  1653
5616  5323G

   t    t N
6521  6123
5616  5321
.111  2321
3212  .165G suwuk

   t    t N
.612  .165
.612  .165
.612  .165
11..  3216G]
```

Réna-réna/Rina-rina, Lancaran,
sléndro pathet sanga [nem ?] (6).

buka: 235 6532N/G

```
 N N   N N
[3235  6532G
3235  2356G
1632  3216G
1632  3216G
2321  6532G]
```

Rèndèh, Gendhing, kethuk 2 kerep, minggah
kethuk 4, sléndro pathet nem (16).

buka: 5 .612 .2.2 .321 .3.2 .165N/G

mérong:
```
        t       t    N
   [.2.2 .321 ..32 .165
    22.. 2321 ..32 .165
    22.. 2321 ..32 .165
    .615 .615 1216 5323G

        t       t    N
    .... 5235 .616 5323
    .... 5235 .616 5323
    .... 5235 11.. 1121 →
    .... 1121 3212 .165G]
```

umpak:
```
        t       t    N
   →.2.1 .2.1 .3.2 .6.5G
```

minggah:
```
   t    t    t    t N
  [.2.1 .2.1 .3.2 .6.5
   .2.1 .2.1 .3.2 .6.5
   .2.1 .2.1 .3.2 .6.5
   .6.5 .6.5 .1.6 .5.3G

   t    t    t    t N
   .5.3 .6.5 .1.6 .5.3
   .5.3 .6.5 .1.6 .5.3
   .5.3 .6.5 .1.6 .5.3
   .2.1 .3.2 .3.2 .6.5G]
```

Rentet, Gendhing, kethuk 2 kerep, dhawah
kethuk 4, sléndro pathet nem (5).

buka: 223 2161 22.. 2165 3365 22.2N/G

lamba:
```
        t       t    N
   .3.6 .3.6 .3.5 .3.2
   .3.6 .3.6 .3.5 .3.2
   .3.6 .3.6 .3.5 .2.3
   56.1 6532 5653 2126G
```

dados:
```
       t            t    N
   [2321 6535 35325 2356
    2321 6535 35325 2356
    2321 6535 35325 2353
    56.1 6535  3365 3232G
```

```
       t        t   N
.356 .356 .356 3532
.356 .356 .356 3532
.356 .356 .356 3523
56.1 6532 5653 2126G]
```

pangkat dhawah:
```
       t        t   N
2321 6535 35325 2356
2321 6535 35325 2356
2321 6535 35325 2353
.1.6 .1.5  .3.5 .3.2G
```

dhawah:
```
  t    t    t    t N
[.3.6 .3.6 .3.5 .3.2
 .3.6 .3.6 .3.5 .3.2
 .3.6 .3.6 .3.5 .2.3
 .1.6 .3.2 .5.3 .1.6G

  t    t    t    t N
 .2.1 .6.5 .3.2 .1.6
 .2.1 .6.5 .3.2 .1.6
 .2.1 .6.5 .3.2 .5.3
 .1.6 .1.5 .3.5 .3.2G]
```

Renyep, Gendhing, kethuk 2 kerep,
slèndro pathet sanga (3).

buka: ...5 5616 ..51 5321 .65. 5612N/G

mérong:
```
       t        t   N
[[ ...2 5321 .65. 5612
   ...2 5321 .65. 5612
   .365 ..5. 55.6 1656
   ..51 5321 .65. 5612G]
```

ngelik:
```
       t        t   N
11.. 1121 3212 .165
.621 ..1. 3212 .165
.621 ..1. 3212 .126
..51 5321 .65. 5612G]
```

Renyep Gendhing, Gendhing, kethuk 4 awis,
   minggah kethuk 4, sléndro pathet sanga (38).

buka: 5 .5.6 .1.6 ..51 5321 .65. 5612N/G

mérong: t   t
[...2 5321 .65. 5612 ..23 2126 3565 2232
 55.. 55.. 55.6 1656 ..51 5616 3352 3565N
.356 3532 66.1 6535 .356 3532 66.1 6535
.356 3532 66.1 6535 2356 5321 6132 .165N
.61. 1216 532. 2365 .61. 1216 532. 2365
11.. 11.2 3516 5312 5653 2121 3532 .165N
11.. 3216 3565 2232 ..25 2356 3565 2232 →
 55.. 55.. 55.6 1656 ..51 5321 .65. 5612N/G]

umpak minggah:
                                     N
→55.. 55.. 55.6 1656 .5.6 .2.1 .6.5 .3.2G

minggah: t   t   t   t N
    [.3.2 .3.1 .6.5 .3.2
    .3.2 .3.1 .6.5 .3.2
    .3.5 .6.5 .1.2 .1.6
    .5.6 .2.1 .6.5 .3.2G]

Retnaning Sih, Ladrang,
   pélog pathet lima (1).

buka: 2 2165 1612 1645N/G

 t   t N   t   t N
[.612 1645   .555 6465
.612 1645   .555 6465
11.. 5612   6542 1121
1312 .165G   5612 1645G]

Ricik-ricik, Lancaran, sléndro
pathet manyura (2).

buka: 6 .356 .532 .356N/G

```
t tN t tN t tN t tN
.3.5 .6.5 .6.5 .1.6G
.3.5 .6.5 .6.5 .1.6G
.3.2 .3.2 .3.2 .1.6G
.3.2 .3.2 .3.2 .1.6G
```

Rimong, Gendhing, kethuk 2 kerep,
   sléndro pathet manyura (4).

buka: 661 6535 .22. 2356 .365 3212N/G

mérong:
```
          t       t    N
[.32. 232. 232. 2353
..35 1653 ..35 6356
.... 6653 22.3 5653 →
..25 3.25 3.65 3212G

       t       t    N
.126 .123 5653 2126
.16. 6123 5653 2126
.... 66.. 3561 6535
.22. 2356 .365 3212G]
```

umpak minggah:
```
          t       t    N
→ .5.3 .5.3 .1.2 .1.6G
```

minggah: Ladrang Moncèr

Rindhik, Gendhing, kethuk 4 kerep, minggah
   kethuk 8, sléndro pathet nem (16).

buka: 2.35 6.53 ..5. 3.56 1216N/G

mérong:
```
     t        t          t        t     N
[.612 .612 .612 1653 ..35 6532 ..23 5616
 .612 .612 .612 1653 ..35 6532 ..32 1612
 66.1 6523 6532 6165 1632 ..23 5653 2165→
 2356 .523 ..56 5323 ..5. 3.5. 3.56 1216G]
```

umpak:
```
     t        t          t        t     N
→.1.6 .5.3 .5.6 .5.3 .5.3 .5.6 .1.2 .1.6G
```

minggah:
```
   t    t    t    t    t    t    t N
[.3.2 .3.2 .3.2 .5.3 .5.3 .5.6 .1.2 .1..6
 .3.2 .3.2 .3.2 .5.3 .5.3 .5.2 .3.1 .3.2
 .5.6 .5.3 .5.2 .6.5 .3.2 .3.2 .5.3 .6.5
 .1.6 .5.3 .5.6 .5.3 .5.3 .5.6 .1.2 .1.6G]
```

Rondha Maya, Gendhing, minggah
   kethuk 8, sléndro pathet nem (1).

(minggah to Gendhing Mongkok Dhalik)
```
   t    t    t    t    t    t    t    t N
[ 3235 3635 3635 3635 3632 3635 3635 3132
 .1.6 .1.6 .3.6 .3.2 .5.3 .6.5 .6.5 .3.2
 .1.6 .1.6 .3.6 .3.2 .5.3 .6.5 .6.5 .3.2
 .66. 6621 .55. 6621 .55. 6621 5153 6532G ]
```

337

Rondha Nunut, Gendhing, kethuk 2 kerep, minggah
. kethuk 4, slendro pathet manyura (1).

buka: 6616 .12. 2126 1132 .126N/G

mérong: t   t   N
        [..61 22.. 22.3 2121
         ..61 22.. 22.3 2121
         3212 .126 3561 6523 →
         212. 2126 1132 .126G]

umpak: t   t   N
        → .2.1 .2.6 .3.2 .1.6G

minggah: t   t
    [. . . 2   . . . 1   . . . 2̄6̄ 1̄2̄3̄5̄6̄5̄3̄
     2̄5̄3 6 1 2 6 3 2 3 2 6 3 . 2 . 1N
     . . . 2   . . . 1   . . . 2̄6̄ 1̄2̄3̄5̄6̄5̄3̄
     2̄5̄3 6 1 2 6 3 2 3 2 6 3 . 2 . 1N
     . . . 3   . . . 2   . . . 1   . . . 6
     . . . 2   . . . 1   . . . 5   . . . 3N
     . . . 2   . . . 1   . . . 2   . . . 6
     . . . 3   . . . 2   . . . 1   . . . 6N/G]

Rondha Sari, Gendhing, kethuk 2 kerep, minggah
    kethuk 4, slendro pathet manyura (1).

buka: 661 6523 .1.1 .2.1 .3.2 .1.6N/G

mérong: t   t   N
        [.... 6653 22.3 1232
         .... 22.3 55.6 5323
         ..32 1653 11.. 3216 →
         33.. 3356 2321 3216G]

umpak: t   t   N
        → .5.3 .5.6 .2.1 .2.6G

minggah: t   t   t   t N
        [.3.2 .1.6 .3.6 .3.2
         .3.2 .3.2 .5.6 .5.3
         .5.3 .2.1 .3.2 .1.6
         .5.3 .5.6 .2.1 .2.6G]

Rondhon, Gendhing, kethuk 4 awis, minggah
kethuk 8, sléndro pathet sanga (2).

buka: 6.6 .561 .1.6 .561 .612 .165N/G

mérong:

```
.1.1 .1.1 .3.2 .165 ..52 3565 11.. 3216
[..61 6535 11.. 3216 .... 6653 2353 2121N
55.2 3565 1216 5321 .111 2321 3532 .126
.... 6653 22.3 5635 .... 55.6 1656 5321N
.111 2321 5616 5321 5616 5321 3532 .126
.... 6653 22.3 5635 .... 55.6 1656 5321N →
33.. 6532 ..21 3216 3565 2232 ..25 2356
.... 66.. 661. 5561 ..16 5561 .612 .165N/G

      t              t
11.. 1121 3212 .165 ..52 3565 11.. 3216]
```

umpak minggah:

→ .3.2 .1.6 .3.2 .6.5 .6.5 .2.1 .2.1 .6.5N/G

minggah:

```
   t    t    t    t    t    t    t    t N
[.2.1 .6.5 .2.1 .6.5 .6.5 .6.5 .1.6 .2.1
 .6.5 .2.1 .2.1 .6.5 .6.5 .6.5 .1.6 .2.1
 .6.5 .2.1 .2.1 .5.6 .5.6 .3.5 .1.6 .2.1
 .3.2 .1.6 .3.2 .6.5 .6.5 .2.1 .2.1 .6.5G]
```

Ronèng Tawang, Ladrang,
sléndro pathet sanga (3).

buka: 5 .23. 3635 22.3 5635N/G

```
    t    t N
[.352 3565
 323. 3635
 323. 3635
 22.3 5635G

    t    t N
 .352 3565
 323. 3635
 323. 3635
 22.3 5616G
```

ngelik:
```
   t    t N
 .563 5616
 123. 3216
 123. 3216
  55.2 3565G

   t    t N
 66.3 5616
 123. 3216
 123. 3216
  55.2 3565G]
```

Rujak Jeruk, Ladrang, sléndro
   pathet manyura (3).

buka: 2 2356 1653 6532N/G

```
   t       t    N
 .5.2 .5.3 .5.6 .5.2
 .5.2 .5.3 .5.6 .5.2
 6356 2132 5321 6523
 652. 2356 1653 6532G
```

Rujak Sentul, Gendhing, kethuk 2
   kerep, pélog pathet nem (3).

buka: .661 6563 .52. 2365 $\overline{42}$161 2312N/G

mérong:
```
        t       t     N
 .52. 2523 6535 3212
 .52. 2523 6535 3212
 .126 ..6. 2321 6523
 .52. 2365$\overline{42}$161 2312G
```

Sambul Gendhing, Gendhing, kethuk 4 kerep,
    minggah kethuk 8, pélog pathet nem (1).

buka: [123.216.6.]x2 5 .6.5 .616 5323N/G

mérong:
```
          t            t            t            t     N
   [6521  612.  2356  5323  6521  612.  2356  5323
    ....  33..  33.2  3521  6536  3561  2.44  2126
    ...6  .2.6  .2.6  .123  ....  33..  33.2  5321
    .6.3  2132  3123  2123  ....  3353  .5.2  .5.3G

          t            t            t            t     N
    ..56  .535  .352  .356  .5.3  .532  66..  5535
    .35.  5356  ..76  5421  6536  3561  2.44  2126
    ...6  .2.6  .2.6  .123→....  33..  33.2  3561
    .6.3  2132  3123  2126  .6.5  .6.5  .616  5323G]
```

umpak:
```
          t            t            t            t     N
                             →.5.5  .2.6  ..76  5421
    6612  3216  3532  1653  ..35  6532  5654  2126G
```

minggah/unggah:
```
       t    t    t    t    t    t    t    t N
   [.3.2 .1.6 .3.2 .6.7 .6.7 .6.7 .5.6 .3.2
    .3.2 .1.6 .3.2 .6.7 .6.7 .6.7 .5.6 .3.2
    .3.2 .3.2 .3.2 .6.5 2325 2356 6676 5421
    6612 3216 3532 1653 ..35 6532 5654 2126G]
```

Sambul Talèdhèk, Gendhing, kethuk 4 awis,
    minggah kethuk 8, pélog pathet nem (11).

buka: ‾.6 3.‾216 .6.‾.6 3.‾216 .2.‾61 2356 .7.6 .5.3 .6.5N/G

mérong:
```
             t                      t
   [..56  .532  ..13  2161  22.3  5676  .53.  2353
    .53.  53.6  5365  3212  66..  66.5  44..  2245N
    .35.  5365  ..53  2356  ..76  5326  ..76  5421
    612.  2212  33.1  3216  33..  3353  6535  3212N→
    .12.  2132  ..21  6123  ..53  2163  ..53  2161
    23..  33..  3365  .653  ..65  .421  612.  3216N
    ..61  3216  33..  1232  .12.  2123  ..53  2161
    22..  22..  22.3  2161  2356  .7.6  .5.3  .6.5N/G]
```

umpak:
```
   →.12.  2132  ..21  6123  ..53  2163  ..53  2165
                             .5.5  .2.6  .5.3  .6.5N
    .1.6  .5.3  .1.6  .5.3  .5.6  .3.2  .1.6  .3.2N/G
```

minggah:
```
    t    t    t    t    t    t    t    t N
[.3.2 .3.2 .3.2 .5.3 .5.3 .5.6 .2.1 .3.2
 .3.2 .3.2 .3.2 .5.3 .5.3 .5.6 .2.1 .3.2
 .3.2 .3.2 .5.4 .6.5 .6.5 .3.6 .5.3 .6.5
 .1.6 .5.3 .1.6 .5.3 .5.6 .3.2 .1.6 .3.2G]
```

Samiran, Ladrang, pélog
  pathet nem (38).

buka: .66. 6365 .365 2312N/G

```
  t    t N
.3.2 .1.6
.1.6 .5.3
.5.3 .6.5
.365 2312G
```

Sampak, sléndro pathet
  manyura (3).

buka kendhang: 2N/G

```
 P P P P   P P P P   P P P
 NNNNNNNN  NNNNNNNN  NNNNNNNN
[ 2 2 2 2  3 3 3 3  1 1 1 1G
  1 1 1 1  2 2 2 2  6 6 6 6G
  6 6 6 6  3 3 3 3  2 2 2 2G]
```

Sampak, sléndro
  pathet nem (3).

buka kendhang: 5N/G

```
 P P P P   P P P
 NNNNNNNN  NNNNNNNN
[5 5 5 5   3 3 3 3G
 3 3 3 3
 5 5 5 5
 2 2 2 2
 6 6 6 6   5 5 5 5G]
```

Sampak, sléndro pathet
    sanga (3).

buka kendhang: 5N/G

```
P P P P   P P P P   P P P
NNNNNNNN  NNNNNNNN  NNNNNNNN
[ 5 5 5 5   1 1 1 1G
  1 1 1 1   2 2 2 2   6 6 6 6G
  6 6 6 6   1 1 1 1   5 5 5 5G
            5 5 5 5   2 2 2 2G
            2 2 2 2   5 5 5 5G ]
```


Sampak Galong, sléndro
    pathet manyura (35).

buka: 2 2 2N/G

```
    P P  P P  P
    NNNN NNNN NNNN
         [5252 5151G
          5252 5156G
               5156G
    5156 5253 5251G
    5151 5356 5352G
    5252]
```


Sampak Tanggung, sléndro
    pathet sanga (2).

buka kendhang: 5N/G

```
    P P  P P  P P  P P  P P  P P  P
    NNNN NNNN NNNN NNNN NNNN NNNN NNNN
[ 6565 6565 2121 2121 3232 3232 5616G
            1616 1616 2121 2121 3565G
                      6565 6565 3212G
                      3232 3232 3565G]
```

Sangu Pati, Gendhing, kethuk 4 awis, minggah
    kethuk 8, pélog pathet barang (38).

buka: 6 .6.7 6523 .5.5 .5.5 .6.3 .7.6N/G

mérong:
```
            t                    t
[..65 .356 ..65 .356 ..65 3356 ..65 3567
..76 5356 ..65 3567 .... 7765 3565 3272N
5653 2756 33.. 6532 5653 2756 .... 6765
33.. 6532 7232 .756 .... 6656 3567 6532N
5653 2756 33.. 6532 5653 2756 .... 6765
33.. 6532 7232 .756 55.. 55.. 7656 3532N→
55.. 7653 6532 .756 .76. 6723 5653 2756
.... 6656 3567 6532 55.. 55.. 5563 .7.6N/G]
```

umpak:
```
      t         t         t         t    N
→ .5.3 .7.6 .2.3 .7.6 .5.6 .5.3 .5.3 .7.6G
```

minggah:
```
    t    t    t    t    t    t    t    t N
[.2.7 .2.6 .2.7 .5.3 .5.3 .5.6 .2.7 .3.2
 .7.6 .3.2 .3.7 .5.3 .5.3 .5.6 .2.7 .3.2
 .7.6 .3.2 .3.7 .5.6 .5.6 .2.7 .5.6 .5.3
 .5.6 .5.3 .5.6 .5.3 .2.7 .5.6 .3.2 .7.6G]
```


Sangu Pati, Gendhing, kethuk 2 kerep, minggah
    kethuk 4, pélog pathet barang (38).

buka: 667 6523 .5.5 .5.5 .6.3 .7.6N/G

mérong:
```
            t         t    N
[..65 .356 ..65 .356
..65 7653 ..35 6767
..76 5356 ..65 3567
.... 7765 3565 3272G

       t         t    N
5653 2756 33.. 6532
5653 2756 33.. 6532 →
5653 2756 3567 6523
55.. 55.. 5563 .7.6G]
```

umpak:
```
        t         t    N
→ .5.3 .7.6 .2.3 .7.6
  .5.6 .5.3 .5.3 .7.6G
```

```
minggah:
         t    t    t    t N
    [.2.7 .2.6 .2.7 .5.3
     .5.3 .5.6 .2.7 .3.2
     .5.3 .7.6 .2.3 .7.6
     .5.6 .5.3 .5.3 .7.6G]
```

Santri Brahi, Ketawang,
    pélog pathet barang (1).

buka celuk:

```
     t    t N  t    t N
[[.2.3 .2.7 .3.2 .7.6G]x2
 .... 7576 3567 6532G
 .352 .352 5653 2756G]
```

Sapa Ngira, Lancaran,
    sléndro pathet sanga (33).

buka: 1 1235 1652N/G

```
    N N  N N
[ 3232 1615G
  1515 1652G ]
```

Sapu Jagad, Ladrang, sléndro
    pathet manyura (1).

buka: 223 .532 6616 2356N/G

```
  t    t N     t    t N
1516 2356    5653 6532
1516 2356    5653 6532
1516 2356    5653 6532
5563 6532G   6616 2356G
```

Sara Yuda, Ladrang, pélog
pathet nem (1).

buka: 3 .561 .1.1 .6.5 .1.6 .5.3N/G

```
  t    t N           t    t N
[.32. 2321         ..35 6121
 .12. 2321         3265 3561
 .132 .532         3265 3235
 .523 5653G        1216 5323G]
```

Sari Laya, Ladrang, pélog
pathet lima (1).

```
   t    t N
[[22.. 2232    ⎞
 ..23 5653     ⎬ x2
 .321 3212     ⎟
 3321 6535G]   ⎠

   t    t N
 11.. 1121
 3212 .165
 ..23 5656
 3565 3212G

   t    t N
 66.. 6656
 ..76 5323
 .321 3212
 3321 6535G]
```

Sari Madu, Gendhing, kethuk 2 kerep,
minggah kethuk 4, sléndro
pathet manyura (1).

buka: 661 6563 ..35 6532 1232 .126N/G

mérong:
```
   t            t    N
[..61 6132 ..61 2321
 ..32 .161 2353 2121
 3212 .126 3561 6535→
 66.1 6532 1232 .126G
```

```
ngelik:t          t   N
    .... 6656 3561 6523
    .516 .... 3561 6523
    55.. 55.. 55.. 6356
    ..35 6532 1232 .126G]
```

```
umpak: t          t   N
    → .5.6 .3.2 .3.2 .1.6G
```

```
minggah:
    t    t    t    t N
   [.2.3 .5.3 .2.3 .2.1
    .2.1 .2.3 .5.3 .2.1
    .3.2 .1.6 .2.1 .5.3
    .5.6 .3.2 .3.2 .1.6G]
```

Sawung Galing, Gendhing, kethuk 2 kerep,
    minggah kethuk 4, pélog pathet lima (1).

buka: 556 4565 .4.4 .4.4 .5.6 .545N/G

```
mérong: t          t    N
    [.... 5654 22.4 5.65
     .... 5654 22.4 5.65
     66.. 6656 7765 4254
     22.4 5654 2165 6121G
```

```
         t          t    N
     3212 .165 15.6 1.21
     3212 .165 15.6 1.21
     .... 11.2 456. 4566
     44.. 44.. 4456 .545G]
```

```
minggah:
    t    t    t    t N
   [656. 6545 4254 2165
    656. 6545 4254 2165
    6123 55.. 55.6 4565
    656. 6545 4254 2165G]
```

Sawung Galing, Ladrang,
  pélog pathet barang (3).

buka: 235. 5756 7727 6535N/G

t t N	t t N
235. 5756	22.. 2327
235. 5756	3265 2327
235. 5756	55.. 2356
7727 6535G	7727 6535G

Sèdhet, Gendhing, kethuk 4 kerep, minggah
  kethuk 8, sléndro pathet manyura (4).

buka: 2 2165 .63. 3561 .312 .126N/G

mérong:
```
     t         t        t        t   N
[.2.1 .2.6 .2.1 6123 .... 3353 6535 3212
 .321 .3.2 ..21 6123 .... 3353 6535 3212
 .321 .3.2 ..21 6123 .... 3353 6535 3212→
 5653 2165 .63. 3635 .63. 3561 .3.2 .1.6G]
```

badhé minggah [umpak]:
```
      t        t        t        t   N
→.6.1 .5.3 .6.1 .5.3 .2.1 .2.1 .2.6 .3.2G
```

minggah:
```
   t    t    t    t    t    t    t    t N
[.3.2 .3.2 .3.2 .3.1 .2.1 .2.1 .2.6 .3.2
 .3.2 .3.2 .3.2 .3.1 .2.1 .2.1 .2.6 .3.2
 .3.2 .3.2 .3.2 .3.1 .2.1 .2.1 .2.6 .3.2
 .6.1 .5.3 .6.1 .5.3 .2.1 .2.1 .2.6 .3.2G]
```

Segaran, Ketawang, pélog
pathet nem (1).

buka: 356 5323 5676 5352N/G

```
    t   t N  t    t N
[[.356 5323 5676 5352G] x2
 ..16 1232 .356 5352G
 66.. 6656 2165 3565G
 .653 ..23 5676 5323G
 6521 6.56 2165 3561G
 22.3 1232 .165 3561G
 23.. 3333 6532 3565G
 .... 5535 6676 5352G]
```

Sekar Gadhung, Ladrang, sléndro
pathet manyura (3).

buka: 2 2165 .612 .1.6N/G

irama II:
```
        t    t N
    [.1.6 .3.2
     .1.6 .3.2
     .3.2 .3.5
     .1.6 .1.6G]
```

irama III:
```
        t         t    N
    [.3.1 .3.6 .3.5 .3.2
     .3.1 .3.6 .3.5 .3.2
     .3.5 .3.2 .3.6 .3.5
     .3.1 .3.6 .3.1 .3.6G]
```

Sekar Gadhung Pagelèn, Gendhing (Santiswaran),
sléndro pathet sanga (39).

```
                      •
 .  . 1 16616    . 6 1 .51 .65
 .  . 2 2 216 1   2 152    232 1
. 5 5 615 .32 3   5 132    616 5
 .  . 2 2 216 1   2 152    232 1
. 5 1 2 23216 1   2 152    232 1
 .  . 1 1 1 2 3  . 5 6 .15 266
 .  . 6 6 6 1 2  . 231 .26 165
 .  . 5 5 6 1    . 232    616 5
1 6 5   1 6 5 5   6 6 615 23355G
```

Sekar Téja, Gendhing, kethuk 2 kerep,
minggah kethuk 4, pélog pathet lima (1).

buka: ⌊3 .21 65.5. ⌋ x2   .3.3 .321 .1.5 6121N/G

mérong: t   t   N
    [...1 .561 .561 .561
    .3.2 .165 15.6 1232
    .... 2212 33.. 1232→
    11.. 5612 1312 .165G

          t   t   N
    .65. 5612 1312 .165
    33.. 3353 6535 3212
    .... 2212 33.. 1232
    11.. 5612 1312 .165G

          t   t   N
    .65. 5612 1312 .165
    11.. 1121 3212 .165
    .... 55.6 1216 5421
    3212 .165 15.6 1.21G]

umpak: t   t   N
    →.3.1 .3.2 .3.2 .6.5G

minggah:
```
    t    t    t    t N
[.6.5 .3.2 .3.2 .6.5
 .2.3 .5.3 .6.5 .3.2
 .3.2 .5.3 .5.3 .1.2
 .3.2 .6.5 .6.5 .2.1G]
```

Semang, Gendhing, kethuk 8 kerep, minggah
   kethuk 16, pélog pathet nem (1).

buka: [123. 2165] x2 .5.6 .1.6 .1.2 .321N/G

mérong:
```
  t          t          t          t
[.1.6 .1.6 .1.2 .321 .5.6 .1.2 .4.5 .421
 41.2 6123 2.32 .165 6123 .... 3356 .535N
 ..53 22.. 22.3 5653 .323 5654 2144 2121
 41.2 41.2 41.2 6123 ...3 6532 .523 5676N
 .... 66.. 66.5 6356 .567 5676 .532 3565
 .... 55.. 55.. 6356 .567 5676 .535 3212N
 ..21 .2.. 12.1 6123 ...3 6532 .321 6123
 ...3 6532 66.. 6656 776. 5424 .521 6121N/G
```

```
  t          t          t          t
 .5.6 .1.6 .1.2 .321 .5.6 .1.2 .4.5 .421
 41.2 6123 ..32 .165 6123 .... 3356 .535N
 .653 22.. 22.3 5653 .523 5654 2.44 2121
 ..12 41.2 11.2 6123 ...3 6532 .523 5676N
 .... 66.. 66.3 6356 .567 5676 .532 3565
 .... 55.. 55.. 6356 .567 5676 .535 3212N
 ..21 .2.. 12.1 6123 ...3 .652 .321 6123
 ...3 6532 66.. 6656 ..65 .6.5 .6.3 .7.6N/G
```

```
  t          t          t          t
 .... 66.. 6567 6535 .635 66.. 6567 6535
 .635 66.. 6576 5352 66.. 6654 2.44 2121N
 ..12 41.2 41.2 6123 55.6 5654 2.44 2165
 .... 5535 66.. 1653 22.. 2321 6123 2126N
 ..63 2132 3123 2161 2356 7654 2.44 2165
 .... 5535 66.. 1653 .3.3 .3.3 .532 3565N
 ..56 7654 22.3 5.65 2325 2356 6676 5421
 6612 3216 3532 3216 22.. 2621 6535 2232N/G]
```

minggah:
```
  t    t    t    t    t    t    t    t
[.444 5654 .444 5654 .444 5654 2.44 2165
..6. 5.6. 3565 2232 .444 5654 2.44 2165N
..6. 5.6. 3565 2232 .... 2123 .123 5616
..1. 6.12 3216 5612 .... 2123 .123 5612N
323. 3235 3216 5612 323. 3235 3216 5612
356. 3565 4245 2165 6123 .123 6532 3565N
..56 1653 22.3 5.65 2325 2356 6616 5421 →
6612 3216 3532 3216 22.. 2621 6535 2232N/G]
```

suwuk:
```
   t    t    t    t    t    t    t    t
→ 6156 2165 61.6 2165 ..54 24.2 4254 2165N/G
```

Semang, Ladrang, pélog
    pathet nem (38).

buka: 612 3612 .1.6N/G

```
  t    t N
.3.2 .1.6
.3.2 .1.6
.3.2 .3.5
.6.4 .6.5G
```

demung imbal:
```
  t    t N
[.555 3235
.555 3561
3265 6656
53.. 5653G
```

```
  t    t N
.323 5653
.323 5653
.323 5653
56.. 5356G
```

```
  t    t N
.666 5356
5565 3561
3265 3565
32.. 3532G
```

```
  t    t N
.222 3532
.222 3532
.222 3532
35.2 3565G
```

```
  t    t N
.555  3235
6656  3532
.235  6532
16.1  2353G

  t    t N
.1.2  3523
.1.2  3523
.1.2  3523
11.2  3565G]
```

kanggé sabetan:
```
   t    t N
[.1.2  3523
 .1.2  3523
 .1.2  3523
 11.2  .523G]
```

Semang Gita, Gendhing, kethuk 4 awis,
    pélog pathet lima (1).

buka: .556 .532 ..13 .212 3321 6535N/G

mérong:
```
      t                              t
[..22 2232 ..23 2121 ..32 .165 22.. 2321
 ..32 .165 22.. 2321 ..32 .16. 5616 5323N
 ...3 6532 ..23 5653 ...3 6532 ..23 5616
 .... 6656 11.. 3216 ..1. 6.5. 3.23 5635N
 .... 5565 612. 2165 612. 2165 .616 5323
 ...3 6532 ..23 5623 .... 6532 5654 2121N
 .2.6 1261 ..21 6123 55.. 5421 ..21 6123
 55.. 55.. 55.6 .532 ..13 .212 3321 6535N/G]
```

Semar Mantu, Ladrang, sléndro
    pathet nem (35).

buka: 5365 2132 6516 2166N/G

```
 t    t N       t    t N       t    t N
[2123 2126     1612 1615      5365 2132
 2123 2126     1612 1615      5365 2132
 2123 2126     1612 1615      5365 2132
 5565 6165G    2312 3532G     6516 2126G]
```

Sembawa, Ladrang, pélog
   pathet lima (3).

buka: 3 .323 5653 5323 2121N/G

t	t N	t	t N	t	t N
.111	2321	55..	5535	.333	2121
.111	2353	..56	7656	.111	2353
.356	7653	.653	6535	.356	7653
5323	2121G	6621	2353G	5323	2121G

Sembung Gilang, Ladrang,
   sléndro pathet sanga (2).

buka: 222 5321 5612 1635N/G

t tN t tN t tN t tN
[2.25 2.25 2.25 6561G
  2.25 2.25 2.25 6561G
  6356 2126 2321 3216G
  2312 5321 5612 1635G]

'Sembur Adas, Gendhing, kethuk 4 kerep,
   pélog pathet barang (38).

buka: 2.2 .2.7 65.2 .2.2 .765 .2.2 .3.5
             .632 7232N/G

mérong: t   t   t   t   N
[.... 2235 7632 7232 66.. 66.. 6676 5323
  27.. 77.2 3423 2767 ...7 6563 2765 3567
  .3.2 .765 ..56 7232 ..23 4327 .765 3567
  .3.2 .765 66.. 5535 ..53 6532 ..23 5235G

    t   t   t   t   N
76532 7232 ..35 3272 66.. 66.. 6676 5323
  27.. 77.2 3423 2767 ...7 6563 2765 3567
  .3.2 .765 ..56 7232 ..23 4327 .765 3567
  .3.2 .765 22.. 2232 .... 2235 7632 7232G]

minggah: Ladrang Longgor Lasem

Sembur Adas/Sambul Raras/Sembu Raras,
Gendhing, kethuk 2 kerep,
pélog pathet lima (1).

buka: .556 5424 .24. 4521 61.5 6121N/G

mérong: t   t   N
  [.21. 2165 15.6 1232
  ..2. 22.4 5654 .521
  3212 .165 22.3 1232
  ..21 .265 ..56 4565G

    t   t   N
  .532 11.. 11.2 3212
  ..2. 22.4 5654 .521
  6123 55.. 55.6 7653
  .356 5421 61.5 6121G]

minggah: Tamba Oneng

Semèru, Gendhing, kethuk 2 kerep,
sléndro pathet sanga (1).

buka: 55 616. 51.6 521. 5323 2121N/G

mérong:t   t   N
  [..56 1.21 3212 .126
  3532 ..23 5321 6535
  ..5. 55.. 55.6 1656
  .51. .652 1523 2121G

    t   t   N
  22.. 22.3 5321 6535
  22.. 22.3 5321 6535
  22.. 22.3 5321 6535
  22.. 2356 .2.1 .6.5G

    t   t   N
  2353 2165 2321 6535
  2353 2165 2321 6535
  66.. 66.. 3565 3212
  .35. 235. 2353 2126G

    t   t   N
  3532 ..23 5323 2121
  3261 22.. 2321 6535
  ..5. 55.. 55.6 1656
  .51. 1621 5323 2121G]

Semirang/Semiring, kethuk 2 kerep,
   minggah kethuk 4, sléndro pathet sanga (4).

buka: 2 2165 .65. 5612 1312 .165N/G

mérong: t   t   N
    [.65. 5612 1312 .165
     22.. 22.3 5653 2126
     ..21 .653 22.3 5635 →
     .65. 5612 1312 .165G

        t   t   N
     .65. 5612 1312 .165
     11.. 1121 3212 .165
     ..21 .... 3212 .165
     1216 5312 1312 .165G

        t   t   N
     .65. 5612 1312 .165
     66.. 66.. 2321 6535
     ..21 .... 3212 .165
     1216 5312 1312 .165G]

badhé minggah [umpak]:
        t   t   N
     →.6.5 .3.2 .3.2 .6.5G

minggah: t   t   t   t N
    [.6.5 .3.2 .3.2 .6.5
     .3.2 .3.2 .5.3 .1.6
     .2.1 .5.3 .2.3 .6.5
     .6.5 .3.2 .3.2 .6.5G

     t   t   t   t N
     .6.5 .3.2 .3.2 .6.5
     .2.1 .2.1 .3.2 .6.5
     .2.1 .2.1 .3.2 .6.5
     .1.6 .3.2 .3.2 .6.5G

     t   t   t   t N
     .6.5 .3.2 .3.2 .6.5
     .3.6 .5.6 .2.1 .6.5
     .2.1 .2.1 .3.2 .6.5
     .1.6 .3.2 .3.2 .6.5G]

Semu Kirang, Gendhing, kethuk 2 kerep,
  minggah kethuk 4, sléndro pathet nem (2).

buka: 2356 .6.1 .2.1 .2.6 .3.5N/G

mérong: t   t   N
           .3.3 .3.3 .6.5 .3.2
      [.52. 2623 6535 3212
       .52. 2623 6535 3212
       66.. 6656 3565 3212G

             t   t   N
           .52. 2325 6535 3212
           ..1. 6.1. 6.3. 2312
           ..1. 6.1. 6.3. 2312 →
           ..1. 6.1. 6.21 6535G

             t   t   N
           33.. 3353 6535 3212]

umpak minggah:
             t   t   N
        → .1.6 .1.6 .2.1 .6.5G

minggah:
         t   t   t   t N
      [.2.3 .5.3 .6.5 .3.2
       .3.2 .5.3 .6.5 .3.2
       .3.2 .5.3 .6.5 .3.2
       .5.6 .5.6 .3.5 .3.2G

         t   t   t   t N
       .3.2 .5.3 .6.5 .3.2
       .1.6 .1.6 .2.3 .1.2
       .1.6 .1.6 .2.3 .1.2
       .1.6 .1.6 .2.1 .6.5G]

Sénapati, Gendhing, kethuk 2 kerep, minggah
   kethuk 4, sléndro pathet sanga (4).

buka: 2 2165 .612 .165N/G

mérong:

  [2 3 2 1   2 3 2 1   2 3 2 1   6 5 3 5
   2 3 2 1   2 3 2 1   2 3 2 1   6 5 3 5
   2 2 3̅5̅6̅   . 1 6 5̲   . 2 . 1   6 5 3 5
   2 2 3̅5̅6̅   . 1 6 5̳3̳5̳3̳5̳6̳5̳2̳3̳2̳1   6 5 3 5G

```
         t           t           t           N
. . 5 6    1 6 5 3    2 3 2 1    6 5 3 5
. . 5 6    1 6 5 3    2 3 2 1    6 5 3 5
2 2 3̄5̄6    . 1 6 5    . 2 . 1    6 5 3 5
2 2 3̄5̄6    . 1 6  5̄3̄5̄3̄5̄652321  6 5 3 5G

         t                       t           N
. 2 . 1    . 2 . 1    . 2 . 1    6 5 3 5
. 2 . 1    . 2 . 1    . 2 . 1    6 5 3 5
. 2 . 1    . 2 . 1    . 2 . 1    6 5 3 5
. 2 . 6    . 3 . 5    . 2 . 1    . 6 . 5G]
```

minggah:
```
    t      t      t      t N
[.2.1  .2.1  .2.1  .6.5
 .2.1  .2.1  .2.1  .6.5
 .2.6  .3.5  .2.1  .6.5
 .2.6  .3.5  .2.1  .6.5G

    t      t      t      t N
 .1.6  .5.3  .2.1  .6.5
 .1.6  .5.3  .2.1  .6.5
 .2.6  .3.5  .2.1  .6.5
 .2.6  .3.5  .2.1  .6.5G]
```

Sengkawa, Gendhing, kethuk 4 kerep, minggah
   kethuk 8, pélog pathet nem (1).

buka: [1̄23.216.6] x2   .6.6 .7.6 .535 3212N/G

mérong:
```
   t            t            t            t      N
[....  3123  .532  3123  .532  5654  2.44  2126
 ...6  .2.6  .2.6  .123  5676  5421  6123  5676
 ....  66..  66.5  6356  .567  .656  .535  3212
 .321  6132  .321  6123  56..  6676  .535  3212G

    t           t            t            t      N
 ....  3123  .532  3123  .532  5654  2.44  2165
 ....  5535  66..  1653  22..  2321  6123  2126 →
 ..61  2132  3123  2123  ....  33..  33.2  3561
 .6.3  2132  3123  2161  ....  6676  .535  3212G]
```

umpak:
```
    t           t            t            t      N
→ ..63  2132  3123  2165  .5.5  .2.6  ..76  5421
  6653  2356  .653  2365  22..  3216  3565  2232G
```

```
minggah:
     t    t    t    t    t    t    t    t N
[..25 2356 .132 .165 .555 2356 .132 .165
 .555 2356 .132 .165 6356 532. 2321 6132
 ..23 5356 5323 5356 5323 .53. 5654 2126
 1653 2356 1653 2356 22.. 3216 3565 2232G

     t    t    t    t    t    t    t    t N
 .... 2352 5654 2165 .22. 2352 5654 2165
 .22. 2352 5654 2165 6356 532. 2321 6132
 ..23 5356 5323 5356 5325 .53. 5654 2126
 1653 2356 1653 2356 22.. 3216 3565 2232G

     t    t    t    t    t    t    t    t N
 .77. 7656 .5.3 .6.5 .77. 7656 .5.3 .6.5
 .77  7656 .5.3 .6.5 6356 532. 2321 6132
 ..23 5356 5323 5356 5323 .53. 5654 2165
 1653 2356 1653 2356 22.. 3216 3565 2232G]
```

Senthir, Ladrang, pélog
    pathet nem (1).

buka: 22. 2132 5561 3216N/G

```
   t    t N
5651 5616
5651 5616
.22. 2132
5561 3216G
```

Serang, Ladrang, pélog
    pathet barang (23).

(minggah to Gendhing Bandhilori)

```
     t        t   N
[. 2 . 3   . 2 . 7
 . 2 . 3   . 2 . 7
 . 2 . 3   . 2 . 7
 72.7.6.5  .356767G

     t          t   N
 72.7.6.5   .356767
 72.7.6.5   .356365
 55.55235   56765356
 7 .76567   7324327G]
```

Sida Mukti, Gendhing, kethuk 4 awis, minggah
kethuk 8, sléndro pathet nem (1).

buka: 2 .2.6 .2.1 .3.2 .165 32.3 5635N/G

mérong: t   t
[612. 2165 1653 6535 612. 2165 1653 6535
33.. 3353 6535 3212 5653 2165 32.3 5635N
612. 2165 1653 6535 612. 2165 1653 6535
33.. 3353 6535 3212 5653 2165 32.3 1232N
..23 6532 66.1 6535 2356 3532 66.1 6535
2356 3532 66.1 6535 2356 5321 6132 .165N →
11.. 3216 3565 2232 ..25 2356 3565 2232
33.. 3353 6535 3212 5653 2165 32.3 5635N/G]

umpak:
→.1.6 .5.3 .5.6 .5.3 .5.3 .5.3 .5.2 .6.5G

minggah:
 t   t   t   t   t   t   t   t N
[.6.5 .6.5 .6.5 .3.2 .3.2 .3.2 .5.3 .1.6
.1.6 .1.6 .3.6 .3.2 .6.5 .3.2 .5.3 .1.6
.3.2 .3.2 .5.6 .5.3 .5.6 .5.3 .2.3 .6.5 →
.1.6 .5.3 .5.6 .5.3 .5.3 .5.3 .5.2 .6.5G]

[umpak sabetan]:
 t   t   t   t   t   t   t   t N
→3635 3632 3635 3632 3635 3632 3532 3635G

sabetan:
 t   t   t   t   t   t   t   t N
[3635 3632 3635 2232 5325 3253 2523 5653
6365 6365 6365 6532 5325 3253 2523 5653
11.. 1123 5616 5321 2356 1653 5653 2165
3635 3632 3635 3632 3635 3632 3532 3635G]

Sidawayah, Gendhing, kethuk 4 kerep, minggah
kethuk 8, sléndro pathet nem (1).

buka: 2.2. 3212 6.61 2165 3365 2232N/G

mérong: t   t   t   t   N
[..23 6532 ..21 3216 ..61 2165 3365 2232
..23 6532 ..21 3216 ..61 2165 3365 2232
..23 6532 ..21 3216 ..61 2165 3365 2232
66.. 6656 3561 6535 ..56 1656 3565 3212G

```
       t         t         t         t    N
 ..23 6532 66.1 6535 ..56 1656 3565 3212
 ..23 6532 66.1 6535 ..56 1656 3565 3212
 ..23 6532 66.1 6535 ..56 1656 3565 3212 ⇥
 .... 22.. 2321 6132 5653 2165 3365 2232G]
```

umpak:
```
       t         t         t         t    N
⇥.3.2 .3.2 .3.1 .3.2 .5.3 .6.5 .6.5 .3.2G
```

minggah:
```
   t    t    t    t    t    t    t    t N
[.3.2 .3.2 .5.3 .1.6 .3.2 .6.5 .6.5 .3.2
 .3.2 .3.2 .5.3 .1.6 .3.2 .6.5 .6.5 .3.2
 .3.2 .3.2 .5.3 .1.6 .3.2 .6.5 .6.5 .3.2
 .5.6 .5.6 .2.1 .6.5 .6.5 .1.6 .3.5 .3.2G

   t    t    t    t    t    t    t    t N
 .3.2 .3.2 .5.6 .3.5 .6.3 .5.6 .3.5 .3.2
 .3.2 .3.2 .5.6 .3.5 .6.3 .5.6 .3.5 .3.2
 .3.2 .3.2 .5.6 .3.5 .6.3 .5.6 .3.5 .3.2
 .3.2 .3.2 .3.1 .3.2 .5.3 .6.5 .6.5 .3.2G]
```

Silir Banten, Gendhing, kethuk 4 kerep, minggah
kethuk 8, pélog pathet barang (1).

buka:[2.7.2765.] x2 6 72.. 2327 .676 2765N/G

mérong:
```
      t         t         t         t    N
[..56 .765 22.2 327.6̄7̄2̄.. 2327 .676 2765
 ..56 .765 22.2 327.6̄7̄2̄.. 2327 .676 2765
 ..56 .765 .7̄.6 .532 72.7 .567 .676 2765
 6̄7̄2.. 23276̄7̄2.. 23276̄7̄2.. 2327 .676 2765G]
```

minggah:
```
   t    t    t    t    t    t    t    t N
[...5 .672 3532 7672 3532 7672 3532 7675
 ...5 .672 3532 7672 3532 7672 3532 7675
 ...5 .672 3532 7672 3532 7672 3532 7675
 ..55 5356 7276 5356 7276 5763 2232 7675G]
```

Singa Nebak/Nebah, Lancaran,
    sléndro pathet manyura (2).

buka: .532 .532 .653N/G

```
   t tN t tN t tN t tN
[ .5.3 .5.3 .5.3 .6.1G
  .6.1 .6.1 .6.1 .3.2G
  .3.2 .3.2 .3.2 .5.3G ]
[ 1653 1653 1653 6561G
  3561 3561 3561 6532G
  6532 6532 6532 5653G ]
```

Singa-singa, Ladrang, pélog
    pathet barang (3).

buka: .767 2327 6765 3567N/G

```
umpak:  t    t N
      [.767 2327
       .767 2327
       .767 2327
       6765 3567G

ngelik: t    t N
       .777 6532
       .235 6532
       .235 6532
       4327 3532G

        t    t N
       ..23 4323
       .32. 2327
       .767 2327
       6765 3567G]
```

Sinom, Gendhing, kethuk 4 kerep, minggah
    kethuk 4, pélog pathet barang (1).

buka:[2.2.7276.5..]x2   .3.3 .2.7 .2.6 .3.2N/G

mérong:
```
      t            t            t            t     N
 [..27 .6.5 ..56 7567 ..72 .532 .327 .6.5
  ..56 .765 ..56 7567 .... 7767 22.7 .6.5
  .2.7 .3.2 .327 .6.5 22.. 2327 .2.3 .532→
  .327 .6.5 .672 .765 22.. 2327 .2.6 .3.2G]
```

umpak:
```
      t            t            t            t     N
→.327 .6.5 .672 .765 7675 7672 3532 7675G
```

minggah Sinom:
```
     t    t    t    t N
 [7675 7672 3532 7675
  .6.7 .6.7 .3.2 .6.5
  .2.7 .3.2 .327 .6.5
  33.. 6532 3532 7675G]
```


Sinom Parijatha, Ketawang,
    sléndro pathet sanga (3).

buka: .66. 2321 3216 2165N/G

umpak: t   t N   t   t N
  [[6616 2321 3216 2165G]

ngelik:
```
     t    t N   t    t N
 11.. 2356 3532 1615G
 .621 3216 .2.1 .6.5G
 22.. 3532 1165 2321G
 5621 3216 .2.1 .6.5G
 1615 2321 3216 2321G]
```

Siring, Gendhing, kethuk 4 kerep, minggah
  kethuk 8, pélog pathet barang (1).

buka:[.2.2727.65.5..]x2 .5.5 .567 .2.7 6535N/G

mérong:t   t   t   t   N
  [.5.5 .567 .2.7 6535 7656 5323 ...3 6532
  4.43 2756 33.. 6532 4.43 2767 .2.7 6563
  21.. 1235 .6.5 3235 67.. 5676 .532 .765 →
  32.. 2327 .2.7 6535 32.. 2327 .2.7 6535G]

ompak inggah:
       t   t   t   t   N
→ 32.2 .765 32.2 .765 32.. 2523 6563 6765G

inggah:
  t   t   t   t   t   t   t   t N
  [6763 6765 6763 6765 6763 6765 6536 3567
  2.27 2.27 2.27 6765 3235 3235 6536 3567
  2.27 2.27 2.27 6765 3235 3235 6536 3567
  2343 2765 2343 2765 32.. 2523 6563 6765G]

Sita Mardawa, Ketawang,
    pélog pathet barang (1).

buka: 6. 223. 2.7. 2.33 7676N/G

    t   t N t   t N
  [.2.3 .2.7 .2.3 .2.6G
   .2.3 .2.7 33.. 3356G
   .765 33.. 7756 .532G
   .77. 6723 .732 .756G]

Siyem, Ladrang, sléndro
    pathet sanga (1).

buka: 6.1 23.3 .3.3 .5.3 .6.5 .3.2G

    t   t   N
  [.... .... 2.23 2352
  6156 ...2 ..12 1253
  .... ..53 ..53 5235
  5235 .6.5 ..35 3565G

```
   t       t    N
..61 6126 ..16 1253
...6 ...5 ..32 35.2
.... ..53 ..53 5253
.... ..53 ..53 52.1G

   t        t    N
...3 ...2 ..16 12.6
.... .1.5 ...6 1561
2561 ...5 ..16 1253
...6 ...5 .323 2352G]
```

Slébrak, Gendhing, kethuk 4 awis, minggah
   kethuk 8, pélog pathet lima (1).

buka:[5.53.1235]x2 22.5 .22. 2321 ..32
                    .165 4524 5645N/G

mérong:
```
    t       t         t         t
[.6.4 5645 22.. 2321 ..32 .165 4524 5645
.6.4 5645 22.. 2321 ..32 .165 4524 5645N
.6.4 5645 22.. 2321 ..32 .165 4524 5645
.... 55.. 2454 2121 23.. 33.. 3321 6121N
..12 4565 .... 5654 .254 .212 45.. 5654
.254 .212 45.. 5654 .254 .21. 6.21 6545N→
.... 55.. 2454 2121 .41. 1245 .424 2121
55.. 55.. 22.. 2321 ..32 .165 4542 5645N/G]
```

umpak:
```
          t                    t
→2 4 5 4  2 1 2 1  4 2 1 4  1 2 4 5
 . .6545  . .6545  .612165  4 2 4 5N/G
```

minggah:
```
     t          t          t          t
[. .6545   . .6545   .612165   4 5 6 2
 . 6 2 .   6 2 . 6   2 1 2 3   2 1 6 5N
 . .45454 5454545   .612165   4 5 6 2
 . 6 2 .   6 2 . 6   2 1 2 3   2 1 6 5N
 . .45454 5454545   .612165   4 5 6 2
 . 6 2 .   6 2 . 6   2 1 2 3   2 1 6 5N
 4 2 5 4   2 1 2 1   4 2 1 4   1 2 4 5
 . .6545   . .6545   .612165   4 2 4 5N/G]
```

Slébrak, Lancaran, pélog
pathet nem (2).

buka: .2.1 .2.1 .6.5N/G

```
t tN t tN t tN t tN
4545 4545 4545 .6.1G
.2.1 .2.1 .2.1 .6.5G
```

Sobah, Ladrang, sléndro
pathet manyura (16).

buka: 6 123. 3361 2312N/G

```
  t   t N     t    t N
[.3.1 .3.2   .1.6 .1.6
 .3.1 .3.2   .3.6 .3.2
 .3.1 .3.2   .3.1 .3.2
 .6.5 .1.6G  .6.1 .3.2G]
```

Sobanlah, Gendhing, kethuk 2,
pélog pathet lima (38).

buka: 55 3.12 .5.5 53.1
        2.5. 21.2 1.23 .532N/G

mérong:
```
       t       t    N
[ ..31 ..21 ..23 .532
  ..67 6532 ..67 6532
  .22. 2356 .22. 2356
  ..21 ..21 ..23 .532G ]
```

minggah: Ladrang Sobanlah

Sobanlah, Ladrang, pélog
pathet lima (38).

(minggah to Gendhing Sobanlah)

```
t    t N
.365 2312
.365 2356
.123 2165
2361 2312G
```

Sobrang, Ladrang, pélog
pathet barang (1).

buka: 356726 3356 .532N/G

```
t    t N
3532 3576
.576 .532
767. 7632
.3.2 .765G
```

```
t    t N
..56 7232
.276 5672 →
.276 3323
.576 .532G
```

badhé ngelik:
```
  t    t N
→ .276 ..56
  ..72 .356G
```

ngelik:
```
 t    t N
..72 .356
7767 6523
5653 2767
3265 .756G
```

```
t    t N
33.5 6767
.765 3567
.765 3323
.576 .532G
```

(Kenong I and II use
system kenongan goyang sungsun:

```
Nt N P       N
. . .   . . .)
```

Somantara, Gendhing, kethuk 4 awis, minggah
kethuk 8, sléndro pathet nem (1).

buka: 2. 356. 6.1. 2165 32.3 5616N/G

mérong:
```
           t                          t
[..21 .621 .621 6563 ..35 6532 ..23 5616
 ..21 .621 .621 6563 ..35 6532 ..23 5616N
 ..21 .621 .621 6563 ..35 6532 ..23 5616
 22.. 22.. 2321 6123 .... 33.. 3365 .653N
 ..35 1653 66.1 6535 ..56 1653 66.1 6535
 235. 235. 6535 3212 .... 22.3 5653 2165N →
 11.. 3216 3565 2232 ..25 2356 3565 2232
 66.. 66.1 2321 6563 ..35 6532 ..23 5616N/G]
```

umpak:
```
→ .1.2 .1.6 .3.2 .1.6 .1.6 .3.2 .6.5 .1.6N/G
```

minggah:
```
   t    t    t    t    t    t    t    t N
[.1.6 .3.2 .6.5 .1.6 .1.6 .3.2 .6.5 .1.6
 .1.6 .3.2 .6.5 .1.6 .1.6 .3.2 .6.5 .1.6
 .1.6 .3.2 .6.5 .1.6 .2.3 .5.3 .5.2 .6.5
 .1.2 .1.6 .3.2 .1.6 .1.6 .3.2 .6.5 .1.6G]
```

sabetan:
```
   t    t    t    t    t    t    t    t N
[2123 2165 3532 5356 2123 2165 3532 5356
 2123 2165 3532 5356 33.. 33.. 6532 3635
 3632 3635 3632 3635 22.. 22.3 5653 2165
 22.3 5616 .653 2356 22.. 2165 3532 5356G]
```

Sonto Loyo, Ladrang, pélog
pathet nem (19).

[buka celuk]:
```
  t    t N        t    t N
[..65 .653       ..23 6532
 3325 .352       ..23 5.65
 ..25 .653       .35. 6532
 3325 .352G      6612 3216G]
```

Srepegan, Ketawang, pélog
   pathet nem (38).

buka: 321 6563 11.. 3216N/G

```
     t        t  N    t        t  N
[2 3 2 1   6 5 6 3   1 1 . .   3 2 1 6G
 2 3 2 1   6 5 6 3   5 2 3 .   5 2 3 5G
 6̄1̄2̄ 6̄1̄2̄   6̄1̄2̄ 1 6   2 3 2 1   6 5 3 5G
 2 3 5 6   3 5 3 2   6 6 . .   3 3 5 6G
 3 3 . .   6 5 3 2   5 6 5 4   2 1 2 6G
 2 3 2 1   6 5 6 3   1 1 . .   3 2 1 6G
 2 3 2 1   6 5 6 3   5 2 3 .   5 2 3 5G]
```


Srepegan, sléndro pathet
   manyura (3).

buka kendhang: 2N/G

```
  P P   P P   P
  NNNN NNNN NNNN
[ 3232 5353 2121G
  2121 3232 5616G
  1616 5353 6532G]
```

suwuk: P P   P
           NNNN NNNN
           5616 3212G

Srepegan, sléndro pathet nem (2).

buka kendhang: 5N/G

```
  P P   P P   P P   P
  NNNN NNNN NNNN NNNN
            6565 2353G
  5353 5235 1653 6532G
            3232 3565G
       6161 3212 1656G
  1616 1561 3265 3235G
            [6565 2353G
  5353 5235 1653 6532G
            3232 3565G]
```

Srepegan, sléndro pathet sanga (2).

buka kendhang: 5N/G

```
 P P   P P   P P   P
NNNN NNNN NNNN NNNN
               6565 2321G
          5621 3212 3565G
     1656 5356 5312 3565G
     6565 2356 5152 5321G
         [2121 3232 5616G
          1616 2121 3565G
               6565 3212G
               3232 3565G suwuk
               6565 2321G]
```

Srepegan Kemuda, pélog
    pathet nem (3).

buka kendhang: 6N/G

```
  P     P     P
N N   N N   N N   N N
               2626 2626G
ngelik:
          5612 5321 6545G
     4245 4245 3356 3532G
     5653 5653 5245
     4245 4245 3212 1656G
              [2626 2626G
          3323 2121 6545G
     4245 4245 3212 1656G]
suwuk:         2626 3216G
```

Srepegan Kemuda, pélog
pathet nem (6).

buka kendhang: 6N/G

```
   P    P    P    P
 N N  N N  N N  N N  N N
1616 1616 5612 5321 6545G
     6165 6165 3356 3532G
5653 5653 6545 4245
          4245 3212 5356G
[1616 1616 3323 2121 6545G
     4245 4245 3212 5356G]
```

suwuk: 1616 3216G

Srepegan Rangu-rangu, pélog
pathet barang (36).

[buka kendhang: 7N/G]

```
   P P  P P  P
  NNNN NNNN NNNN
 [2727 2727
  3523 5653
  5653 6765 3237G]
```

Srepegan Sri Martana, sléndro
pathet sanga (16).

buka celuk: 5N/G

```
   P    P    P    P    P    P    P    G
 N N N  N N N  N N N  N N N
[.6.5.6.5 .2.1.2.1 .5.6.1.2 .5.6.1.6G
          .1.6.1.6 .2.1.2.1 .3.2.6.5G
 .6.5.6.5 .1.6.5.6 .5.1.5.2 .5.3.2.1G]
```

Srepegan Tlutur, sléndro
pathet sanga (2).

buka kendhang: 5N/G

```
   P P   P P   P
  NNNN  NNNN  NNNN
[6565  1656  5323G
 2121  6535  2321G
 3565  3212  3565G
 3565  3212  3565G]
```

suwuk: 3232 3565G

Sri Biwadha, Ladrang, pélog
pathet barang (41).

buka: 6 6765 7632 4327N/G

```
   t     t N
[3276  2327
 .767  2353
 66..  6765
 7632  4327G]
```

```
   t     t N
[3276  2327
 .767  2353
 ..35  6532
 ..23  5653G]
```

```
   t     t N
 ..35  6756
 3567  6523
 5653  2756
 22..  4327G]
```

Sri Biwadha Mulya, Ladrang
   sléndro pathet manyura (41).

buka: 235 6.1. 1.3. 2126N/G

```
   t    t N
[2321 3216
 2321 3216
 2261 2232
 .3.2 .126G]
```

```
   t    t N
[2321 3216
 33.. 6532
 .5.6 .3.2
 .3.2 .126G
```

```
   t    t N
 ..6. 1216
 3532 .126
 22.3 5653
 .132 .126G]
```

Sri Dayita, Ladrang,
   pélog pathet barang (38)

buka: 7 3267 2356 6732 .7.6N/G

```
   t    t N
[.567 .3.2
 ..67 .3.2
 .767 23.7
 23.5 6356G]
```

```
   t    t N
[.535 6756
 .535 6756
 33.. 3327
 6535 3272G
```

```
   t    t N
 6567 6532
 723. 3532
 6732 6327
 .3.2 .756G]
```

Sri Dayita Linuhur, Ladrang,
 pélog pathet nem (38).

buka: 352 1123 2126N/G

```
   t   t N
 [2321 3216
  3356 3532
  5352 5352
  1123 2126G]

   t   t N
 [2321 3216
  3356 3532
  55.. 5565
  1216 3532G

   t   t N
  5654 2126
  2123 2126
  33.. 6532
  1123 2126G]
```

Sri Dayita Minulya, Ladrang,
 sléndro pathet manyura (38).

buka: 2 2356 5321 3216N/G

```
   t   t N
 [2126 3532
  5321 3216
  33.. 3356
  5321 3216G]

   t   t N
 [2126 3532
  5321 3216
  3561 6523
  ..32 5321G

   t   t N
  33.. 6532
  5653 2126
  11.. 3216
  5321 3216G]
```

Sri Dayita Wibawa, Ladrang,
    pélog pathet barang (38).

buka: 555 7653 2723 2756N/G

```
   t   t N
[2327 3276
 2327 3276
 55.. 7653
 2723 2756G]
```

```
   t   t N
[2327 3276
 2327 3276
 55.. 7653
 ..35 6767G
```

```
   t   t N
 ..7. 6672
 6327 3532
 66.. 7576
 .732 .756G]
```

Sri Dirga Yuswa, Ladrang,
    pélog pathet barang (41).

buka: 732 3327 3276N/G

```
   t    t N
[2726 2327
 5653 2756
 33.. 6532
 3327 3276G]
```

```
   t    t N
[2726 2327
 5653 2756
 ..32 6523
 7756 .523G
```

```
   t    t N
 5653 2756
 33.. 6532
 77.. 5653
 6532 .756G]
```

Sri Hascarya, Ladrang,
   sléndro pathet sanga (41).

buka: 51 6.53 2.11 .561 .561 2165N/G

```
    t    t N
[.6.5 .2.1
 .2.1 .6.5
 .2.1 .6.5
 .3.2 .6.5G]
```

ciblon:
```
   t          t   N
[1 6 5 6    5 3 2 1
 6 6 . 1    6 5 3 5
 3 2 1 .    5 6 1 2
 . 6 2 1    6 5 3 5G

   t          t   N
 1 6 1 5    2 3 2 1
 5 5 . .    5 5 6 1
 3 2 1 2    . 1 6 5̄1̄
 6̄5̄6̄5̄3̄2̄1̄6̄ 6 1̄6̄5̄3̄5̄3̄
 2̄1̄.5̄6̄1̄2 6̄2̄1̄6̄5̄3̄5G]
```

Sri Kacaryan, Ketawang, sléndro
   pathet manyura (41).

buka: 2 .2.3 .6.1 2353 2126N/G

```
  t    t N  t     t N
[232. 2361 2353 2126G
 33.. 3356 3561 6532G
 321. 1123 ..35 6121G
 3263 6532 321. 3532G
 321. 6123 .132 .126G]
```

Sri Kaloka, Ladrang, sléndro
pathet manyura (38).

buka: 6 .123 .3.3 .6.1 .2.3 .1.2N/G

   t   t N
.3.2 .5.3
.1.6 .5.3
.2.1 .2.6
.5.3 .1.2G

Sri Karongron, Ladrang,
   sléndro pathet sanga (1).

buka: .2.1 .2.1 2211 .6.5N/G

   t   t N
[2126 2165
6165 2321
55.. 6165
3216 2165G]

ciblon:
   t
[. 2 . 1 . 2 . 6 . 2 . 1 . 6 . 5
6 6 . . 2 1 6 5 2 3 5 6 5 3 2 1
5 5 . . 6 1 6 $\overline{52}$ $\overline{5612}\overline{5612}$ $\overline{5612}\overline{165}$
2 2 5 3 2 1 2 6 . 2 . 1 . 6 . 5G]

Sri Kastawa, Ladrang, pélog
   pathet barang (1).

buka: 2276 .3.3 .2.2 .7.6N/G

```
    t    t N
[.7.6 .3.2
 .3.2 .7.6
 .7.6 .3.2
 .3.2 .7.6G]

    t    t N
[.7.6 .3.2
 .3.2 .7.6
 .7.6 .3.2
 .3.2 .7.6G

    t    t N
 .3.5 .6.7
 .3.2 .7.6
 .7.6 .3.2
 .3.2 .7.6G]
```

Sri Kasusro, Ladrang, sléndro
   pathet manyura (41).

buka: 2 2321 3212 .126N/G

```
    t    t N
[123. 3216
 3532 .126
 22.. 2321
 3532 .126G]

    t    t N
[123. 3216
 3532 .126
 ..6. 1653
 11.. 3216G

    t    t N
 .... 6656
 3561 6532
 ..61 2321
 3532 .126G]
```

378

Sri Katon, Ladrang, sléndro
    pathet manyura (2).

```
    t    t N
[.2.1 .2.6
 .2.1 .2.6
 .2.1 .2.6
 .3.6 .3.2G
```
ngelik:
```
    t    t N
 .5.6 .5.3
 .1.6 .5.3
 .2.1 .2.6
 .2.1 .2.6G]
```

Sri Kawuryan, Ladrang, pélog
    pathet barang (3).

buka: .3.2 .3.2 3322 .7.6N/G

```
    t    t N
[2756 2756
 3276 3532
 5376 3532
 5327 3276G]
```

irama III:
```
    t         t    N
[.2.7 .5.6 .2.7 .5.6
 .3.2 .7.6 3567 6532
 5653 2756 3567 6532
 6732 6327 .3.2 .7.6G]
```

Sri Kretarta, Ladrang,
    pélog pathet nem (3).

buka: .2.1 .2.1 2232 .165N/G

```
    t   t N
  [2126 2165
   1216 2321
   3265 2321
   3216 2165G]
```

irama III/ciblon:

```
     t       t    N
 [[.2.1 .2.6 .2.1 .6.5
  ..56 1216 2152 5321
  .3.2 .6.5 .2.3 .2.1
  5621 5216 .2.1 .6.5]
```

[badhé ngelik:]
```
    t       t    N
  5621 5216 .2.1 .561
```

ngelik:
```
     t       t    N
  ..1. 3212 ..24 5645
  11.. 3216 2154 6542
  ..24 5645 1216 5421
  5621 5216 .2.1 .6.5G]
```

Sri Kuncara, Ladrang,
    pélog pathet nem (3).

buka: 3 3216 2123 2126N/G

umpak: t   t N
      2123 2126
      2123 2126
      33.. 6532
      5654 2126G

ngelik: t   t N
     [2123 2126
      33.. 6532
      11.. 3216
      3565 3212G

      t   t N
      66.. 6545
      1216 3532
      3565 2126
      3532 3126G]

Sri Linuhung, Ladrang, pélog
    pathet barang (41).

buka: 576 .532 .11. 1612
      .327 6535N/G

     t   t N
   [7672 7675
    33.. 6532
    55.. 7632
    1132 1635G]

     t   t N
   [1672 7675
    33.. 6532
    66.. 7567
    .756 .532G

     t   t N
    7732 5327
    5653 2756
    55.. 7632
    1132 1635G]

Sri Malela, Ketawang, pélog
   pathet barang (22).

buka: .335 2353 .3.5 6765 3237N/G

```
dados:  t            t        N
[. 2 . 7_  . 2 . 7  3 5 3 2  . 7 6 5
  3 3 . b̄b̄ 3 3 . 5  6 7 6 5  3 2 3 7G

                      t        N
                    6 7 . 5  6 7 6 7G

       t            t        N
. 7̄7̄7 7̄7̄ 7 7 . 7̄7̄ 7 7 . 6  5 3 5 6
  3 5 6 7  2 7 6 5  3 5 . 2  3 5 6 5G

       t            t        N
2 3 5 b̄b̄ 5 5 . 6  7 7 3 2  6 3 5 6
3 5 6 7  6 5 3 2  7 2 . 6  7 2 3 2G

       t            t        N
4 3 4 3  2 7 5 6  3 3 . 5  6 5 3 2
3 7 2 3  2 7 6 7  . 2 . 7  6 5 3 5G

       t            t        N
7 6 7 .  5 6 7 2  . 3 . 2  . 7 6 5
3 3 . b̄b̄ 3 3 . 5  6 7 6 5  3 2 3 7G]
```

Sri Minulya, Ladrang,
   sléndro pathet sanga (3).

buka: .52. 2635 .1.6 .1.5N/G

```
umpak:   t    t N
       [.1.6 .1.5
        .1.6 .1.5
        .1.6 .1.5
        .1.6 .1.5G

ngelik:  t    t N
        .615 2321
        3532 .126
        ..6. 5561
        3212 .165G

         t    t N
        1656 5351
        5621 5216
        22.. 5351
        6612 .165G]
```

Sri Nassau, Ladrang, pélog
   pathet barang (41).

buka: 3 3276 2723 2756N/G

```
   t    t N
[ 2723 2756
  2723 2756
  33.. 6532
  7732 .756G ]

   t    t N
[ 2723 2756
  2723 2756
  3567 6532
  7732 .756G

   t    t N
  ..65 3567
  3532 .756
  .732 6327
  .3.2 .756G ]
```

Sri Nata Wibawa, Ladrang,
   sléndro pathet manyura (41).

buka: 6 .123 1132 .1.6N/G

```
   t    t N
[.2.1 .2.6
 .5.6 .3.5
 .321 3216
 2321 3216G]

    t        t     N
[. 2 . 1  . 2 . 6
 .6.66561 1 .32653
 31253213 532 1263
 3 .33216 1232126G]
```

Sri Nindhita, Ladrang,
   pélog pathet nem (38).

buka: 2.1 .2.1 2211 .6.5N/G

```
  t    t N
[.2.1 .6.5
 .2.1 .6.5
 .6.5 .2.1
 .2.1 .6.5G]
```

Sri Raharja, Ketawang,
   pélog pathet barang (38).

buka: 3.2 .3.2 3322 .7.6N/G

```
  t    t N   t    t N
[.2.7 .2.6 .2.7 .2.6G
 .2.7 .2.6 .2.7 .2.6G
 .... 7576 .765 3356G
 3567 6532 7656 3532G
 3532 6732 5653 2756G]
```

Sri Raja Putri, Ladrang,
   sléndro pathet manyura (41).

buka: 661 6532 1132 .1.6N/G

```
  t    t N
[.1.6 .1.6
 .5.3 .2.1
 .3.2 .3.1
 .5.3 .1.6G]
```

Sri Rinengga, Ladrang,
   sléndro pathet manyura (38).

buka: 2 2163 3132 .126N/G

```
   t    t N
[2126 2321
 3532 .126
 22.3 5653
 6532 .126G]

   t    t N
[2126 2321
 3532 .126
 3561 6532
 1216 2126G

   t    t N
 33.. 6532
 5321 3216
 22.3 5653
 6532 .126G]
```

Sri Sekar Ing Puri, Ketawang,
   pélog pathet barang (38).

buka: 3.2 .3.2 3322 .7.6N/G

```
   t    t N  t    t N
[.2.7 .2.6 .3.2 .7.6G]
[.... 6672 4323 .756G
 3567 6523 77.. 3276G
 .732 6327 5653 2756G]
```

Sri Sinuba, Ladrang,
    pélog pathet nem (1).

buka: 2 2165 1612 1615N/G

   t   t N
[1612 1615
 1612 1615
 33.. 6532
 3216 2165G

   t   t N
 1612 1615
 1612 1615
 11.. 2321
 3212 .165G

ngelik:
   t   t N
 ..56 1654
 2321 3216
 33.. 6532
 3216 2165G]

Sri Sudhana, Ladrang,
    sléndro pathet sanga (38).

buka: 2 2165 1216 2165N/G

    t   t N
[[2321 3265
   2321 3265 →
   22.. 6165
   2621 6535G]

ngelik:

→ ..56 1656
  2321 6535G

   t   t N
 1653 5312
 3532 1635
 11.. 3216
 3532 1635G]

386

Sri Utama, Ladrang, sléndro
pathet manyura (41).

buka: 6.12 3113 2.16N/G

```
   t    t N
[.2.3 .2.1
 .3.2 .1.6
 .2.3 .2.1
 .3.2 .1.6G]

   t    t N
[.2.3 .2.1
 .3.2 .1.6
 33.. 3356
 3561 6523G

   t    t N
 11.. 3216
 3561 6523
 22.. 5653
 6532 .126G]
```

Sri Wibawa, Ladrang,
    sléndro pathet sanga (3).

buka: 2 2165 1612 1615N/G

```
   t    t N
[1612 1615
 1612 1615
 22.. 5321
 6621 6535G

   t    t N
 1612 1615
 1612 1615
 1656 5321
 6621 6535G
```

ngelik:
```
   t    t N
 ..53 2356
 2321 6535
 1656 5321
 6621 6535G]
```

Sri Widada, Ladrang, pélog
 pathet barang (3).

buka: 235. 7653 2723 2756N/G

```
    t    t N
 [2726 2726
  3567 6523
  235. 7653
  2723 2756G]
```

irama III:
```
     t         t
 [2327 3276 2327 3276
 ..6. 7576 3567 6523
 235. 7653 235. 7653
 7756 7523 2723 2756G]
```

Sri Yatno, Ladrang, sléndro
 pathet manyura (38).

buka: .3.2 .3.2 3322 .1.6N/G

```
    t    t N
 [.2.1 .2.6
  .2.1 .2.6
  33.. 6532
  1132 .126G]
```

```
    t    t N
 [.2.1 .2.6
  .2.1 .2.6
  ..6. 2321
  3265 3561
```

```
    t    t N
 ..1. 6612
 6321 3532
 6132 6321
 .3.2 .126G]
```

Srundèng Gosong, Minggah, kethuk
2, pélog pathet nem (3).

```
       t          t    N
[565. 5653 121. 1312
 565. 5653 121. 1312
 .356 2321 3212 1656

     t          t          t    N
 535. 5356 .22. 3123 1216 1312G]
```

Suba Kastawa, Ketawang,
sléndro pathet sanga (3).

buka: .2.1 .2.1 2211 .165N/G

umpak:
```
    t    t N t    t N
  [[.1.6 .1.5 .1.6 .1.5G]
```

ngelik:
```
     t    t N t    t N
 [.2.1 .6.5 .2.1 .6.5
  .2.1 .6.5 .2.1 .6.5
  .2.1 .2.6 .2.1 .6.5G]
```

Sukar Sih, Ladrang,
   pélog pathet nem (1).

(follows Gendhing Gendhiyeng)

```
  t     t N
[.5.6 .5.6
 .2.1 .6.5
 .3.2 .3.5
 .1.6 .3.2G

  t     t N
 .3.2 .3.5
 .1.6 .3.2
 .6.5 .3.2
 .5.4 .2.1G

  t     t N
 .2.1 .2.1
 .3.5 .3.2
 .6.5 .3.2
 .5.4 .2.1G

  t     t N
 .2.1 .2.1
 .3.5 .3.2
 .6.5 .3.2
 .5.4 .1.6G]
```

Sukma Ilang, Ketawang, sléndro
   pathet manyura (2).

```
  t    t N  t    t N
[..26 1232 6123 6532G
 33.. 3353 6165 1653G
 ..35 6356 3561 3216G
 11.. 3216 3561 3216G
 33.. 6532 6123 6532G]
```

Sumar/Sumyar, Gendhing, kethuk
   2 kerep, minggah kethuk 4,
   sléndro pathet sanga (38).

buka: 2 2165 .65. 5612 1312 .165N/G

mérong:
```
    [.... 55.6 1232 1656
     11.. 11.2 35.6 3565
     .... 5535 6635 .321
     .... 1121 3212 .165G

          t    t    N
     .... 55.6 1232 1656
     11.. 11.2 35.6 3565
     1656 5321 3532 .165 →
     .65. 5612 1312 .165G
```

ngelik: t   t   N
```
     11.. 1121 3212 .165
     .235 1121 3212 .165
     1656 5321 3532 .165
     .65. 5612 1312 .165G]
```

umpak: t   t   N
```
     →.6.5 .3.2 .3.2 .6.5G
```

minggah:
```
     t    t    t    t N
    [.6.5 .3.2 .3.2 .1.6
     .2.1 .2.1 .5.6 .3.5
     .1.6 .2.1 .3.2 .6.5
     .6.5 .3.2 .3.2 .6.5G]
```

Sumedhang, Gendhing [Ketawang], kethuk
   2 kerep, sléndro pathet sanga (2).

buka: 22 165. .22. 2356 .2.1 .6.5N/G

mérong: t   t   N
```
    [.2.1 .2.1 .2.1 .6.5
     .22. 2356 .2.1 .6.5G

          t         t    N
     .2.1 .2.1 .2.1 .561
     ..32 .165 ..56 1.21G

          t         t    N
     ..32 .165 66.. 3356
     ..21 .653 22.3 5616G
```

```
        t       t    N
    ..21 .653 22.3 5.65
    ..56 1653 2321 6535G

        t       t    N
    ..56 1653 2321 6535→
    .22. 2356 .2.1 .6.5G]
```

umpak minggah:
```
        t       t    N
    →.22. 2356 .2.3 .2.1G
```

Sumedhang, Ketawang,
  pélog pathet nem (1).

buka: 2 .2.1 .6.5 .22. 2356
              .2.1 .6.5N/G

```
    t    t N  t    t N
 [..32 .165 ..56 1.21G
  ..32 .165 66.. 3356G
  ..21 .654 22.4 5.65G
  ..56 .2.1 .2.1 .6.5G
  .2.1 .2.1 .2.1 .561G]
```

Sumekar, Gendhing, kethuk 2 kerep, minggah
  kethuk 4, sléndro pathet nem (14).

buka: 3561 5323 .212 3216N/G

mérong: t   t   N
  [.532 .356 .535 3212
   .156 .253 6365 3216
   .312 .321 .216 6523
   .561 .523 .212 .126G]

minggah:
     t   t   t   t   N
  [.123 6532 3235 2356 .123 2365 2123 2132
   .321 2356 5352 5253 .235 6523 2321 2356
   .523 5312 .123 5321 .532 .356 3235 2123
   .532 5321 .253 5352 .123 5321 .532 5356G]
```
```

Sumirat, Gendhing, kethuk 2 kerep, minggah
   kethuk 4, sléndro pathet manyura (1).

buka: 1 .1.2 1656 .516 .5.3N/G

mérong:
                          N
   [..36 3561 ..16 5356
   ..65 3561 ..16 5356
   ..65 3561 ..16 5356
   55.. 5565 1656 5323G

                          N
   .13. 1235 1656 5323
   .13. 1235 1656 5323
   .13. 1235 1656 5323
   11.2 1656 .516 .5.3G]

minggah:
                          N
   [.5.3 .2.1 .2.1 .5.6
   .1.6 .2.1 .2.1 .5.6
   .1.6 .2.1 .2.1 .5.6
   .3.5 .6.5 .1.6 .5.3G

                          N
   .5.3 .6.5 .1.6 .5.3
   .5.3 .6.5 .1.6 .5.3
   .5.3 .6.5 .1.6 .5.3
   .6.1 .2.1 .5.6 .5.3G]

Sumirat, Ladrang, sléndro
   pathet manyura (2).

buka: 156. 1653 5652 5653N/G

   t   t N   t   t N
  [5652 5653   156. 1653
   5652 5653   156. 1653
   5652 5653   156. 1653
   156. 1653G   5652 5653G]

Sumiyar, Ladrang, pélog
    pathet barang (3).

buka: .365 2726 7673 7672N/G
    t   t N
    [7372 7372
    7372 5653
    5756 5257
    3576 7372G]

        t   t   N
    [7673 7672 7673 7672
    7673 7672 5.56 5.53
    5.57 5.56 7732 5327
    3365 2756 7673 7672G]

Sundawa, Ketawang, pélog
    pathet nem (1).

buka: 6 .6.2 .6.3 .6.5N/G
    t   t N t   t N
    [.632 ..23 5356 5323G
    6521 6.56 2165 3561G
    2.23 1232 .165 3561G
    22.3 1232 .165 3561G
    2216 ..56 2165 3565G]

Sunggèng, Gendhing, kethuk 2 kerep, minggah
    kethuk 4, sléndro pathet sanga (2).

buka: 2 .2.6 .2.1 .3.2 .165 .2.3 .2.1N/G
mérong: t   t   N
    [..32 .165 22.. 2321
    ..32 .165 22.. 2321
    ..32 .165 66.. 3356
    .... 2321 3212 .165G

        t   t   N
    .352 .523 ..36 3565
    .352 .523 ..36 3565
    .... 55.6 1216 5321 →
    3532 .165 22.. 2321G]

umpak minggah:
```
           t          t    N
→ .3.2 .6.5 .2.3 .2.1G
```

minggah:
```
         t    t    t    t N
[ .3.2 .6.5 .2.3 .2.1
  .3.2 .6.5 .2.3 .2.1
  .3.2 .6.5 .3.6 .5.6
  .5.6 .2.1 .3.2 .6.5G

   t    t    t    t N
  .3.2 .5.3 .5.6 .3.5
  .3.2 .5.3 .5.6 .3.5
  .3.5 .6.5 .1.6 .2.1
  .3.2 .6.5 .2.3 .2.1G]
```

Sura Laya, Gendhing, kethuk 2 kerep,
    pélog pathet barang (38).

buka: .66. 6656 7765 .3.2N/G

mérong:
```
         t          t    N
[ ..3. 23.. 5567 6535
  .235 .... 5567 6535
  .235 ..62 ..23 6532
  .66. 6656 7765 .3.2G]
```

Surabayan, Lancaran, sléndro
    pathet sanga (2).

buka: .2.1 .2.1 .6.5N/G

```
  t tN t tN t tN t tN
[ .6.5 .3.2 .6.5 .2.1G
  .2.1 .2.6 .2.1 .6.5G]
```

Surung Dhayung, Ladrang,
  pélog pathet nem (3).

buka: .556 4565 6521 3265N/G

```
   t        t  N
[[. . 5 6  1 2 3 2
 . 2 1 6  5 6 1 2
 . 2 3 5  . 6 4 5
 656 2 1  3 2 6 5G]

   t        t  N
 656 2 1  . 5 6 1G
```

ngelik:
```
   t        t  N
 . . 3 2  . 1 6 5
 1 2 1 6  5 3 1 2
 6 6 . .  6 5 4 5
 656 2 1  3 2 6 5G]
```


Surung Dhayung, Ladrang,
  sléndro pathet sanga (35).

buka: 5. 161. 1615 1621 5555N/G

```
 t   t N    t   t N    t   t N
[..5. 5612  ..5. 5612  3532 1635
 .165 .612  .165 .612  1216 3532
 .165 1615  .165 1615  6356 2165
 1621 3265G 1621 6561G 1621 3265G]
```


Suwignya, Ladrang, pélog
  pathet barang (31).

buka: 35. 2356 7756 .532N/G

```
 t   t N    t   t N
[6567 6532  7672 7675
 6567 6532  7672 7675
 7372 7675  235. 2356
 7672 7675G 7756 .532G]
```

Swala Gita, Ketawang,
  pélog pathet nem (3).

buka: 6 6123 .2.1 3312 2̄1̄6̄2̄1̄6N/G

umpak: t   t N   t   t N
   [[.2.3 .2.1 .3.2 .1.6G]

ngelik: t   t N   t   t N
   33.. 3356 2321 6532G
   5321 6654 6521 3216G]

Talak Bodin, Ladrang, sléndro
  pathet manyura (16).

      t   t N
[[. 3 . 1 . 3 . 2
 . 3 . 1 . 3 . 2
 1̄3̄2 1̄3̄2 1̄3̄2̄6̄1̄2̄3→
 3̄3̄.3̄3̄6̄1 2 3 1 2G]

    t̄   t N
→ 3̄3̄.3̄3̄6̄1̄2 2 3 5 6G

ngelik:
     t   t N
 . 5 . 3 . 1 . 6
 . 5 . 3 . 1 . 6
 3̄6̄5 3̄6̄5 3̄6̄5̄2̄3̄5̄6
 6̄6̄.6̄6 1̄2 2 6̄1̄2̄3̄2G]

Tali Murda, Gendhing, kethuk 4 kerep, minggah
kethuk 8, sléndro pathet manyura (2).

buka: 3 .3.2 .321 ..12 3212 .1.6 .5.3N/G

mérong: t   t   t   t   N
  [..35 1653 ..32 5321 ..12 3212 .126 .532
  ..35 1653 ..35 6.56 .... 1653 22.3 5653
  ..35 1653 11.. 3216 .... 6653 22.3 5653⟶
  .516 .... 6165 3231 ..13 .212 .126 .523G]

umpak minggah:
     t   t   t   t   N
⟶ .5.6 .5.6 .3.5 .2.1 .2.1 .3.2 .1.6 .5.3G

minggah:
  t   t   t   t   t   t   t   t N
  [.5.3 .5.3 .5.3 .2.1 .2.1 .3.2 .1.6 .5.3
  .5.3 .5.3 .5.3 .5.6 .5.6 .5.3 .2.3 .5.3
  .5.3 .5.3 .2.1 .5.6 .5.6 .5.3 .2.3 .5.3
  .5.6 .5.6 .3.5 .2.1 .2.1 .3.2 .1.6 .5.3G]

Tali Wangsa, Gendhing, kethuk 4 awis, minggah
kethuk 8, pélog pathet lima (1).

buka: 556 5424 55.6 5421 61.5 6121N/G

·mérong: t   t
  [.21. 2161 .5.6 1232 .... 22.4 5654 2121
  .21. 2161 .5.6 1232 .... 22.4 5654 2121N
  .21. 2161 .5.6 1232 .... 22.4 5654 2121
  561. 1323 .321 6545 32.. 2323 56.7 5676N⟶
  .... 6654 22.4 5.65 .... 5654 22.4 5.65
  .... 5654 22.4 5.65 .... 5654 216. 5616N
  ..61 3216 2321 6545 2456 5452 66.. 2165
  .... 55.. 5456 5424 55.6 5421 61.5 6121G]

umpak: N
⟶ .556 7653 22.3 5.65 2325 2356 5676 5421
  5612 1645 .612 1645 .55. 5545 4212 1645G

minggah:
  t   t   t   t   t   t   t   t N
  [.55. 6545 .212 1645 .55. 6545 4212 1645
  .55. 6545 4212 1645 .612 1656 .666 5356
  .556 7653 22.3 5.65 2325 2356 6676 5421
  5612 1645 .612 1645 .... 6545 4212 1645G]

Tamba Oneng, Minggah,
pélog pathet lima (1).

(minggah to Gendhing Sembur Adas)
                N
[3231 3235 3635 3231
 3231 3235 3635 3231
 55.. 55.. 5356 .532
 3132 3635 3635 3231G]

Tamèng Gita, Gendhing, kethuk 2 kerep,
    minggah kethuk 4, pélog pathet nem (38).

buka: 6 3.21 65.5 .63. 2165 6123 5654
                        .2.4 2165N/G
mérong:
    [61.1 .1.1 .1.2 .321
     .3.2 .165 ..56 1.21
     ..21 6123 5654 2165
     6123 5654 2.44 2165G

        t   t   N
     61.. 11.. 1132 .321
     ..32 .165 ..56 1.21
     ..21 6123 5654 2165
     66.. 6656 .2.3 5676

        t   t   N
     .... 6656 .2.3 5676
     .567 5676 .535 3212
     ..23 .532 6535 2353
     .... 3353 .6.1 2353G

        t   t   N
     6535 .421 612. 3212
     ..23 5676 .535 3212
     ..23 .532 6535 2321
     .... 1121 3212 .165G]

umpak: t   t   N
     ..56 11.. 1132 .321
     ..32 .165 .3.6 .3.5
     .6.3 .6.5 .254 2165
     .22. 2523 6563 6535G

minggah:
```
       t    t    t    t N
  [.55. 5561 2165 3323
   .... 3353 6532 3565
   7653 6535 2454 2165
   .22. 2523 6563 6535G
```

ngelik:
```
       t    t    t    t N
   .77. 7723 4327 6567
   .77. 7767 3265 3565
   7653 6535 2454 2165
   .22. 2523 6563 6535G]
```

Tanjung Gunung,
    pélog pathet nem (19).

buka celuk:

```
[.    2    .    1    .    2    .    66.5
 66.5 66.5 6 5  6    .    .    .    .
 .    .    .    33.2 33.2 33.2 3 2  3
                                    33.2
 .    .    .    .    .    .    .    
 33.2 33.2 3 2  3    6    5    2    1
 6 6  . 6  1 2  3    6    1    3    2G

 6    1    2    3    6    1    3    2
 6    1    2    3    1 1  . 1  2 3  1
 2 1  . 1  2 3  1    2 1  . 1  2 3  1
 1 3  2    6    5    3    6    5    3G]
```

Taru Pala, Ketawang, sléndro
    pathet manyura (1).

buka: 111 3322 3321 3216N/G

```
      t    t N  t    t N
 [[11.. 3532 5321 3216G]
```

ngelik:
```
      t    t N  t    t N
 ..6. 2321 3265 1653G
 ..3. 5321 3212 5321G
 33.. 3532 .5.3 6532G
 616. 6523 6521 3216G]
```

Tebu Kéyong, Gendhing (Santiswaran),
pélog pathet nem (39).

```
.   . 1 1 1 2 3   . 1 2 3 1 216
. 5 3 5 5 6 6 1   2 6 5   56532
.   . 1 1 1 2 3   . 1 2 3 1 216
. 5 3 5 5 6 6 1   2 6 5   56532
. 2 3 5 5 6 5     6 2 3 .56   5
. 2 3 5 5 6 5     6 231   1 216
.   . 1 1 1 2 3   . 1 2 3 1 216
. 5 3 5 5 6 6 1   2 6 5   56532G
```

Tebu Sak Uyon, Ladrang,
sléndro pathet manyura (15).

```
  t    t N        t    t N
[ 2123 2126      22.6 1232
  2123 1561      11.2 5321
  3265 3235      3356 1653
  1216 1523G     6521 3216G ]
```

Tedhak Saking, Ladrang,
pélog pathet barang (1).

buka: .767 2327 6765 3567N/G

```
   t    t N
[2326 2327
 2326 2327
 2326 2327
 6765 3567G
```

ngelik:

```
   t    t N
 .777 6567
 5676 3532
 ..35 7632
 7675 7632G
```

```
        t    t N
       ..23 4323
       2767 3567
       2343 2767 →
       6765 3567G]
```

umpak:
```
        t        t     N
    →  5672 .765 .3.5 .6.7G
```

```
        t        t     N
    [.77. 77.. 7765 3567
     55.. 55.. 5576 3532
     .22. 22.3 5576 3532
     .7.6 .7.5 .7.6 .3.2G
```

```
        t        t     N
     .22. 22.3 4434 2343
     434. 4323 2765 3567
     434. 4323 2765 3567
     5672 .765 .3.5 .6.7G]
```

Teguh Jiwa, Ladrang, sléndro
     pathet sanga (22).

buka: 1561 5312 3532 55.5N/G

dados:
```
        t    t N
     [1612 1615
      22.3 5635
      ..56 1216
      5152 5321G
```

```
        t    t N
      66.. 2126
      2321 3216
      1561 5312
      3532 1635G
```

t			$\overline{}$	$\overline{}$	t		N
.	.	.	$\overline{.62}$	$\overline{62.6}$	$\overline{262}$	$\overline{35.6}$	5
.	.	.	$\overline{.62}$	$\overline{62.6}$	$\overline{262}$	$\overline{35.6}$	5
.	.	5	6	1	6	5	3
2	1	3	2	1	6	3	5G]

Téja Nata, Gendhing, kethuk 2 kerep,
   minggah kethuk 4, pélog pathet lima (19).

buka: [3 .... 2165]x2 .3.3 .321 .1.5 6121N/G

mérong: t   t   N
       .233 .121 .233 .121
    [[33.. 3353 6535 3212
     .... 2212 33.. 1232 →
     11.. 5612 1312 .165G

          t   t   N
       .621 .65. 5621 .645]

ngelik: t   t   N
       .621 .65. 5621 .645
       11.. 1121 3212 .165
       .... 5545 66.. 4565
       44.. 4245 4645 .421G]

umpak minggah:
          t   t   N
     → .3.1 .3.2 .3.2 .6.5G

minggah: t   t   t   t N
      [.2.1 .2.1 .3.2 .6.5
       .2.3 .5.3 .6.5 .3.2
       .3.2 .5.3 .5.3 .1.2
       .3.1 .3.2 .3.2 .6.5G
ngelik:
          t   t   t   t N
       .2.1 .2.1 .3.2 .6.5
       .2.1 .2.1 .3.2 .6.5
       .6.5 .4.6 .5.4 .6.5
       .6.4 .6.5 .6.5 .2.1G

          t   t   t   t N
       .2.3 .2.1 .2.3 .2.1
       .2.3 .5.3 .6.5 .3.2
       .3.2 .5.3 .5.3 .1.2
       .3.1 .3.2 .3.2 .6.5G]

Téjaning Sih, Gendhing, kethuk 2
   kerep, pélog pathet lima (1).

buka: [3.2165.]x2 33. 3321 6123 2121N/G

mérong: t   t   N
     [.11. 1123 5323 2121
      55.. 5535 66.5 3212
      11.. 1123 5323 2121
      33.. 5321 6123 2121G

       t   t   N
     .11. 1123 5323 2121
     .11. 1121 3212 .165
     ..5. 5561 3212 .165
     33.. 33.. 5532 3123G

       t   t   N
     33.. 33.. 5532 3123
     55.. 5535 6535 3212
     ..2. 2235 6535 3212
     11.. 1123 5323 2121G]

Téja Sari, Gendhing, kethuk 2
   kerep, pélog pathet lima (3).

buka: 3. 2165 .3.2 165. 33.. 3321
            6123 2121N/G
mérong: t   t   N
     [[.11. 1123 5323 2121
      55.. 55.. 5356 .532
      11.. 11.. 112. 6121
     .11. 1123 5323 2121G]

ngelik: t   t   N
     .11. 1123 5323 2121
     ..1. 1121 3212 .165
     .621 ..1. 3212 .165
     33.. 3321 6123 2121G]

Temantèn, Ladrang, sléndro
pathet manyura (15).

buka: 6561 6563 6535 6156N/G

```
 t    t N
[1516 1516
 1516 3561
 2321 6563
 6535 6156G

 t    t N
 3523 5653
 6165 3232
 5321 6532
 5323 5653G

 t    t N
 6563 6563
 6563 6532
 6526 5265
 2523 5653G

 t    t N
 6563 6563
 6563 6561
 2321 6563
 6535 6156G]
```

Tembung Alit/Kagot Manyura/
Kagok Nem, Ladrang,
pélog pathet nem (19).

buka: 5 .23. 3635 6616 5323N/G

```
 t    t N
[.23. 3635
 .23. 3635
 .23. 3635
 6616 5323G

 t    t N
 11.. 1312
 561. 1312
 561. 1312
 3353 2121G
```

```
  t    t N
561. 1312
561. 1312
561. 1312
3353 2121G
```

```
  t    t N
23.. 3353
5676 5323
6521 6.56
1216 5323G]
```

Tembung Gedhé, Ladrang,
    pélog pathet nem (38).

buka: 5 .23. 3635 6616 5323N/G

```
  t    t N
[.23. 3635
.635 6165
.635 6165
6616 5323G
```

ngelik:
```
  t    t N
55.. 5535
..67 6535
..67 6535
..67 5676G
```

```
  t    t N
33.. 3353
..56 5323
..56 5323
56.3 5676G
```

```
  t    t N
.... 6656
.765 3565
..21 .235
6654 2121G
```

```
  t    t N
..6. 5365
..3. 1235
..3. 1235
6654 2121G
```

```
 t    t N
55.. 5535
..3. 1232
.216 5612
3321 6535G

 t    t N
..3. 1235
..3. 1232
.216 5612
3321 6535G

 t    t N
.33. 3353
5676 5323
6521 6656
1216 5323G]
```

Tirta Kencana/Tirto Kencana,
  Ladrang, pélog pathet nem (3).

buka: 1561 3216 5424 5645N/G

umpak: t   t N
     [[2126 2165 ⎫
       2126 2165 ⎬ x2
       1561 3216 ⎪
       5424 5645G] ⎭

[ngelik:] t   t   N
          $\overline{5612}\overline{5612}$ $\overline{5612}\overline{165}$
          $\overline{5612}\overline{5612}$ $\overline{5612}\overline{165}$
          1 5 6 1 3 2 1 6
          5 4 2 4 5 6 4 5G]

Titi Pati, Gendhing, kethuk 2 kerep, minggah
kethuk 4, sléndro pathet nem (3).

buka: .6.6 .126 .6.1 .2.1 .2.6 .3.5N/G

mérong: t   t   N
  [.65. 5612 .621 .635
    .65. 5612 .621 .635→
    2356 3532 ..25 2356
    11.. 3216 3356 3532G

       t   t   N
    5653 2121 ..12 3532
    5653 2121 ..12 3532
    .126 ..6. 3561 6523
    ..3. 5653 2353 2165G

       t   t   N
    33.. 6532 5653 2165
    33.. 6532 5653 2165
    1216 3532 66.. 3356
    3561 6535 2356 3532G

ngelik: t   t   N
    11.. 3216 3565 3212
    11.. 3216 3565 3212
    .126 ..6. 3561 6523
    ..3. 5653 2353 2165G]

umpak minggah:
       t   t   N
  → 2356 3532 .5.3 .5.6
    .2.1 .2.6 .3.6 .3.2G

minggah: t   t   t   t N
  [.3.2 .3.1 .2.1 .3.2
    .3.2 .3.1 .2.1 .3.2
    .3.2 .1.6 .2.1 .5.3
    .1.6 .5.3 .2.3 .6.5G

    t   t   t   t N
    .6.5 .3.2 .3.2 .6.5
    .6.5 .3.2 .3.2 .6.5
    .1.6 .3.2 .5.3 .1.6
    .2.1 .2.6 .1.6 .3.2G]

Titi Sari, Gendhing, kethuk 4 kerep, minggah
    kethuk 8, sléndro pathet nem (1).

buka: 661 5616 .3.3 .6.5 .253 2126N/G

mérong:
```
        t           t           t           t    N
  [.3.3 .6.5 .253 2126 22.. 22.3 5653 2121
   3265 3235 .352 .356 .3.2 .1.6 22.. 2321
   3265 3235 .352 .356 .3.2 .1.6 22.. 2321→
   66.. 66.. 66.5 3356 33.. 3365 .253 2126G]
```

umpak:
```
        t           t           t           t    N
 →.5.6 .5.6 .5.3 .5.6 .5.3 .6.5 .2.3 .1.6G
```

minggah:
```
   t    t    t    t    t    t    t    t N
 [.5.3 .6.5 .2.3 .1.6 .3.2 .3.2 .5.3 .1.6
  .6.5 .3.5 .3.2 .5.6 .3.2 .1.6 .2.3 .2.1
  .6.5 .3.5 .3.2 .5.6 .3.2 .1.6 .2.3 .2.1
  .5.6 .5.6 .5.3 .5.6 .5.3 .6.5 .2.3 .1.6G]
```


Tlutur, Gendhing [Ketawang], kethuk 2
    kerep, pélog pathet lima (1).

buka: [3 .216 5.5.] x2   .2.2 .2.2 .321 2612N/G

mérong:
```
    [.... 22.. 2321 2612
     33.. 1121 .216 1561

        t       t    N
     .... 11.. 1216 1561
     22.. 22.. 2321 2612G

        t       t    N
     .... 22.. 2321 2612
     33.. 1121 .412 4565G

        t       t    N
     .... 5654 22.4 5.65
     .654 22.. 56.7 5676G

        t       t    N
     .654 22.. 22.4 5.65
     .654 1121 .412 4565G
```

```
      t       t    N
 .... 5654  22.4 5.65
 .654 1121  3212 .165G

      t       t    N
 .... 33..  3212 .165
 33.. 3353  6532 3123G

      t       t    N
 .... 33..  3532 3123
 55.. 1121  .216 1561G]
```

Tlutur/Talutur, Gendhing [Ketawang],
   kethuk 2 kerep, sléndro
   pathet sanga (2).

buka: 1 .235 .5.5 .3.2 1132 .165N/G

```
mérong:  t        t    N
   [.... 5532  1312 .165
    33.. 3353  5616 5323G

         t        t    N
    .... 3356  1656 5323
    11.. 1121  55.2 3565G

         t        t    N
    ..21 ....  11.2 3565
    .... 5532  1312 .165G

         t        t    N
    .65. 5612  1312 .165 →
    66.. 6656  33.. 5653G]
```

umpak minggah:
```
         t        t    N
   →.... 3353  5616 5323G
```

minggah: Ladrang Tlutur

410

Tlutur, Ladrang, sléndro
pathet sanga (2).

(minggah to Gendhing Tlutur)

```
   t   t N        t    t N
[.6.5 .2.1      .2.1 .6.5
 .6.5 .2.1      .2.1 .2.3
 .3.2 .3.2      .5.3 .5.3
 .3.2 .6.5G     .1.6 .5.3G]
```

Topèng Arum, Gendhing (Santiswaran),
sléndro pathet sanga (39).

```
. 5 6 2 1 5 2 2   2 231 5 653 2 5
3 1 6 5 1 2 32.   . 5 6 2 1 5 2 2
2 231 5 653 2 5   3 1 6 5 6 1 2 3
2 3 2 3 2 5 3 1   6 1 5 1 2 6 1 .6
2 .61 6 5 6 1 .6  2 .61 6 5 6 1 5
5 5 615 32532 6   5 1 6 2 316 5G 555
55555223532 1111  111112226 1122
.    . 2 5 6 6    . 1 2   616 5
.5615   .5615 2   2 1 615 653 2 .1
1 .11 5 56611 2   61523 51216 5G
```

Tropong Bang, Lancaran,
   pélog pathet nem (2).

buka: 3132 5612 1645N/G

```
t tN t tN t tN t tN
[[3132 3132 5612 1645G
  3132 3132 5612 1645G
  1216 1216 5612 1645G
  1216 1216 5612 1645G]
```

ngelik:
```
t tN t tN t tN t tN
..5. 6465 1216 5412G
66.. 6465 1216 5412G
11.. 3532 1612 1645G
3132 3132 5612 1645G
3132 3132 5612 1645G]
```

Tropongan, Lancaran, pélog
   pathet nem (2).

buka: 321 .312 3565N/G

```
t tN t tN t tN t tN
[6356 1656 5424 2165G
 2165 2165 2156 1232G
 3123 5653 5653 2321G
 2321 2321 2312 3565G]
```

Tukar Maru/Kenceng, Ladrang,
   pélog pathet barang (38)

buka: 2 .356 3565 7653N/G

```
t   t N      t    t N
[.735 6756   ..23 5635
 .735 6756   ..23 5635
 .735 .635   .22. 2356
 .7.6 .5.3G  3565 7653G]
```

412

Tukar Maru/Kenceng, Ladrang,
pélog pathet nem (38).

buka: 356 2765 7654 2165N/G

```
      t    t N
    [2356 2765
     2356 2765
     2356 2765
     7654 2165G
```

ngelik: t   t N
```
     11.. 1121
     2165 3561
     2165 3561
     6532 3561G
```

```
      t    t N
     2165 3561
     2165 3561
     2165 3561
     6532 3565G]
```

Tukung, Gendhing, kethuk 4 kerep, minggah
kethuk 8, pélog pathet barang (1).

buka:[2. 2727 65.5]x2   .5.5 .5.5 6727 6535N/G

mérong: t   t   t   t   N
```
  [6727 6535 6727 6535 33.1 2353 .7.. 5676
   .653 2353 6765 3272 ..7. 5672 .7.. 5676
   .653 2353 6765 3272 ..7. 5672 .7.. 5676→
   54.2 4542 141.2 4565 .... 55.. 6727 6535G]
```

umpak minggah:
```
    t        t        t        t    N
→ .76. 6723 276. 6723 434. 434. 4346 4342G
```

minggah:
```
    t    t    t    t    t    t    t    t N
  [4346 4342 4346 4342 4346 4323 .333 2756
   3567 6563 6535 6532 5325 3253 .333 2756
   3567 6563 6535 6532 5325 3253 .333 2756
   .76. 6723 276. 6723 434. 434. 4346 4342G]
```

Tunggul, Gendhing, kethuk 2 kerep,
  pélog pathet barang (38).

buka: 667 5676 .672 7653 2356 2353N/G

mérong: t   t   N
  [...3 6532 ..23 5653
  ...3 6532 ..23 5653
  .576 .... 6567 5676⁺
  .672 7653 2356 5323G]

umpak: t   t   N
  ⁺.22. 2356 .5.2 .5.3G

minggah: Ladrang Pacul Gowang

Tunggul Kawung, Gendhing, kethuk
  2 kerep, pélog pathet barang (3).

buka: 6 6̄7̄5̄6̄7̄6̄ 7672 7653 2356 2353N/G

mérong: t   t   N
  ...3 6532 ..23 5653
  ...3 6532 ..23 5653
  .576 ..6. 6567 5676
  7672 7653 2356 2353G

minggah: Ladrang Pacul Gowang

Tunjung Keroban, Gendhing, kethuk 4 kerep,
  minggah kethuk 8, sléndro pathet nem (16).

buka: 2.2. 3.12 6.61 2165 3565 .3.2N/G

mérong:
       t   t   t   t   N
  [..23 6532 ..21 3216 ..61 2165 3565 2232
  ..23 6532 6621 6523 6535 .321 6123 5.65
  1656 2321 66.1 6523 6535 .321 6123 .165
  .555 2235 2353 2126 ..61 2165 3532 .356⁺
  22.. 22.3 5653 2126 33.. 6521 6535 2232G]

umpak:
       t   t   t   t   N
  ⁺.3.2 .3.2 .5.3 .1.6 .3.2 .6.5 .3.5 .3.2G

minggah:
```
     t    t    t    t    t    t    t    t N
 [.3.2 .3.2 .5.3 .1.6 .3.2 .6.5 .3.5 .3.2
  .3.2 .3.2 .5.6 .5.3 .6.5 .2.1 .2.3 .1.2
  .3.2 .3.2 .5.6 .5.3 .6.5 .2.1 .3.2 .6.5
  .6.5 .6.5 .2.3 .1.6 .3.2 .6.5 .3.2 .1.6
  .3.2 .3.2 .5.3 .1.6 .3.2 .6.5 .3.5 .3.2G]
```

Turi Rawa, Gendhing, kethuk 2 kerep, minggah
    kethuk 4, sléndro pathet nem (2).

buka: 2 .356 .6.1 .2.1 .2.6 .3.5N/G

mérong: t   t   N
      [.1.6 .532 66.1 6535
       22.1 6123 ..56 .535
       22.. 22.3 55.6 3356
       3561 6535 2356 3532G

            t   t   N
       .52. 2523 6535 3212
       .52. 2523 6532 .126
       33.. 33.5 6165 3231→
       3532 .126 .532 .365G]

umpak minggah:
             t   t   N
      →.3.2 .1.6 .3.2 .3.5G

minggah:
           t   t   t   t N
      [.1.6 .3.2 .5.6 .3.5
       .3.2 .5.3 .5.6 .3.5
       .3.2 .3.2 .5.3 .5.6
       .5.6 .3.5 .6.5 .3.2G

       t   t   t   t N
      .3.2 .5.3 .6.5 .3.2
      .3.2 .5.3 .5.2 .1.6
      .2.3 .5.3 .6.5 .2.1
      .3.2 .1.6 .3.2 .3.2G]

Tutur, Gendhing, kethuk 2 kerep, minggah
kethuk 4, sléndro pathet manyura (1).

buka: 6 6165 23.2 12.6 12.3 .2.1N/G

mérong: t   t   N
      [.... 1121 3265 3561
      .... 1121 3265 3561
      ..32 .126 3561 6523
      212. 2123 ..61 2321G]

minggah: t   t   t   t N
      [.2.3 .2.1 .2.6 .2.1
      .2.3 .2.1 .2.6 .2.1
      .3.2 .1.6 .2.1 .5.3
      .2.1 .2.6 .2.3 .2.1G]

Udan Arum, Gendhing, kethuk 4 kerep, minggah
kethuk 4, sléndro pathet nem (1).

buka: 2.2 .161 23.3 .5.6 .6.3 .6.5N/G

mérong: t   t   t   t   N
  [16532 1232 ..21 6123 .... 3356 ..61 6535
  16532 1232 ..21 6123 .... 3356 ..61 6535
  16532 1232 ..21 6123 .... 3356 ..61 6535
  22.. 22.3 5653 2121 3212 .165 32.3 5635G

     t   t   t   t   N
  .555 2235 33.. 6532 5653 2121 3265 3235
  .555 2235 33.. 6532 5653 2121 3265 3235
  .555 2235 33.. 6532 5653 2121 3265 3235→
  22.. 22.. 22.1 6123 .... 3356 .532 3565G]

umpak: t   t   t   t   N
 → 22.. 22.. 22.1 6123 .513 .5.6 .3.2 .6.5G

minggah: t   t   t   t N
      [.6.5 .3.6 .3.2 .6.5
      .6.5 .1.6 .3.2 .3.2
      .3.2 .3.2 .3.2 .5.6
      .5.6 .5.6 .3.2 .6.5G]

Udan Asih, Gendhing; kethuk 4 kerep, minggah
kethuk 4, sléndro pathet nem (1).

buka: 365. 2161 23.3 .3.3 .5.6 .3.5 .3.2N/G

mérong:
```
       t        t        t        t   N
[..21 6132 ..21 6123 .... 3353 6535 3212
..21 6132 ..21 6123 .... 3353 6535 3212
..21 6132 ..21 6123 .... 3353 6535 3212
.... 22.. 2321 6132 .... 2321 3265 2232G

     t        t        t        t   N
..23 6532 ..25 2356 ..61 2321 3265 2232
..23 6532 ..25 2356 ..61 2321 3265 2232
..23 6532 ..25 2356 ..61 2321 3265 2232 →
.... 22.. 22.1 6123 .... 3353 6535 3212G]
```

umpak:
```
      t        t        t        t   N
→ .3.2 .5.3 .6.5 .3.5 .6.5 .1.6 .3.5 .3.2G
```

minggah:
```
     t    t    t    t N
[.3.2 .1.6 .3.2 .3.2
 .5.6 .5.3 .5.3 .5.2
 .3.2 .5.3 .6.5 .3.5
 .6.5 .1.6 .3.5 .3.2G]
```

Udan Mas, Bubaran, pélog
pathet nem (3).

buka: 3323 1235 .424 2165N/G

```
 t  tN t  tN t  tN t  tN
[2165 2165 .656 2165G
 2165 2165 .656 2165G
 3323 1235 .424 2165G
 3323 1235 .424 2165G]
```

Udan Soré, Gendhing, kethuk 2 kerep, minggah
    kethuk 4, sléndro pathet nem (2).

buka: 6.6 .126 .6.1 .2.1 .2.6 .3.5N/G

mérong: t   t   N
       ..5. 5612 .621 .635
       ..5. 5612 .621 .635
      [2356 3353 ..35 2353
       66.1 6532 3565 2126G→

          t   t   N
       3561 6532 3565 2126
       3561 6532 3565 2126
       1121 3216 3532 .356
       22.. 2321 3265 3235G

          t   t   N
       ..5. 2356 .2.1 .6.5
       ..5. 2356 .2.1 .6.5]

minggah:
        t   t   t   t N
     →[.1.6 .3.2 .3.5 .1.6
       .1.6 .3.2 .3.5 .1.6
       .2.1 .2.6 .3.2 .5.6
       .3.2 .3.1 .6.5 .3.5G

        t   t   t   t N
       .6.5 .1.6 .2.1 .6.5
       .6.5 .1.6 .2.1 .6.5
       .1.6 .5.3 .5.6 .5.3
       .6.1 .3.2 .3.5 .1.6G]

Uga-uga, Ladrang, sléndro
    pathet sanga (2).

buka: 232. 2325 6121 6535N/G

    t   t N   t   t N
  [232. 2325   1612 1615
   232. 2325 x2   1612 1615   x2
   232. 2325   1612 1615
   6121 6535G   6121 6535G]

418

Uler Kambang, Jineman,
    sléndro pathet sanga (3).

buka: 5651 5222 1̲2̲3̲5̲16N/G

          N
  1165 .216
[2356 5321
  6562 6521
  3216 2165G

         N
    2521 suwuk
  5621 5216G]

Uluk-uluk, Ladrang, sléndro
    pathet sanga (2).

buka: 2.1 .2.1 2211 .6.5N/G

     t   t N
[[.3.2 .3.5
   .3.2 .5.6
   .2.1 .2.1→
   .2.1 .6.5G]

     t   t N
→.2.1 .5.6G

ngelik:
     t   t N
  .5.6 .5.6
  .2.1 .5.3
  .2.3 .5.3
  .6.5 .3.2G

     t   t N
  .3.2 .5.6
  .2.3 .5.6
  .2.1 .2.1
  .2.1 .6.5G]

Undur-under Kajongan/Calapita, Ketawang,
    sléndro pathet manyura (11).

buka: 2 .2.3 .5.3 5325 2356 ..56 .5.3N/G

[mérong:]
```
     t         t    N    t         t    N
  3333 3335 6536 3565 6565 6535 6536 3565G
  6565 6535 6536 3561 2353 2321 6535 2222G
 [5353 5653 5653 5652 5653 5253 3235 2222G
  5322 2223 5325 2356 6666 6656 6665 3653G
  6533 3335 6536 3565 6565 6535 6536 3565G
  6565 6535 6536 3561 2353 2321 6535 2222G
  5353 5653 5653 5652 5653 5253 3235 2222G
  5322 2223 5325 2356 6666 3561 1116 5165G
  1655 5556 1651 5616 1616 1656 1651 5616G
  1616 1656 1651 5612 3565 3532 1656 3333G
  6565 6165 6165 6163 6165 6365 5356 3333G
  6533 3335 6536 3561 2353 2321 6535 2222G]
```

ngelik:
```
     t         t    N    t         t    N
  2222 2223 5653 6532 6666 6663 3335 6535G
 [6563 6563 6563 6563 6563 6563 6563 6535G
  2222 2223 5663 6532 6666 6663 3335 6535G
  6563 6563 6563 6563 6563 6563 6563 6535G
  2222 2223 5663 6532 1111 1115 5556 1656G
  1615 1615 1615 1615 1615 1615 1615 1656G
  3333 3335 6115 1653 1111 1115 5556 1656G
  1615 1615 1615 1615 1615 1615 1615 1656G  suwuk
  3333 3335 6115 1653 6666 6663 3335 6535G]
```

Utama, Ladrang, sléndro
pathet sanga (3).

buka: .211 .211 2211 .6.5N/G

```
     t    t N
  [.2.3 .2.1
   .2.6 .2.1
   .2.6 .2.1
   .2.1 .6.5G

     t    t N
   .2.3 .2.1
   .2.6 .2.1
   .2.6 .2.1
   .2.1 .2.1G
```

ngelik:
```
     t    t N
   .3.2 .6.5
   .1.6 .5.6
   .5.6 .3.5
   .2.1 .6.5G]
```

Wangsa Guna, Gendhing, kethuk 2 kerep, minggah
kethuk 4, sléndro pathet sanga (4).

buka: 5 .612 .2.2 .121 .3.2 .165N/G

mérong:
```
    t                      t           N
 [. . . 5  2 3 5 6  2 2 . .  2 3 2 1
  . . 3 2  . 1 2 6  2 2 . .  2 3 2 1
  . . 3 2  . 1 2·6  2 2 . .  2̲ 3̲ 2̲ 1
  2 3 5 6  1 6 5 6  5 3 2 1  2̲3̲5̲6̲1̲2̲1̲G
```

```
    t           t    N
 .... 1121 3212 .165
 ..61 .... 3212 .165
 ..61 .... 1216 5312
 66.. 6535 3352 3565G
```

```
    t         t
 1656 5323 6532 3565
 11.. 1121 3212 .165
 22.. 5321 .111 6535→
 .22. 2356 .2.1 .6.5G]
```

umpak:
```
      t         t    N
 → .3.2 .5.6 .2.1 .6.5G
```

minggah:
```
     t    t    t    t N
[.6.5 .1.6 .1.6 .2.1
 .2.1 .2.6 .1.6 .2.1
 .2.1 .2.6 .1.6 .2.1
 .6.5 .1.6 .2.3 .2.1G

     t    t    t    t N
 .2.1 .2.1 .3.2 .6.5
 .3.5 .2.1 .3.2 .6.5
 .3.5 .2.1 .2.6 .3.2
 .5.6 .3.5 .3.2 .3.5G

     t    t    t    t N
 .1.6 .5.3 .5.2 .3.5
 .2.1 .2.1 .3.2 .6.5
 .2.5 .2.1 .2.1 .6.5
 .3.2 .5.6 .2.1 .6.5G]
```

Wani-wani, Ladrang, sléndro
    pathet sanga (2).

buka: 2 .5.3 .5.2 .6.3 .6.5N/G

```
     t    t N
[.1.6 .3.5
 .1.6 .3.5
 .2.3 .5.3
 .6.5 .3.2G

    t        t   N
. 5 . 3   . 5 . 2
. 5 . 3   . 5 . 2
36523652  356 216
.6615613  2653235G]
```

Wedhi Kengser, Gendhing, kethuk 4 awis, minggah
kethuk 8, pelog pathet barang (1).

buka: [3.277766.6..]x2 .6 .6.6 .6.7 .6.5N/G

merong:

[.6.5 .6.5 .6.5 3567 .765 3567 .765 3235
..23 5.23 5.76 5323 ..24 .324 .323 .2.7N
.2.7 .2.7 .3.2 .756 3567 6563 ..36 3567
234. 234. 2343 2765 .... 55.. 22.3 .6.5N→
..36 .535 323. 3235 ..36 .535 323. 3235
67.. 77.. 77.6 5356 3567 6532 7232 .765N
.67. 5676 .535 3232 767. 7656 .535 3232
66.. 66.. 66.5 3567 .765 3567 .765 3235G]

ompak unggah:
```
        t         t         t         t    N
→ 3635 3235 3635 3235 3635 3234 .444 3237
  3234 3237 3234 3237 33.. 3276 5653 6567G
```

unggah:
```
   t    t    t    t    t    t    t    t N
[3234 3276 5653 6567 3234 3276 5653 6567
 3234 3237 5653 6567 55.. 55.. 5532 3635
 3635 3235 3635 3235 3635 3234 .444 3237
 3234 3237 3234 3237 33.. 3276 5653 6567G]
```

Welas Tangis/Welas Nangis, Ladrang,
pelog pathet lima (38).

buka: .21. 2165 ..56 1232N/G

```
      t    t N
[.... 2232
 ..23 2121
 .21. 2165
 ..56 1232G
```
```
      t    t N
 .... 2232
 ..23 2121
ngelik: .21. 2165
 ..52 3565G
```
```
      t    t N
 .... 5565
 ..56 7767
 ..76 5323
 55.2 3565G
```

423

```
t    t N
.... 5535
..56 7656
..76 5323
.232 5321G

t    t N
.111 2321
.111 2321
.21. 2165
..56 1232G]
```

Weling-weling, Ladrang,
    sléndro pathet nem (16).

(minggah to Gendhing Lara Nangis)

```
t    t N
[.5.6 .3.5
.1.6 .3.5
.2.3 .5.2
.6.5 .3.2G

t    t N
.1.6 .3.5
.1.6 .3.5
.1.6 .3.5
.5.3 .1.6G

t    t N
.5.3 .1.6
.5.3 .1.6
.5.6 .5.6
.3.5 .3.2G

t    t N
.6.5 .3.2
.6.5 .3.2
.3.2 .3.2
.6.5 .3.2G]
```

424

Westminster, Ladrang, sléndro
    pathet sanga (22).

buka: 612. 5321 3532 55.5N/G

sesegan:
```
     t    t N
    1612 1615
    1652 5321
    612. 5321
    3532 1635G

     t    t N
    .... 5162
    2615 1562
    2615 1111
    2321 3265G
```

antal:

```
1 6 1 2  1 6 1 5
. .1̄6̄52 5 3 2 1
6 1 2 .  5 3 2 1
3 5 3 2  1 6 3 5

   t          t   N
. . . .   . .5̄1̄62
. .2̄6̄15  . .1̄5̄62
. .2̄6̄15  1 1 1 1
2 3 2 1   3 2 6 5G
```

Wida Sari, Gendhing, kethuk 2 kerep, minggah
    kethuk 4, pélog pathet barang (3).

buka: .667 6563 672. 2327 .276 3532N/G

mérong: t   t   N
```
  [[..23 2727 ..72 3532
    ..23 2727 ..72 3532→
    .726 ..6. 3567 6523
    ..67 2327 3276 3532G
```

ngelik: t   t   N
```
    66.. 6656 3567 6523
    77.. 3276 3567 6523
    2732 7726 3567 6523
    ..67 2327 3276 3532G]
```

umpak minggah
```
         t        t    N
→ .5.6  .5.6  .2.7  .5.3
  .2.7  .2.3  .7.6  .3.2G
```

minggah, irama III:
```
      t        t        t        t    N
[...3...2  ...3...7  ...2...7  ...3...2
 ...3...2  ...3...7  ...2...7  ...3...2
 ...3...2  ...7...6  ...2...7  ...5...3
 ...2...7  ...2...3  ...7...6  ...3...2G]
```


Wida Sari, Gendhing, kethuk 2 kerep, minggah
    kethuk 4, sléndro pathet manyura (3).

buka: .661 6563 612. 2321 .216 3532N/G

mérong: t   t   N
```
     [[..23 2121 ..12 3532
       ..23 2121 ..12 3532→
       .126 ..6. 3561 6523
       ..61 2321 3216 3532G]
```

ngelik: t   t   N
```
       66.. 6656 3561 6523
       11.. 3216 3561 6523
       2132 1126 3561 6523
       ..61 2321 3216 3532G]
```

umpak minggah:
```
        t        t    N
→.5.6  .5.6  .2.1  .5.3
 .2.1  .2.3  .1.6  .3.2G
```

minggah:
```
      t        t        t        t    N
[...3...2  ...3...1  ...2...1  ...3...2
 ...3...2  ...3...1  ...2...1  ...3...2
 ...3...2  ...1...6  ...2...1  ...5...3
 ...2...1  ...2...3  ...1...6  ...3...2G]
```

Wilujeng, Ladrang, sléndro
    pathet manyura (3).

buka: .132 6123 1132 .126N/G

umpak: t   t N
    [[2123 2126
      33.. 6532
      5653 2126
      2123 2126G]

ngelik: t   t N
    ..6. 1516
    3561 6532
    66.. 1516
    1132 .126G]

Winangun, Ladrang, pélog
    pathet barang (8).

```
  t    t N      t    t N      t    t N
[.767 3532    ..27 6535    .555 6765
 .765 3576    .555 3567    .555 3567
 .635 6676    .723 4327    .723 4327
 5327 3532G   2765 3235G   2765 3567G]
```

Witing Klapa, Lancaran,
    sléndro pathet manyura (1).

buka: 6263 .6.5 .3.2N/G

    N N N N
   [5653 5321G
    6123 5616G
    356. 1561G
    2163 6535G]

Wrahat Bala/Raha Bala, Lancaran,
sléndro pathet nem (2).

buka: .1.6 .1.6 .3.2N/G

```
   t tN t tN t tN t tN
[.3.2 .1.6 .1.6 .3.2G
 .3.2 .1.6 .5.3 .2.6G
 .5.3 .2.3 .2.1 .2.6G
 .5.3 .2.3 .2.1 .2.6G
 .2.3 .2.1 .6.5 .3.2G]
```

Yasangka, Ladrang, pélog
pathet lima (1).

buka: 612 1645 1612 1645N/G

```
        t    t N
    [.612 1645
     .612 1645
     ..56 1232
     3132 1645G
```

```
ngelik: t    t N
     .555 6465
     .555 6465
     6542 1645
     1612 1645G]
```

APPENDIX 3

BIOGRAPHIES OF AUTHORS

Gitosaprodjo, Drs. R. M. [Radèn Mas] Sulaiman

Born on May 13, 1934, at Purwakerta, Gitosaprodjo lived in Solo (Surakarta) from 1935 to 1958. His formal education included courses in economics and the training program for high school teachers. He received his degree in 1958 from the Teachers' Training Institute (Economics, B.A. in 1968, Drs. in 1976). Informal training in karawitan began at the age of ten, with lessons from his uncle. Later he studied general karawitan, sindhèn, gérong, and bawa privately with teachers from the Indonesian Conservatory of Karawitan at Surakarta [Konservatori Karawitan Indonesia Surakarta], from the Indonesian Academy of Karawitan at Surakarta [Akademi Seni Karawitan Indonesia, Surakarta], and from the gamelan group of Radio Republic Indonesia at Surakarta. From 1958 to 1960 he was a teacher of economics at senior high schools in Palembang and Salatiga, and from 1961 to 1966 he served as a civil servant with the Indonesian Mining Department at Cilacap. He then spent ten years teaching at high schools and teachers colleges in Majakerta and Malang. From 1977 to the present he has been a civil servant with the Indonesian Department of Public Works at Solo. In the field of karawitan, between 1969 and 1976, he served as director of the gamelan ensemble at Radio Republic Indonesia at Malang and director of various gamelan ensembles there.

Information supplied by the author. Translated by J. Becker.

Martopangrawit, R. L. [Radèn Lurah]

On Wednesday *Wagé*, the third day of the month of *Mulud*, in the year 1845 [A.J.], *Jimawal Mongso* the sixth, *Windu Sengara*—or, 4 April 1912 [A.D.]—God gave a boy-child ·to the family of Mas Ngabèhi Wirawiyaga of Surakarta. He was given the name Soejitno, and is now a famous figure in *karawitan* called Martopangrawit. His father was *mantri niyaga* [court musician] of the *kadipatèn* and his mother was *abdi dalem niyaga* [court musician] of the *kasepuhan*.[1]

On 25 April 1984, Pak Marto was given the title Bupati Anom Anom-anom by Paku Buwana XII of Surakarta, with the name Radèn Tumenggung Martodipura. However, although he holds the title Tumenggung, he prefers to be called simply "Pak Marto" because he is not interested in titles and the like.

His father died when he was four years old. Soejitno was adopted by his grandfather, whose name was Mas Ngabèhi Purwapangrawit, the elder. His grandfather always took the boy with him on his travels and gave him instruction in karawitan. Thus the soul of *pengrawit* was formed within Soejitno, who soon immersed himself in karawitan.

Pak Marto's mother died when he was thirteen years old and only his grandfather was left to care for him. As he was intelligent, he quickly absorbed the knowledge imparted by his grandfather. Because he was resolute and determined (indeed, he clearly took the initiative in his study of karawitan), when he was very young he became an abdi dalem niyaga in the *kraton* of Surakarta.

In the year 1935, Bapak Martopangrawit was already teaching about the hidden truths of karawitan. Among these is a theory of *pathet*, which is much discussed by scholars from both the West and from Indonesia. Many topics were researched by Pak Marto; matters that were unclear became clear, and matters that became clear were spread to every person who studied karawitan.

In the year 1948, at the request of Governor Sutardjo of Central Java, Pak Marto became director of karawitan activities in Central Java. At that time, despite the fact that he was still a court musician, he became a civil servant of the Republic of Indonesia, in the Ministry of Education and Culture, along with Bapak Warsopangrawit, Bapak Mloyowidodo, and Bapak Puspalalito. Only a short time later the Ministry of Education and Culture was forced to disband as a result of the Second World War.

In the year 1951, the Indonesian Music Conservatory was opened. The faculty absorbed Bapak Pangrawit's knowledge, for the benefit of the public at large.

In the year 1964, the Akademi Seni Karawitan Indonesia [ASKI] was opened in Surakarta, and at that time Pak Marto continued to contribute to the upper levels of artistic studies. He wrote books about karawitan, published by both ASKI and the conservatory, which were widely dispersed throughout the world. In addition, Pak Marto was a major contributor to informal discussions, seminars, meetings, and conferences concerned with the Javanese arts.

It may be said that his compositions are so numerous that they cannot be counted, ranging from gendhing that stand alone to suites of gendhing that accompany *sendratari*, for example, suites for the Ramāyaṇa Prambanan [dance-dramas performed at the Prambanan temple complex], the National Ramāyaṇa Festival, and the International Ramāyaṇa Festival at East Java, along with the sendratari *Bangun Majapahit*, produced by the Pusat Pengembangan Kesenian Jawa Tengah [PKJT, the Center for the Development of the Arts of Central Java] at Surakarta, and many others.

Pak Marto also documented in notation *gendhing bedhayan* and *gendhing pakurmatan* such as *gendhing sekatèn, monggang, kodhok ngorèk,* and *cara balèn,* for which the method of playing the instruments was almost forgotten. His vast contributions to the people have been recognized by the government from the regional level (the city of Surakarta), to the provincial level (the province of Central Java), to the national level (the Republic of Indonesia).

In the year 1973, Mayor Bapak Koesnandar designated him as a model citizen of the city of Surakarta.

In the year 1977, he received the "Hadiah Seni" [Arts Gift] from the province of Central Java, along with the "Anugerah Seni" [Arts Gift] from the government of Indonesia.

[Bapak Martopangrawit died on 17 April 1986.]

Sri Hastanto
[Director of ASKI, Surakarta]

Translated by J. Becker.

Poerbapangrawit, R. M. K. [Radèn Mas Kangjeng]

The intimate name of Poerbapangrawit was Kodrat Lesyan. He was the son of K. R. M. T. [Kangjeng Radèn Mas Tumenggung] Poerbadipuro. He became *surah niyaga* [head of musicians] at the palace in Solo. Poerbapangrawit was the brother of Poerbatjaraka.

Information supplied by Radèn Mas Johny Lesnar, half-brother of Poerbapangrawit. Translated by J. Becker.

Poerbatjaraka, Prof. Dr. R. M. Ng. [Radèn Mas Ngabèhi]

[The following are excerpts from the introduction to Poerbatjaraka, *Tjerita Pandji Dalam Perbandingan.* The introduction was written by Drs. Zuber Usman.]

Mpu Professor R. M. [Radèn Mas] Ngabèhi Poerbatjaraka.

Born January 1, 1884; died July 25, 1964.

The first time the writer encountered the intellectual named above was in 1938, when he [Poerbatjaraka] worked at the Jakarta Museum as researcher and cataloguer of manuscripts written in Javanese. The writer was attracted and impressed by his parental kindness and the friendships he maintained with the young people. Later the writer became his student in the degree program of the literature faculty of the National University in Jakarta (1957-1959). . . . At that time there was a demand for his services in other places, especially in Yogyakarta. Several times scheduled lectures were cancelled. One afternoon, when it had already been announced that we would not receive a lecture, he knocked on my door; summoning us in his usual way, he said, "This afternoon, we will have a lecture."

That day he had not left town and apparently had walked from his house on Sumenap Street to my house on Sumatra Street. It was hot. I invited him to ride in a pedicab to the lecture hall, the Kanisius Building, but he refused, saying, "Why should we ride in a pedicab? It is better that we walk."

I had known of his fondness for walking since our first meeting in 1938, when he lived across from the Tanah Abang Mosque and my house was nearby. The people who lived in the neighborhood of the Tanah Abang Mosque, Karet Street, the Kebun Kacang [Peanut garden], or the Bali village, still remember him wearing a white jacket with a stiff collar, a *batik kain* [traditional Javanese skirt worn by both men and women], and a *blangkon* [traditional, close-fitting, batik hat]. Sometimes when it was hot he wore a hat on top of the blangkon. The people recall that each day he walked to the museum and home again. Sometimes on Sunday morning he could be found playing gamelan at the museum *pendhapa* [open-sided, pillared, audience hall] along with all the other musicians. His sharp and lively glance would be directed at the audience, which always packed in to listen. Until his old age, until he was eighty, Pak Poerbo stood erect, not bent, simply but neatly dressed, a reflection of his personality.

Education and Work. His intimate name was Lesiya. He was born in Solo. At first, Lesiya entered a Javanese elementary school, later he entered ELS[?], which was exclusively for Dutch children, Javanese children of high government officials, and the children of other prominent Javanese. After leaving ELS (in 1900) he worked and studied at the government office of archaeology. Although Lesiya Poerbatjaraka graduated from a Dutch school, he remained attached to his own language and culture. He loved reading Old Javanese books. While working at the office of archaeology, he already displayed a talent and expertise that astonished the Dutch scholars there. Based upon his knowledge and wide reading of *kakawin* literature and other Javanese books, he performed no small service to the interpretation of Indonesian temple reliefs and statues. . . .

When Poerbatjaraka was working as a government official at the Hadiningrat Surakarta Kraton [palace] with the rank of *mantri* [minister], Dr. G. A. J. Hazen recognized his talents and enthusiasm. He was sent to the Netherlands to further his studies and graduated with a degree from Leiden

University. During that year, he submitted his thesis, entitled "Agastya in den Archipel," which was brilliantly defended. After receiving his doctorate, he returned to his homeland. **Professor Poerbatjaraka as Father and Pioneer of the Study of Indonesian Literature.** He was granted the title Professor by Gajah Mada University in Yogyakarta, the first university of the Republic of Indonesia, a school with which he was involved since its inception. . . . In the study of Old Javanese literature, or Kawi literature, Professor Dr. R. M. Ngabèhi Poerbatjaraka has no equal. . . .

Translated by J. Becker.

Purbodiningrat, Prof. Ir. [Engineer] B. K. R. T.
[Bupati Kangjeng Radèn Tumenggung]

Purbodiningrat was born in Yogyakarta on March 23, 1904. He was the son of K. G. P. A. A. [Kangjeng Gusti Pangéran Anom Angabèhi] Sudibya Raja Putra Naréndra Mataram, the crown prince [the son of Sultan Hamengku Buwana VII], who died before his coronation as sultan.

He began his schooling at the palace, attended Dutch colonial primary, junior, and senior high schools, and graduated from the School of Engineering, Technische Hoge School, Bandung, in 1929, with a degree in civil engineering. Purbodiningrat held various jobs as a public works engineer in Yogyakarta, taught mathematics in a high school, and was at one time associate director of the Sana Budaya Museum in Yogyakarta. In 1948 he was a lecturer in physics and chemistry at University Islam Indonesia in Yogyakarta, and from 1950 until his death he was a professor of civil engineering at Gajah Mada University in Yogyakarta.

Information supplied by Radèn Mas Wasisto Surjodiningrat, a nephew of Purbodiningrat. Translated by J. Becker.

Probohardjono, R. Ng. [Radèn Ngabèhi] Samsudjin

[The author used no first-person pronouns in the autobiography translated and reproduced below. The original style has been maintained as far as possible.]

[I was] born on Sunday, July 2, 1916, in the village of Tegalmulya, the ward of Purwasari, subdistrict Lawinyan, regency of the city of Surakarta, the child of Hardjowikarto, whose business was making *batik* at Lawiyan and who had a total of five children, three sons and two daughters. Schooling only as far as the first year of junior high school, called MULO (Meer Uitgebreid Lager Onderwijs). Schooling finished in 1935.

While still small [I] was very fond of watching wayang kulit performances, and thus bought wayang puppets made of cardboard, which were sold at the market, until [I] had collected hundreds of cardboard puppets. Then played at being a *dhalang*, imitating what [I] heard and saw. Since the age of ten was active in studying karawitan, especially singing, and also a little dancing. Since at that time [I] was already well known as a singer of *bawa* and *gérong* at parties, festivities, and the like, [I] was asked to give lessons in bawa and gérong to the young men and women in karawitan groups in the villages. [I] also used to join small gamelan ensembles (*siter, gendèr, kendhang, kemodhong*) that wandered along the paths of the village areas in the city of Surakarta.

At the age of nineteen [I] began studying the art of the dhalang under the guidance of Ki Sororeso at the dhalang school at Surakarta, PADASUKA (Pasinaon Dhalang Surakarta) at the museum Radya Pustaka Sri Wedari, the first school for dhalang studies in all of Indonesia. In 1935 for the first time [I] performed all night. The story was Irawan Rabi [Irawan's wedding] for the celebration of the wedding of a member of my family from the village of Tegalmulya. The performance was a success and was praised by all the experts and by the audience.

Following that event [I] performed as dhalang in many places: in 1948 at the palace of the President in Yogyakarta; at RRI [Radio Republic Indonesia], Yogyakarta; at RRI, Solo [Surakarta]; at RRI, Madiun; at the palace in Solo; and also at various places in Central Java, West Java, East Java, Sumatra, Kalimantan, and, in the year 1955, in Malaysia.

In the time of Sri Sunan Paku Buwana X of Solo, [I] was called to become a court servant at the palace, but left shortly thereafter because [I] had so much work outside the palace and also was helping with the business of my parents. In 1938, assisted teaching at the school for dhalangs, PADASUKA, which had moved to Kesatriyan Kraton Surakarta [male quarters of the palace] and also helped with the contents of the monthly magazine *Pedalangan* [Art of the dhalang]. However, all that stopped with the occupation of Solo by the Japanese army.

In 1939, [I] became a member of the Pengurus Perkumpulan Dalang [Organization of dhalangs] in Surakarta, and also became a member of several arts organizations in the city of Solo. In 1950, after Indonesian independence, along with all prominent artists and intellectuals, helped to found the organization Himpunan Budaya Surakarta [Surakarta cultural association], became its first director, and later became the editor-in-chief of the monthly magazine *Pedalangan* from 1951 to 1957.

[I] helped to found the conservatory school in Surakarta and later, in 1953, taught dhalang studies there. [I] helped to found Panunggaling Dalang Republik Indonesia [Union of Indonesian dhalangs] (PADRI), which had its center in Solo, and became its director. [I] became the first secretary responsible for organizing the All-Indonesia Congress of Dhalangs (Konggres Dalang Seluruh Indonesia), the first meeting of which was held at the Prangwedanan Mangku Negaran [the mansion of the prince Prangwedana of the Mangku Negara palace], Solo, in the year 1958.

Since the PADRI organization had not been active for a long time, in the year 1966, along with other dhalangs, we founded the Himpunan Kebaktian Dhalang [Association of dedicated dhalangs] and [I] was appointed to the Dewan Ahli [Council of experts]. However, within one year it was replaced by the Lembaga Pembina Seni Pedalangan Indonesia [Council for the development of the art of the dhalang in Indonesia], abbreviated GANASIDI. Also [I] was appointed director of the Dewan Ahli, a position [I] still hold. [I] gave support and helped to found the Universitas Negeri Surakarta "Sebelas Maret" [State University Surakarta, "11th March"] and gave lectures there in the fields of literature and history.

In 1961, [I] was ordered to offer classes on the art of the dhalang, bawa, and gérong for the commoners and the royal family at the palace, and was given the title Radèn Ngabèhi Samsudjin Probohardjono. In 1968 was appointed to teach at the Akademi Seni Karawitan Indonesia in Solo, as assistant teacher in the Department of Dhalang Studies. In 1977, was asked to offer classes at the Akademi Sekretaris Manajemen Indonesia [Indonesian academy of secretarial and management studies], abbreviated ASMI, by the Yayasan Dharma Pancasila [Foundation for the support of *pancasila*] in Solo.

In 1931, [I] was a contributor of articles for the weekly Jakarta journal *Kejawèn* [Javanese culture], which was published by a semiofficial agency of the colonial administration. Later, was active in writing articles for several Javanese magazines, including *Penyebar Semangat* [The spread of enthusiasm] at Surabaya; *Jayabaya* [the title of a book of prophecy named after a legendary thirteenth-century king of East Java] at Kedhiri; *Candra* [Moon] at Semarang; and others. At the present time, am a member of the Council of Editors, whose names are listed on the cover of the magazine/newspaper *Dharma Kanda* at Surakarta, the magazine *Mekar Sari*, and correspondent for the daily newspaper *Berita Yudha* at Jakarta. Also, was the editor-in-chief of the magazine *Pedalangan* from 1951 to 1957, and also was the person responsible for the police newspaper in Surakarta from 1969 to 1972.

Writings that have been published as books total sixteen, including:

Sulukan Sléndro, published nine times.

Sulukan Pélog.

Pakem Lakon Wayang Purwa [Plot summaries from the wayang kulit repertoire], five volumes, some of which have been published three times.

Gending-gending Wayangan Kulit Purwa [Gendhing from the wayang kulit repertoire], published three times

Tuntunan Andalang Lengkap Lakon Parta Krama [A complete manual for the dhalang's performance of the story "Parta Krama"], already performed and also used as a source of instruction at ASKI [Akademi Seni Karawitan Indonesia].

Langen Swara, the most complete collection of bawa, gérong, sekar ageng, tengahan, and macapat.

There are many others.

Within the organization Ikatan Penerbit Indonesia [Union of Indonesian publishers], abbreviated IKAPI, in the year 1966, [I] was chosen to become the manager of the Surakarta branch, and in 1968 was chosen to be the chairman of the Surakarta branch.

From 1961 to 1963, became the head of the organization Persatuan Wartawan Indonesia [Union of Indonesian journalists], abbreviated PWI, and now am cosecretary of the Surakarta branch.

Information supplied by the author. Translated by J. Becker.

Sastrapustaka, B. Y. H. [Benedictus Yusuf Harjamulya]

This entry is a translation of a document supplied by B.Y.H. Sastrapustaka. The undersigned attests that the life history below is truthful. Included are letters of appointment and official statements. [The latter are not included here.]

Born 1910. Short name—Harjamulya.
From birth I lived at the palace [Yogyakarta] because my mother was the wet nurse for the son of Sri Sultan [Hamengku Buwana] VIII. At that time he was not yet sultan. The sultan was still his father, Sultan [Hamengku

Buwana] VII. At the Yogyakarta palace, the employment of a wet nurse to suckle the son of the sultan was common practice. I was still a baby and was also suckled by my mother. I suckled first, and when I was full, only then did my mother suckle the son of the sultan.

Since the age of eight I have always been happy playing gamelan. My great-grandfather, my grandfather, and my father were singers for *bedhaya* and *srimpi*, and dance teachers at the palace. My siblings were two. My elder brother danced *wayang orang* and my elder sister danced bedhaya or srimpi at the palace. Every Saturday night there was a wayang kulit performance at the palace. I would approach the player of the *saron* and he would allow me to play. The saron musician was afraid that I might be a son of the sultan. I was eight years old at that time. When I was nine years old I entered primary school. In 1924 I received my certificate. I became a female dancer in wayang orang. At that time all female parts in wayang orang were danced by male children, for in those days females were forbidden to dance wayang orang.

In 1929 I became a court servant. I wished to continue my education. I was granted permission to enter a school for elementary teachers, passed the examination, graduated, and received my certificate. I then returned to the palace and worked in the library. In 1942 I married Christina Suhartati. In 1950 I became a teacher in the elementary school of the Institute Kanisius Yogyakarta.

Beginning in the year 1926 I studied karawitan wherever there was a gamelan ensemble; I did not use notation. In 1950 I became a teacher of karawitan with the Paguyubab Katulik Cipta Budaya [Catholic cultural association]. In 1955 I received a letter of appointment from the Netherlands, from the director of the Kanisius School, Pastor D. C. Wammes, Order of Jesuits, who had decided to make me head of the school. In 1955 I also received an appointment from the Vicarate Apostolic in Semarang to be one of the members of the committee for arranging Javanese songs accompanied by gamelan for use in the Church. I was given this appointment by Archbishop A. Soegiyapranata, Order of Jesuits. In 1953 I became a teacher at the Sokawati Junior High School (Yogyakarta). It was built by all the nobility and the commoners who still were connected with the family of Sri Sultan Hamengku Buwana I. From 1955 to 1960 I was a teacher of karawitan at a seminary school.

In 1962 I received a certificate of appreciation from the Indonesian National Armed Forces because I had once been a member of the armed forces. Also in 1962 I became a teacher of karawitan at KONRI [Konservatori Tari Indonesia, a high school of dance in Yogyakarta]. In 1963 I became a teacher at ASTI [Akademi Seni Tari Indonesia, a dance college in Yogyakarta]. To this day I am a court official of arts at the palace, looking after all the old books that concern the arts.

Written November 29, 1978.
Signed: B. Y. H. Sastrapustaka.

Translated by J. Becker.

In August 1979, Sastrapustaka received the Anugerah Seni award from the Indonesian government for his activities connected with karawitan.

Sindoesawarno, Ki [Radèn Mas]

Ki Sindoesawarno was born in Solo during the Dutch occupation. He attended the Techniese Hoge School in Bandung, which was later to become the Institut Teknologi Bandung. Since he was not from a wealthy family, he had to leave school before he received his degree.

The deep concern of Ki Sindoesawarno with the issue of national art and culture led him to become a member of Anggauta Pamong Luhur Taman Siswa, the highest council of education within the Taman Siswa school system. He was a close friend of Ki Hadjar Dewantara and for a time taught at the Taman Siswa School in Bandung.

During the revolution Ki Sindoesawarno moved to Solo where he became head of the Jawatan Kebudayaan Pusat [Central department of culture] with an office in the Mangku Negaran.

Around 1948, following Indonesian independence, he conceived the idea of opening a school for the study and dissemination of karawitan. He founded the Panitya Kemungkinan Berdirinya Konservatori Karawitan [Committee for the possibility of the founding of the karawitan conservatory] whose membership included R. C. Hardjosubrata; Dr. Suharso; Dr. Moerdawa (who later became the cultural attaché in London, ca. 1955); R. M. P [Radèn Mas Panji] Banakamsi (the conductor of the western court orchestra); R. Ng. [Radèn Ngabèhi] Prajapangrawit (who later became Warsadiningrat); G. P. H. [Gusti Pangéran Harya] Suryahamijaya; R. M. H. [Radèn Mas Harya] Yudadiningrat; R. M. [Radèn Mas] Sartiyatma from the Mangku Negaran; Dr. Patmanegara; and the chairman, G. P. H. [Gusti Pangéran Harya] Surya Hamijaya.

This group met regularly and formed a second committee, called the Panitya Peresmian Berdirinya Konservatori Karawitan Indonesia [Official committee for the founding of the Indonesian conservatory of karawitan], which was headed by K. R. M. T. [Kangjeng Radèn Mas Tumenggung] Bratadiningrat. The second committee developed the curriculum for the proposed school, which consisted of the theory of karawitan, cultural history, history of literature, theory of Western music, musicology, English and Indonesian, gamelan performance, and dance. The inauguration of the Konservatori Karawitan Indonesia took place August 27, 1950, at the Dalem Ngabèhian, the home of the first son of Pangéran Hangabèhi.

Sindoesawarno taught *ilmu karawitan* [theory of karawitan] at the new school and later taught at the Akademi Seni Karawitan Indonesia. His colleagues there included R. Ng. [Radèn Ngabèhi] Prajapangrawit; R. Ng. Purwapangrawit; R. Ng. Wirawiyaga; R. Ng. Wirapradangga; R. L. [Radèn Lurah] Prawirapangrawit; R. L. Mlayareksaka; and R. L. Pancapangrawit. In 1954 they were joined by R. M. [Radèn Mas] Sumadarmaka and R. M. Sukanto.

Sindoesawarno had many innovative ideas including the concept of a shortened, four-hour, wayang kulit. He died around 1965.

Information supplied by R. M. Sukanto. Translated by J. Becker.

Sumarsam

Born in Dander, Bajanegara, East Java, on July 27, 1944, Sumarsam began to play gamelan at the age of eight. He studied at the Konservatori Karawitan Indonesia at Surakarta from 1961 to 1964, and at the Akademi Seni Karawitan Indonesia at Surakarta from 1965 to 1968. In 1965 he taught gamelan at a junior high school in Surakarta. From 1966 to 1971 he taught at the conservatory in Surakarta and from 1967 to 1971 he was an assistant lecturer at the academy in Surakarta. From 1971 to 1972 he taught gamelan at the Indonesian Embassy in Canberra, Australia. He has performed in major cities throughout Java; at the 1970 "Expo" in Osaka, Japan; in the Philippines; and in Australia. In 1972 he was appointed visiting artist in Indonesian music at Wesleyan University in Connecticut, and from 1974 to the present he has been artist-in-residence there. In that capacity he has performed and lectured widely in the United States. He is the author of several articles on gamelan music published in *Ethnomusicology*, *Asian Music*, and *Indonesia*. Mr. Sumarsam is married, the father of two children, and continues an active career as a teacher and performer in the United States.

Information supplied by the author.

Warsadiningrat, K. R. T. [Kangjeng Radèn Tumenggung]

Born in 1882, K. R. T. Warsadiningrat was a gamelan expert from the palace of Surakarta. Recognition of his activities in karawitan began at age sixteen when he became *jajar nyaga* (lowest-ranking gamelan official) with the title Pradangga. In 1941, after several elevations in rank, he became *ordenas* of the Surakarta palace by order of Paku Buwana X. His final promotion occurred in 1972 when, by order of the Sunan Paku Buwana XII, he was named *bupati sesepuh niyaga* with the title Kangjeng Radèn Tumenggung Warsadiningrat. In the field of karawitan, he is known as one of the founders of the Konservatori Karawitan Indonesia at Surakarta (1950). He composed many gamelan gendhing and many suluk for wayang. His written legacy, six volumes entitled *Serat Wréda Pradangga* [*Wédha Pradangga*] represents an effort to develop traditional Javanese karawitan. In 1972, before his death on September 6, 1975, K. R. T. Warsadiningrat was given the award Anugerah Seni from the Indonesian government for his role as composer of Surakarta-style gamelan pieces and wayang songs.

From M. Soeharto, Kamus Music Indonesia. *Jakarta: P. T. Gramedia, 1978. Translated by J. Becker.*

His Royal Highness the Most Glorious and Wise
Kangjeng Susuhunan Paku Buwana X

Paku Buwana X was born November 29, 1866, crowned March 30, 1893, and died February 20, 1939. His story need not be told at length, because at his death there was a great deal written about him. Here we will just relate that which is important.

His Highness, the son of Paku Buwana IX, was born to Queen Gusti Kangjeng Ratu Paku Buwana. When he was three years old he was named Prince Kangjeng Gusti Pangéran Adipati Anom Hamengku Negara Sudibya Raja Putra Naréndra Mataram V [Lord ruler, young prince, holding the country in his lap, more than wise child-king of Mataram V]. He was circumcised at age sixteen. On August 27, 1884, he was appointed a lieutenant colonel in the Dutch army. On May 5 [188?] he became head of the court of law. On August 1, 1890, he married Bendara Radèn Ajeng Sumasti, who then took the name Gusti Kangjeng Ratu Paku Buwana, the daughter of Gusti Pangéran Adipati Harya Mangku Negara IV. On August 10, 1890, he was promoted to the rank of colonel. On March 30, 1893, he became king. He took a second wife, the daughter of Sampéyan Dalem, the Sinuhun Kangjeng Sultan VII, of Yogyakarta. This queen took the name Gusti Kangjeng Ratu Emas and bore a child, Gusti Kangjeng Ratu Pambayun. His Highness died at age seventy-four, having reigned for forty-five years.

His Highness was famous for his wide knowledge. He dedicated himself to the study of many matters, physical and spiritual. His special talents and abilities, beyond those of ordinary men, included the following.

1. He was a master of gamelan and vocal music, beginning his studies at a young age. While still a prince, he often would dance *wirèng* [fragments from *wayang wong*], which he describes in his book *Sri Mataya.* So also with wayang.
2. His Highness was unusually skilled at oral composition and his servants recorded what he composed. On the first try he could compose a *tembang* [Javanese sung verse]. A great many of his writings have been published; many more are still stored [in manuscript form]. Below is a quotation from one addressed to his father, composed while he was still a prince. Three verses of *dhangdhang gula* [prose translation only]:

1. May this my greeting reach you, my father, who rules Surakarta. I have already received the writing on the slate, the message of the *kidung,* along with the 10,000 in paper money. I receive this generous gift with happiness.

2. I understand that I must use this money to purchase for my *biyada* [female dancers, food bearers, servants] clothing that is matching, so that they are not envious of one another, but are obedient and loyal. From your blessing to all the servants under my rule, may everyone be contented and eternally happy by the grace of Your Majesty.

3. Finally, this letter I offer on the evening of *Sukra Paing* [Friday *Paing*], on the sixteenth of *Jumadilawal,* in the year *Jimakir, Wuku Galungan,* seventh month. The appropriate *candra sangkala* is:

8   1   8   1

[1818, the Javanese year, 1886 A.D.]

SALIRA PUTRA ATI RAJA

body child heart king

[the body of a child, the heart of a king]

Thus concludes my letter, Pangéran Adipati Anom Mangku Negara.

3. His Highness was an expert on the subject of horses. His abilities included not only riding but also mastery of the equestrian science. Often he inspected his horses at the Langen Sari stable. And he would inspect the horses offered to him and would ride them himself [to test their quality].
4. His Highness stood out from ordinary people in his expertise on magic weapons. He knew exactly which *krises* he had entrusted to the members of his family and to his hundreds of servants. With just a glimpse of the handle he would know the name of the *kris*. Not only could he remember their names, but he could remember their character and special qualities as well.
5. In addition to sharp weapons [such as swords], he also was masterful in the use of guns. Once a spotted tiger escaped from its cage and climbed to the top of a banyan tree near the tiger cage. His Highness Paku Buwana X fired his weapon and the tiger fell dead to the ground.

To the excellence of His Highness, there seemed to be no end. His memory was formidable. If he saw someone just once, he would not forget when he met that person again several decades later. He had an amazing memory for stories as well, and could be called *awicarita* [storyteller].

Most people considered the late Paku Buwana X to be—a thousand pardons—conservative. But this is a false opinion. As for exercise, His Highness always maintained a rigid daily schedule: sitting, eating, sleeping, and recreation all occurred at fixed times. Regarding his spiritual training, although it was not immediately apparent, one can see that he kept well and that he could not have lived long had he not kept his mind and body in harmony. He guarded his health by always being a perfectionist. His spirit was pure—this is all quite evident.

His Highness took an active part in the process of modernization [and development]. At the beginning of this modern era, he sent all his children to school. It was his idea always to send those who graduated from high school to continue their studies in Holland.

As for government, his opinions were progressive. In the realms of education, religion, health, economy, government, and agriculture, to name a few, the process of modernization was evident. Whoever knows about the conditions in Surakarta past and present will certainly concur.

His Highness's generosity and kindness were felt by all the governing bodies and groups that passed through Surakarta, and so Surakarta was chosen as the location for the Konggres [Congress]. To put it simply, many people were indebted to his generosity; indeed, his gifts flowed like water. His socializing flourished. With no end there were foreign guests who came to his palace and were touched by his warmth. Furthermore, his friendship with the kings of other countries is a proven fact.

As a last impression of the late Paku Buwana X, his real spiritual perfection meant that he was a god. Whatever he said really happened, and there is no need to feel apprehensive about his eternal life in the hereafter. Fortunate are all those who have been given a bit of his knowledge.

May his blessing flow continuously forever.

Information supplied by Radèn Mas Tumenggung Sapardi Josodipuro. Translated by R. Anderson Sutton.

TRANSLATOR'S NOTE

[1]See Susan Pratt Walton's "Translator's Introduction" to *Wèdha Pradangga*, in volume 2, for an explanation of Javanese calendrical terms, titles of the nobility, and the various courts of Surakarta.

APPENDIX 4

BIBLIOGRAPHY OF SOURCES MENTIONED BY
AUTHORS, TRANSLATORS, EDITORS,
AND CONSULTANTS

ABBREVIATIONS

BKI   Bijdragen tot de Taal-, Land- en Volkenkunde van het Koninklijk Instituut voor Taal-, Land- en Volkenkunde (van Nederlandsch-Indië).

KBG   Koninklijk Bataviaas Genootschap van Kunsten en Wetenschappen (Museum Pusat Kebudayaan Indonesia, Jakarta).

KITLV   Koninklijk Instituut voor Taal-, Land- en Volkenkunde.

TBG   Tijdschrift voor de Indische Taal-, Land- en Volkenkunde, uitgegeven door het Koninklijk Bataviaasch Genootschap van Kunsten en Wetenschappen.

VBG   Verhandelingen van het Bataviaasch Genootschap van Kunsten en Wetenschappen. Batavia.

VKI   Verhandelingen van het Koninklijk Instituut voor Taal-, Land- en Volkenkunde.

BIBLIOGRAPHY

Ādi Parwa. Old Javanese prose version of the first book of the *Mahābhārata*, dated ca. eleventh century A.D. See Juynboll 1906.

Arjuna Wiwāha. Old Javanese *kakawin* by Mpu Kaṇwa, dated eleventh century A.D. See Poerbatjaraka 1926.

Aśvaghoṣa. "The Buddha-Karita [Buddhacarita]." Translated from Sanskrit by E. B. Cowell. In *Buddhist Mahâyâna Texts*, edited by F. Max Müller.

Sacred Books of the East, no. 49, 1894. Reprint. New York: Dover Publications, 1969.

Atmadarsana, F. *Mardawa Swara.* Semarang: Jajasan Kanisius, 1956.

Atmadarsana, F. *Mardawa Swara, Bagian Praktijk I, Seni Suara Djawa.* Yogyakarta: n.p., 1957.

Babad Demak. History of the Javanese kingdom of Demak, north-central Java, dated ca. eighteenth century A.D. See Pigeaud 1967–70, vol. 1, 138–42.

Babad Mataram. History of the Javanese kingdom of Mataram, central Java, dated ca. eighteenth century A.D. See Pigeaud 1967–70, vol. 1, 138–42.

Bandem, I Made; I Gusti Bagus Arthanegara; I Ketut Rota; I Ketut Rindi; I Nyoman Rembang; and I Gusti Putu Geria. *Panitihalaning Pegambuhan.* Den Pasar: Seni Budaya dan Pembelian Benda-Benda Seni Budaya, 1975.

Becker, A. L. "Literacy and Cultural Change." In *Literacy for Life: The Demand for Reading and Writing,* edited by Richard W. Bailey and Robin Melanie Fosheim. New York: Modern Language Association of American, 1983.

Becker, A. L. "The Poetics and Noetics of a Javanese Poem." In *Spoken and Written Language,* edited by D. Tannen. Norwood, N.J.: Ablex, 1982.

Becker, A. L. "Text-building, Epistemology, and Aesthetics in Javanese Shadow Theatre." In *The Imagination of Reality: Essays in Southeast Asian Coherence Systems,* edited by A. L. Becker and A. Yengoyan. Norwood, N.J.: Ablex, 1979.

Becker, Judith. *Traditional Music in Modern Java.* Honolulu: University Press of Hawaii, 1980.

Berg. C. C. "*Kidung Sunda*: Inleiding, Tekst, Vertaling en Aanteekeningen." BKI 83 (1927):1–161.

Bhārata Yuddha. An Old Javanese *kakawin* version of the Indian epic. The *kakawin* is by Sedhah and Panuluh (see Sedhah and Panuluh 1157). Also see Gunning 1903 and Sutjipto Wirjosuparto 1968.

Bharati, Agehananda. *The Tantric Tradition.* Garden City, N.J.: Anchor Books, 1970.

Bibliotheca Javanica. Bandung: Weltevreden, 1930–49.

Bonokamsi, R. M. P. W. *Samboja.* Solo: Prodjosoejitno, 1957.

Brandes, J. L. A. "*Pararaton (Ken Arok)* of het Boek der Koningen van Tumapel en van Majapahit." VBG 49 (1896). 2d ed., revised by N. J. Krom et al. VBG 62 (1920).

Brandon, James. *On Thrones of Gold: Three Javanese Shadow Plays.* Cambridge, Mass.: Harvard University Press, 1970.

Bratakésawa, R. *Katrangan Tjandrasangkala.* Batavia: Balé Poestaka, 1928. 2d ed. (in romanized transcription). Jakarta: Balai Pustaka, 1952. Reprint, with translation into Indonesian by T. W. K. Hadisoeprapta.

Jakarta: Projek Penerbitan Buku Sastra Indonesia dan Daerah. Dep. Pendidikan dan Kebudayaan, 1980.

Brata Yuda, kawi miring. See Yasadipura I, *Brata Yuda*.

Budha Carita. See Aśvaghoṣa.

Campbell, Joseph. *The Mythic Image*. Princeton, N.J.: Princeton University Press, 1974.

Chevé, Emile. *Methode Galin-Paris-Chevé: Methode Elementaire de Musique Vocale*. Paris: Chez Les Auteurs, 1884.

Cohen Stuart, A. B. "Brata-Joeda, Indisch-Javaansch Heldendicht [by R. Ng. Yasadipura I]: Javaansche Tekst en Critische Aanteekeningen." VBG 28 (1860):1–198. In Javanese script.

Cohen Stuart, A. B. *Kawi Oorkonden in Facsimile, met Inleiding en Transcriptie*. 2 vols. Leiden: n.p., 1875. Collection of transcriptions of Old Javanese charters.

Cohen Stuart Collection, KBG, Jakarta.

Dahm, Bernard. *History of Indonesia in the Twentieth Century*. Translated by P. S. Falla, New York: Praeger, 1971.

Darmoredjono, Kenang. *Gending Djawi Sekarsari*. Solo: Djawatan Penerangan Kabupaten Wonogiri, 1968.

Devi, Sudarshana. See Singhal.

Dewantara, Ki Hadjar. "Rancangan Wewatoning Kawroeh Toewin Pasinaon Gending Djawi." *Wasito* 2, no. 3 (1936):61–72. Reprinted, with translation into Indonesian, in *Karja Ki Hadjar Dewantara*, vol. 2a, *Kebudajaan*. Jogjakarta: Madjelis-Luhur Persatuan Taman Siswa, 1967.

Dewantara, Ki Hadjar. *Serat Sari Swara*. Djakarta: Pradnjaparamita, 1964.

Déwa Ruci. See Yasadipura I, *Déwa Ruci*.

Dhani Nivat, Prince. "The Dalang." *Journal of the Siam Society* 43, no. 2 (1956):113–35.

Dharmaja, Mpu. *Smara Dahana*. An Old Javanese *kakawin* story of the begetting of Ganesha by Śiwa and Umā, dated ca. twelfth century A.D. See Poerbatjaraka 1931.

Djumadi. *Tuntunan Belajar Rebab*. Surakarta, 1972. Typescript.

Djajadipoera, R. M. "Gegevens met betrekking tot den gamelan," *Djawa* 1, Prae-adviezen 2 (1921):91–108.

Djakoeb and Wignjaroemeksa. *Lajang anjurupaké pratikelé bab sinaon nabuh sarto panggawéné gamelan* [Dutch title: *Over de Gamelan*]. Batavia: Papyrus, 1913.

Djakoeb and Wignjaroemeksa. *Serat Enoet Gending Sléndro*. Batavia: Landsdrukkerij, 1919.

Drewes, G. W. J. "Ranggawarsita, the Pustaka Raja Madya and the Wayang Madya." *Oriens Extremus* 21, no. 2 (1974):199–215.

Ḍusun, Mpu. Kuñjarakarṇa Dharmakathana. Edited and translated by A. Teeuw and S. O. Robson. Bibliotheca Indonesia, no. 21. The Hague: Martinus Nijhoff, 1981.

Dwidjasewaya, M. Ng. Lajang Paramasastra Djawa. 2 vols. Jogjakarta: H. Buning, 1908.

Echols, John M., and Hassan Shadily. An Indonesian-English Dictionary. Ithaca, N.Y.: Cornell University Press, 1970.

Encyclopaedie van Nederlandsch-Indië. 2d ed. 9 vols. The Hague: Martinus Nijhoff, 1917–40. Vol. 1, 1917; vol. 2, 1918; vol. 3, 1919; vol. 4, 1921; vol. 5, 1927; vol. 6, 1932; vol. 7, 1935; vol. 8, 1939; vol. 9, 1940.

Errington, Joseph. "Changing Speech Levels among a Traditional Javanese Elite Group." Ph.D. diss., University of Chicago, 1981.

Favre, Plieppe Etienne Lazare. Dictionnaire javanais français. Vienna: Imprimerie Impériale et Royale, 1870.

Fokker, A. A. "Wirāṭaparwa. Opnieuw Uitgegeven Vertaald en Toegelicht, I." Ph.D. diss., University of Leiden, 1938.

Forrester, Geoffrey. "'The Dharmaśunya' (The Philosophy of the Void): An Old-Javanese Treatise on Yoga and Liberation." Honors sub-thesis, Australian National University, Canberra, 1968.

Fox-Strangeways, Arthur H. The Music of Hindostan. Oxford: Clarendon Press, 1914.

Ganda, ed. "Pakem Purwatjarita pangruwatan mataram. Lampahan lakon 'Amurwa Kala Ngruwat.'" Pandjangmas 2, no. 2 (1954):17–18; no. 3 (1954):16–18; no. 4 (1954):17–18; no. 5 (1954):17–18; no. 10 (1954):17–18.

Geertz, Clifford. The Interpretation of Culture. New York: Basic Books, 1973.

Geertz, Clifford. The Religion of Java. Chicago and London: University of Chicago Press, 1976.

Gericke, J. T. C., and T. Roorda. Javaansch-Nederlandsch Handwoordenboek. Edited by A. C. Vreede. 2 vols. Amsterdam: Muller; Leiden: E. J. Brill, 1901.

Groneman, J. De gamelan te Jogjakarta. Amsterdam: Koninklijke Akademe van Wetenschappen, 1890.

Grote Winkler Prins: Encyclopedie in Twintig Delen. 10th ed. Amsterdam: Elsevier, 1972.

Gunasentika II, Kyai Demang. Serat Titi Asri. Edited by Sapardal Hardasukarta and Mas Ngabehi Mlajadimedja. Surakarta: Budi Utama, 1925. Reprinted as Titi Asri, Sapardal Hardasukarta, ed. Jakarta: Departemen Pendidikan dan Kebudayaan, 1978. Reprint (in romanized script), with summary in Indonesian by A. Hendrato. Jakarta: Balai Pustaka, 1983.

Gunning, J. G. H., ed. *Bhārata-Yuddha, Oudjavaansch Heldendicht.* The Hague: Martinus Nijhoff, 1903.

Hardjasubrata, R. C. *Serat Tuntunan Aku Bisa Nembang.* Jakarta: Ministry of Education and Culture [Dep. P. P. dan K.], 1951.

Heins, E. L. "Cueing the Gamelan in Javanese Wayang Performance." *Indonesia* 9 (1970):101–27.

Herrfurth, Hans. *Djawanisch-deutches Wörterbuch.* Leipzig: Verlag Enzyklopädie, 1972.

Hikayat Panji Kuda Semirang: Transkripsi. Transcribed and compiled by Lukman Ali and H. S. Hutagalung. Jakarta: Direktorat Jendral Kebudayaan, Departemen Pendidikan dan Kebudayaan, 1973. Transcription of Lembaga Kebudayaan Indonesia MS 125C, Cohen Stuart Collection.

Hood, Mantle. "The Effect of Medieval Technology on Musical Style in the Orient." *Selected Reports* 1, no. 3 (1970):148–70.

Hood, Mantle. *The Ethnomusicologist.* 2d rev. ed. Kent, Ohio: Kent State University Press, 1982.

Hood, Mantle. "Music of Indonesia." In *Music*, edited by M. Hood and J. Maceda. Leiden and Köln: E. J. Brill, 1972.

Hood, Mantle. *The Nuclear Theme as a Determinant of Patet in Javanese Music.* Groningen and Djakarta: J. B. Wolters, 1954.

Hood, Mantle, and Hardja Susilo. *Music of the Venerable Dark Cloud.* Los Angeles: Institute of Ethnomusicology, University of California, 1967. Booklet accompanying the recording of the same title.

Hooykaas, C. *Kama and Kala: Material for the Study of Shadow Theatre in Bali.* Amsterdam: North-Holland Publishing Co., [1973].

Hooykaas, C., ed. *Tantri Kāmandaka.* Bibliotheca Javanica, no. 2. Bandung: A. C. Nix, 1931. Old Javanese adaptation of Sanskrit *Pancatantra.*

Hornbostel, E. M. von. *Hornbostel Opera Omnia I*, edited by Klaus P. Wachsmann. The Hague: Martinus Nijhoff, 1975.

Horne, Elinor C. *Javanese-English Dictionary.* New Haven: Yale University Press, 1974.

Juynboll, H. H. *Ādiparwa: Oudjavaansch Prozageschrift, uitgegeven door Dr. H. H. Juynboll.* The Hague: Martinus Nijhoff, 1906. The Old Javanese version of the first book of the *Mahābhārata.*

Juynboll, H. H. *Oudjavaansch-Nederlandsche Woordenlijst.* Leiden: E. J. Brill, 1923.

Juynboll, H. H., ed. *Udyoga Parwa.* BKI 69 (1913):219–96. The Old Javanese version of the fifth book of the *Mahābhārata.*

Juynboll, H. H. "Vertaling van sarga VII–XXVI van het Oud-Javaansche *Rāmāyaṇa.*" BKI 78 (1922) through BKI 94 (1938).

Juynboll, H. H. *Wirātaparwa: Oud-Javaansche Prozageschrift.* The Hague: Martinus Nijhoff, 1912. The Old Javanese version of the fourth book of the *Mahābhārata.*

Kahin, George McT. *Nationalism and Revolution in Indonesia.* Ithaca: Cornell University Press, 1952.

Kaṇwa, Mpu. *Arjuna Wiwāha.* Old Javanese *kakawin,* dated eleventh century A.D., which relates the story of Arjuna's wedding. See Poerbatjaraka 1926.

Kartomi, Margaret. *Matjapat Songs of Central and West Java.* Canberra: Australian National University Press, 1973.

Keboedjaan Timoer. Djakarta: Kantor Besar Pusat Kebudajaan, Keimun Bunka Sidosho, [1942].

Kern, Hendrik, ed. "De legende van Kuñjarakarṇa." *Verspreide Geschriften* 10 (1922):1–76. Text and translation of *Kuñjarakarṇa.*

Kern, Hendrik, ed. *Rāmāyaṇa Kakawin: Oud-Javaansch Heldendicht.* The Hague: n.p., 1900.

Kern, Hendrik. "Zang I-VI van het Oud-Javaansch *Rāmāyaṇa* in vertaling." BKI 73 (1917):1–29, 155–74, 472–94.

Khin Zaw, U. "Burmese Music: A Preliminary Enquiry." *Journal of the Burma Research Society* 30, pt. 3 (December 1940):389.

Kidung Sunda. Historical ballad based on an episode of the history of Majapahit, East Java, dated ca. 1300–1400 A.D., written in *sekar tengahan* meters. See Berg 1927.

Kitab Jitapsara. See Ranggawarsita, n.d.

Kodiron. *Lelagon Dolanan.* Solo: Toko Buku Pelajar, 1969.

Kodiron. *Sinau Tembang Djawa.* Solo: Toko Buku Pelajar, 1968.

Kodiron. *Tuntunan Karawitan Gending Djawi.* Solo: Trijasa, 1964.

Koesoemadilaga, K. P. A. *Pakem Sastramiroeda: Oegering Padalangan ingkang Sampoen Moepakat Kangge Abdi-Dalem Dalang in Karaton Soerakarta Adiningrat.* Surakarta: De Bliksem, 1930. Manual for the *wayang* performer including passages referring to gamelan and details of *wayang* puppets.

Kramaleya. Unidentified work.

Kuñjarakarṇa See Kern 1922; Dusun 1981. Old Javanese *kakawin.*

Kunst, Jaap. *De Toonkunst van Java.* 2 vols. The Hague: Martinus Nijhoff, 1934.

Kunst, Jaap. *Hindu-Javanese Musical Instruments.* The Hague: Martinus Nijhoff, 1968.

Kunst, Jaap. *Music in Java: Its History, its Theory and its Technique.* 2 vols. 3d ed., enlarged. The Hague: Martinus Nijhoff, 1973. Translation of Kunst 1934.

Kunst, Jaap, and R. Goris. *Hindoe-Javansche Muziekinstrumenten, Speciaal die van Oost-Java.* Batavia: n.p., 1927.
Kunst, Jaap, and C. J. A. Kunst-van Wely. *De Toonkunst van Bali.* Weltevreden: G. Kolff, 1925.
Kusumadilaga, K. P. A. See Koesoemadilaga 1930.
Langendriya, Inggih Punika Pakem Padhalangan Ringgit Krucil Cariyos Lalampahanipun Radèn Damar Wulan. 7 vols. Batavia: Balé Poestaka, 1932. See also Tandhakusuma 1939, 1954. Text of the dance drama, *Langen Driya*, of the Mangku Negaran court.
Lindsay, Jennifer. *Javanese Gamelan.* Kuala Lumpur: Oxford University Press, 1979.
Mangku Negara IV, K. G. P. A. A. "Sendhon Langen Swara: Katrangan sarta Tegesipun Bawa sarta Gendhingipun." In *Serat-serat Anggitan-dalem,* by Mangku Negara IV, vol. 4, 142–78. Jakarta: N. Kolff, 1953. Collection of poems for sung performance.
Mangku Negara IV, K. G. P. A. A. *Serat-serat Anggitan-dalem.* 4 vols. Jakarta: N. Kolff, 1953. Collected works of Mangku Negara IV.
Mantra Yoga. Unidentified work. "Mantra Yoga" refers to a Tantric discipline for controlling the vital winds with the help of mantras.
Manuscript Museum C 125. Undated manuscript in the Cohen Stuart Collection, Museum Pusat Kebudaijaan Indonesia, Jakarta.
Mardiwarsito, L. *Kamus Jawa Kuna-Indonesia.* 2d ed., rev. Ende, Flores: Nusa Indah, 1981.
Martopangrawit, R. L. *Catatan-catatan Pengetahuan Karawitan.* 2 vols. Surakarta: Pusat Kesenian Jawa Tengah and Dewan Mahasiswa Akademi Seni Karawitan Indonesia, 1972.
Martopangrawit, R. L. *Gérong Bedhayan.* Surakarta: Akademi Seni Karawitan Indonesia, 1971.
Martopangrawit, R. L. *Tetembangan.* Solo: Dewan Mahasiswa Akademi Seni Karawitan Indonesia, 1967.
Martopangrawit, R. L. *Titilaras cengkok-cengkok genderan dengan wiletannya.* 2 vols. Surakarta: Akademi Seni Karawitan Indonesia, 1973.
Martopangrawit, R. L. *Titilaras Gending dan Sindenan Bedaya-Srimpi Kraton Surakarta.* Surakarta: Akademi Seni Karawitan Indonesia, 1975.
Martopangrawit, R. L. *Titilaras Kendangan.* Surakarta: Konservatori Karawitan Indonesia, 1972.
Martopangrawit, R. L. *Vocaal Karawitan.* Surakarta: Konservatori Karawitan Indonesia, 1967.
McDermott, Vincent, and Sumarsam. "Central Javanese Music: The Pathet of Laras Slendro and the Gendèr Barung." *Ethnomusicology* 19, no. 2 (1975):233–44.
McPhee. Colin. *Music in Bali.* New Haven: Yale University Press, 1966.

Moertono, Soemarsaid. *State and Statecraft in Old Java: A Study of the Later Mataram Period, 16th to 19th Century.* Ithaca, N.Y.: Modern Indonesia Project, Southeast Asia Program, Department of Asian Studies, Cornell University, 1968.

Mugi Baswara. *Sekar lan Ubarampénipun.* Malang: n.p., n.d.

Naradha Purana. Unidentified work.

Nartosabdho, Ki *Gendhing-gendhing Djawi Saha Dolanan Gagrag Enggal.* Semarang: Ngesti Pandawa, 1969.

Nojowirangka, M. Ng. *Centhangan terhadap Preadvis Ki Hadjar Dewantara Bab Gendhing.* Yogyakarta: n.p., 1936.

Ong, Walter J. *The Presence of the Word.* New Haven: Yale University Press, 1967.

Ortega y Gasset, José. "The Difficulty of Reading." *Diogenes* 28 (Winter 1959):1–17.

Padmasusastra, Ki. *Serat Sekar-sekaran.* N.p., 1914.

Paku Buwana IV, S. D. I. S. K. S. *Serat Wulangrèh.* Edited by R. Tanojo. Solo: Toko Buku Pelajar, n.d.

Panji Semirang. One version of the numerous stories of the marriage between the crown prince of Koripan, Radèn Panji (Inu Kartapati), and the princess of Daha. See Poerbatjaraka 1940b, 1968. Also see *Hikayat Panji Kuda Semirang.*

Picken, Laurence. "The Music of Far Eastern Asia. 1. China." In *The New Oxford History of Music. Ancient and Oriental Music,* edited by Egon Wellesz. London: Oxford University Press, 1957.

Pigeaud, Th. "De *Serat Tjabolang* en de *Serat Tjentini*: Inhouds-opgaven." VBG 72, no. 2 (1933):1–89.

Pigeaud, Th. *Javaans-Nederlands Handwoordenboek.* Batavia and Groningen: J. B. Wolters, 1938.

Pigeaud, Th. *Literature of Java: Catalogue Raisonne of Javanese Manuscripts in the Library of the University of Leiden and Other Public Collections in the Netherlands.* 3 vols. The Hague: Martinus Nijhoff, 1967–70.

Poerbatjaraka, R. Ng. "*Arjuna-Wiwāha,* Tekst en Vertaling." BKI 82 (1926):181–305.

Poerbatjaraka, R. Ng. "Déwa-Roetji." *Djawa* 20 (1940a):5–55.

Poerbatjaraka, R. Ng. "Historische gegevens uit de Smaradahana." TBG 58 (1919):461–89.

Poerbatjaraka, R. Ng. *Kapustakan Djawi.* Jakarta: Djambatan, 1952.

Poerbatjaraka, R. Ng. *Nītiçāstra: Oud-Javaansche Tekst met Vertaling.* Bibliotheca Javanica, no. 4. Bandung: A. C. Nix, 1933. Old Javanese moralistic maxims in Indian meters, ca. fifteenth century A.D.

Poerbatjaraka, R. Ng. *Pandji-Verhalen Onderling Vergelekan.* Bibliotheca Javanica, no. 9. Bandung: A. C. Nix, 1940b.

Poerbatjaraka, R. Ng. *Smaradhana: Oud-Javaansche Tekst met Vertaling.* Bibliotheca Javanica, No. 3. Bandung: A. C. Nix, 1931.
Poerbatjaraka, R. Ng. *Tjerita Pandji Dalam Perbandingan.* Jakarta: Gunung Agung, 1968. Translation of Poerbatjaraka 1940b.
Poerbatjaraka, R. Ng., and C. Hooykaas. "*Bhārata-Yuddha* vertaald." *Djawa* 14 (1934):1–87.
Poerwadarminta, W. J. S. *Baoesastra Djawa.* Batavia and Groningen: J. B. Wolters, 1939.
Poerwadarminta, W. J. S. *Kamus Umum Bahasa Indonesia.* 5th ed. Jakarta: Balai Pustaka, 1976.
Poesaka Djawi 1926. Unidentified work.
Prawiradihardja, Ki. *Serat Mardi-Laras.* Surakarta: Privately published, 1939.
Prawiradihardja, R. [Title unidentified.] *Sasadara* 4, no. 11 (*Besar* 1833 A.J.) (1904 A.D.).
Prawirasudirja, K., and R. M. Sulardi. *Pakem Wajang Purwa, Wiwit purwakala gnantos dumugi sabibaripun Bratajuda.* 2 vols. Surakarta: N.p., n.d.
Prijohoetomo. "Nawaruci: Inleiding, Middel-Javaansche Prozatekst, Vertaling, Vergeleken met de Bimasoetji in Oud-Javaansch Metrum." Ph.D. diss., University of Utrecht, 1934.
Probohardjono, R. Ng. Samsudjin. *Gending Djawi: Tuntunan Bawa, Dumugi Dawahing Gending Dipun-Gérongi, dalah Sindenan Sarta Ura-uranipun.* 5th ed. (2 vols. in 1). Solo: Sadu Budi, 1963.
Probohardjono, R. Ng. Samsudjin. *Gending-gending Ingkang Kanggé Nabuhi Wajang Purwa.* 5th ed. Jogjakarta: Puspa Rahaju, 1964.
Probohardjono, R. Ng. Samsudjin. *Primbon Langen Swara.* Solo: Ratna, 1961.
Probohardjono, R. Ng. Samsudjin. *Serat Sulukan Slendro: Ingkang Djangkep lan Baku Kanggé Njuluki Titingalan Wajang Purwa Katambahan Kawruh-kawruh Padhalangan.* 7th ed. Solo: Ratna, 1966.
Probohardjono, R. Ng. Samsudjin. *Sulukan Pelog.* Solo: Budhi Laksana, 1954.
Pustaka Raja. See Ranggawarsita 1884–1906.
Raffles, Thomas Stamford. *The History of Java.* London: Black, Parbury and Allen, 1817. 2d ed. London: J. Murray, 1830. 3d ed. New York: Oxford University Press, 1965.
Rama, kawi miring. See Yasadipura I, *Rama.*
Rāmāyana, kakawin/kawi. Old Javanese version of the Indian epic, dated ca. ninth century A.D. See Kern 1900.
Ranggawarsita, R. Ng. *Kitab Jitapsara.* Unpublished manuscript, n.d. Late nineteenth-century cosmogony.
Ranggawarsita, R. Ng. *Mardawalagu: Amratélakaké Laguning Lajang Watjan Patang Pangkat, Ija Iku, Matjasa Lagu Matjaro Lagu, Matjatri Lagu lan*

Matjapat Lagu. Translated into Low Javanese by R. Tanojo. Solo: Sadu Budi, 1957.

Ranggawarsita, R. Ng. *Pustaka Raja Purwa.* See Ranggawarsita, *Serat Poestaka Radja Poerwa.*

Ranggawarsita, R. Ng. *Serat Aji Pamasa,* vols. 1–10. Surakarta: N.p., 1896.

Ranggawarsita, R. Ng. *Serat Poestaka Radja Poerwa.* 9 vols. Yogyakarta: H. Buning, 1884–1906. 2d ed., 1906. 3d ed., 1912.

Ranggawarsita, R. Ng. *Serat Poestokorodjo* [Madya], edited by Dirdjaatmadja. 8 vols. Surakarta: n.p., 1904–08.

Rassers, W. H. *Panji, the Culture Hero: A Structural Study of Religion in Java.* The Hague: Martinus Nijhoff, 1959.

Ricklefs, Merle C. *A History of Modern Indonesia: c. 1300 to the Present.* Bloomington: Indiana University Press, 1981.

Ricklefs, Merle C. *Jogjakarta Under Sultan Mangkubumi, 1749–1792: A History of the Division of Java.* London: Oxford University Press, 1974.

Ricklefs, Merle C. *Modern Javanese Historical Tradition: A Study of an Original Kartasura Chronicle and Related Materials.* London: School of Oriental and African Studies, University of London, 1978.

Ricoeur, Paul. "The Model of the Text: Meaningful Action Considered as a Text." *Social Research* 38 (1971):529–62.

Ronggosworo, R. *Primbon Gendhing Umbul Donga.* Surakarta: [Krida?], 1951.

Rouffaer, G. P. "Vorstenlanden." *Adatrechtbundel* 34, ser. D, nos. 80–82 (1931):194–379. Originally published in *Encyclopaedie van Nederlandsch-Indië,* 1st ed., vol. 4 (1905), pp. 587–652.

Sana Budaja. Jogjakarta: Pertjetakan Taman Siswa, 1956–57.

Sapardal Hardasukarta, M. Ng. Mlayadimeja, and Kyai Demang Gunasentika II. *Serat Titi Asri.* See Gunasentika II, 1983.

Sasadara. Javanese-language monthly published in Surakarta in the early twentieth century, edited by Padmasusastra.

Sastra Gendhing. A section of a longer work on Javanese Islamic mysticism, entitled *Serat Purwa Campur.*

Sastra Miruda. See Koesoemadilaga 1930.

Sastrasumarta, R. Ng. *Wangsalan.* Jakarta: Balai Pustaka, 1958.

Sastrasoewignja, Soehardha; R. Wiradat; and R. Kodrat. "Ringkesaning kawroeh padalangan ringgit poerwa ing Soerakarta," *Kadjawen,* nos. 70–74 (1931–32).

Schrieke, B. J. O. *Indonesian Sociological Studies, Selected Writings of B. Schreike.* Part II. The Hague: W. van Hoeve, Ltd., 1957.

Schumacher, Rüdiger. *Die Suluk-Gesänge des Dalang im Schattenspiel Zentral-javas.* Serie NGOMA, no. 7. München: Musikverlag Emil Katzbichler, 1980.

Sedhah, Mpu, and Mpu Panuluh. *Bhārata Yuddha. Kakawin,* 1157 A.D. Old Javanese version of the Indian epic, in verse. See Gunning 1903 and Sutjipto Wirjosuparto 1968.

Seeger, Charles. "Prescriptive and Descriptive Music Writing." In *Readings in Ethnomusicology,* edited by David McAllester, pp. 24–34. New York: Johnson Reprint Corp., 1971.

Séno-Sastroamidjojo, R. A. *Renungan tentang Pertundjukan Wayang Kulit.* Djakarta: Kinta, 1964.

Séno-Sastroamidjojo, R. A. *Tjeritera Dewa Rutji Dengan Arti Filsafatnja.* Djakarta: Kinta, 1962.

Serat Cabolong. A Section of the *Serat Centhini.* See Yasadipura II and Ranggasutrasna 1912–15.

Serat Centhini. See *Serat Tjentini.*

Serat Dharma Śūnya. Śaivite *kakawin* poetry, 1418–1419 A.D. See Forrester 1968.

Serat Karawitan, kumpulan pelajaran kursus tembang gedhé. Kusumayudan, n.p., 1866.

Serat Niti Sastra. See Poerbatjaraka 1933.

Serat Panitisastra. See Poerbatjaraka 1933.

Serat Panji Semirang. See Poerbatjaraka 1940b. Also see *Panji Semirang.*

Serat Purwa Campur. Unpublished manuscript, Jakarta.

Serat Rama. See Yasadipura I, *Rama.*

Serat Tjentini: Babon Asli Saking Kita Leiden ing Negari Nederland, edited by R. Ng. Soeradipoera, R. Poerwasoewignja, and R. Wirawangsa. 8 parts in 4 vols. Batavia: Ruygrof, 1912–15.

Sindoesastra, R. Ng. *Ardjoena-Sastra-Baoe: Javaansch gedicht, in kleine dichtmaten opgesteld.* Edited and translated by W. Palmer van den Broek. Batavia: Lange, 1868. Reprint. VBG 34 (1870).

Singhal, Sudarshana Devi, ed. *Wrhaspatī-tattwa.* New Delhi: International Academy of Indian Culture, 1957.

Smara Dahana. See Dharmaja.

Soebardi. "Calendrical Traditions in Indonesia." *Madjalah Ilmu-ilmu Sastra Indonesia* 3, no. 1 (March 1965):49–61.

Soebardi. "Radèn Ngabèhi Jasadipura I, Court Poet of Surakarta: His Life and Works." *Indonesia,* no. 8 (October 1969):81–102.

Soebardi. "Santri Religious Elements as Reflected in the Book of *Tjentini,*" BKI 127 (1971):331–49.

Soedarsono, B. Suharto, Y. Sumandijo Hadi, Djoko Walujo, and R. B. Sudarsono. *Kamus Istilah Tari dan Karawitan Jawa.* Jakarta: Projek Penelitan Bahasa dan Sastra Indonesia dan Daerah, 1978.

Soehari, S. (Prime Hadiwidjaja). "Gamelan Lokanata." *Poesaka Djawi* 1 (1922):10–.

Soeharto, M. *Kamus Musik Indonesia.* Jakarta: Gramedia, 1978.

Soekanto Sastrodarsono, R. M. *Teori Nabuh Gamelan: Sistem Konservatori Karawitan Indonesia.* Surakarta: Jajasan Lektur Kesenian/Kebudajaan Nasional, Kemudawati, 1966.

Soelardi, R. B. *Serat Pradongga.* Widya Pustaka, no. 2, Weltevreden: s.n., 1918.

Soemonagoro [Sumonagara], K. R. M. T. *Serat Karawitan.* Sragen: n.p., 1935.

Soeradipoera, Poerwasoewignja, and Wirawangsa, eds. See *Serat Tjentini.*

Soetrisno, R. *Kuliah Teks-Verklaring Sulukan Pedalangan.* 2d ed. Surakarta: Akademi Seni Karawitan Indonesia, 1977.

Soetrisno, R. *Pitakonan lan Wangsulan bab Wanda Wajang Purwa.* Surakarta: Mahabarata, 1964. Reprint. Surkarta: Akademi Seni Karawitan Indonesia, 1977.

Soetrisno, R. *Sejarah Karawitan.* Surakarta: Akademi Seni Karawitan Indonesia, 1976.

Soewardi. *Peladjaran Bawa dan Gérong.* Surabaya: Direktorat Jendral Kebudayan Jawa Timur, 1967.

Stutterheim, W. F. *Studies in Indonesian Archaeology.* The Hague: Martinus Nijhoff, 1956.

Sumarsam. *Céngkok gendèran.* Surakarta: Akademi Seni Karawitan Indonesia, 1971.

Sumarsam. "Gendèr Barung: Its Technique and Function in the Context of Javanese Gamelan." *Indonesia* 20 (1975):161–71.

Sumarsam. *Kendhangan Gaya Solo: Kendhang Kalih dan Setunggal Dengan Selintas Pengetahuan Gamelan.* Surakarta: Akademi Seni Karawitan Indonesia, 1976.

Sumonagara [Soemonagoro], K. R. M. T. *Titiswara.* Surakarta: Persatuan, 1936.

Surjodiningrat, R. M. Wasisto. *Gending Beksan Mataraman.* Yogyakarta: Dewan Pembina Olah Raga dan Seni Budaya, Universitas Gajah Mada, 1976.

Surjodiningrat, R. M. Wasisto, with P. J. Sudarjana and Adhi Susanto. *Penjelidikan dalam Pengukuran Nada Gamelan-Gamelan Djawa Terkemuka di Jogjakarta dan Surakarta.* Jogjakarta: Universitas Gadjah Mada, 1969.

Susilo, Hardja. "Drumming in the Context of Javanese Gamelan." Masters thesis, University of California, Los Angeles, 1967.

Sutjipto Wirjosuparto, ed. and trans. *Kakawin Bhārata-Yuddha.* Djakarta: Bhratara, 1968.

Sutrisno, R. See Soetrisno.

Suwito, R. M. Author of an article published in three parts on the history of gamelan (title unidentified) in *Sasadara* (Surakarta) 5, no. 1 (1904):2–26; no. 2 (1904):86–96; no. 4 (1904):161.

[Tandhakusuma, R. M. H.]. *Langendrija Mandraswara: Babon Saking Mangkoenagaran.* Batavia: Balé Poestaka, 1939.

[Tandhakusuma, R. M. H.]. *Patine Menak Djingga.* Jakarta: Sari Pers, 1954.

Tanojo, R. *Pawukon: Pasemon Dalah Pardikan.* Surabaya: Jajasan Penerbitan Djaja Baja, 1967.

Tantri Kāmandaka. See Hooykaas 1931.

Tedjosumarto, R. *Mbombong Manah.* 5 vols. Djakarta: Penerbit Djambatan, 1958.

Teeuw, A. *Het Bhomakawya: een Oudjavaans Gedicht.* Groningen: J. B. Wolters, 1946. Ph.D. diss., University of Utrecht.

Teeuw, A.; Th. P. Galestin; S. O. Robson; P. J. Worsley; and P. J. Zoetmulder, eds. *Siwarātrikalpa of Mpu Tanakung.* Bibliotheca Indonesia, no. 3. The Hague: Martinus Nijhoff, 1969.

Tembang Djawa. Djakarta: Djawa Gunseikanbu, 1943.

Tiknopranoto, R. M. Ng. [R. M. Diposoetarno]. *Titi Laras Gending-Gending Djawi Muljaning Agesang.* Surakarta: Trijasa, 1963.

Tirtaamidjaja, Nusjirwan. "A Bedaja Ketawang Dance Performance at the Court of Surakarta." *Indonesia* 3 (1967):31–61.

Titi Asri. See Gunasentika II, 1983.

Tjan Tjoe Siem. *Hoe Koeroepati Zich Zijn Vrouw Verwerft: Javaansche Lakon in het Nederlandsch Vertaald en van Aanteekeningen Voorzien.* Leiden: Luctor et Emergo, 1938. Ph.D. diss., University of Leiden.

Tjiptosuwarso, S. *Tembang Jawi.* Solo: Keluarga Karawitan Studio R.R.I., 1971.

Tjitrosomo, A. S. *Poenarbawa,* vol. 1. Djakarta, Batavia: J. B. Wolters, 1949.

Udan Mas. Vol. 1, nos. 1–7 (1960). A Javanese-language periodical published for one year, in Surakarta, by the Konservatori Karawitan Indonesia.

Udyoga Parwa. See Juynboll 1914.

Uhlenbeck, E. M. *A Critical Survey of Studies on the Languages of Java and Madura.* KITLV, Bibliographical Series, no. 7. The Hague: Martinus Nijhoff, 1964.

Uhlenbeck, E. M., and J. Soegiarto. "Aantekeningen bij Tjan Tjoe Siem's Vertaling van de Lakon Kurupati Rabi," VKI 29 (1960):i–vii, 1–67.

Usman, Zuber. *Kesusasteraan Lama Indondesia.* Djakarta: Guning Agung, 1954.

Vogel, Jean Phillippe. *Buddhist Art in India, Ceylon, and Java,* translated by A. J. Barnous. Oxford: Clarendon Press, 1936.

Vogel, Jean-Phillippe. *De Buddhistische kunst van Voor Indië.* Amsterdam: H. J. Paris, 1932.

"Vokalia dan Instrumentalia pada Gamelan." *Udan Mas* 1, no. 1 (1960):22–23. Author not identified.

Wasitodipura, K. R. T. *Kumpulan Catatan Vokal.* Unpublished manuscript.

Werlich, Robert. *Orders and Decorations of All Nations Ancient and Modern, Civil and Military.* Washington, D.C.: Quaker Press, 1974.

Wesleyan World Music Archives, tape no. WA 6.2.493, n.d.

Wignjosoeworo, Bonokamsi R. M. P. *Sekar Matjapat, Tengahan dan Sekar Ageng.* Solo: R. Ng. Prodjosoejitno, 1957.

Winter, C. F. "Romo; Een Javaansch Gedicht, naar Bewerking van Josodhipoero," VBG 21 (1846–47):1–596.

Wiraguna, K. R. T. *Noot Pakem Wirama wileting Gending Pradangga laras Slendro utawi Pelog.* 5 vols. Yogyakarta: Kraton Library, 1897–[?].

Wirāta Parwa. See Juynboll 1912.

Wṛhaspatī-tattwa. See Singhal 1957.

Yasadipura I. *Brata Yuda,* kawi miring. Ca. late eighteenth century. See Soebardi 1969, 86.

Yasadipura I. *Déwa Ruci,* kawi miring. Late eighteenth century. Story concerning the second Pahdhawa brother, Bimaséna, found in prose texts, *kawi miring,* and *macapat* meters.

Yasadipura I. *Rama.* See Yasadipura I, *Serat Rama.*

Yasadipura I. *Serat Rama,* kawi miring. Late eighteenth century. 3 vols. Weltevreden: Balé Poestaka, 1925. A rewriting of the Old Javanese *Rāmāyaṇa.*

Yasadipura II and Ranggasutrasna. *Centhini.* See *Serat Tjentini.*

Zoetmulder, P. J. *Kalangwan: A Survey of Old Javanese Literature.* The Hague: Martinus Nijhoff, 1974.

Zoetmulder, P. J., and S. O. Robson. *Old Javanese-English Dictionary.* The Hague: Martinus Nijhoff, 1982.

Zurbuchen, Mary. *The Shadow Theater of Bali: Explorations in Language and Text.* Ph.D. diss., The University of Michigan. Ann Arbor: University Microfilms, 1981.

GENERAL INDEX

aba-aba. II: 345-47. III: 5
abon-abon. III: 5. See also sindhènan isèn-
isèn
ada-ada. I: 392, 424-26, 443, 449, 453-56,
460, 464-66, 469-70, 479-81, 484, 487-88,
490. II: 42, 46, 50, 89-90, 110, 209, 269,
270, 271. III: 5. See also lelagon;
sulukan; sulukan, proper names of
ada-ada, proper names of. See sulukan,
proper names of
adangiyah. See odangiyah
Adi Parwa, kakawin. II: 280
adu manis. See kempyung
ahata. I: 392n
aja ngono. I: 269. III: 5
Akademi Seni Karawitan Indonesia. I: xiii,
256, 519n. II: 29, 68. III: 431, 432, 437,
438, 441
aksara. III: 5. See also Javanese script
alok. II: 124. III: 5
alusing gendhing. I: 414. See also gendhing,
study of
ambitus. I: 223
anahata. I: 392n
andhegan. I: 12n. II: 212. III: 5. See also
mandheg
andhegan gawan. III: 5. See also andhegan
andhegan gendhing. III: 5. See also
andhegan
andhegan selingan. III: 5. See also andhegan
angkat-angkatan. II: 212, 251. III: 5
angkat dhawah. III: 6, 52. See also umpak
minggah; umpak inggah
angkaton. III: 5
angkatan ciblon. I: 367. II: 181-82, 200. III:
6. See also ciblon drumming
angkatan seseg. III: 6
angkatan sindhèn. III: 6

angkep. See gembyangan
angklung. I: 404. II: 37, 304-5. III: 6
angkub. II: 80
antal. III: 6. See also irama
antawacana. I: 443, 492-96. III: 6
antecedent. See padhang
arah nada. I: 82, 227. See also direction of
tones
arang. I: 291. III: 6
Arjuna Sasra Bau. I: 502
Arjuna Wiwāha, kakawin. I: 467, 476. II:
314n
ASKI. See Akademi Seni Karawitan
Indonesia
avoided tone. I: 402
awis. See arang
ayak-ayakan. I: 17-18, 279, 291, 293, 373,
427, 431, 434, 435. II: 42, 46, 49, 372.
III: 6
ayo yok-oyokan, cèngkok. I: 106-7
ayu kuning, cèngkok. I: 14, 113, 266-67.
III: 6

Babad Demak. II: 236
Babad Mataram. II: 70n
babarengan. II: 351. See also barangan
babon nada. II: 333-34
badhaya. I: 426, 429. II: 300. See also
bedhaya
bahiri. II: 36, 301. See also bèri
baku. III: 6
baku swara. I: 402. III: 6. See also tonic
balungan. I: 13, 249-56, 272-77, 353, 393-94,
417, 420, 429-30. III: 6. See also melody
balungan, changes in. I: 191-200
balungan beats. I: 85-88
balungan gantungan. I: 77, 111, 430

ladrang. I: 19, 21, 291–92, 367. II: 43–44, 48–49, 248–49, 367–69. III: 27
ladrang, as inggah. I: 21, 293–94, 369. See also *inggah ladrang*
ladrang, padhang-ulihan in. I: 75–76
ladrang lancaran. II: 44–45, 49. III: 27. See also *lancaran*
ladrangan. I: 367, 432. II: 43, 301, 302–3. See also *ladrang*
ladrangan ageng. II: 97
ladrangan alit. II: 97
ladrangan tengahan. II: 97
lagon. II: 41, 252, 270, 362. III: 27. See also *lelagon; sulukan*
lagon, proper names of. See *sulukan, proper names of*
lagon jugag. I: 425, 426. II: 252. III: 27. See also *pathetan*
lagon pathet. See *lagon*
lagon wantah. II: 425, 426. III: 27. See also *pathetan*
lagu. I: 11, 392–93, 397–99, 521n. II: 210, 358–86. III: 27. See also *guru-lagu*
lagu, fixed. I: 17, 100. See also *lagu mati*
lagu, form of. II: 359–61
lagu, influence of *irama* on. I: 16–17. II: 377
lagu, influence on *irama.* I: 16–17
lagu, kalimat. See *kalimat lagu*
lagu, supervisor of. I: 13, 25. See also *pamurba lagu*
lagu, upholder of. I: 12–13. See also *pamangku lagu*
lagu gecul. I: 402, 404. III: 27
lagu gedhé. II: 372. III: 27
lagu gendhing. II: 366. III: 27
lagu leutik. III: 27
lagu mati. I: 17, 100, 228. III: 27
lagu ngelik. I: 38. See also *ngelik*
lagu pathet. I: 156. III: 27
lagu pokok. I: 38
lagu sedheng. II: 372. III: 27
lagu sekar. II: 366. III: 27
lagu sumèlèh. I: 68
lagu tengah. II: 372. III: 27
lajengan. I: 374. III: 27. See also *gendhing lajengan*
lakon. I: 190, 328, 329, 448
lakuning balungan. See *density of balungan*
lalagon. II: 41. See also *lelagon; lagon*
lamba. I: 99. III: 27
lampah. II: 211–12, 225–29, 252. III: 27–28

lancaran. I: 18–19, 276–78, 291–92, 365–66. III: 28
langen driya. II: 154, 166, 220. III: 28
Langen Sekar (by Hardjosubrata). I: 403
Langendrija Mandraswara. II: 218, 219
langgam. III: 28
langgam jawa. I: 353. III: 28
laras. I: 40, 257, 345, 414–16, 421–24. II: 35, 37–39, 303, 324–25, 361–62. III: 28. See also *tuning system*
laras barang. II: 38, 40. See also *barang tuning; pathet barang*
laras bremara. II: 256. III: 28. See also *laras mleng*
laras cilik. I: 421. III: 28
laras degung. II: 362
laras gedhé. I: 421. III: 28
laras madya. I: 199, 210, 419. II: 167. III: 28
laras mleng. II: 255–56. III: 28
laras nyliring. See *laras silir*
laras pélog. See *pélog, laras*
laras pleng. See *laras mleng*
laras sedhengan. I: 421. III: 28
laras silir. II: 256. III: 28
laras sléndro. See *sléndro, laras*
laras suréndra bawana. II: 301
laras tengah. II: 38. See also *laras sedhengan*
laras umyung. II: 256. III: 28
large *gendhing.* II: 247. See also *gendhing ageng*
lawung. II: 168, 302, 305–7
laya. I: 10, 31. II: 351–52, 354–55. III: 28. See also *tempo; mlaya*
laya, metronomic measurements of. II: 355
lelagon. I: 392, 424–26. III: 28. See also *lalagon; lagon; sulukan*
lelagoning gendhing. I: 422
lenggot. II: 298
lengut. II: 385–86. III: 28
let. II: 325. III: 28. See also *interval*
lik. See *ngelik*
lima. I: 47–48, 311–16, 332. III: 28
lingkaran-kempyung. I: 401
lintasan. I: 223, 402
logondhang. III: 28
Loro Kidul, Nyai. II: 82, 83, 115–17
luk. I: 395. II: 383–84. See also *eluk*

sampak. **I**: 17, 68–69, 291, 293, 373, 423, 427,
    431, 434, 435. **II**: 42, 372. **III**: 37
samyaswara. **II**: 341, 343, 360. **III**: 37
Sana Budaja (periodical/museum). **I**: 407.
    III: 435
Sang Hyang Éndra. See *Éndra, Bathara*
Sang Hyang Guru. **II**: 34–35, 63, 297–98. See
    also *Śiwa*
Sang Hyang Wisnu. See *Wisnu, Sang Hyang*
sanga. See *pathet sanga*
sanggit. **II**: 378
sanggitan. **II**: 378
sangka. **II**: 298, 301, 309n. **III**: 37. See also
    songka
sangkala. **I**: xi, 307, 331n. **II**: 4–6, 31, 34, 36,
    69n, 70n, 75, 99n, 108, 114, 297–302. **III**:
    443. See also *calendrical systems*
santi swara. **I**: 210, 217, 419. **II**: 128, 166–67.
    III: 37
saptaswara. **II**: 279–80, 288
sarayuda. **I**: 426. **III**: 37. See also
    kendhangan sarayuda
sariswara notation. See *notation, sariswara*
saron. **II**: 239. **III**: 37
saron, arrangement of keys and *pathet.* **II**:
    253–54
saron barung. **I**: 13, 250, 272–74, 339. **II**: 239.
    III: 37. See also *instruments*
saron demung. **II**: 287. **III**: 37. See also
    demung
saron demung ageng. **II**: 39. **III**: 38
saron demung lantakan. **II**: 39. **III**: 38
saron demung pencon. **II**: 39. **III**: 38
saron melody. **I**: 249–50, 256, 277. See also
    balungan; melody
saron paringgitan. **II**: 129
saron panerus. **I**: 13, 251, 252, 272, 279–82,
    339. **II**: 39, 239. **III**: 38. See also
    instruments
saron panitil. **II**: 39. See also *saron panerus*
saron peking. **II**: 39. See also *saron panerus*
saron penerus. See *saron panerus*
saron slenthem. See *saron demung ageng*
saron wayangan. **II**: 129. **III**: 38
Sasadara. **II**: 33, 70n
sasmita. **I**: 385. **II**: 81, 95, 345. **III**: 38
Sastra Gendhing. **II**: ix
Sastra Miruda. See *Serat Sastra Miruda*
sebawa. **II**: 323
sedheng. **I**: 10. **III**: 38
sekar. **II**: 205–31, 255, 313, 351. **III**: 38
sekar in *gendhing.* **II**: 220–24

sekar ageng. **I**: 358, 521n. **II**: 34, 35, 113, 125,
    128, 207, 213–14, 225–29. **III**: 38. See
    also *sekar gedhé*
sekar ageng (tembang gedhé), proper names
    of
lagu basonta tilaka. See *sekar ageng
    basonta tilaka*
lagu prethitala. **I**: 451. See also *sekar
    ageng prethitala*
lagu rajanī. **I**: 469. See also *sekar ageng
    rajanī*
lagu saradula wikridhita. **I**: 449, 450, 476,
    521n. See also *sekar ageng sardula
    wikridhita*
lagu widara gumulung. See *sekar ageng
    sasadara kawekas*
lagu wisarjita. See *sekar ageng sasadara
    kawekas*
sekar ageng bangsa patra. **I**: 463, 521n.
    See also *sekar ageng patra suratma*
sekar ageng basonta. **I**: 464, 465, 521n
sekar ageng basonta tilaka. **I**: 461, 467
sekar ageng bremara ngingsep sari. **I**: 211
sekar ageng bremara wilasita. **I**: 453, 475
sekar ageng candra kusuma. **I**: 210
sekar ageng candra wilasita. **II**: 81, 251
sekar ageng citra mengeng. **II**: 213, 251
sekar ageng dura dasih. **II**: 112
sekar ageng ganda kusuma. **I**: 464, 465
sekar ageng garjita watang. **II**: 308
sekar ageng hasta kuswala. **I**: 453
sekar ageng jagad gita. **II**: 351
sekar ageng kawitana. **I**: 469
sekar ageng kilayu nedheng. **I**: 458, 465.
    II: 351
sekar ageng kusumastuti. **I**: 31
sekar ageng madayanta. **I**: 360
sekar ageng madu retna. **II**: 251
sekar ageng maésa bayangan. **I**: 521n
sekar ageng manda malon. **II**: 351
sekar ageng manggala gita. **II**: 251, 308
sekar ageng minta jiwa. **II**: 251
sekar ageng naga bandha. **I**: 454
sekar ageng padma wicitra. **II**: 83
sekar ageng pamular sih. **I**: 462
sekar ageng patra suratma. **I**: 463
sekar ageng prawira lalita. **I**: 461, 521n
sekar ageng prethitala. **I**: 451
sekar ageng prit anjala. **I**: 456
sekar ageng raga kusuma. See *sekar
    ageng wohing rat*
sekar ageng rajanī. **I**: 469

INDEX TO MUSICAL PIECES
(GENDHING)

488